Coaching the No-Huddle Multiple Offense

Vince McMahon
Kevin McMahon

COACHES CHOICE™

ISBN: 978-1-60679-388-6
Library of Congress Control Number: 2017938965
Book layout: Cheery Sugabo
Cover design: Cheery Sugabo
Front cover photo: © Anthony Nesmith/Cal Sport Media via Zuma Wire

Coaches Choice
P.O. Box 1828
Monterey, CA 93942
www.coacheschoice.com

Dedication

To my wife Pat, who typed this manuscript and acted as my personal editor; to Kurt and Kara, our high-achieving children; and to our son-in-law Jim, an avid sports fan. It was their love and support that made it possible for me to coach for 50 years. Through thick and thin, they encouraged my life-long pursuit of the great game of football.

—Vince McMahon

To my wife Dina and our children, Sirena, Shaunna, Shayne, and Staci. Their unconditional love, patience, and understanding allowed me to spend so much time away from them in the pursuit of football coaching dreams. Nothing can repay them for their sacrifice, but they will always have my heart-felt appreciation, thanks, and love.

—Kevin McMahon

Acknowledgments

As an assistant coach at all levels, I have been blessed to work for great head coaches. Ed Bender, Monte Charles, Jim Scott, and Jon Cooper all allowed me the opportunity to learn and develop as a coach. Of these outstanding coaches, Ed Bender was the one who first taught me how to coach, and he served as my mentor for a number of years.

During my coaching career, I have been fortunate to associate with excellent assistant coaches from whom I learned much. They became my friends as well as colleagues. To Jack, Bob, Larry, Joe, Walt, Dave, John, Pete, Brad, Keith, Camillo, Chuck, Paul, Kevin, Brian, and Jim I owe much of my success.

It has been a real pleasure to work with my nephew, Kevin McMahon, on this book. He is an outstanding football coach in his own right, and his work on this endeavor was much appreciated. In addition to preparing all the diagrams in the book, he contributed Chapter 15 on game planning.

To the thousands of young men it has been my honor to coach, I owe any success that I've had. It is my hope that I have in some way had a positive effect on their lives.

—Vince McMahon

I wish to acknowledge the author of this book, my uncle Vince McMahon, for his wisdom and guidance on coaching football given to me over the years. I also wish to thank him for allowing me to have a part in this educational endeavor.

—Kevin McMahon

Contents

Preface

Coaching the No-Huddle Multiple Offense is a summary of the offensive ideas I have been associated with during 50 years as a football coach. This book is an attempt to communicate to young coaches what I have learned about offensive football. In this book, I have collaborated with my nephew, Kevin McMahon, who has been a successful head high school football coach in Florida for many years.

As mentioned in the preface to my previous book, Coaching the Option Wing Offense, my offensive ideas stem from experience as a player, assistant coach, and head coach at many levels. As a high school player, I was exposed to the split-T offense. Playing for a team that won 25 games in a row, I became sold on the impact of option football. I became familiar with the wing-T offense as an assistant coach in Sioux City, Iowa.

During my time as assistant coach at Rochelle (IL) High School, I was fortunate to work in a program that had a 35-game winning streak. Head coach Ed Bender taught me how to coach. The flip-flop offense, tackle trap counter, and inside belly series originated with the Rochelle program.

As an assistant at the University of Wisconsin at Superior, I worked with the shotgun or spread offense, where we were always aligned in a five-wide formation. I became familiar with the no-huddle offensive concept while working with offensive coordinator, Paul Hefty, at Aurora (IL) University.

As a head football coach in three different junior college programs, I developed a hybrid wing-T offense. This offense helped me win 127 games over 20 years. This offense ranked in the top 10 in the nation in scoring, rushing, and total offense.

The no-huddle multiple offense allows the coach to do the following:

- Control game tempo.
- Stretch the defense vertically and horizontally.
- Do something different from what other coaches do.
- Use various forms of the option.
- Use wing-T principles and plays.
- Feature a strong physical running game.
- Use misdirection.
- Promote ball control and field position.
- Create defensive conflicts through shifting, motion, and formations.
- Have the ability to be a one-back, two-back, or three-back attack.

- Be a series offense.
- Have a run and pass balance.
- Make big plays with play-action passes.
- Score.

CHAPTER 1

Why the No-Huddle Multiple Offense?

Success on offense is based on one of two principles. The first of these is doing the same things other people are doing, but doing them better than your opponent. This can be due to better coaching or better players, but if coaches are equal, personnel will determine the outcome of games.

A second way to be successful is to do things differently from the way others are doing them. The no-huddle multiple offense is based on this principle of doing things in a different way.

In order to succeed, the offense must be versatile enough so it can adapt to various types of personnel. Not all players have the same skill sets, and the offense must be able to succeed with players of very different abilities. The no-huddle multiple offense allows the coach to emphasize the offensive skills that best fit the players' abilities.

The no-huddle multiple offense is a high-volume offense. It includes a sizeable number of run and pass plays. By using a flip-flop offensive system, several different types of plays may be run with less learning involved.

The no-huddle multiple is a series-based offense. A series consists of a group of plays that have a similar origin, but hit varying areas of the defense. A series typically has base running plays, a counter play, and play-action passes off the base run-action. Seven series constitute the no-huddle multiple offense:

- Buck series
- Veer series
- Belly series
- Power series
- Zone series
- Quick pass series
- Five-step dropback pass series

Multiple types of run plays are used in this attack. The wing-T and the veer option offenses are the basis for the no-huddle multiple offense. It is a run-first attack. The wing-T is the best single offensive system ever developed, but its basic weakness is the compact nature of the wing, tight end side of the formation. The no-huddle multiple offense uses two true wide receivers that stretch the defense vertically and horizontally. The result is a more dangerous passing game threat.

At its core, a football team must develop toughness both offensively and defensively. A strong physical ground game develops that hardness that leads to physical domination. The no-huddle multiple offense has, as its basis, the physical attack that leads to that toughness. This offense can be run from goal line to goal line. Special short-yardage or goal line plays are not necessary.

Most football games are won by big plays. The definition of a big run play is one that gains 15 or more yards; a big pass play is one that gains 20 or more yards. Five big offensive pass plays will result in a team winning at more than a 75 percent clip.

Big pass plays from the no-huddle multiple offense most often come off play-action passes executed in a down-and-distance that is more likely a running down. Big run plays will normally come from option or counter plays. Use of the no-huddle multiple offense provides a platform for numerous big play opportunities. A basic game plan for the offense is to initially attack the perimeter of the defense. This is done in the following ways:

- Buck sweeps designed to attack outside with some type of inside threat to hold defensive pursuit
- Bootleg passes to both the strongside and quickside of the formation
- Outside zone or stretch plays, including the jet sweeps
- Outside veer play, using zone blocking
- Sprint-out passes run to the quickside of the formation
- Bubble screens and wide receiver screens

After the defense adjusts to contain the perimeter attack, the offense then attacks off-tackle to the inside. The whole principle of offensive football is to create conflicts for defensive players and to take advantage of those conflicts. One example is running the outside veer strongside. When the read defender slow-plays the option, the offense runs the strongside belly down play and traps that read man. A second example is running the quickside jet sweep and, as the defense flows to the outside, running the quickside belly play with jet sweep action.

One way in which this offense is multiple is through the use of various blocking schemes. Gap blocking and trap blocking are used for wing-T-type plays. Veer blocking combined with zone blocking is used for the option game. Pure zone blocking is utilized for the jet sweep plays and the outside zone play.

This offense features multiple types of passes. Five-step drop passes and one- or three-step drop passes are used featuring four receiver patterns. Play-action passes are run off option play or power play fakes. Full flow and split flow bootleg passes are run to both the quickside and strongside of the formation. Sprint-out passes to the quickside may be run from any formation.

Multiple types of misdirection plays are featured in this offensive attack, including tackle trap counters, counter trey plays, double handoff counter crisscross runs, counter bootleg passes, and bootleg actions from full or split flows. These types of plays slow defensive pursuit and have big play potential.

The quarterback operates from the gun in the pistol, but in most cases he will be under center for the following reasons:

- Under center is the best position from which to run the dive option since the defense has less time to react.
- The quarterback is able to have his eyes on the secondary for keys as he drops back to pass because he does not have to worry about catching the football.

- The quarterback under the center provides for more of a downhill running game.
- This position improves the opportunity for faking for the run game and play-action passing.
- The center becomes more effective when he does not have to execute a shotgun snap.
- Fewer bad snaps occur.
- Timing in the quick passing game is better.

At least one option play is run from every offensive formation. Extensive use of the option running attack has the following advantages:

- The dive portion of the option hits quickly, forcing immediate defensive reaction.
- The option forces defenses to play assignment football. On every snap, some defender must cover the dive, quarterback, and pitchback. This need tends to limit the number of fronts, stunts, and coverage employed by the defense.
- Option football is effective against superior defensive players because they don't have to be blocked and can be optioned instead.
- This attack spreads ball-carrying responsibilities to three backs and makes it difficult for the defense to concentrate on stopping one player.
- The option attacks the defensive interior, off-tackle, and perimeter of the defense with one play.
- Running play-action passes from the dive fake results in opportunities for big plays.

The no-huddle multiple offense is a flip-flop offensive system. The offensive line has a strongside and a quickside. A right formation has the strongside to the right with the quickside left. The offensive personnel flip over for a left formation. A primary advantage of this system is that multiple types of plays may be run to the strongside, and different plays may be run to the quickside. For the no-huddle multiple offense, the following plays are run to the strongside:

- Tackle trap counter
- Belly down
- Power off-tackle
- Buck sweep
- Jet sweep by 2-back

Plays run only to the quickside of the formation include the following:

- Jet sweep by the 4-back
- Inside belly
- Midline option
- Outside zone
- Counter crisscross
- Counter bootleg pass
- Sprint-out passes

The most efficient use of practice time has been to run right formation one day and left formation the next day. This method eliminates confusion for the center, 3-back, and quarterback as to the strength of the formation. It also saves practice time since the offense does not have to flip between plays.

Multiple formations are featured in this offensive system. The five basic formations used are: strong, I, wing, doubles, and pistol. Right and left formations are used for each. Thus, 10 distinct formations have been created. Use of motion further distorts the alignments. Strong is used as a pre-shift alignment. Plays are run from strong, or the offense may shift from it to other formations. The formation to be used is based on the first number in the play call. Strong is the 5 alignment, I is 6, wing is 7, doubles is 8, and pistol is 9.

A big advantage of the no-huddle multiple offense is the ability to control the tempo of the game. This offense allows the team to play at four distinct speeds.

Normal tempo has the quarterback call right or left to set the strength of the offense. He next calls any motion to be used. Following the motion, he makes a play call. In normal tempo, the formation, shift, and snap count are determined by the play called. The use of normal tempo results in the offense running plays at a rapid pace, which will result in the ball being snapped in much less than the allotted clock time. Over the course of a game, this tempo allows the offense to run many more plays than if they huddled.

A second tempo, NASCAR, is used as a hurry-up pace for two-minute situations or if the coach simply wants to speed up play. In this case, the quarterback says "NASCAR" and makes a call of right or left to set strength; motion (if desired) is called, and then a formation. The offense immediately aligns in the called formation, and the quarterback calls the play. When using this tempo, the snap count is always on set, which is the first sound in the cadence. This tempo eliminates shifting, thus saving clock time.

A third tempo is Indy. The quarterback calls Indy prior to making a direction call to set formation strength. He then makes his play call. The offense aligns in strong, runs a play, or shifts to another formation and executes the play called. After that play is run, the offense quickly aligns in the same formation and repeats the previous play with the ball being snapped on set. Since the defense must always be prepared for this tempo, it probably cannot substitute personnel, and the defensive players must be ready to line up immediately. This tempo will result in more vanilla defensive alignments, coverage, and stunts.

The fourth tempo used is a slow, deliberate speed, where the ball is snapped with less than five seconds on the play clock. This tempo may be used late in a game or half when leading, and the team needs to run time off the clock. An additional use of slow tempo could be when a team is playing a far superior opponent. In this case, it is desirable to shorten the game as much as possible to limit the number of possessions for the opposition.

Use of the no-huddle offense is a huge benefit in terms of practice time. The offensive team never huddles during practice. All plays are signaled to the quarterback—the same procedure used for game action. Thus, the quarterback and offense in general become more familiar with the signaling and play calling process. The coach who is responsible for signaling plays in games should do so in practice. This coach becomes more and more comfortable with the process. For this system to be effective, a script of plays needs to be written for each offensive period.

After a play is run in practice, the offense immediately returns to the line of scrimmage, and the quarterback sets strength with a right or left call. After receiving the play signal, he will call the play using the same system used in games. In reality, it has been found to be more efficient to run only right formations one practice and left formations the next practice.

Experience using the no-huddle concept in practice has shown that about one-third more plays can be run in the same period of time than are executed if the team has to huddle. If players tire or injuries occur, substitutions should be made promptly so that the pace of practice does not slow. If a coach absolutely must talk to an individual in order to make a correction, substitution for that player should be made, and the pace of practice maintained. Coaches in this offense must learn to coach on the run when no-huddle multiple offense team periods are being utilized. Valuable team time cannot be wasted while lengthy discussions with a player are conducted. Individual and group periods are used to explain concepts and correct errors.

The ability to run more plays per game is one purpose of the no-huddle concept of offense. A typical college team that huddles will run somewhere in the neighborhood of 70 plays per game. The goal of the no-huddle multiple offense is to run 90 offensive plays each game. Eliminating the huddle, time used to form the huddle, and time to get to the line of scrimmage saves a significant amount of time per play. A sense of urgency is fostered among offensive players that results in their hustling to get aligned after the previous play is completed.

Another concept in this offense that speeds up play is that, other than right or left, no formations have to be signaled. The formations are based on the first number of the play called. If all other things are equal, the no-huddle concept allows the offense to run about one-third more plays than if it huddled. This approach creates more scoring opportunities.

Many defenses like to substitute personnel for specific down-and-distance situations. When facing the no-huddle multiple offense and threat of a hurry-up tempo, such substitution patterns become problematic; the threat of being caught in the substitution process is always present.

Defenses that face the no-huddle multiple offense are typically limited in the number of fronts, stunts, and coverages they can use. The defense must align quickly, communicate information to each player, and be ready as soon as the ball is marked ready for play. The need for speedy alignment and the need to adjust to shifts and motions tend to make the defense more vanilla. The extensive use of the veer option by the no-huddle multiple offense forces the defense, in order to be sound in their option responsibilities, to limit the number of fronts, stunts, and coverages they employ.

Conditioning for the offensive players is built in practice by use of the no-huddle offensive concept. This concept allows for a tempo of play in games that eventually tires an opponent's defense when it is not accustomed to that speed of play. A virtue of using the no-huddle offense is that practice tempo is such that the team does not have to spend a lot of additional time conditioning.

A quarterback using this offense has more time after the ball is marked to change plays if necessary. In addition, he has much more time to read pre-snap secondary coverages. Rarely should a no-huddle team incur a delay-of-game penalty.

A team using the no-huddle multiple offense conserves valuable energy for the offensive players. They don't waste energy going to a huddle seven yards behind the line of scrimmage and then running seven yards back up to the line. This conservation of energy is important in games and practice.

Two-minute situations find this offense in a very comfortable position. The team practices the hurry-up offense on a regular basis. Shifting is eliminated in a two-minute situation to conserve time, but all else remains the same. As a result of constant exposure to a hurry-up tempo, the offense is not as stressed when faced with a two-minute situation.

The no-huddle multiple offense provides a great system for attacking defenses. It is tremendously versatile and flexible.

CHAPTER 2

Formations, Motion, Terminology, Shifting, and Cadence

Formations

A number of abbreviations and terms apply to no-huddle multiple offensive positions:

- *QS (Quickside):* The side of the offensive formation opposite the callside is termed the quickside. In right formation, the quick side is the left side of the offensive alignment. For a left formation, the quick side is the right side of the alignment.
- *QG (Quick guard):* The quick guard is the guard aligned to the quick side of the formation.
- *QT (Quick tackle):* The tackle on the quick side of the formation is the quick tackle.
- *SS (Strongside):* An offensive call of right or left establishes the strongside of the formation. For a right call, the right side of the formation is the strongside. But if left formation is employed, the strongside is to the left.
- *SG (Strong guard):* The strong guard is aligned to the direction call for the offensive formation.
- *ST (Strong tackle):* The strong tackle always lines up to the direction call of strength. For a right formation, he aligns on the right side, and he aligns on the left side for a left formation.
- *Y (Y-receiver):* Y is the tight end. He aligns in a number of positions, often shifts, and may be in motion. For a strong set, he is aligned on the line of scrimmage one yard outside the quick tackle. In this position, he assumes a two-point stance since he is covered by the X-receiver and often shifts to the strongside. When wing formation is used, Y shifts to a position one yard outside the strong tackle on the line of scrimmage and assumes a three-point stance. For a doubles call, Y shifts strongside to a position on the line halfway between the strong tackle and the 4-back. Y is in a two-point stance in doubles with the inside foot back. If pistol is called, Y shifts strongside and aligns on the line of scrimmage two yards outside the strong tackle in a three-point stance. For I formation, Y aligns one yard outside the quick tackle and one yard off the line of scrimmage.
- *2B (2-back):* This player is the tailback or 2-back. He always uses a two-point stance. When I or pistol formations are used, the 2-back lines up seven yards deep directly behind the center in a traditional I alignment. For wing formation, the 2-back is aligned five yards deep with his inside foot on the outside foot of the quick tackle. A doubles formation has him positioned one yard outside the quick tackle and one yard deep. In strong formation, the 2-back lines up five yards deep with his inside foot on the strong guard's outside foot.
- *3B (3-back):* The 3-back is the fullback. For wing, doubles, and I formations, his alignment is directly behind the quarterback with his heels four yards from the line of scrimmage. In strong formation, he aligns four yards deep with his inside foot on the quick guard's outside foot. His alignment for the pistol formation is one yard off the line of scrimmage and one yard outside the strong tackle. He is always in a three-point stance.
- *4B (4-back):* The 4-back is the flanker in the no-huddle multiple offense, but is aligned in a number of positions. For wing and doubles formations, the 4-back aligns on the numbers strongside two yards off the line of scrimmage. In pistol

formation, he lines up two yards off the line, halfway between the quick tackle and the X-receiver on the quickside. For pistol, wing, and doubles, the 4-back uses a two-point stance with the inside foot back. When a strong formation is used, the 4-back aligns one yard outside Y and one yard deep on the quick side. In strong formation, the 4-back utilizes a three-point stance. For I formation, he aligns on the line of scrimmage on the numbers to the strongside.

- *X (X-receiver):* The X-receiver is the split end. He is always aligned on the line of scrimmage on the numbers to the quick side of the formation. He uses a two-point stance with the inside foot back.
- *QB (Quarterback):* In pistol formation, the quarterback lines up four yards deep directly behind the center. He is under center for all other formations.
- *C (Center):* The center long snaps for the pistol formation, but makes a normal center-to-quarterback exchange in other formations.

The no-huddle multiple offense is a 2-back offense using a hybrid player as a flanker. The offense is built around five basic formations and uses wing-T, zone, and veer concepts married to pro sets. It is a flip-flop offensive system rather than a mirrored system. The strong guard and strong tackle are always aligned to the direction call for the formation; the quick guard and quick tackle line up opposite the direction call. An I right formation has the strong guard and strong tackle on the right side of the center, and the quick guard and quick tackle aligned to his left. A left formation would have the strong guard and strong tackle on the center's left side, with the quick guard and quick tackle on his right side. By flipping formations, the offense creates 10 different sets. The X-receiver always aligns on the formation's quick side, but Y and the 4-back have alignments to either side, depending on the specific formation used.

A goal of this offense is the use of multiple formations without personnel substitution. This approach makes it impossible for the defense to anticipate formations or plays to be utilized based on personnel groupings and to substitute defensive players to match offensive alignments.

Formations, shifting, motion, and no-huddle are weapons employed to attack defenses. Some of these weapons are designed to outflank the defense; others force the defense to expand and remove players from the box. Still other alignments may cause the defense to contract. Forcing the defense to adjust to shifting and motion is designed to make it less aggressive and force simplification of the defensive game plan. Use of the no-huddle approach with varying tempos forces the defense to be immediately ready to play and to simplify its approach. One benefit of this offense is that it makes the defense spend much of its practice time adjusting to these multiple offensive approaches.

Much of the no-huddle multiple offense's success is based on creating defensive conflicts. An example of the use of formations to create conflict is to set formation strength into the shortside of the field. If the defense fails to adjust to formation strength, the offense gains advantages into the boundary. When the defense shifts its strength to the boundary, the offense may change strength by shifting or motioning to the wideside of the field. Many offensive series are designed to create defensive conflicts. The quick side belly series features motion across the formation from which the quick side jet sweep is run. When linebackers pursue the motion, the offense runs the belly play to the quick side. Formations with three or four quick receivers force the defense to expand and remove defenders from the box, enhancing the running game opportunities.

By shifting players before the snap and changing offensive strength, the offense forces the defense to adjust. Motion by the 4-back, Y, or the 2-back also changes formation strength and requires defensive adjustments.

Figure 2-1 shows a wing right formation with the hole numbers. The holes are numbered with even numbers on the strongside and odd numbers on the quick side. When formations flip, the hole numbers also flip. As seen in this diagram, the numbers 3 and 5 are both assigned to the quick side B gap. Hole numbers for an I left formation are shown in Figure 2-2.

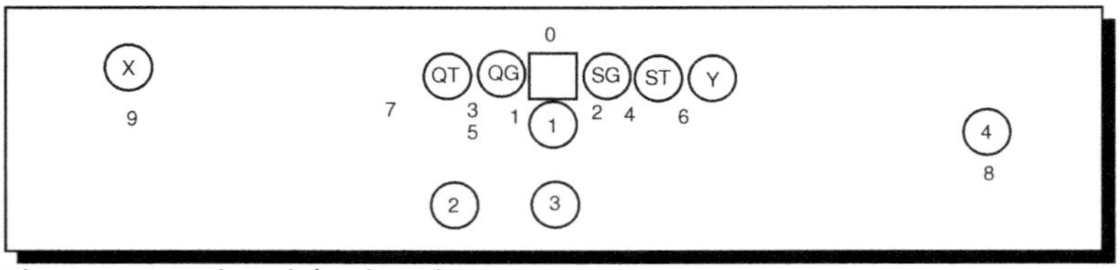

Figure 2-1. Wing right (700)

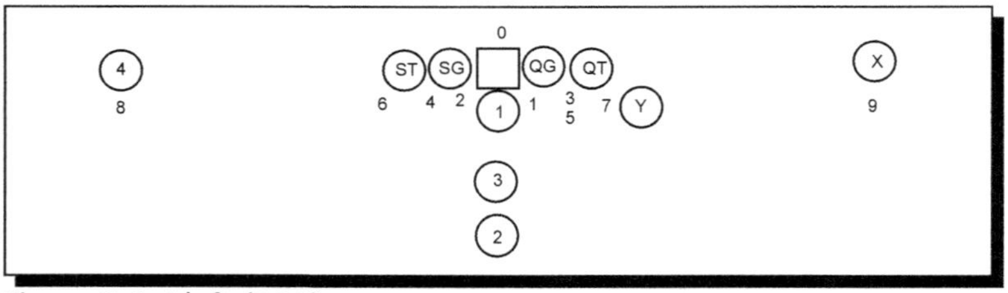

Figure 2-2. I left (600)

A flip-flop offensive system gives the offense several distinct advantages, including the following:

- *Use of a strongside and a quick side allows the offense to run a greater variety of plays.* Not every play is run to both the strongside and quick side of the formation, but by flipping the formation, any play may be run to the right or left. Plays run only to the quick side of the formation include the outside zone, inside belly, midline option, counter crisscross, 3-back dive, shovel option, off-tackle trap, jet sweep by the 4-back, and sprint-out passes. Plays that are run only to the strongside of the formation include tackle trap counter, power off-tackle, jet sweep by the 2-back, and the belly down.
- *A flip-flop offensive system neutralizes physical disadvantages of individual players.* In a mirrored system, the offense may find itself unable to operate to a side where

defensive personnel clearly outman offensive players to that side. This would result in the offense being able to attack only one side of the defense. With a flip-flop system, the formation is flipped over to create a match of the best offensive players against the defensive strength.

- *A flip-flop system allows for more specialization by offensive linemen.* The two tackles are an example of this. The quick tackle pulls and traps for the tackle trap counter, and he pulls and leads through the hole for the counter trey. A strong tackle is never asked to pull.

The best method for practicing a flip-flop offense is to run only right formation one practice and left formation the next practice. This method seems to eliminate any confusion that may be caused by flipping the offense. The center, 3-back, and quarterback positions are the positions most likely to become confused.

Alignment

Offensive linemen align as far off the ball as is legal. Their helmets should line up on the center's belly button. They assume a three-point stance as soon as the quarterback calls a play. Depth of alignment facilitates a number of types of blocks used in the no-huddle multiple offense, including trap blocks, down blocks, zone blocks, and pass protection.

Splits between the guards and the center are always two feet. These splits remain constant since the guard's outside hip is the aiming point for the 3-back for inside veer plays. Both tackles split two feet from the guard, but these splits may be expanded up to four feet for plays such as the inside veer and midline option.

Formations and Shifts

Strong formation is used as a pre-shift alignment. All plays from strong formation are run on set. Any shifts to other formations are also made on set.

The first number in the play call determines the formation to be used. Strong formation is 5, I is 6, wing is 7, doubles is 8, and pistol is 9. All run plays from strong formation begin with the number 5. The second number is the back carrying the ball, and the third number is the hole. For example: a call of right 525 has the offense aligned in strong right and the 2-back carrying the ball in the 5 hole. The only passes thrown from strong are bootleg strongside, bootleg quick side, and sprint-out quick side. A call of eastern is bootleg action to the quick side; a western call is bootleg action to the strongside. Eastern 537 would be a bootleg quick side from strong formation, and the ball is faked to the 3-back running 34. The pass pattern would be 7. For a sprint-out pass quick side, the call could be 597. The number 5 is strong formation, 9 is sprint-out protection to the quick side, and 7 is the pass pattern. Figures 2-3 and 2-4 show right and left strong formations.

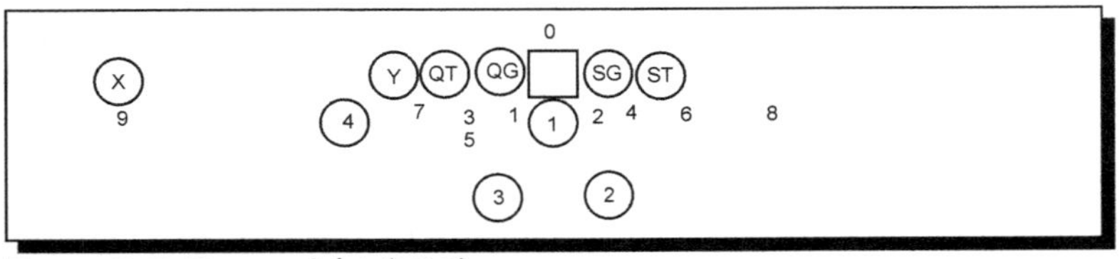

Figure 2-3. Strong right (500)

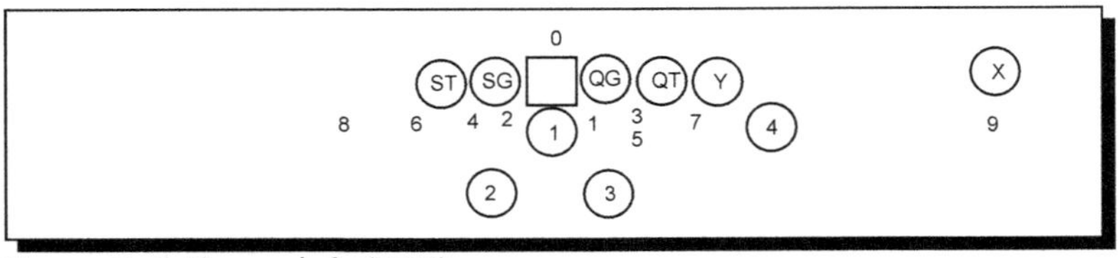

Figure 2-4. Strong left (500)

I formation, which is numbered 6, is shown in Figures 2-5 and 2-6. Any play call with a first number of 6 is run from I. Right 626 would be I right, and the 2-back would carry the ball into the 6 hole on the counter trey. Figure 2-7 shows the shift pattern from strong right to I right. Y is aligned one yard off the line of scrimmage and one yard outside the quick tackle. The 4-back shifts to the line of scrimmage strongside on the numbers.

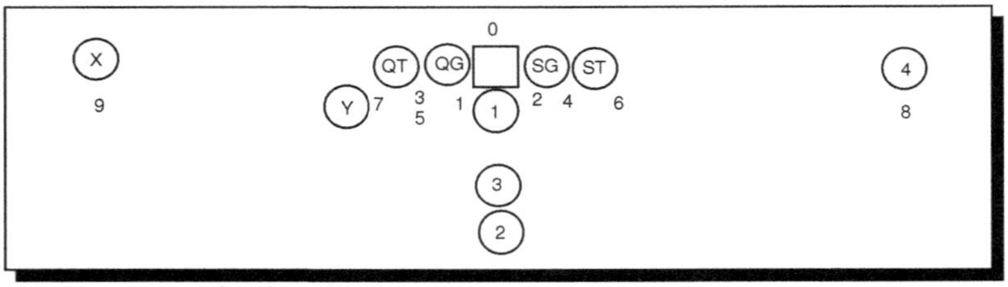

Figure 2-5. I right (600)

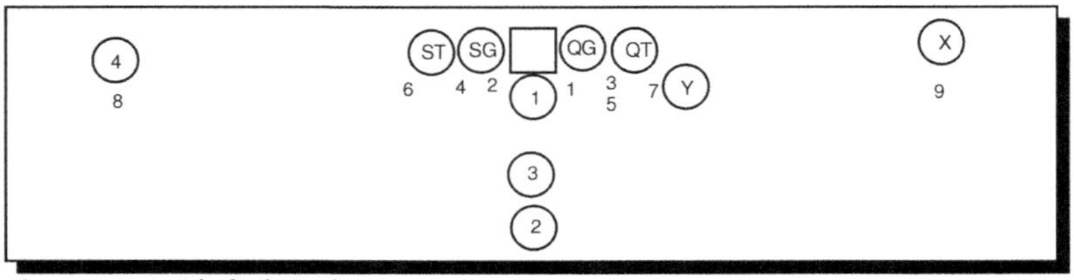

Figure 2-6. I left (600)

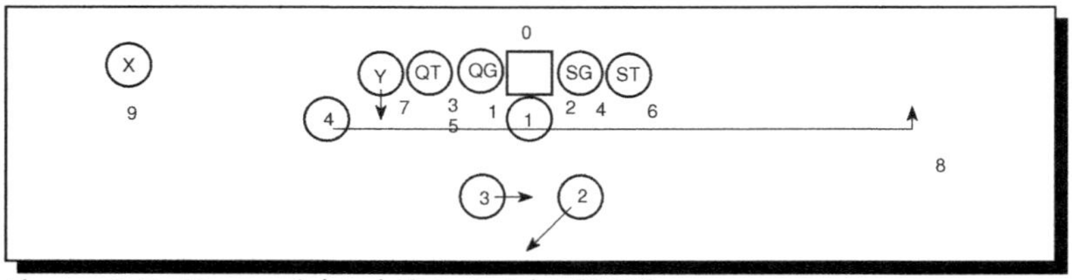

Figure 2-7. Strong right shift to I right (600)

Figures 2-8 and 2-9 show wing right and left. The number 7 means wing formation. A shift from strong left to wing left is shown in Figure 2-10. A call of right 724 would be a wing right with the 2-back carrying the ball in the 4 hole. This is the power off-tackle play to the strongside. This formation represents a typical wing-T alignment, except that the 4-back is positioned as a flanker. He may be sent in motion to create a tight wing formation.

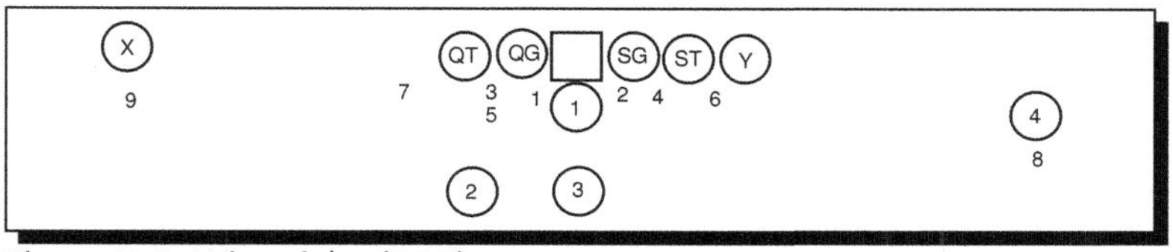

Figure 2-8. Wing right (700)

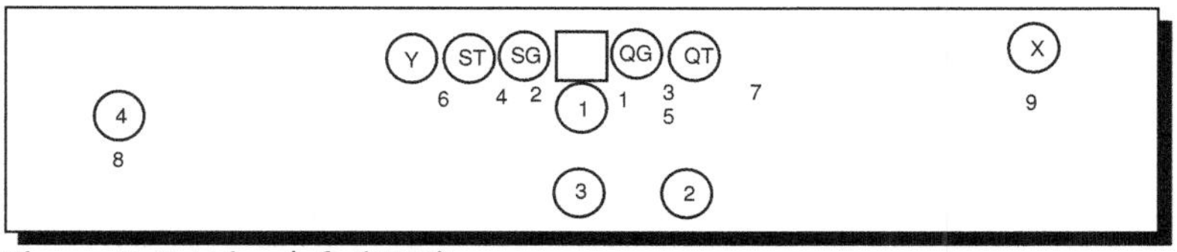

Figure 2-9. Wing left (700)

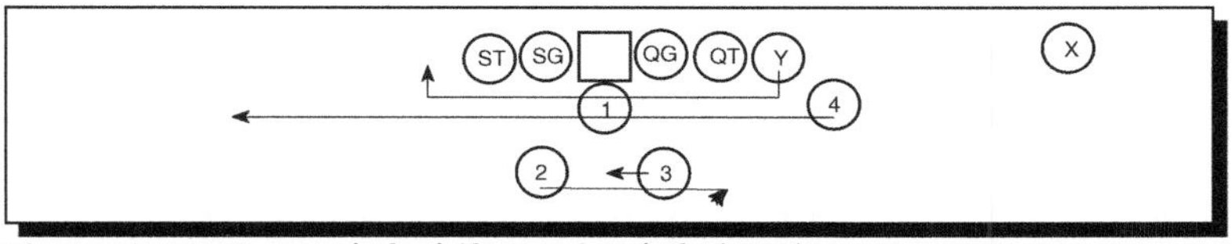

Figure 2-10. Strong left shift to wing left (700)

The fourth formation used in the no-huddle multiple offense is doubles (Figures 2-11 and 2-12). Y shifts from the quick side to a position on the strongside halfway between the strong tackle and the 4-back. He is on the line of scrimmage in a two-point stance with his inside foot back. The 4-back shifts strongside and aligns on the numbers two yards off the line. A wing alignment on the quick side is created by the 2-back shifting to a position one yard outside the quick tackle and one yard off the line of scrimmage. The 3-back shifts to align directly behind the quarterback with his heels at four yards of depth. Figure 2-13 shows a shift from strong right to doubles right. Doubles spreads the defense horizontally and threatens it vertically. All plays run from doubles have a first number of 8.

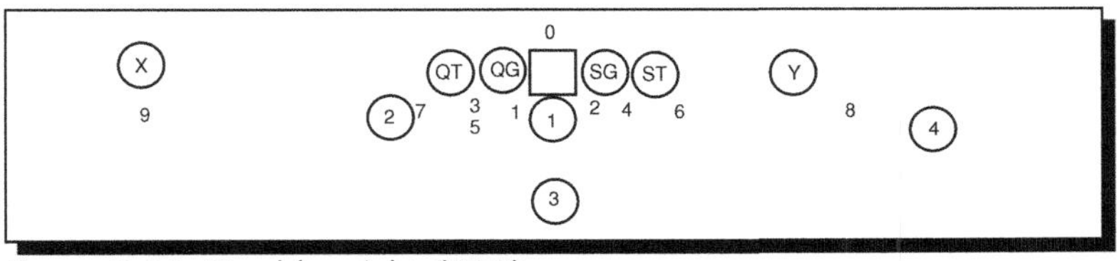

Figure 2-11. Doubles right (800)

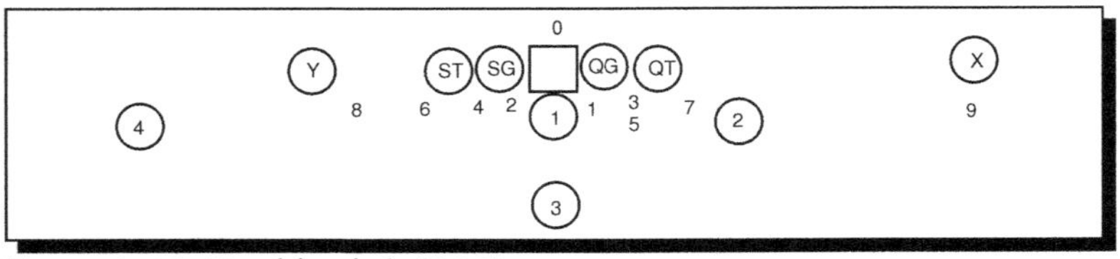

Figure 2-12. Doubles left (800)

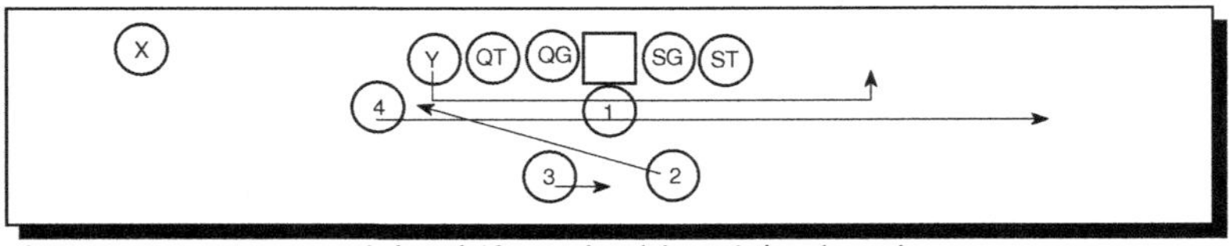

Figure 2-13. Strong right shift to doubles right (800)

Each of the first four formations used in the no-huddle multiple offense has the quarterback under the center. For the pistol formation, the quarterback shifts to a position four yards deep in the backfield. The 2-back shifts to the I alignment seven yards from the line of scrimmage directly behind the quarterback. Y shifts from the quick side to the strongside and lines up two yards outside the strong tackle on the line. He assumes a three-point stance. The 3-back shifts strongside to a position one yard outside the strong tackle and one yard off the line of scrimmage. He will be in a three-point stance. A shift by the 4-back from a tight wing alignment quick side to a position halfway between the X-receiver and the quick tackle creates a twins look quick side. The 4-back is two yards off the line in a two-point stance with his inside foot back. Figures 2-14 and 2-15 show pistol formations. The shift from strong left to pistol left is diagrammed in Figure 2-16.

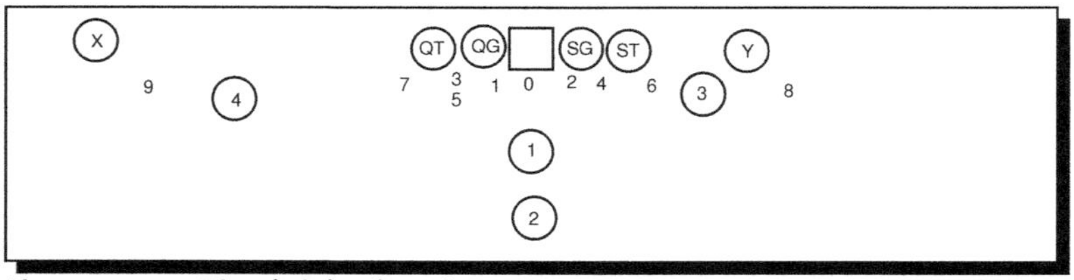

Figure 2-14. Pistol right (900)

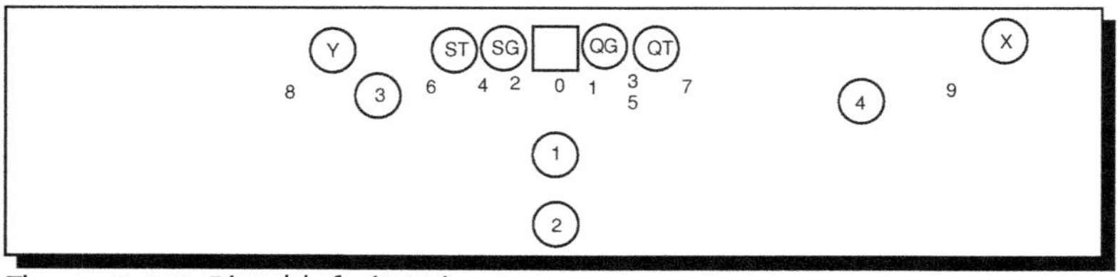

Figure 2-15. Pistol left (900)

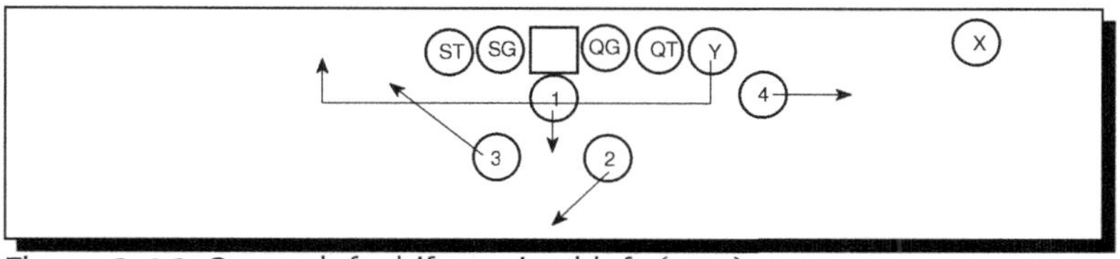

Figure 2-16. Strong left shift to pistol left (900)

All plays run from the pistol have a first digit of 9. Veer option plays are not run from pistol, but the shovel option play and zone read are. The pistol alignment places the quarterback in a shotgun set that allows him to throw the football using short drops. This position makes it more difficult for the defense to create a strong pass rush while retaining a downhill running attack.

Motion

Motion is used extensively in the no-huddle multiple offense. It is employed by the 4-back, 2-back, and Y or tight end. Reasons for the use of motion are as follows:

- Motion is used to gain blocking angles for some players.
- A player may be positioned to carry the ball for some plays through use of motion. One such example is the jet sweep.
- Motion is used to help identify man-to-man pass coverage.
- Receivers are placed in motion to avoid bump and run pass coverage.
- Extensive use of motion forces the defense to limit fronts, stunts, and pass coverages because of the need to make multiple adjustments and still remain sound versus the option attack.
- Motion may be used as window dressing for plays to cause confusion for the defense.
- Variations in pass patterns are created by putting receivers in motion.

Two types of motion are used by the 4-back. The first is zac motion, which sends the 4-back completely across the formation. Zac is used to change formation strength, add an additional blocker to one side, or position the 4-back to run a particular pass route. It also positions the 4-back to run the jet sweep to the quick side. Figures 2-17 through 2-19 show examples of zac motion. This motion is started by the quarterback raising his heel. It should always be run at full speed.

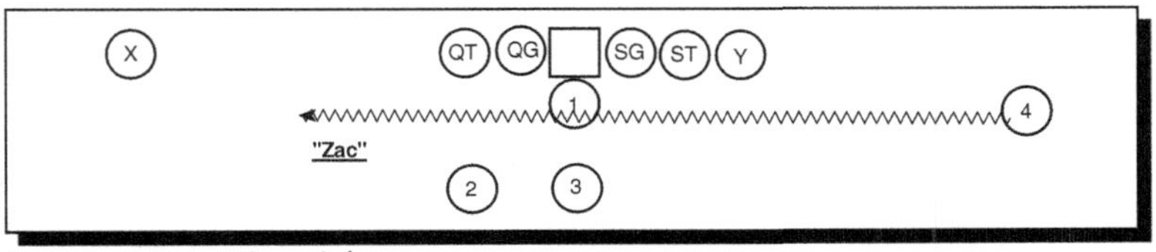

Figure 2-17. Wing right zac

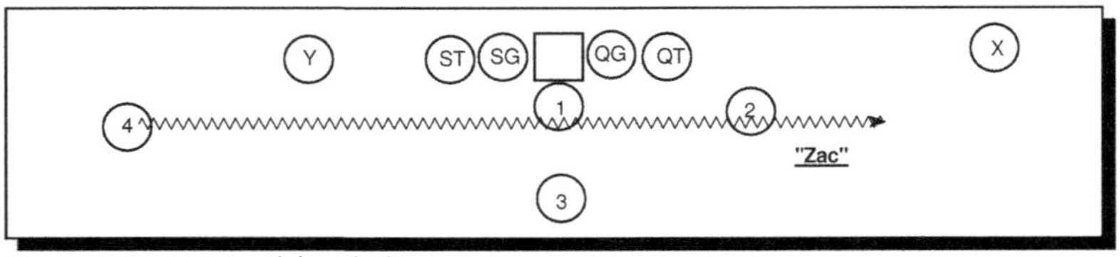

Figure 2-18. Doubles left zac

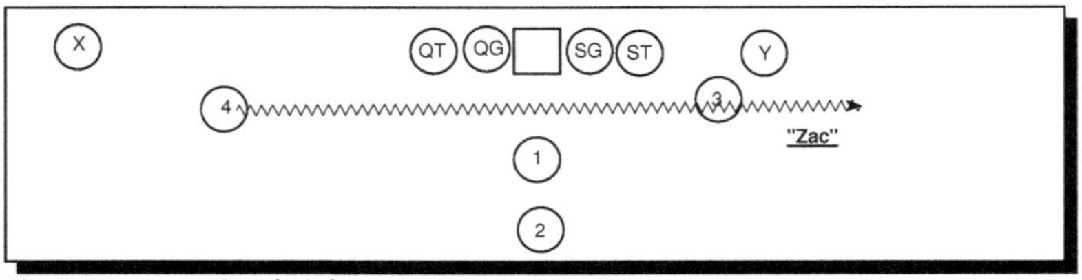

Figure 2-19. Pistol right zac

Figures 2-20 through 2-22 show zin, the second type of motion run by the 4-back. Zin has the 4-back motion in to a wing alignment. This motion starts as full-speed movement, but the 4-back will slow as he approaches a position one yard outside the last offensive lineman, who is aligned tight to the formation. He may even come to a complete stop and chop his feet when he reaches the desired position if the ball has not been snapped. Zin motion is used to position the 4-back as a blocker, ballcarrier, or pass receiver. It is sometimes used strictly as window dressing.

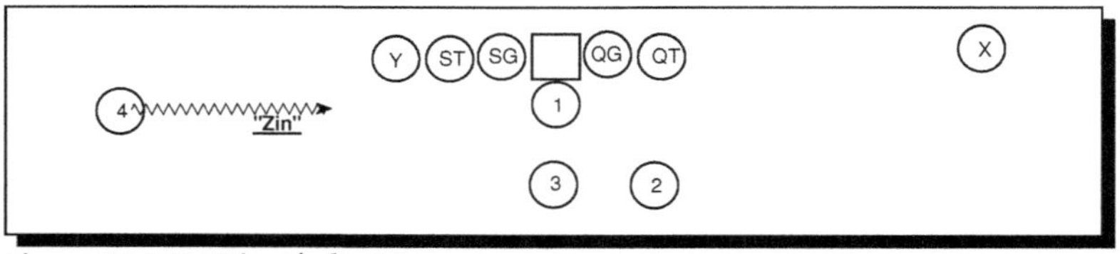

Figure 2-20. Wing left zin

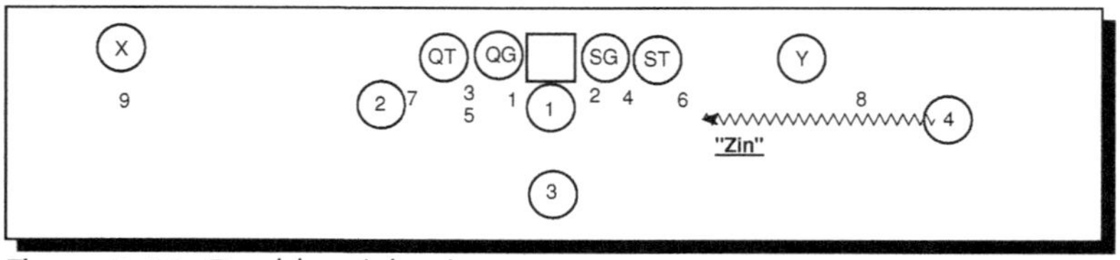

Figure 2-21. Doubles right zin

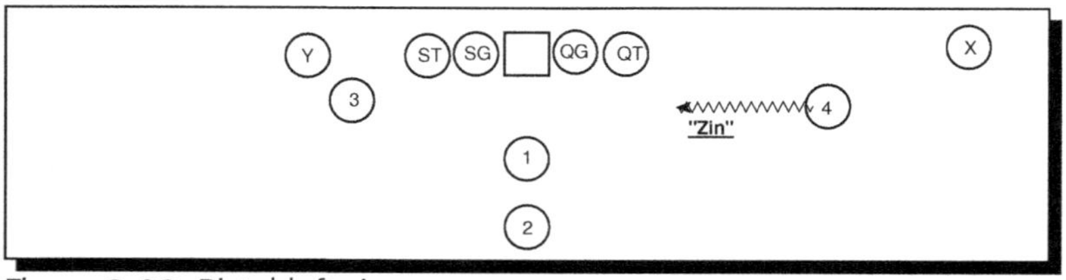

Figure 2-22. Pistol left zin

Fast motion flat across the formation by the 2-back in a doubles alignment is called jet. This motion is started by the quarterback raising his heel. It is used to run the jet sweep to the strongside or to position the two-back as a pitchman for the inside veer play run to the strongside. Jet motion creates a trips formation strongside from which the 2-back is positioned as a receiver in some pass patterns. Figures 2-23 and 2-24 show doubles formations with jet motion by the 2-back.

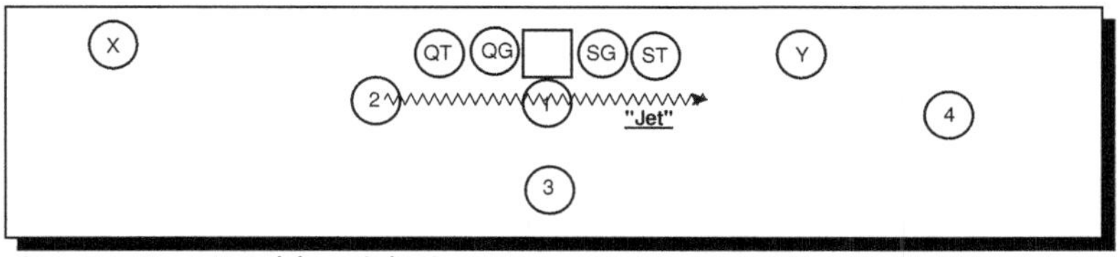

Figure 2-23. Doubles right jet

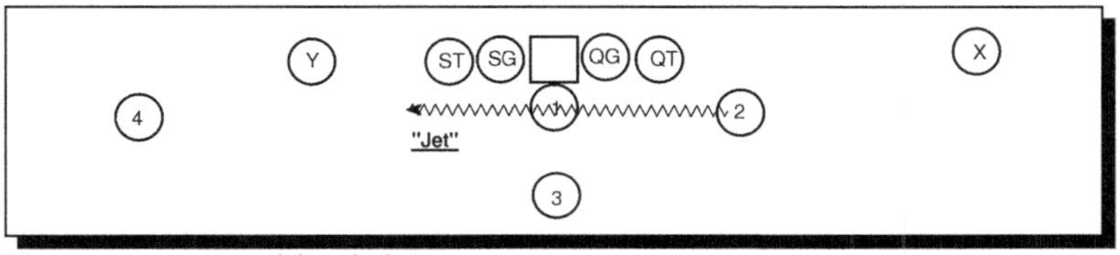

Figure 2-24. Doubles left jet

Two motions are run by Y, which are only used from the I formation. Flip motion (Figures 2-25 and 2-26) crosses the formation from the quickside to the strongside, which presents a change of strength to the defense and positions Y as a blocker or as a pass receiver. Y leaves in motion when the quarterback raises his heel. Fast motion is used until he crosses behind the quarterback. At this time, Y turns parallel to the line of scrimmage and shuffles until the ball is snapped, which allows him to have his body in better position to release on a pass route or execute a block.

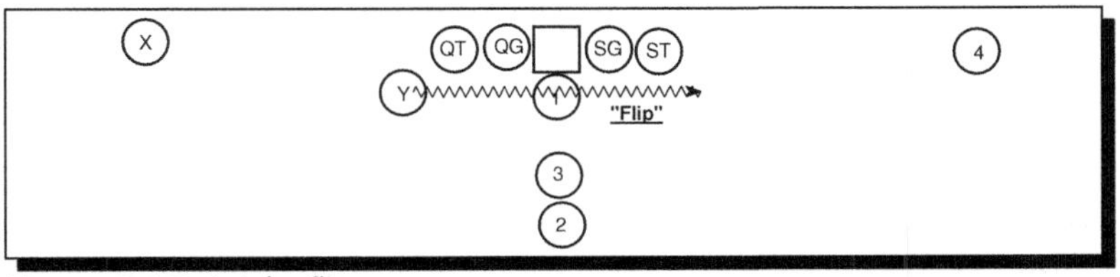

Figure 2-25. I right flip

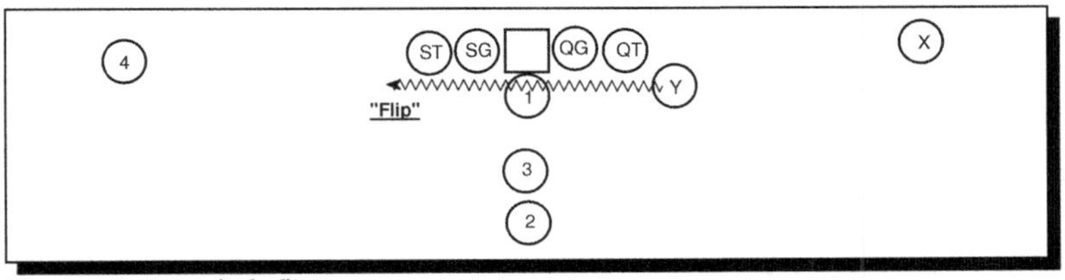

Figure 2-26. I left flip

Flop (Figures 2-27 and 2-28) is the second motion used by Y. He starts as though he will run flip. However, when he reaches the quarterback, Y will turn to face the line of scrimmage and shuffle back to the quick side. The purpose of flop movement is to make it harder for the defense to react by rolling secondary coverage, move linebackers, or slant toward flip motion. If any of these adjustments are used versus flip, the defense must redirect when flop is executed since formation strength is returned to the quick side.

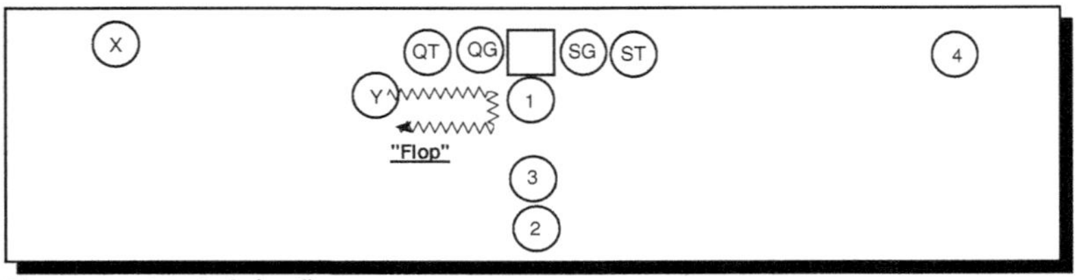

Figure 2-27. I right flop

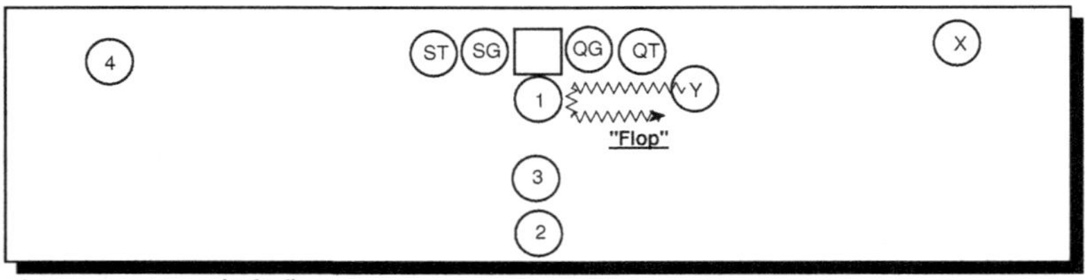

Figure 2-28. I left flop

Cadence

The no-huddle multiple offense uses a rhythm cadence. An advantage of this cadence is that offensive linemen are able to anticipate the snap of the ball and fire off the line quickly. The biggest disadvantage of a rhythm cadence is that the defense may anticipate the snap. To offset such, the offense must vary the snap count. This variation is built into the no-huddle multiple offense. All plays run from the strong formation are run on the call of "set." Shifts from strong to other alignments are also made on set. Plays run from the I or wing formations always have the ball snapped on two. Doubles or pistol formation plays are run on one. When no shift is desired, NASCAR is called, and the quarterback calls the formation and direction of strength. When no shift is used, the ball is always snapped on set.

A normal cadence for the quarterback would be as follows:

- *Right or left:* This call sets formation strength.
- *Red or blue:* Red or blue is used for calling plays from the line of scrimmage. If blue is used, the first play called after using it is the play to be run. When red is called, the second play called will be used. Any color combination could be used, and it could be changed each game.

- *A play is called:* A play such as 542, 597, or some other play is called. If preceded by blue, this is the play to be run, and it determines the formation and snap count.
- *A second play is called:* When blue is called, this is dummy; if red is called, the second play is the play to be run.
- *Any motion is called:* Examples of motion would be zac or zin.
- *Set:* All shifts are executed on the quarterback's call of set, and any play run from the strong formation has the ball snapped on set.
- *Ready:* The call of ready is used for spacing and to give offensive players time to get set after shifting.
- *Go:* If the ball is to be snapped on one, the snap will occur on the first go.
- *Go, go:* When the ball is to be snapped on two, it will be snapped on the second go.

A typical cadence call by the quarterback would be as follows:

- *Right*
- *Blue 624, 688:* The power off-tackle from the I formation (24) will be run.
- *Flip:* This motion call sends Y across to the strongside when the quarterback raises his heel.
- *Set:* A shift is made from a strong right alignment to an I right formation.
- The quarterback raises his heel and Y motions to the strongside.
- *Ready:* Ready is called before Y reaches his desired position.
- *Go, go:* The ball is snapped on the second go, and the power off-tackle play to the strongside is run.

Calling Plays

All running plays are called using three digits. The first number indicates the formation, the second number is the back carrying the ball, and the third number is the hole. Thus, 728 is a running play from wing alignment and the 2-back carries the ball in the 8 hole.

Dropback, quick, sprint-out, and play passes where the ball is faked into the 4 hole are also called with three digits. The first number is the formation, the second is the pass protection scheme and quarterback action, and the third number is the pattern to be run. A 688 call would mean the play is run from the I, 80 protection is play-action protection with a fake of 24, and 8 is the pattern to be used.

Bootleg passes are called with a direction call of east, west, north, south, eastern, or western as the first command. This call is followed by three digits. The first number designates the formation, the second the back to whom the fake is made, and the third number is the pattern run. The direction call is the pass protection scheme and the quarterback action for the play. A call of east 727 would indicate bootleg protection quick side from the wing formation. The quarterback fakes to the 2-back and bootlegs quick side and throws using the 7 pattern.

For dropback and quick passes, the depth of the quarterback's drop is determined by the pass pattern. Patterns 0 through 3 are one- or three-step drop quick passes. Patterns 4 through 9 are five-step drop passes. The 50 or 60 protection is used for quick or dropback passes. For example, 658 would indicate an I formation five-step drop pass with 50 protection and an 8 pattern.

Tags may be added to pass patterns. These words alter the routes of one or more receivers in the pattern. An example would be a call of right 854 Utah. This call is a pass run from doubles using 50 pass protection and a 4 pattern. It is a five-step drop, and the 4 pattern is four verticals. The tag tells the X-receiver to run a shallow crossing route. Figure 2-29 shows right 854 Utah. Other tags used to change patterns are covered in Chapter 4.

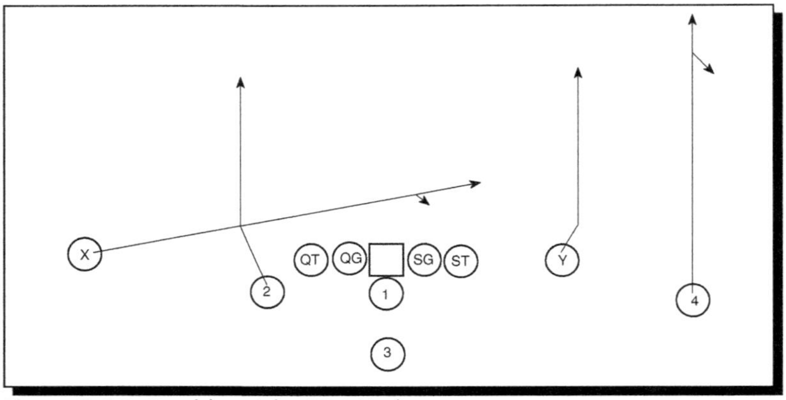

Figure 2-29. Doubles right 854 Utah

CHAPTER 3

Personnel

The most important phases of coaching have little to do with the X's and O's of the game. Long-term coaching success is most dependent upon the following:

- The ability to evaluate players' talents and to place them in positions where they have the best chance to succeed and consequently help the team to win
- The ability to teach individual skills and techniques
- The ability to motivate and lead student athletes and assistant coaches

This chapter discusses the abilities needed to play various positions in the no-huddle multiple offense. College coaches can recruit players who fit the needs of this offense, but a high school coach must take the players available and place them properly in the offense. Young players must be constantly evaluated as they mature and develop. A coach needs to be flexible and have the imagination to move players to new positions as they grow.

The no-huddle multiple offense flip-flops the offensive line, which allows the offense to utilize the individual abilities of linemen to the fullest extent. No two players are ever exactly alike in their ability, and flipping the linemen allows for the maximization of individual skills. An example would be the strong guard position. This player should be the best offensive lineman. He finds himself as the crucial blocker on many of the best offensive plays. He is the kick-out blocker on the buck sweep, counter trey to the quickside, and the strongside belly play.

A discussion of the ideal requirements for each position in the no-huddle multiple offense follows. Few programs have players who meet the ideal skills for each position, but coaches may use the following guidelines to select players for each offensive position.

Quarterback

A coach selects his quarterback first from all the available athletes. If a team uses a two-platoon system, the defense should have first choice of all available talent with the exception of the quarterback and the 2-back or tailback.

Leadership ability is an intangible quality that the quarterback must possess. This is not necessarily vocal in nature, but is shown through setting an example of how things should be done. He needs to be the hardest worker on the practice field, in the weight room, in the film room, and in the classroom. Leadership is also demonstrated by the quarterback's show of confidence in pressure situations in games or practice. The ability to handle failure is essential for a quarterback. Being calm when all others are excessively excited gives his teammates confidence. A good leader does not belittle teammates, even the least-talented member of the squad. Instead, he praises and compliments others and deflects praise from himself to teammates.

An effective quarterback must understand the offense better than any other player on the team. He should see the offense's total picture and know the assignments for all offensive players for all plays. The quarterback becomes a coach on the field.

Through film study and meetings with coaches, the quarterback must learn as much about defenses and secondary coverages as possible.

The quarterback should be a good athlete. He needs to be both an adequate runner and passer. The offense is versatile enough to allow a player who is an outstanding passer, but a mediocre runner, to succeed. Conversely, a player who is a highly skilled runner but an average passer can have success. Ideally, the quarterback has both skills, but that is unlikely. Foot speed is not necessary for the quarterback to run the option effectively, but it makes him a more dangerous threat.

A player with decent throwing technique can be coached to become a better passer. The quarterback ideally has decent-sized hands. If he has small hands, he will probably fumble more often and have a difficult time handling the ball in wet weather.

Potential quarterbacks may often be spotted by high school coaches by watching baseball pitchers, shortstops, catchers, or outfielders who have strong arms. Flag football teams in park district programs, physical education classes, or intramurals are other places where potential quarterbacks may be found.

Physical toughness is an attribute the quarterback must possess. He will take some hits running the option, but most big hits come from a pass rush by the defense.

Having a quarterback with height presents an advantage in the quick and dropback passing game because height allows him to see over offensive linemen and on- rushing defenders. A shorter player who is athletic can be very successful with this offense. The shorter player may be more effective at sprint-out and bootleg-type passes.

2-Back

Filling the position of 2-back or tailback should be a coach's second priority. This player will have the majority of carries in the offense and, as a result, must be the best ballcarrier available.

Speed is a desirable quality for the 2-back because it increases the effect of the perimeter running attack. Speed by itself, however, is not the most important attribute for the 2-back to possess. Being able to change directions without losing speed and making tacklers miss are the most sought-after qualities for a 2-back.

Having good size is a bonus for the tailback; it makes him harder to tackle and more durable when asked to carry the ball a great deal. Physical toughness is essential for this athlete since he averages 25 to 30 carries per game. A smaller player can compensate for lack of size if he runs with low pad level.

Ball security is of primary importance because the 2-back handles the ball so much. This skill can be taught through daily drills and emphasis on it in practice and in games.

Because of the heavy workload for the 2-back, it is a good idea for the coach to try to find an adequate backup and play him on a regular basis. This approach allows the starting tailback to remain strong and fresh during the course of a game or season. It is also a necessary insurance policy against injury.

The 2-back must become an adequate pass protection blocker. He is also called upon to lead block on linebackers for the inside belly and midline option plays. A tailback needs to work on these skills and show a willingness to engage in physical contact.

Pass receiving is an important skill that the 2-back must acquire. From doubles and wing formations, he becomes an important receiver in the dropback and quick pass schemes. He is also a primary receiver in the screen passing attack. Practice time needs to be devoted to improving these receiving skills.

A 2-back needs to become proficient in reading blocks and running to daylight. Drills in practice are used to practice jump cuts, spinning, and using a stiff arm. In addition, the 2-back must make a commitment to physical conditioning. Stamina and a high level of conditioning are achieved by running hard and trying to score on every play during practice.

Because the 2-back will gain a lot of yards and score many touchdowns, he finds himself in the center of public attention. He needs to be humble and publicly appreciate the efforts of his teammates. He should recognize that, without the effort of his blockers, he will not be successful.

3-Back

The 3-back or fullback in the no-huddle multiple offense is a key member of the attack. The first criterion used in selection of a 3-back is his blocking ability. His blocks at the point of attack are crucial to the success of the power off-tackle, the counter crisscross, and the outside zone plays. Most of his other blocks are fill-type blocks for pulling linemen. In college, cut blocking may be used for most assignments other than the power off-tackle or counter crisscross kick-out blocks.

A second skill the 3-back must possess is the ability to be a strong ballcarrier. He runs the ball between the tackles as the dive back for the veer option attack, belly options, and fullback trap. Speed is not an absolute requirement nor is size, but one or the other makes the 3-back a more dangerous weapon. Depending on the defenses faced and the offensive game plan, the 3-back may have a large number of carries. He is often asked to get tough yardage in goal line or short-yardage situations.

The 3-back needs to be a good pass receiver. Most of the routes he runs are relatively short. The exception is the seam route he is responsible for on some patterns from the pistol formation. His routes include a lot of five-yard flat routes, where he may be the primary receiver.

Physical toughness is an absolute requirement for the 3-back. The combination of blocking and inside running responsibilities for this player demand someone who loves contact and accepts the physical challenge presented by his role.

4-Back or Flanker

The fastest wide receiver available should play the 4-back or flanker position. Speed is necessary for him to be an effective ballcarrier on the jet sweep and counter crisscross plays he runs. He is also the home-run threat in much of the passing game.

This player must learn the pass routes for both the #1 and #2 receiver positions. Motion and different formations will place him in either position. He needs to run crisp, disciplined pass routes.

Motion across the formation is often used by the 4-back to change strength of alignment, free him from bump-and-run coverage, or position him as a blocker or ballcarrier. Because of the frequent motion and deep pass routes the 4-back runs, he needs to become one of the best conditioned athletes on the team.

Ability as a runner is important for the 4-back to make the jet sweep, counter crisscross, and tackle trap from strong formation effective. His running ability is important in creating YAC yards, or yards after the catch, in the passing game.

Good hands are an obvious requirement for this position. The receiver must be able to catch the ball with his hands and not with his body.

Blocking ability is important for the 4-back to make the running game effective. He becomes a key blocker for some sweep plays run from the no-huddle multiple offense. Size is not required to do this effectively, but toughness and a willingness to hit are important. Blocking for sweep plays is more of a screen type of block, where the 4-back needs to occupy the defender, but doesn't have to move him a great deal. Stalk blocks, cut blocks, and crackback blocks may also be part of his responsibilities.

X-Receiver or Split End

The X-receiver or split end always aligns to the quickside of the motion on the numbers. He needs to know the pass routes assigned to the #3 receiver.

Speed is a desirable quality for this player, as it enhances the vertical threat to the defense. If he is not fast, the X-receiver should be an outstanding route runner and be adept at faking and breaking on cuts without losing speed. Without this ability, he will have a difficult time getting open versus tight man-to-man pass coverage. Because he always aligns on the line of scrimmage, motion cannot be used to free him from bump- and-run coverage.

Size is a big advantage since defensive cornerbacks are usually relatively short. Good height can offset a lack of outstanding speed. Leaping ability also allows the X-receiver an opportunity to make plays on throws where he is well-covered.

As with the 4-back, the X-receiver must have good hands and be willing to work hard to improve them. He must be able to consistently catch the ball with his hands and not have to trap it against his body. The X-receiver is not used as a ballcarrier, but must be able to gain yardage after he catches the football.

Blocking ability is essential to make the running game effective. In a run-oriented attack such as the no-huddle multiple offense, good blocking on the perimeter of the defense creates big plays. Stalk blocks, cut blocks, and crackback blocks are used by the X-receiver as well as the 4-back. These skills can be developed through constant drills and attention to proper technique. The player requires a physical toughness and a liking for physical contact. Pride in a player's blocking skills can be developed through hard work and encouragement.

Y-Receiver or Tight End

Y is the tight end in the no-huddle multiple offense. He needs to be a very good blocker since many of the best running plays in the offense are directed toward him. His ability to secure the edge of the defense is crucial for the outside veer play. Down blocks are used by Y for the power off-tackle, buck sweep, counter trey, and strongside belly play. He arc blocks the safety when the inside veer is run strongside. Great size is not necessarily needed if Y is physical, has good quickness, and develops good techniques.

Y needs to be a good receiver. He should be adept at releases off the line of scrimmage and have the ability to fake and make good cuts when running pass routes. The ability to read coverages, adjust his routes to coverage, and find open areas in zone coverage is important. Great speed is not absolutely necessary, but is obviously an asset. Y must have very good hands and be willing to catch the ball in traffic.

This position calls for an offensive lineman with receiver skills. Basketball centers and power forwards are possible candidates for the position. Athletic offensive linemen may be converted to become Y candidates.

Strong Guard

The strong guard should be the team's best offensive lineman. He is the focal point of much of the running game. This player will many times be required to pull to the point of attack. He is responsible for blocking the force man when the buck sweep is run. He will also execute kick-out blocks for the strongside belly play and the counter trey to the quickside. He will pull and seal linebackers on the counter crisscross and the quarterback sweep run to the quickside of the formation.

Agility is important so that the guard can block defenders in spaces. Height is not a requirement for offensive linemen in the no-huddle multiple offense, but physical size and strength become a major factor. This is particularly true for the strong guard since so many of the best run plays are directed toward him. When crucial yardage is needed, this is where the offense will attack. In this offense, it is more important for the guards to have size than the tackles. For the inside veer plays to be successful, the guards must get movement at the point of attack. The strong guard will pull quickside to block for bootleg passes run to that side.

Quick Tackle

Quick tackle is the second position on the offensive line to be chosen. The quick tackle should be the better of the two tackles. He must be agile enough to pull and trap the 2 hole for the tackle trap counter. On the counter trey play strongside, the quick tackle pulls and seals the linebackers. For the buck sweep, he releases behind the linebackers and goes strongside to block any defender in the alley. The quick tackle does not have a tight end on his side of the formation; thus, he must seal the edge on the outside zone play and the quarterback sweep.

Agility and quick feet are really important in the passing game. The quick tackle will face wide outside rushers without the benefit of a tight end on his side. He needs to be the offensive line's best pass protector.

Quick Guard

The quick guard should be the next offensive line position to be filled. His skill set is similar to that of the strong guard, but differs in some critical respects. A player with good quickness who lacks the size of some of the offensive linemen can play quick guard effectively. He needs to be mobile to pull strongside and seal linebackers for the power off-tackle and buck sweep plays.

The quick guard is asked to execute the short trap for the 3-back on 0 hole plays and the long trap for the strongside counter trey. He must also be quick enough to pull and get out front on the jet sweep quickside.

Pass protection skills for the guards are normally easier than those for the tackles since they do not need to block wide defensive rushers. The quick guard will be expected to pull strongside to protect on bootleg passes run that way.

Strong Tackle

The strong tackle often has Y aligned tight to his outside. He thus has the potential for double-team or combo blocks for some running plays. Unlike the quick tackle, he does not pull and make long traps or lead through the hole to seal linebackers. Most of his blocks are down blocks with the exception of the jet sweep and outside veer plays to the strongside. The strong tackle does not need to be as good a player as the quick tackle.

Center

Snapping the ball is the center's first responsibility. He executes a shotgun snap of four yards in the pistol formation. The remainder of the time the quarterback is under the center, and a normal center-to-quarterback exchange is used. When practicing snaps with the quarterback, the center must always fire out as he snaps the ball. Poor habits are developed if the exchange is made without the center stepping. Pre-practice is the time for work on the center-quarterback exchange.

The quarterback should never run any type of drill without simulating the quarterback-center exchange initiating it. Failure to have a center snap allows the quarterback to develop the bad habit of not riding the center as he fires out and will disrupt the offense's timing. When centers are not available, the quarterbacks may snap to each other. Kickers and punters can also be trained to snap in drills such as 7-on-7, when centers are involved in other drill work.

The center's most difficult block is cutting off a defender in the strongside A gap on the buck sweep. A cut-and-scramble technique can be used for this block. Zone blocks require a reach block to the playside for the center.

Because the no-huddle multiple offense is a flip-flop offense, the center has the most difficult job of all offensive linemen in remembering which is the strongside or quickside of the offense. Running right formation one practice and left formation the next practice seems to eliminate this possible confusion.

This offense needs to develop three guards and three tackles as well as a second center. One guard and one tackle need to learn both the strongside and quickside positions. These two players should be used regularly in games to develop depth. Normally older, more experienced players should be asked to learn the two positions.

CHAPTER 4

Pass Protection Schemes

Twelve pass protection schemes are used in the no-huddle multiple offense. This number may seem like a lot of learning for the offensive linemen, but in reality a great deal of carryover occurs among a number of the protections. From the point of an offensive lineman, western, west, north, south, and 70 pass protections are identical. East and eastern protections are also identical for the lineman. As a result, these players only have to learn seven different blocking schemes. The 3-back, 2-back, and the quarterback have different assignments for each of the 12 protections.

Pass protection rules are partially based on counting defensive linemen. Guards are asked to make one of three calls on every offensive play. A gap call means that the #1 defensive lineman is aligned on the guard's inside or A gap. Odd is called when a nose man is on the center. This defender is counted as #1 on the line. An even call has the #1 defensive man on the line of scrimmage aligned on or outside the guard. Both guards should call the defense as it appears on their side of the center. The guards' calls are used for pass blocking and run blocking assignments.

Figure 4-1 shows an odd call by both guards, Figure 4-2 is a gap call, and Figure 4-3 illustrates an even call. The defensive alignment is usually different on one side of the offense from the other. Figure 4-4 is a gap call by the strong guard and an even call by the quick guard. The counting rules remain valid whatever the call.

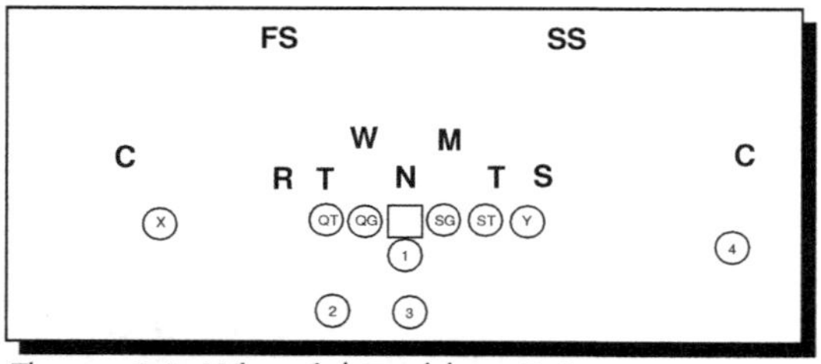

Figure 4-1. Wing right odd vs. 5-2

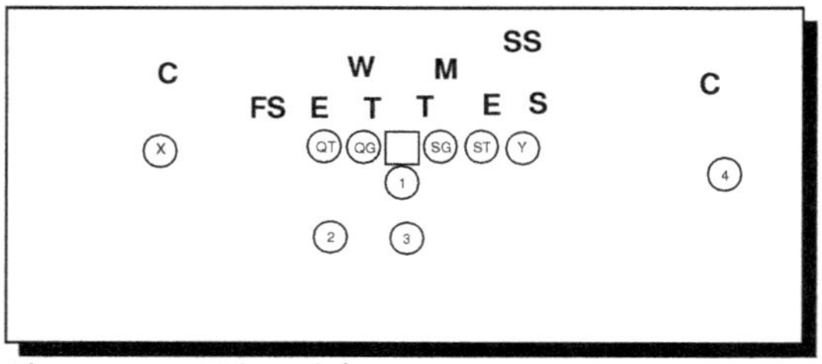

Figure 4-2. Wing right gap vs. 6-2

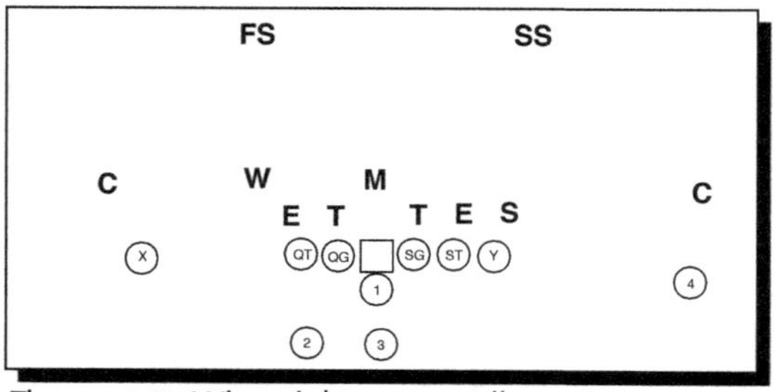

Figure 4-3. Wing right even call vs. 4-3

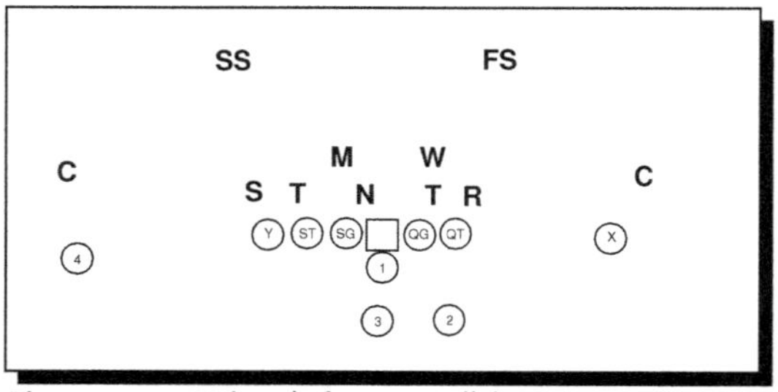

Figure 4-4. Wing left gap call by SG and even by OG

Some blocking rules for pass protection are based on gap designations for the defense. Figure 4-5 shows the gap lettering.

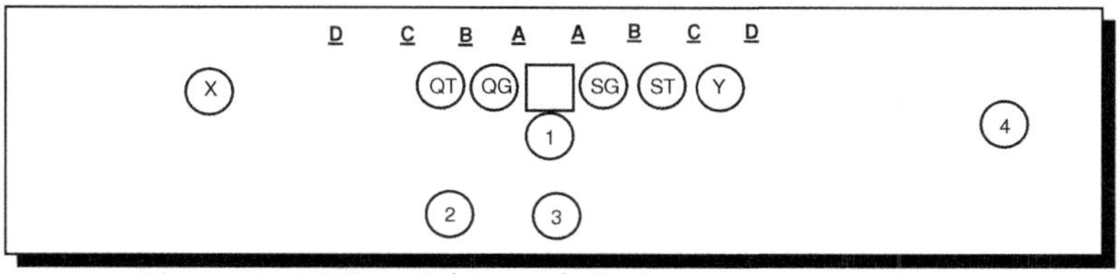

Figure 4-5. Wing right gap lettering

90 Pass Protection

The 90 pass protection and action moves the pocket so that the quarterback can escape inside defensive pressure. The sprint-out action shortens the quarterback's throw and aids a player who does not have a strong arm. This also resembles the quarterback's action for the outside zone play that is run to the quickside. One disadvantage of 90 is that the defense only has to defend the half of the field to which the quarterback sprints. Another problem can occur when the quarterback does not make a decision to throw or run quickly enough and finds himself out of room. Either the ball should be thrown on the quarterback's fifth step, or he should elect to run. By flooding the quickside of the formation, the offense increases the chance that at least one receiver will be open.

Blocking for 90 protection is shown in Figures 4-6 through 4-8. The blocking rules are as follows:

- Y-Receiver: Y runs a pass route unless a stay call is made. If he is on the strongside and stay is called, Y blocks gap, over, or the first defender to the outside. From the quickside, Y zone blocks aggressively to the quickside on a call of stay.
- Quick Tackle: The quick tackle blocks a man over him or the first defender to the outside. This defender must be pinned on the line of scrimmage. The technique for the block is the same as used for 29 or 49.
- Quick Guard: The quick guard blocks aggressively on a defender in the B gap or over him.
- Center: The center is responsible for the A gap quickside or a man over him. If no defensive player is in these areas, the center steps quickside and hinges strongside. He blocks the first defender to show.
- Strong Guard: The strong guard blocks A gap, over, or steps inside and hinges to the strongside, where he blocks the first defensive man to appear.
- Strong Tackle: Any defender in the B gap or over is the strong tackle's responsibility. If no defensive man is in these spots, the strong tackle steps quickside and hinges to the strongside. He blocks the first man to come.
- 3-Back: From I or strong formations, the 3-back runs a five-yard deep route into the quickside flat. In wing or doubles, he blocks the first defensive man who shows to the quickside outside the last reach block on the line of scrimmage. In the pistol alignment, the 3-back steps quickside and hinges strongside, blocking the first defensive man to appear.

- 2-Back: The 2-back's assignment from strong, I, or pistol formation is to block the first defensive man quickside beyond the last reach block on the line of scrimmage. From wing or doubles alignments, the 2-back runs a five-yard deep flat route to the quickside.

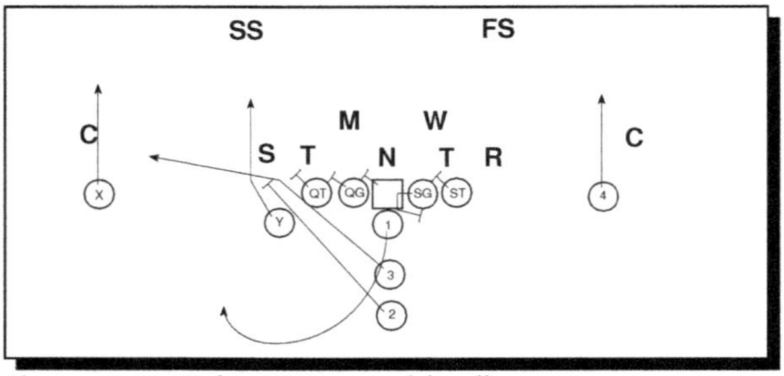

Figure 4-6. Right 697 vs. odd call

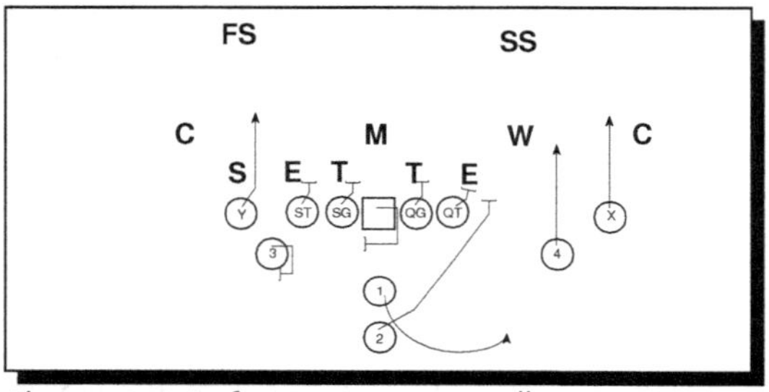

Figure 4-7. Left 997 vs. even call

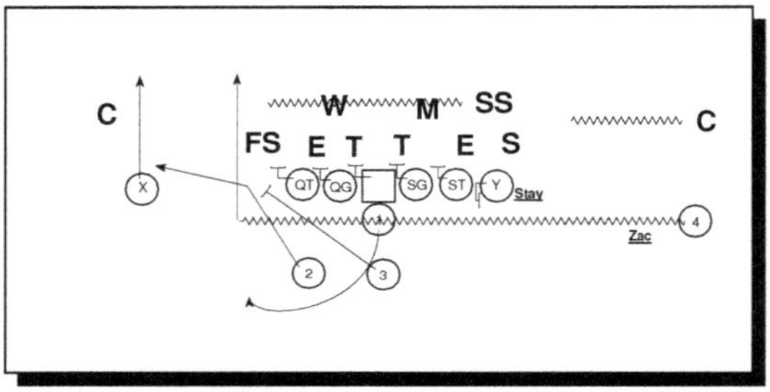

Figure 4-8. Right 797 stay/zac vs. gap call

60 Pass Protection

Figures 4-9 through 4-12 demonstrate 60 pass protection, which can be used for the quick passing game or the five-step drop passing attack. For 60 pass protection, all offensive linemen block their quickside gap to a man over the next offensive lineman to the quickside. When 60 to 63 pass patterns are called, the offensive linemen block low and aggressively as these passes are either one- or three-step drops for the quarterback. Other 60 passes use five-step drops, and the offensive linemen use dropback pass blocking techniques.

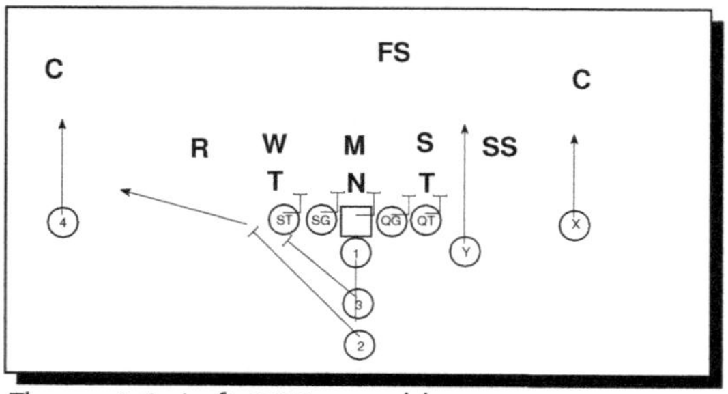

Figure 4-9. Left 663 vs. odd

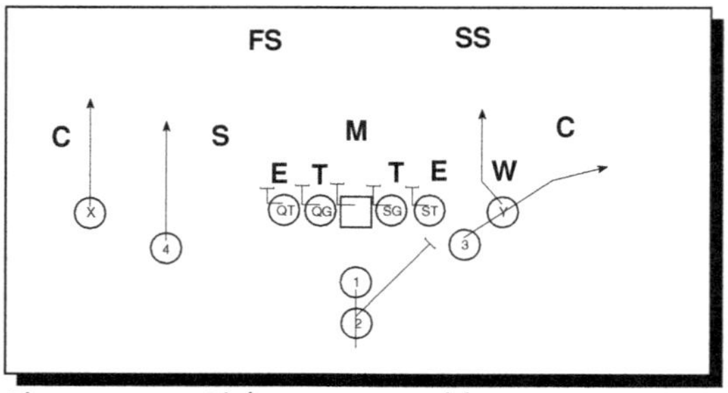

Figure 4-10. Right 968 vs. odd

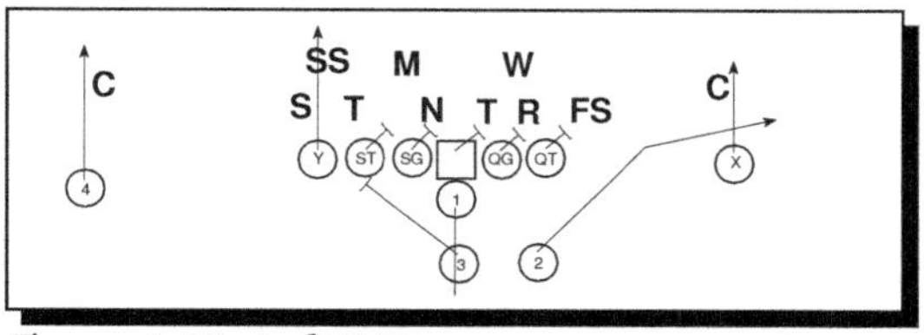

Figure 4-11. Left 769 vs. gap

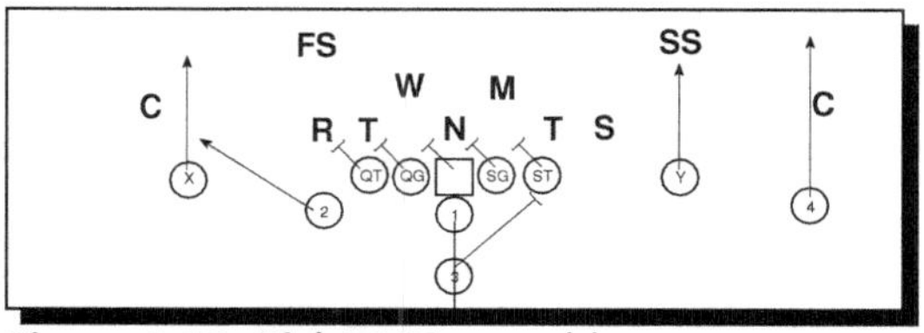

Figure 4-12. Right 861 vs. odd

The 3-back blocks aggressively on the first defender outside the strong tackle's block for all 60 protections unless the pistol formation is used. In this case, the 3-back runs a pass route.

From wing or doubles formations the 2-back runs a pass route. When I is used, the 2-back blocks the first defender outside the 3-back's block. If no defensive man shows, the 2-back runs a five-yard flat route to the strongside. In pistol formation, the 2-back blocks the first defensive player outside the strong tackle's block.

50 Pass Protection

The 50 pass protection is also slide protection, but the slide is to the strongside instead of the quickside of the formation. The offensive linemen block their strongside gap to a man over the next offensive lineman strongside. Figures 4-13 through 4-16 show 50 pass protection. Pass patterns 50 through 53 are one- or three-step drops and require low, aggressive blocks by the offensive linemen.

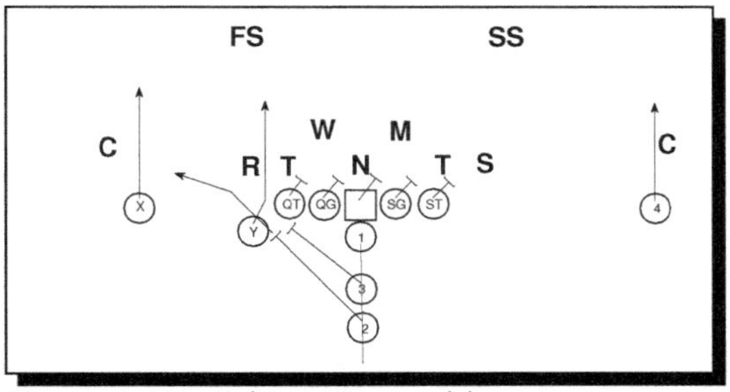

Figure 4-13. Right 658 vs. odd

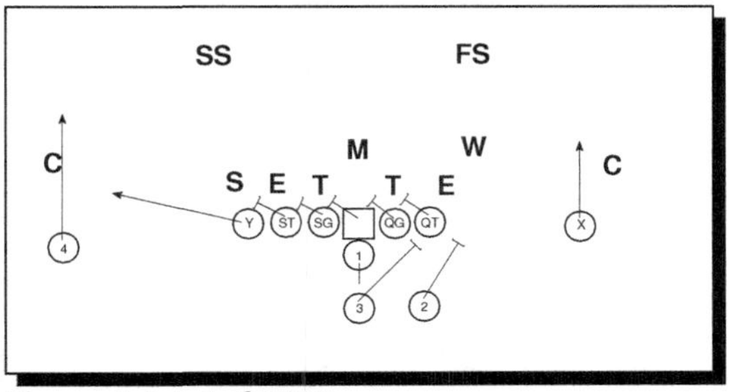

Figure 4-14. Left 752 vs. even

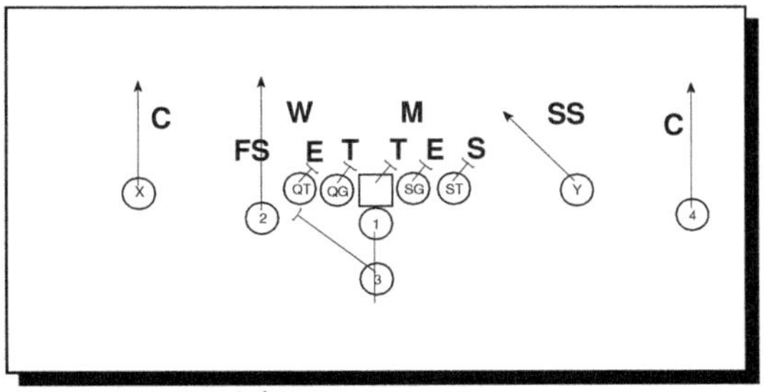

Figure 4-15. Right 859 vs. gap

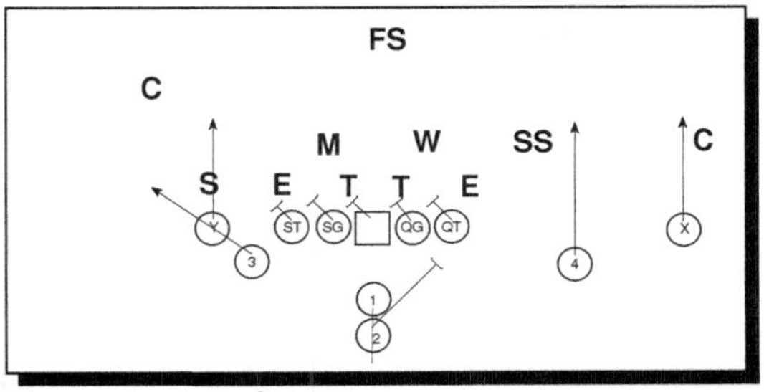

Figure 4-16. Left 953 vs. gap

The 3-back blocks the first defender outside the quick tackle's block. From the pistol alignment, he runs a pass route. From the I formation, the 2-back blocks the first defensive man who appears outside the 3-back's block, and if no defender shows, he runs a pass route. If the pistol formation is used, the 2-back blocks the first defensive player outside the quick tackle's block. A pass route is run by the 2-back from doubles or wing formation.

Both 50 and 60 pass protections provide a solid six- or seven-man protection scheme. They are very effective versus interior blitzes or stunts. All quick passes are thrown from one of these protections. Whenever protection problems occur, 50 or 60 blocking schemes should be used.

80 Pass Protection

The 80 is a combination pass protection. It features man-to-man blocking strongside with slide protection to the quickside. A play-action fake is made to either the 2-back or 3-back running the 4 hole. Figures 4-17 through 4-20 show 80 pass protection from various formations. Blocking assignments for 80 pass protection are as follows:

- Y-Receiver: Y runs a pass route.
- Strong Tackle: Defensive player #2 on the line of scrimmage is blocked by the strong tackle.
- Strong Guard: The strong guard's rule is to block the #1 defender on the line of scrimmage to the strongside.
- Center: The center blocks the quickside A gap to a man over the quick guard.
- Quick Guard: B gap to a man over the quick tackle is the quick guard's blocking assignment.
- Quick Tackle: C gap to the first defender to the outside is the quick tackle's blocking rule.

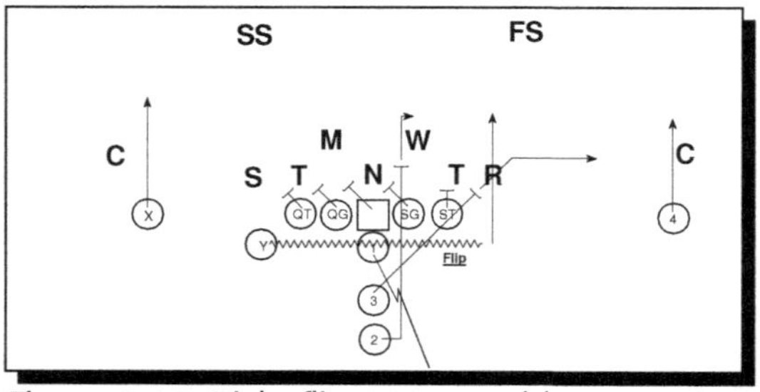

Figure 4-17. Right flip 688 vs. odd

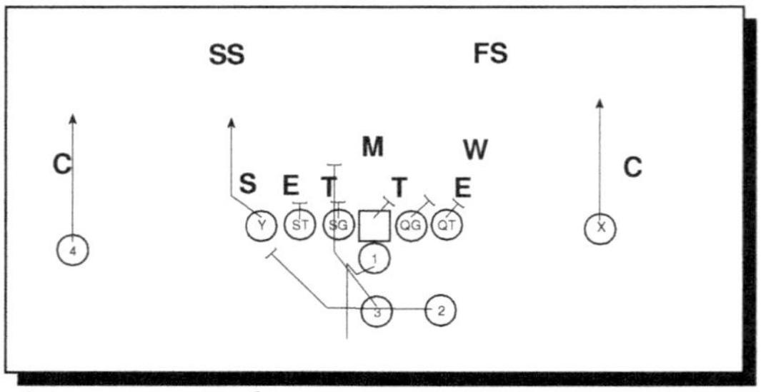

Figure 4-18. Left 785 vs. even

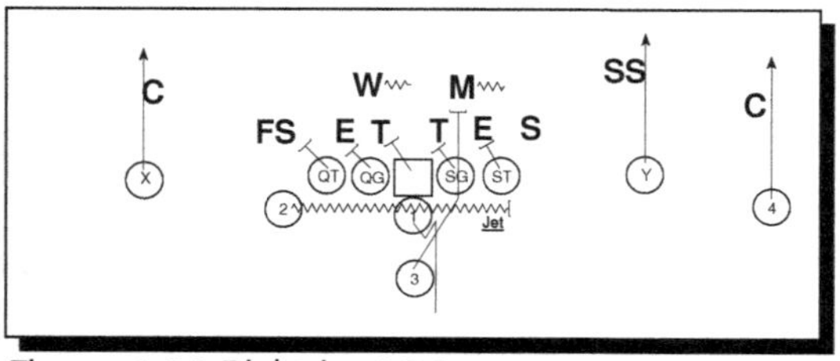

Figure 4-19.Right jet 884 vs. gap

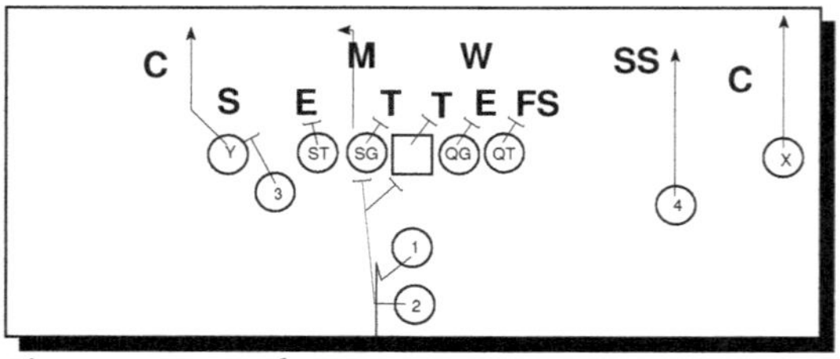

Figure 4-20. Left 989 vs. gap

From the I or pistol formation, the 2-back fakes 24. He blocks any blitz in the B or A gap strongside. If he does not encounter a blitz, he runs a hook-out pass route at six yards deep and becomes the checkdown receiver. When wing or doubles alignments are used, the 2-back blocks the first defensive man outside the strong tackle's block. If no defender shows, he runs a five-yard strongside flat route.

The 3-back runs 14 from wing or doubles and blocks any blitzing linebacker in B gap. He runs the six-yard checkdown route if he does not face a blitz. From I or pistol formations, the 3-back blocks the first defensive man past the strong tackle's block. When no defender appears, he runs a five-yard flat route.

The 80 protection provides for four potential strongside blockers and features a play-action fake to hold linebackers. When no blitz threatens, this protection scheme allows the release of five receivers into the pass pattern.

East and Eastern Pass Protections

East and eastern pass protections are bootleg protections to the quickside of the formation. Offensive line blocking assignments are identical for both. Backfield action differs. East protection is split flow as is shown in Figures 4-21 through 4-24. The running play faked for east pass protection is 26. The 2-back is responsible for blocking the first defensive player outside the strong tackle's block. The 26 is faked from I, wing, pistol, or doubles alignments. From doubles, the 2-back can be sent in jet motion across the formation, and 18, the jet sweep, is faked.

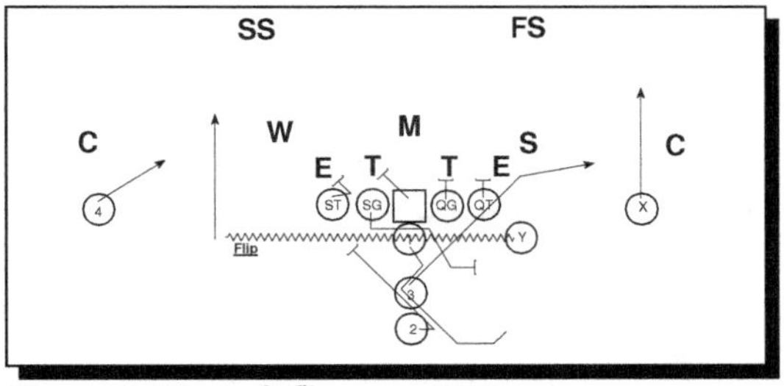

Figure 4-21. Left flip east 627 vs. even

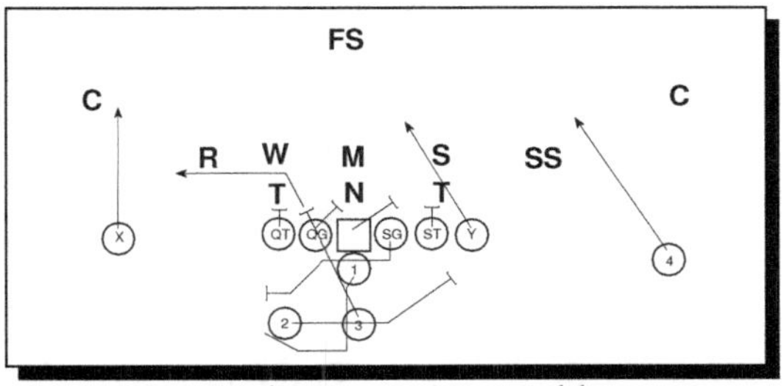

Figure 4-22. Right east 727 vs. odd

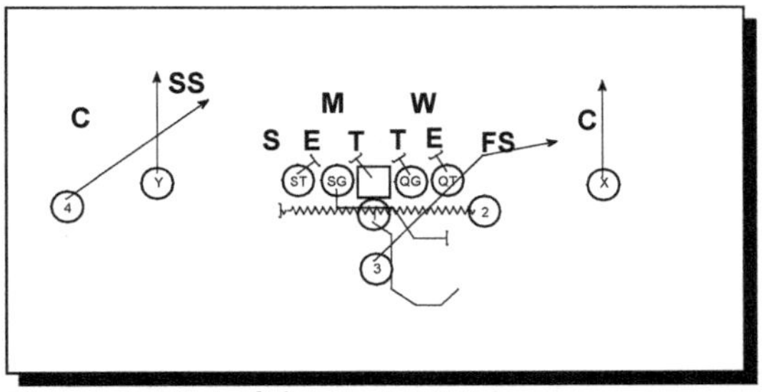

Figure 4-23. Left jet east 827 vs. gap

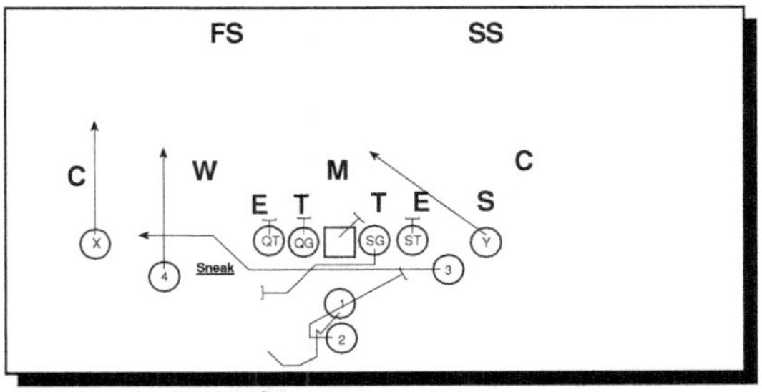

Figure 4-24. Right east 927 vs. even

The 3-back runs a flat route quickside at a depth of five yards. He releases through the quickside B gap and blocks any blitzing linebacker in B gap. If B gap is jammed, he releases outside to run his pass route. Blocking rules for east and eastern pass protection are as follows:

- Y-Receiver: Y runs a pass route for east protection. He blocks gap, over, or outside in eastern pass protection.
- Strong Tackle: The strong tackle blocks gap, over, or the first defensive man to the outside.
- Strong Guard: The strong guard pulls quickside and blocks the first defensive man who shows. He pulls to log the defender he is assigned, but if the defensive man comes upfield hard, he is kicked out.
- Center: The center blocks the first defensive man strongside.
- Quick Guard: The quick guard blocks the #1 defender on the line.
- Quick Tackle: The quick tackle's assignment is the #2 defensive man on the line of scrimmage.

Eastern pass protection has the quarterback fake 34 to the 3-back. The 3-back blocks the first defender outside the strong tackle's block. The 2-back fills for the strong guard's pull. If he does not have a blitzing linebacker to block, the 2-back runs a five-yard late flat route quickside. Eastern pass protection is run from strong formation as shown in Figure 4-25.

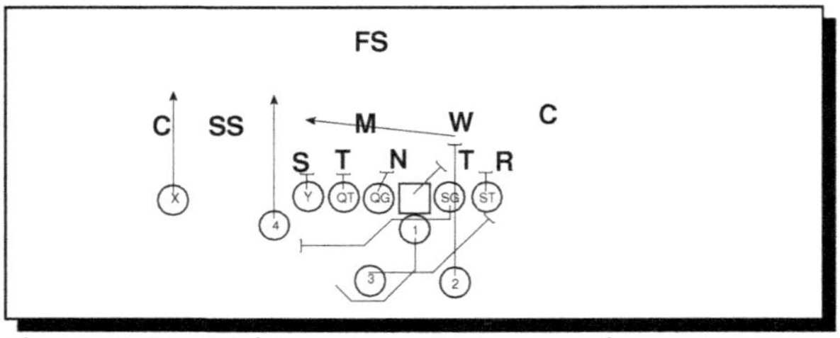

Figure 4-25. Right eastern 534 vs. under

West, Western, South, and North Protections

West, western, south, and north protections are all bootlegs run to the strongside of the formation. They are diagrammed in Figures 4-26 through 4-33. The offensive line blocking rules are identical for all four protections, but the backfield action is different for each of them. Following are offensive blocking rules for west, western, north, and south pass protections:

- Y-Receiver: For western pass protection, which is run only from strong, Y is an ineligible receiver. He blocks gap, over, or the first defensive player to the outside. Y is a pass receiver for west, north, and south protections.
- Strong Tackle: The #2 defender on the line of scrimmage is blocked by the strong tackle.

- Strong Guard: The #1 defensive player on the line is the strong guard's assignment.
- Center: The center blocks the #1 defensive man to the quickside.
- Quick Guard: The quick guard pulls strongside and blocks the first opponent to show. He pulls flat past the center and then gets depth as he attempts to log the defender he is blocking. If the defensive man comes hard upfield, the guard kicks him out.
- Quick Tackle: The quick tackle blocks gap, over, or the first defender to the outside.

Western pass protection (Figure 4-26) is run only from strong formation. The 3-back fakes 30 and runs a five-yard flat route strongside. The X-receiver and 4-back run pass routes. The 2-back fakes 25 and blocks the first defensive man who shows on the strongside. The quarterback reverse pivots to the strongside and fakes 25 before bootlegging to the quickside of the formation.

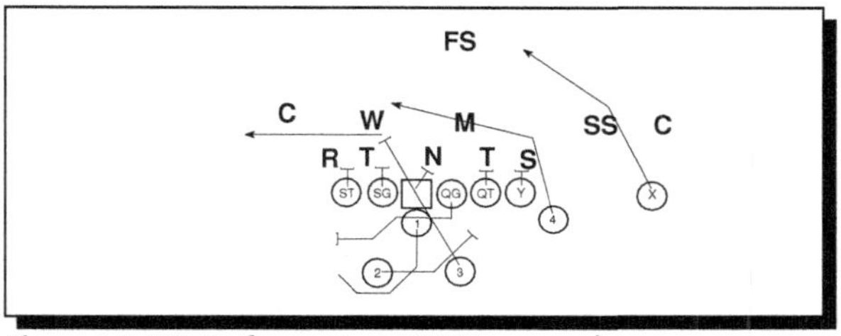

Figure 4-26. Left western 526 vs. under

When west protection is called, I formation or pistol is used. This is full flow bootleg action where the outside zone play to the quickside is faked and the quarterback bootlegs back to the strongside. If run from the I formation (Figure 4-27) the 3-back blocks the first defensive player outside the quick tackle's block. The 2-back fakes 29 and blocks the first defender past the 3-back's block. Y will run a five-yard flat route strongside. From pistol, the 2-back fakes 29 and blocks the first man outside the quick tackle's block. The 3-back blocks gap, over, outside for two counts, and runs the five-yard flat route. Figure 4-28 shows west 926 from pistol.

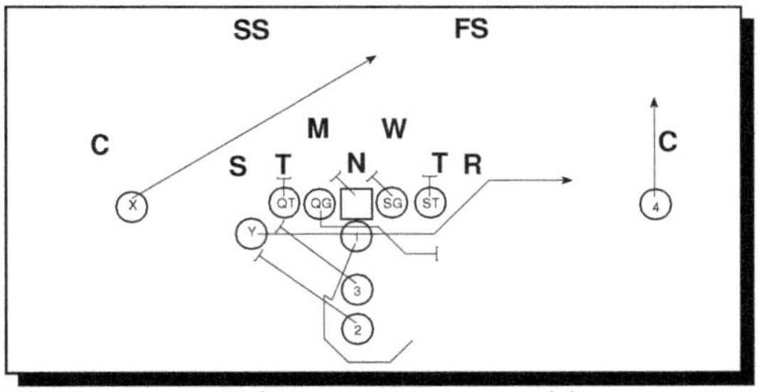

Figure 4-27. Right west 626 vs. odd

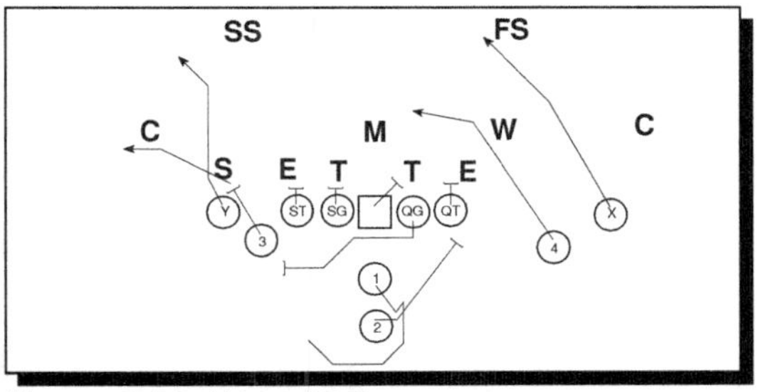

Figure 4-28. West 926 vs. even

South pass protection is run from wing or doubles formations. The 4-back goes in zac motion to the quickside and 49 is faked to him before he runs a pass route. The 2-back blocks the first defender outside the quick tackle's block. The 3-back fakes 31 and he runs a five-yard flat route to the strongside. The quarterback does a 180-degree pivot to the quickside and fakes 49, after which he bootlegs to the strongside. Figures 4-29 and 4-30 show south pass protection.

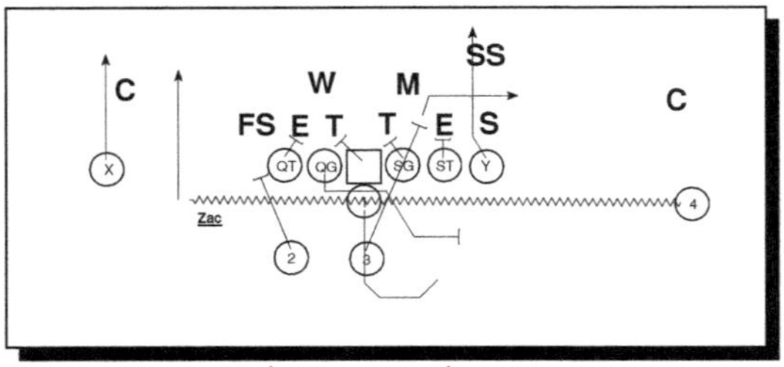

Figure 4-29. Right zac south 746 vs. gap

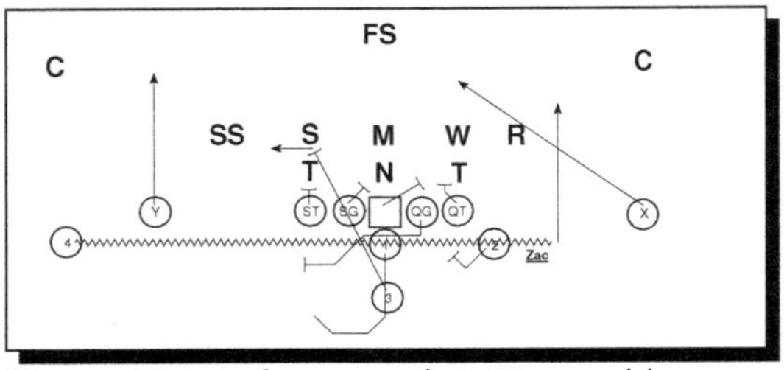

Figure 4-30. Left zac south 846 vs. odd

North protection may be run from I, wing, or doubles formations. The tackle trap, 22, is the running play being faked. Figures 4-31 through 4-33 are north protection. From wing or doubles, zac motion by the four-back is often used. The three-back blocks the first defender outside the quick tackle's block and the two-back runs 22. If the two-back encounters a blitzing linebacker, he blocks him. If not, he runs a five-yard flat route to the strongside. The quarterback reverses out to the quickside and moves to fake to the 2-back. This fake is usually executed on the quarterback's third step. Following the fake, the quarterback goes straight back to a depth of seven yards and then executes the bootleg to the strongside.

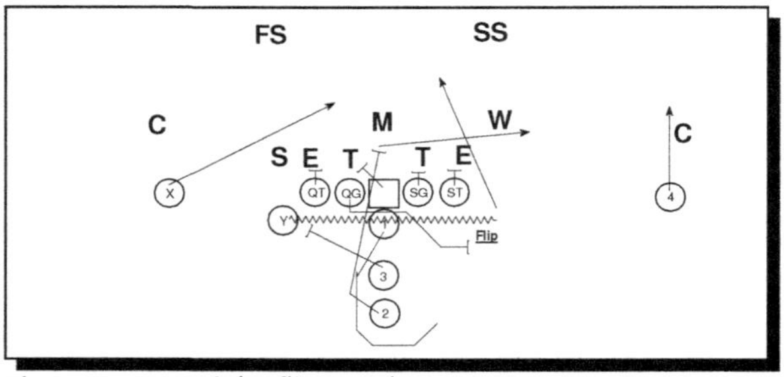

Figure 4-31. Right flip north 625 vs. even

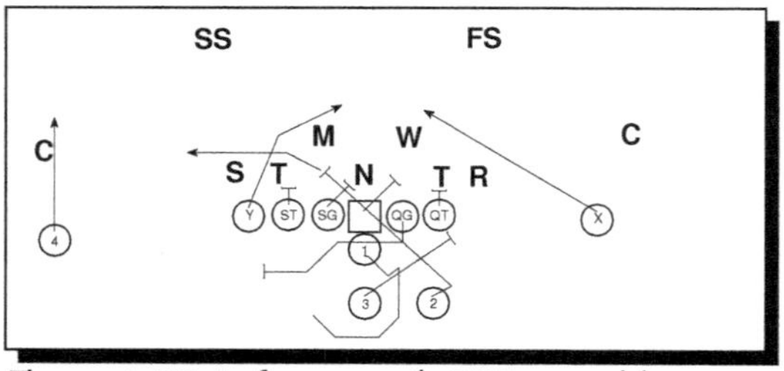

Figure 4-32. Left zac north 725 vs. odd

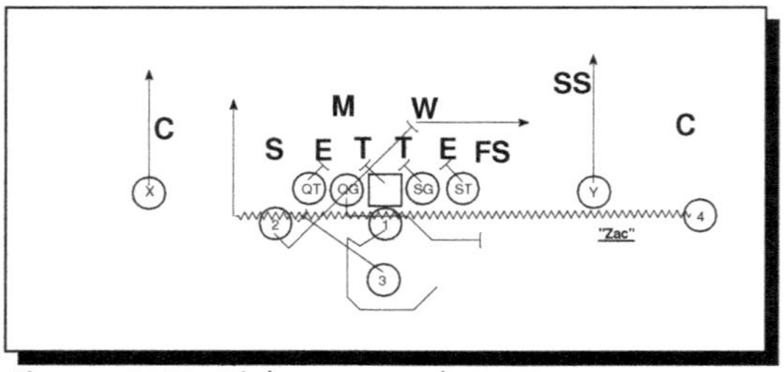

Figure 4-33. Right zac north 825 vs. gap

70 Pass Protection

The 70 is a pass protection from which the counter bootleg pass is thrown. Figures 4-34 through 4-37 are examples of 70 pass protection. The offensive line blocking rules are the same as those for west pass protection. If run from wing or doubles, zac motion is always used to provide another receiver to the quickside of the formation.

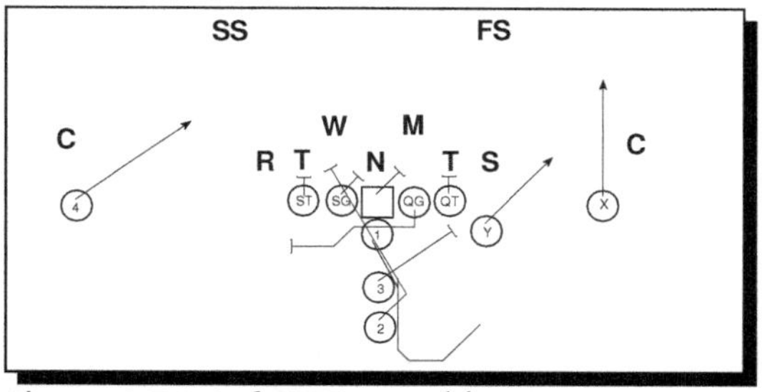

Figure 4-34. Left 677 vs. odd

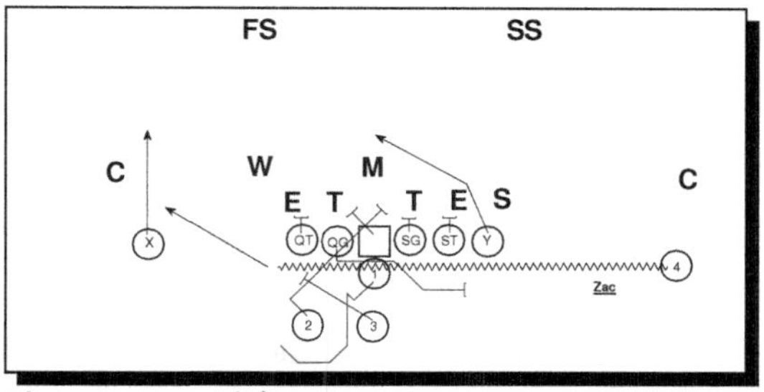

Figure 4-35. Right zac 777 vs. even

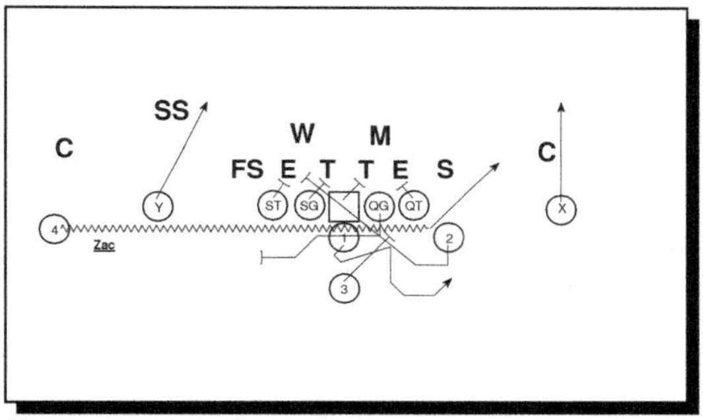

Figure 4-36. Left zac 877 vs. gap

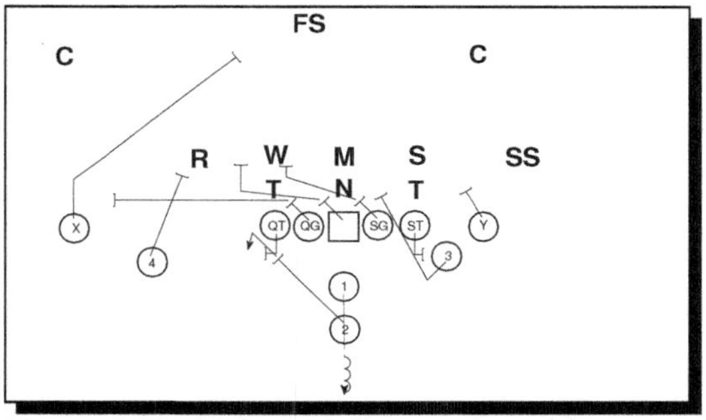

Figure 4-37. Right 980 Denver vs. odd

The 3-back blocks the first defender outside the quick tackle's block. He, like the quick tackle, must hook this man and keep him on the line of scrimmage. The 2-back runs 22 and blocks any linebacker blitz over the center.

The quarterback uses a reverse pivot. He fakes 22 and gains five yards of depth as he continues to roll quickside. This play becomes a true run-or-pass option play. If the receivers are not open, the quarterback runs the football. A great fake by the 2-back and quarterback should limit linebackers' flow toward the attack point. The quick guard pulling opposite the play's direction also holds defensive flow.

Denver is a tag that may be applied to 80 pass protection. This tag means dropback screen pass. The offensive line blocking resembles 80 protection. The strong guard and strong tackle block man protection, and the center, the quick guard, and the quick tackle slide protect to the quickside. The 3-back will double read strongside from the inside linebacker to the outside. Figures 4-38 through 4-40 show 80 pass protection with a Denver tag. Blocking assignments for Denver are as follows:

- Y-Receiver: Y blocks #3 on the line of scrimmage. If there is no #3 or Y is split, he blocks the outside linebacker or strong safety. He uses a pass protection technique for his block on #3 on the line.
- Strong Tackle: The strong tackle blocks the #2 man on the line of scrimmage.
- Strong Guard: The strong guard blocks the #1 defender on the line for two counts and then releases to the quickside flat on the defensive side of the line. When he reaches the quick tackle's position, the strong guard turns back strongside and blocks the first defensive man to show.
- Center: The center blocks A gap quickside to a man over the quick guard for two counts. After two counts, the center releases to the quickside and blocks any defensive man in the alley.
- Quick Guard: The quick guard blocks B gap to a man over the quick tackle for two counts and releases to kick out the cornerback quickside.
- Quick Tackle: The quick tackle's assignment is C gap or outside. He executes a deep pass set and invites the defender to rush upfield to the outside.
- X-Receiver: The X-receiver crack blocks the safety aligned to the quickside.
- 4-Back: The 4-back crack blocks the first second-level defender to his side.

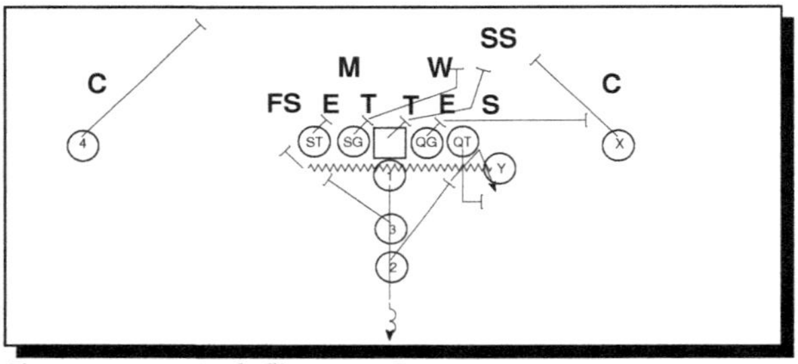

Figure 4-38. Left flip 680 Denver vs. gap

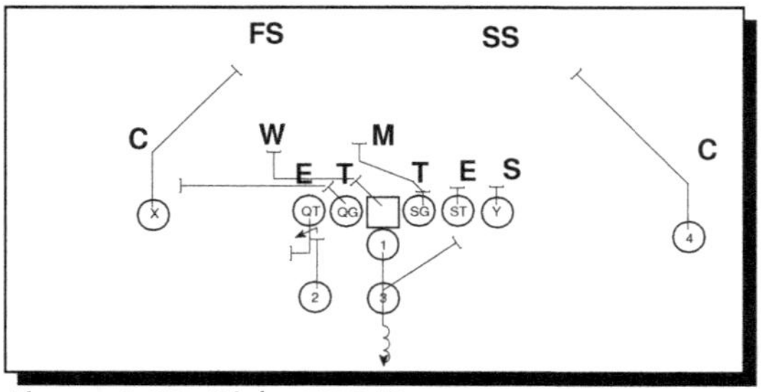

Figure 4-39. Right 780 Denver vs. even

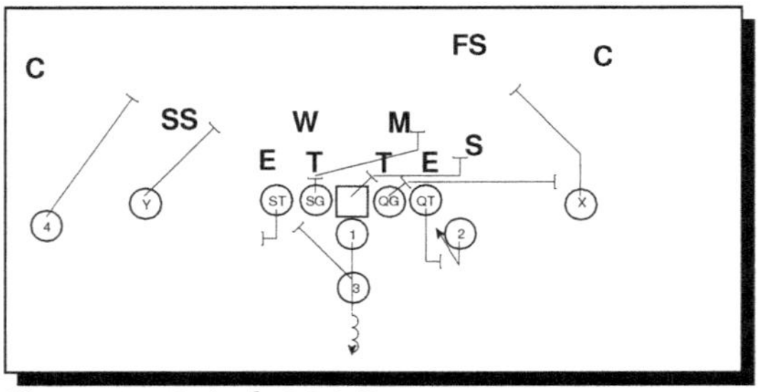

Figure 4-40. Left 880 Denver vs. even

The 2-back steps up to the quickside and simulates a pass block. He keys the quick guard's release. When the guard releases to kick out the corner, the 2-back releases behind the quick tackle's pass block and curls back onto the offensive side of the line of scrimmage. He will sit and turn his body back to the quarterback. After catching the ball, the 2-back calls go to alert the offensive lineman that he has started to run.

The quarterback executes a five-step dropback. He focuses his eyes to the strongside. At five steps of depth, he hesitates and then drifts back two more steps before turning and throwing the ball to the 2-back.

CHAPTER 5

The Quick Passing Game

The quick passing game is used extensively in the no-huddle multiple offense. It has proved to be an effective method of moving the football in this offense. Because of the quarterback's short drops of one to three steps, it is difficult for the defense to apply pressure to him. Other advantages of this phase of the passing game include the following:

- It should result in a high percentage of completions. A 70 percent completion rate is the target.
- The interception ratio should be low since the ball is not in the air for a long period of time.
- The patterns can be thrown versus any secondary coverage.
- Big play potential is present if any tackles are missed.
- Pre-snap reads determine to which side of the formation the quarterback will throw.
- Most of the quarterback's reads are versus only one secondary defender.
- The no-huddle multiple offense views the quick passing game as an extension of the run game using long handoffs.
- It attacks all of the secondary zones.

From under the center, the quarterback uses primarily a three-step drop. A one-step drop is sometimes used for the fade pattern when there is not room to throw the ball deeper. One- or two-step drops are used when throwing the bubble screens. From the pistol alignment, the quarterback uses a catch-and-throw technique with no drop. He is already aligned four yards deep in this formation. The quarterback should always look off the safeties when throwing quick passes.

The quick passing attack normally uses 50 or 60 protections. As described in Chapter 4, these are slide protections with one or two backs blocking opposite the offensive line slide. The offensive linemen use a low, aggressive blocking technique, and the backs in college football cut block the edge. This approach forces the defenders to get their hands down and helps eliminate the possibility of passes being tipped or the quarterback having to change the trajectory of his throw.

Four basic patterns are run in the quick pass series, with the addition of the bubble and wide receiver screens. The basic patterns are numbered 0 through 3.

0 Pattern

A 0 pattern (Figures 5-1 through 5-4) is the shallow mesh route. For a 0 pattern, the Y-receiver runs a shallow crossing route, never getting deeper than six yards. From doubles, wing, or I, the 2-back crosses under Y as close to him as possible. Y sets the depth of the route, and the 2-back running the under cross is responsible for the mesh. When a pistol formation is employed, zin motion is used by the 4-back, and he crosses under Y and creates the mesh. After meshing, the crossers may set down in a void versus zone defensive coverages or continue to the flat at six yards of depth.

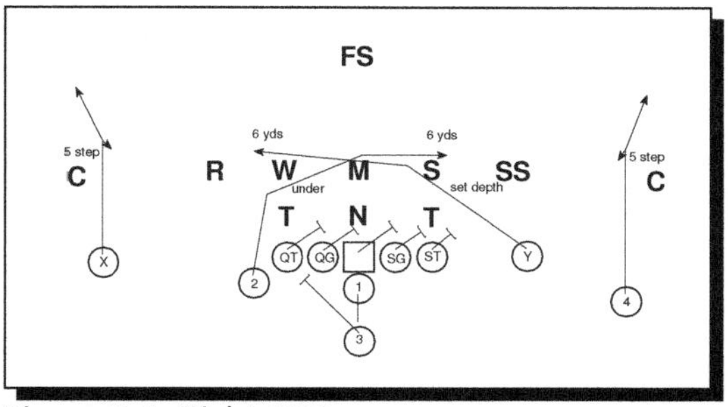

Figure 5-1. Right 850

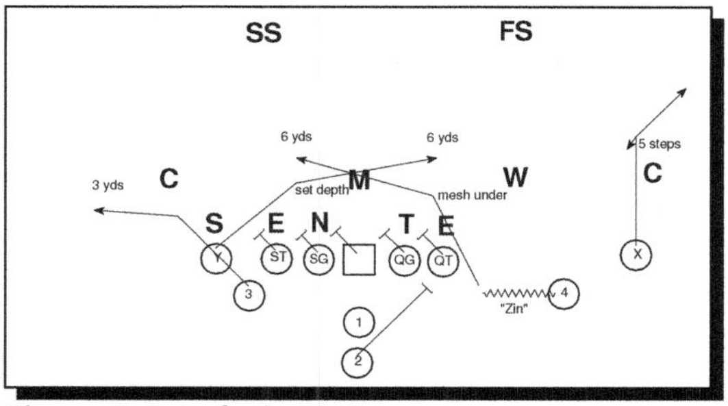

Figure 5-2. Left zin 950

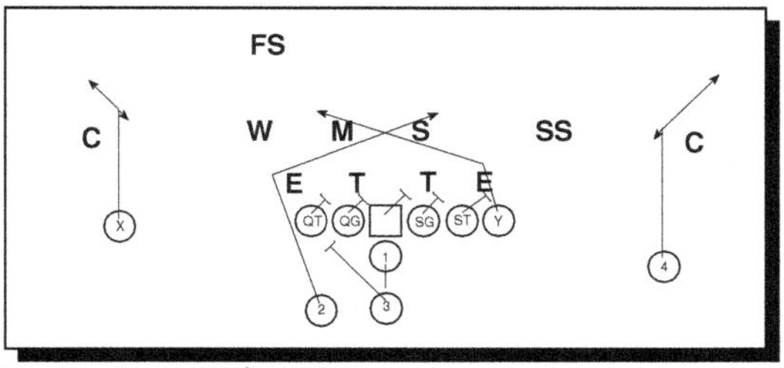

Figure 5-3. Right 750

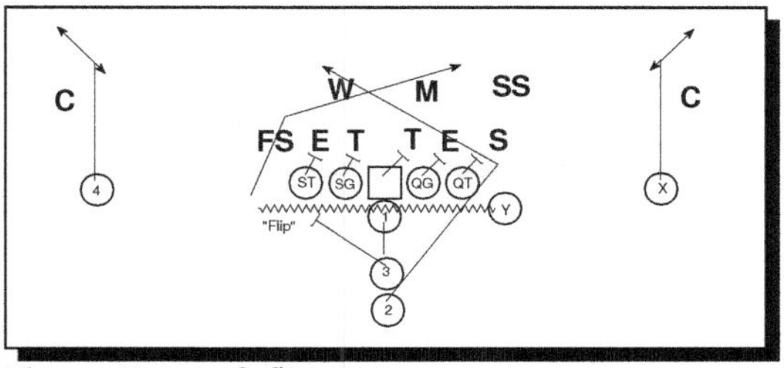

Figure 5-4. Left flip 660

The X-receiver always runs a five-step corner route. He aims for 18 yards of depth after he cuts. From doubles, wing, and I, the 4-back has the same route. The 3-back aligned for the pistol formation runs an arrow route aiming for three yards of depth.

The quarterback throws to one of the crossing players after the mesh is completed. This pattern is very good versus man-to-man pass coverage and also is effective against zone coverages.

Wide receivers and Y are numbered 1 through 3, starting on the strongside of the formation. For some patterns, pass routes are assigned by the receiver's number. Motion may change the number assigned to one or more of the receivers.

1 Pattern

A 1 pattern has six-yard quick out routes run by the #1 and #3 receivers. The #2 receiver, the 2-back from doubles or wing, and the 3-back from the pistol, all run six-yard hitch routes. The quarterback uses a three-step drop. Against a loose corner, the quarterback makes a pre-snap decision as to which side of the formation he will work and throws the quick out. If the corner is rolled up in cover 2 or man coverage, receivers #1 and #3 convert the out cut to a fade. The quarterback throws the fade or works to the hitch routes. The conversion to a fade by receivers #1 and #3 may be a sight adjustment for the quarterback, or it may be signaled by the receiver pre-snap. A simple signal to indicate the change of route is to have the receivers hang their arms in front of them in their normal stance, but place the hands on the hips when they intend to convert the pattern.

The 1 pattern normally uses 60 or 50 pass protection. It is possible to use 80 pass protection with the chance that the 3-back may have an opportunity to run a six-yard hitch over the middle if he does not block a blitzing linebacker. Figures 5-5 through 5-8 are 1 patterns from varying formations. Because of the ability of the outside receivers to convert their routes, this pattern can be effective against any secondary coverage. It is most effective versus cover 3 or 4.

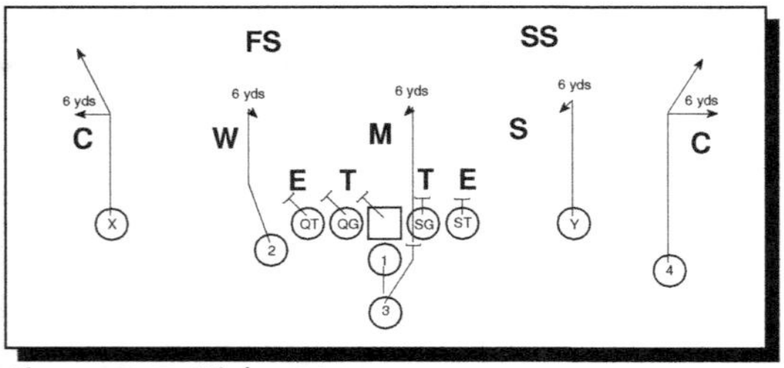

Figure 5-5. Right 881

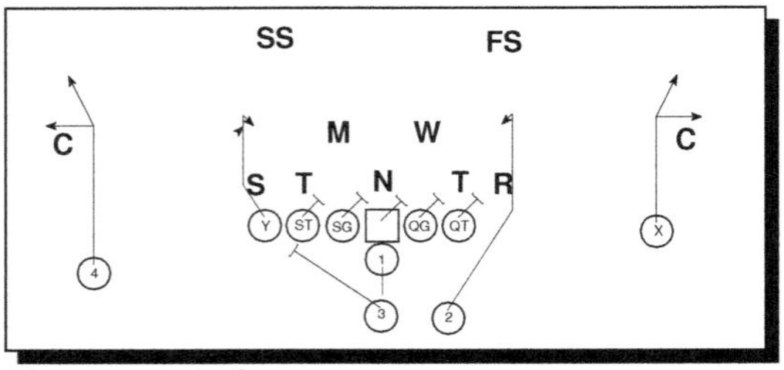

Figure 5-6. Left 761

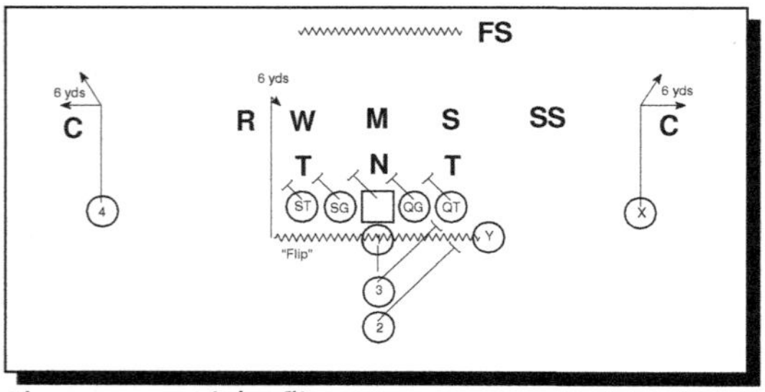

Figure 5-7. Right flip 651

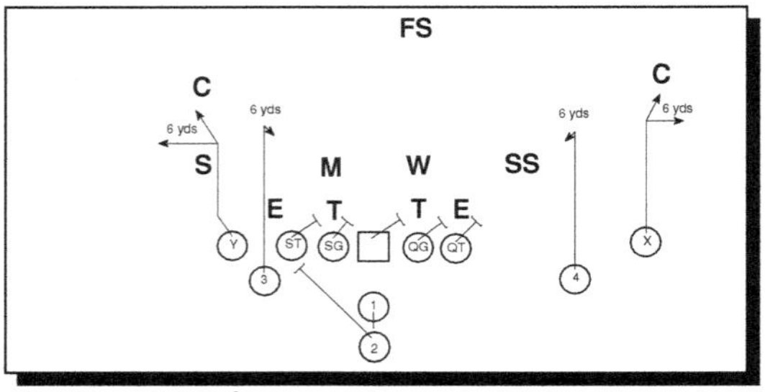

Figure 5-8. Left 961

Gold is a tag that may be added to any quick pass pattern. Figure 5-9 illustrates 851 gold. The call of gold has receivers #1 and #3 run their normal pass cut at six yards and after three steps they turn upfield on a fade route. This tag is a double move for receivers #1 and #3. The quarterback makes a pump fake for the out route and then throws the fade. Receiver #2 and the 2-back or 3-back run hitch routes, and they may also be targeted by the quarterback. This play needs to be run when corners are reading the depth of the quarterback's drop and breaking up on the out cut.

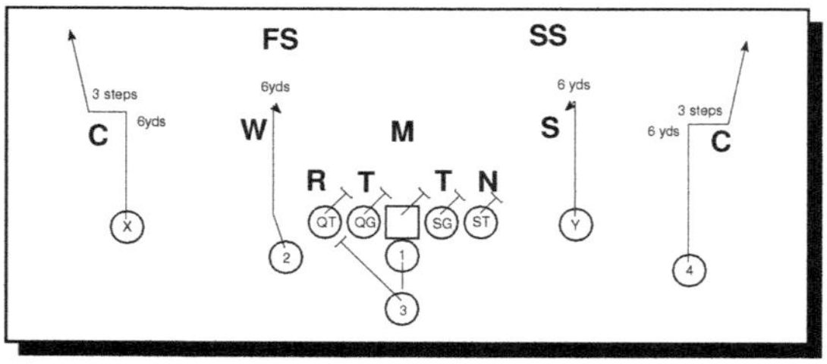

Figure 5-9. Right 851 gold

2 Pattern

The 2 pattern is a third quick pass concept. This pattern is a six-yard slant route for receivers #1 and #3. If the 2-back or the 3-back is in a wing alignment, he runs an arrow cut, aiming for three yards of depth in the near flat. The #2 receiver's route is determined by his alignment. If he is tight to the formation, he will run a three-yard arrow to the flat. When he is split from the formation, receiver #2 will execute a six-yard slant route. When receiver #1 or receiver #3 has a split #2 receiver to their side, the outside receiver runs a six-yard square-in cut.

The quarterback predetermines the side to which he will throw. With flat and slant combination, the read man becomes the flat defender. With a slant and square-in pattern, the quarterback reads inside out. The square-in is an easy pass to throw and has a high completion rate. If a third receiver is to any side of the formation and a 1 or 2 pattern is called, the third receiver runs a seam route.

If a 2 pattern is called, receivers do not convert the routes no matter what the defensive coverage. The slant pattern is effective versus all types of coverages.

Figures 5-10 through 5-15 show examples of two patterns from multiple formations. As shown in these diagrams, the receivers running the slant outside release on an angle to widen the defender covering them.

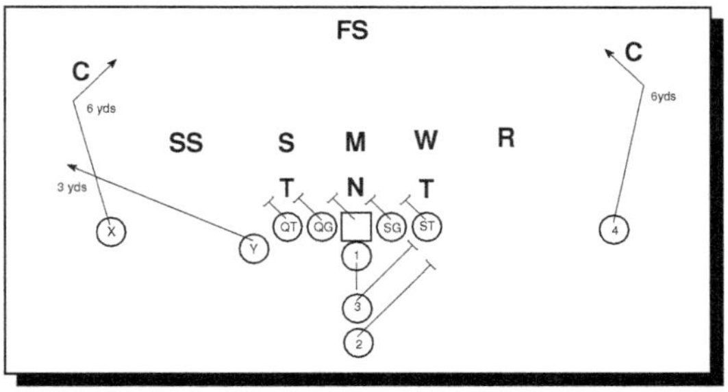

Figure 5-10. Left 662

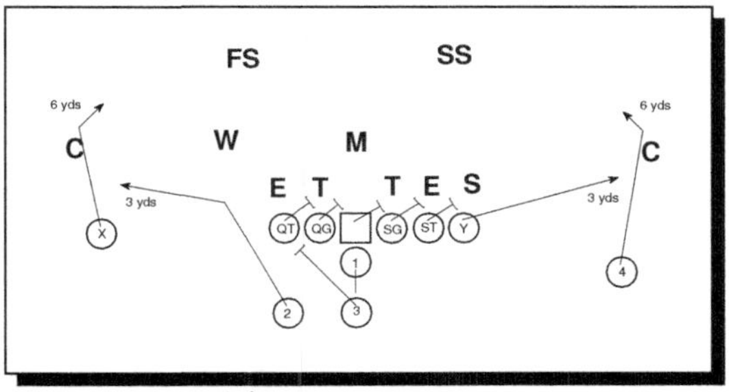

Figure 5-11. Right 752

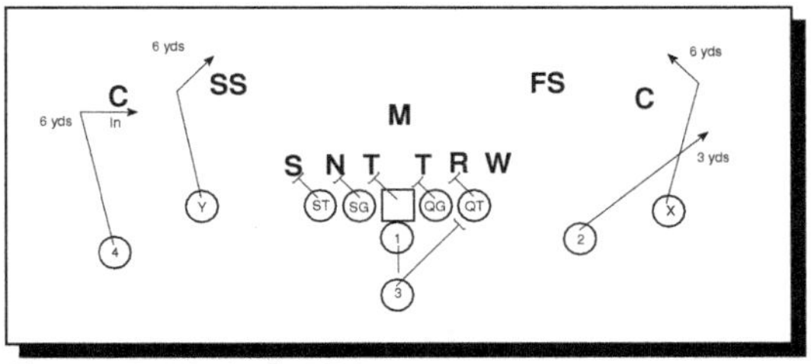

Figure 5-12. Left 852

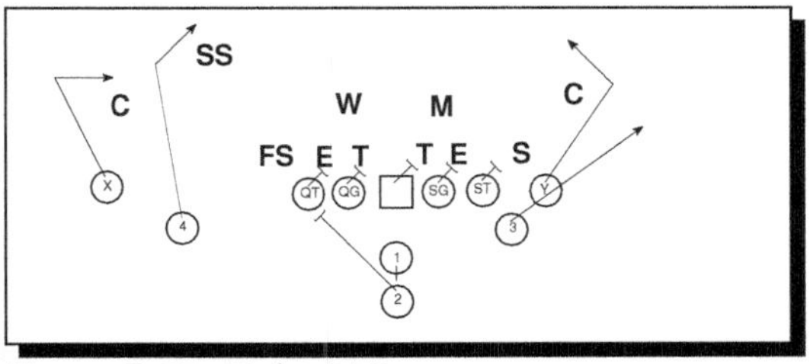

Figure 5-13. Right 952

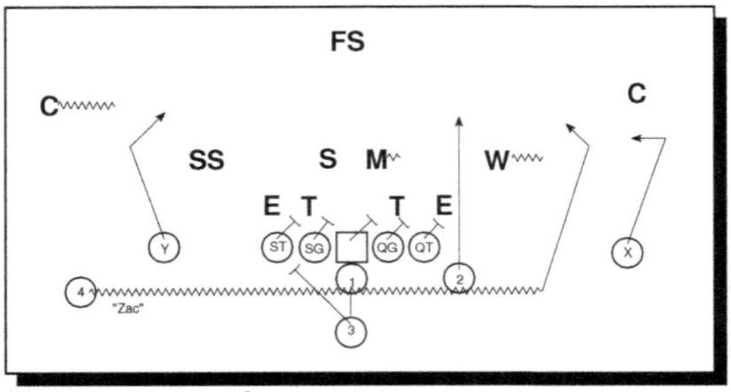

Figure 5-14. Left zac 862

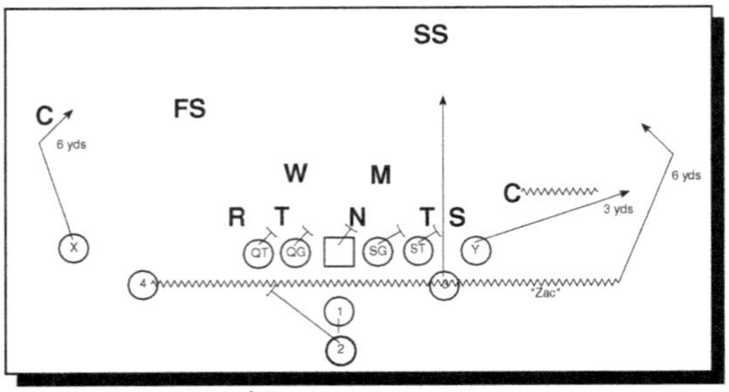

Figure 5-15. Right zac 952

3 Pattern

The 3 pattern (Figures 5-16 through 5-19) is an all-fade concept. This pattern has receivers #1 and #3 run fade routes at the bottom of the numbers. The receiver runs these cuts in such a way as to allow room for the ball to be thrown to the receiver between him and the sideline. The distance from the sideline can never be less than six yards. Once the receiver is able to secure a release from the defender covering him, he must get to the outside edge of the numbers. When possible, he should release to the corner's outside, but the position of the defensive man may force an inside release. In this case, the receiver stems back to the numbers as soon as possible. A well-thrown fade route allows the receiver to use his body to shield the defender away from the ball and still have room to catch the pass inbounds. If the defensive men covering the #1 and #2 receivers are playing off coverage, the receivers convert the fade route to a four-step hitch cut.

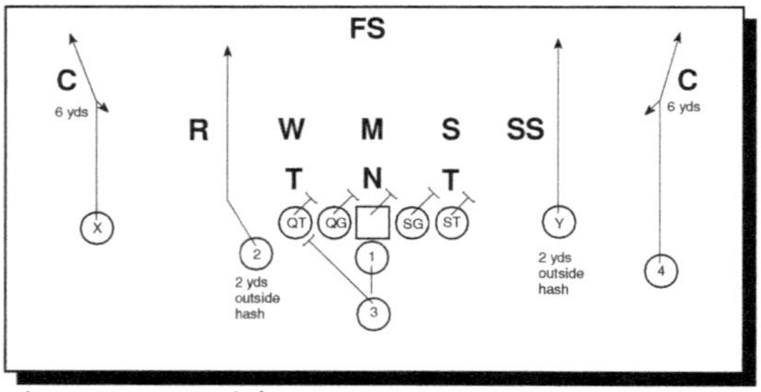

Figure 5-16. Right 853

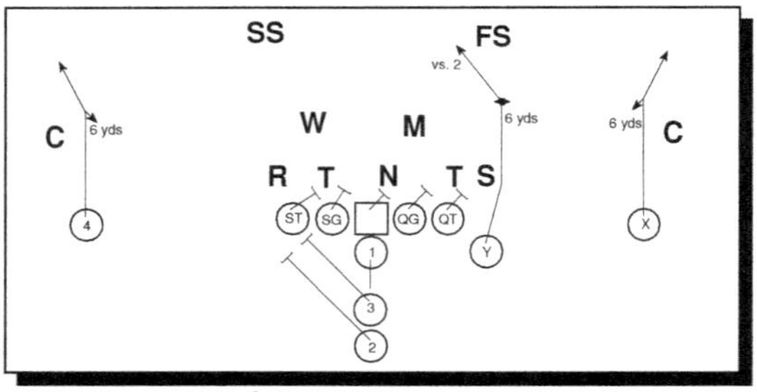

Figure 5-17. Left 663

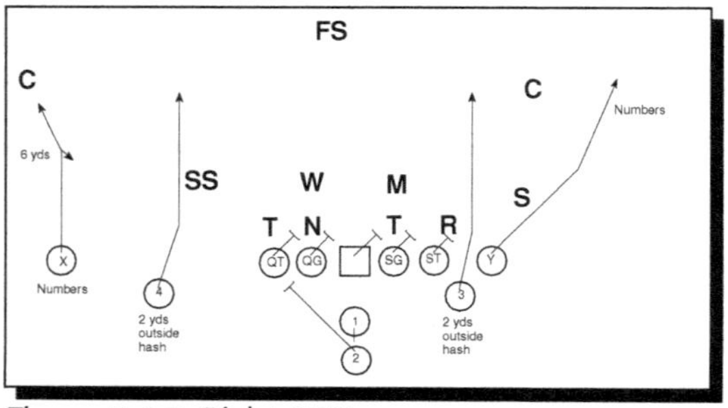

Figure 5-18. Right 953

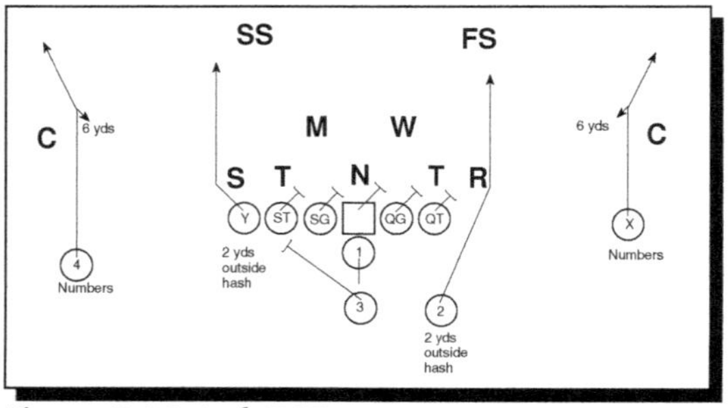

Figure 5-19. Left 763

Receiver #2 and the 2-back or 3-back run seam routes two yards outside the hash marks. These landmarks are the aiming points for the receivers no matter where the ball is located on the field. Versus two high safeties, the #2 receiver bends his route to the middle of the field at six yards of depth.

When faced with a single high safety, the quarterback throws to one of the inside seam routes based on the reaction of the safety. The quarterback can influence the reaction of the safety by looking at the seam route opposite of where he intends to throw. Against two high safeties, the quarterback picks a side of the formation and throws to either the inside seam or the #1 or #3 receiver running the fade. The pre-snap look by the quarterback should help him anticipate whether the fade route by either receiver #1 or #3 will be converted to a four-step hitch cut.

The quarterback normally uses a three-step drop when throwing the 3 pattern, but he may use a one-step drop in some instances, such as goal line. Holding the ball too long is a common fault for quarterbacks throwing the fade pattern.

A tag may be used for the 3 pattern; it is the word two. This tag affects all the receivers running the pattern. If a call such as right 853 two is made, the #1 and #3 receivers are locked into running the fade routes regardless of secondary coverage. Receiver #2 and the 2-back or 3-back are locked into running three-step speed outs at about five yards of depth. Figures 5-20 through 5-23 show the 3 pattern employing a two tag.

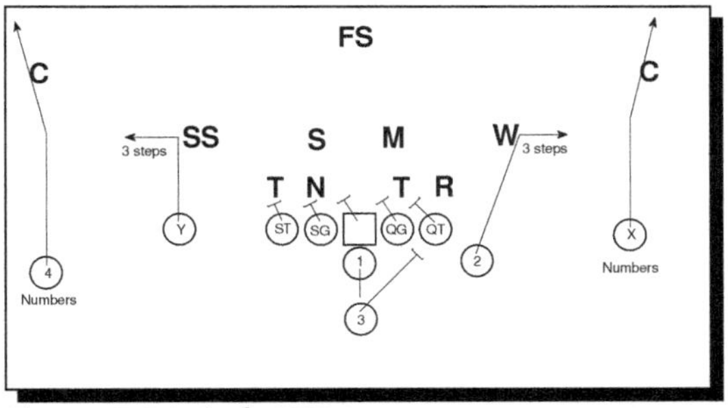

Figure 5-20. Left 853 two

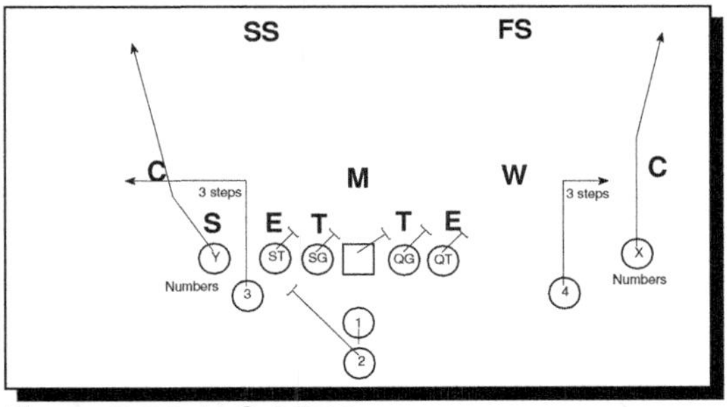

Figure 5-22. Left 963 two

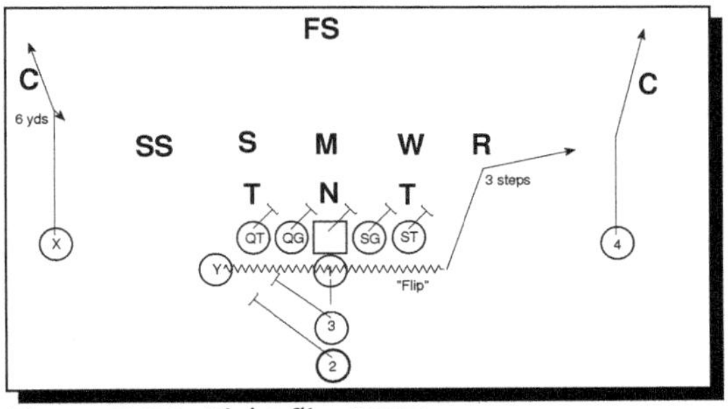

Figure 5-21. Right flip 653 two

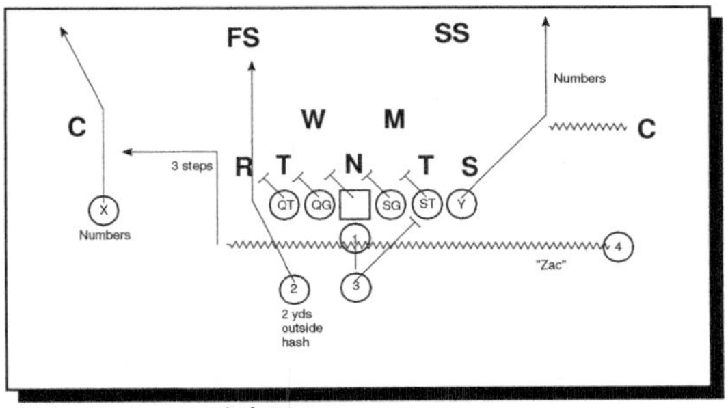

Figure 5-23. Right zac 763 two

When running this pattern, the quarterback will pick a side to which to throw based on his pre-snap read. When the ball is snapped, he reads the corner. If the corner hangs for the speed out, the ball is thrown to the wide receiver in the hole between the corner and the safety. When the corner goes deep with the outside receiver, the quarterback throws the speed out. This pattern is designed to beat cover 2 secondary coverages.

Tags are added to the 0 pattern to call the bubble screen and the jailbreak screen. Figure 5-24 shows 760 Fred. Fred is the tag used to call the bubble screen to the 4-back. Zac motion has the 4-back cross the formation to the quickside. Using motion across the formation sometimes allows the receiver to outleverage the defender assigned to cover him. The X-receiver blocks the man covering him, and the 4-back works off of his block.

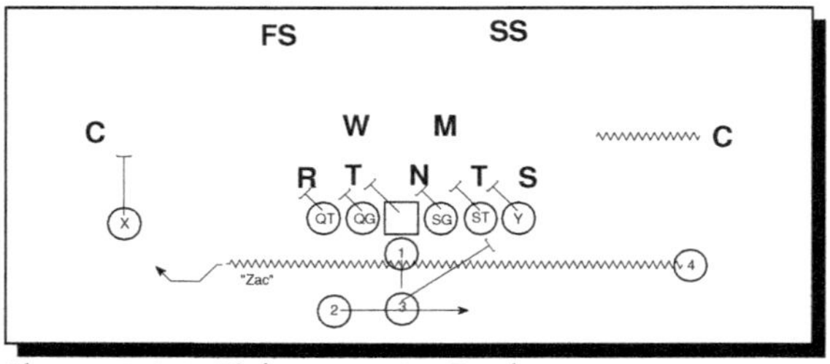

Figure 5-24. Right zac 760 Fred

Figure 5-25 illustrates the other way that the bubble screen is potentially thrown to the 4-back. From the pistol formation, the 4-back runs the bubble screen route and the X-receiver blocks for him. Everyone blocks 60 protection. The quarterback catches the snap and throws at once to the 4-back.

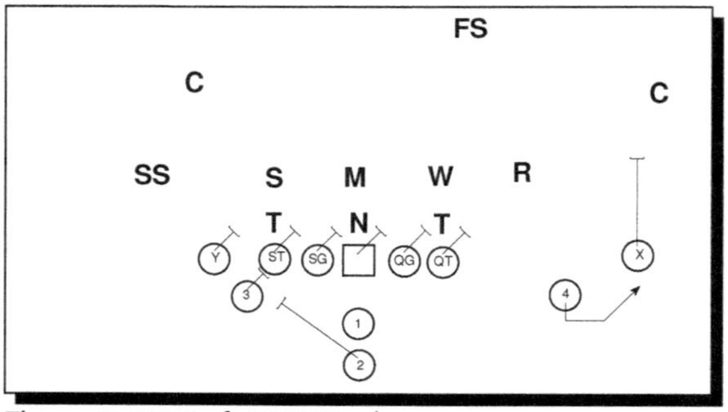

Figure 5-25. Left 960 Fred

A Frank tag on the 0 call has the jailbreak or wide receiver screen thrown to the 4-back. Figure 5-26 shows the I formation with flip motion by Y. He is responsible for blocking the corner covering the 4-back. The 4-back takes one quick step upfield and two steps back so that he is behind the line of scrimmage when the football is thrown to him. The 50 pass protection is used. If the strong tackle does not have a defender to his outside on the line of scrimmage, he releases upfield to block the first defensive man to his outside off the line. This pass could also be run from doubles with jet motion by the 2-back as seen in Figure 5-27. In this case, Y blocks the man covering the 4-back, and the 2-back blocks the second defender from the outside.

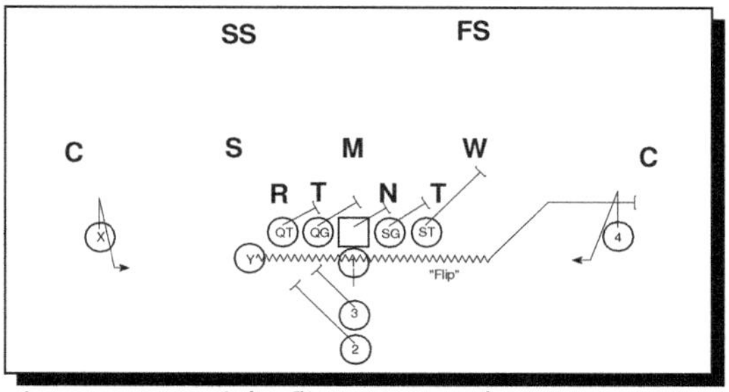

Figure 5-26. Right flip 650 Frank

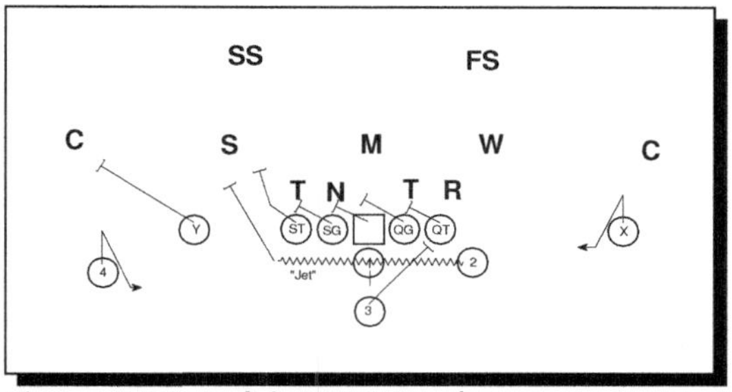

Figure 5-27. Left jet 850 Frank

The Tom tag following a 0 call indicates the bubble screen thrown to the 2-back as shown in Figure 5-28. Jet motion is used to have the 2-back cross the formation to the strongside. Y and the 4-back block the defensive men covering them. In this case, 50 pass protection is used.

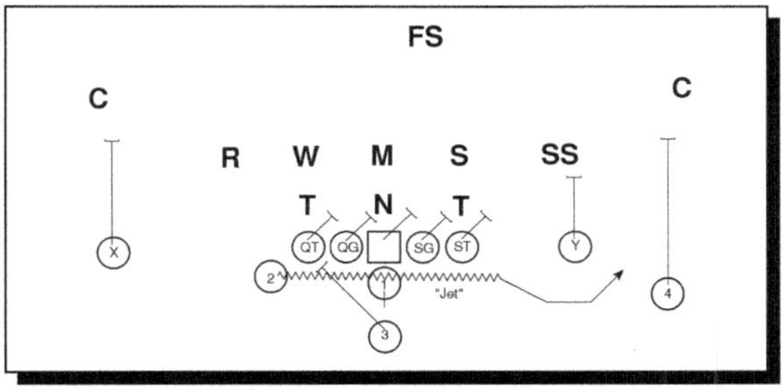

Figure 5-28. Right jet 850 Tom

The no-huddle multiple offense uses the quick screen passing game like a sweep play as another method of attacking the perimeter of the defense as rapidly as possible. Big play potential exists if there is a missed tackle or if the defense fails to adjust properly. The threat of these screens forces the defense to cover each potential receiver. Effective blocking by the wide receivers and Y on the secondary defenders is crucial to the success of the play.

A one- or two-step drop by the quarterback from under the center is used for these passes. When a pistol formation is used, no drop is executed. These passes are easy to throw, but they need to be practiced frequently to ensure that they are thrown forward and that the timing is correct. The quarterback and those receiving the pass must work on the play daily.

The quick passing game has the potential for a high completion percentage and big plays. This passing series is relatively easy to protect because of the quick release of the football. Slide protections seal the interior gaps. As a result, effective pass rushers must come from the outside. When the ball is thrown on time, these rushers should not get to the quarterback. When combined with the play-action passing game, the quick passing attack provides a complete pass offense.

CHAPTER 6

Basic Pass Concepts and Dropback Passes

Chapter 5 covered the 0 through 3 pass patterns and how they are used in the quick passing game. This chapter covers the 4 through 9 pass patterns and how they are used in the five-step dropback pass series. The dropback screen pass is also discussed in this chapter. Patterns 4 through 9 are also used for the play-action and sprint-out passing attack.

Each pattern is taught to the quarterback, the running backs, and the receivers as a concept. As an example, the 7 pattern is a quickside flood pattern that may be thrown from dropback, sprint-out, bootleg, or play-action. Y- and X-receivers and the 4-back are numbered 1 through 3, starting on the strongside. The routes that make up any pattern are assigned by number to the appropriate receiver. For a 7 pattern, the #1 receiver runs a drag quickside, #2 runs a skinny post, and #3 runs a read route that ends up as a curl or post corner based on the secondary coverage. The running backs have complementary routes based on the pass concept. Motion by Y or the 4-back can change their receiver number. Tags are used to alter pass patterns.

Dropback passes are thrown with either 50 or 60 protection, which are slide protections that use dropback pass protection techniques for the linemen and backs. Pass protections are discussed in Chapter 4.

The 4-back and Y may learn pass routes for two different positions for each pass concept as they align or motion to different positions based on the formations used. The 4-back and Y learn pass routes for the #1 and #2 receiver positions. An X-receiver is always the #3 receiver.

4 Pattern

A 4 pattern (Figures 6-1 through 6-4) is an all-vertical concept. This concept is utilized with four or three quick receivers. Receivers #1 and #3 run go routes on the outside of the number. If the defensive back covering them is deep, the routes are converted to 15-yard comeback cuts at 15 yards of depth. Receiver #2 and the 2-back or 3-back run seam routes two yards outside the hash marks. When facing two deep safeties, the #2 receiver bends his seam route inside the near safety.

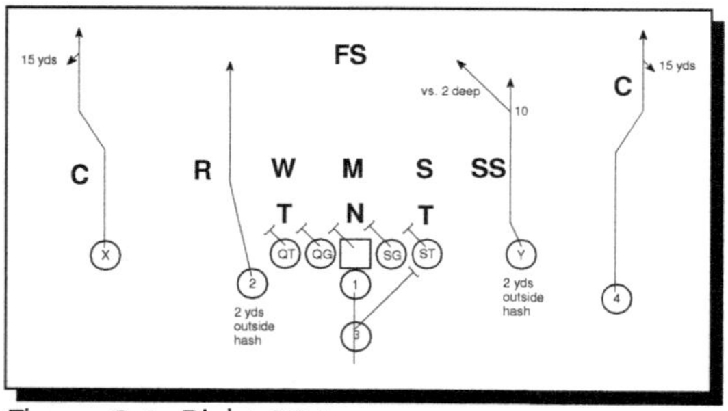

Figure 6-1. Right 864

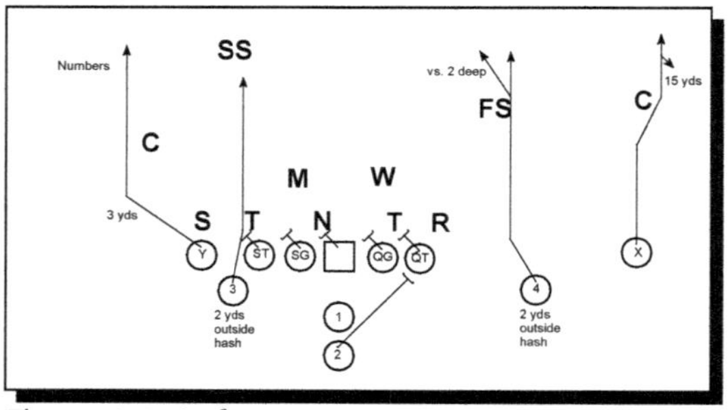

Figure 6-2. Left 954

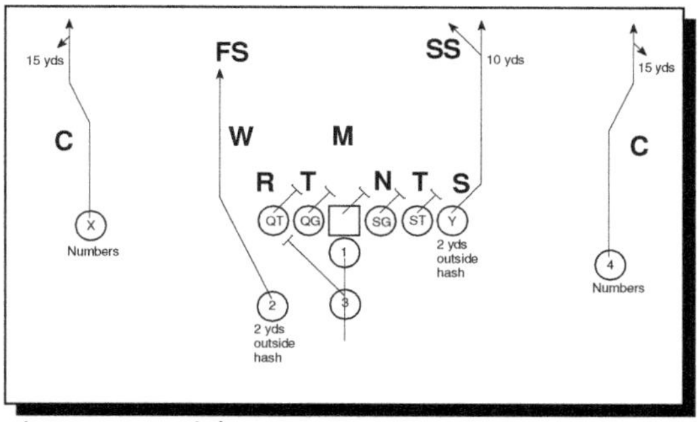

Figure 6-3. Right 754

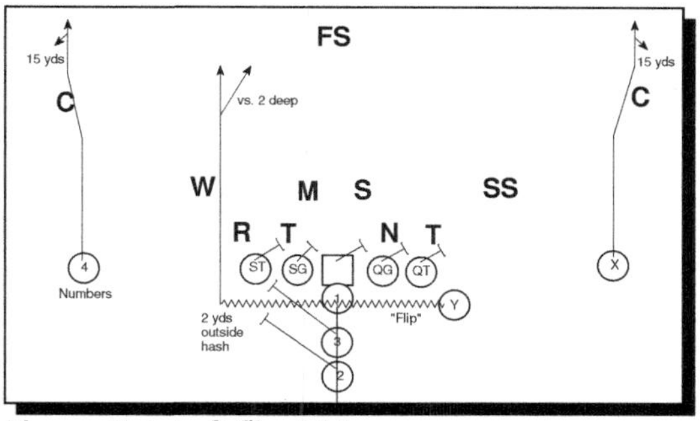

Figure 6-4. Left flip 664

Against one high safety, the quarterback will throw to one of the inside seam routes as his first choice. He must look the safety off to the opposite side before making the throw. The quarterback's second choice is one of the comeback routes. Versus two high safeties, the quarterback's progression has him throw to either the seam route or go route to one side or the other. This read is made on the safety to the side he is working. His second read is the comeback cut by the outside receiver.

Utah is the tag that may be applied to the 4 pattern. This tag affects receivers #1 and #3. Figures 6-5 through 6-8 show 4 patterns using the Utah tag. This variation of the 4 route has the #3 receiver run a shallow crossing route to the strongside of the formation. This route is under the linebackers' drops at a depth of no more than three yards behind the line of scrimmage. The #3 receiver can set down in a hole versus zone coverage any time after he passes the strong guard's position. Versus man coverage, he continues his route to the strongside flat. Receiver #1 runs a square-in route at a depth of 12 yards. He reads linebacker drops and settles down in the first void in the defense he finds after crossing under the seam route run by receiver #2. Against man-to-man coverage, he continues across the field to the quickside of the alignment.

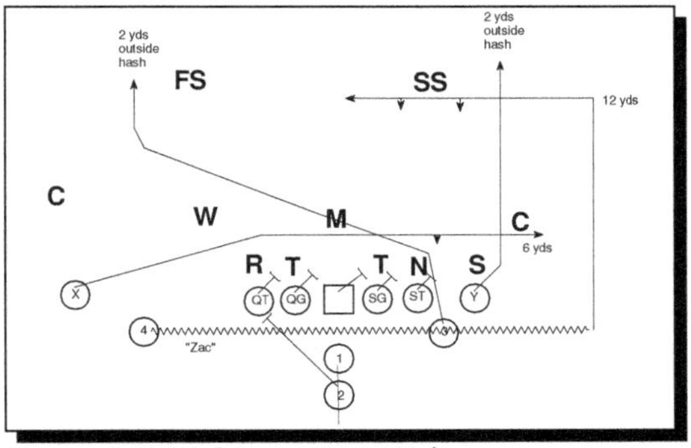

Figure 6-5. Right zac 954 Utah

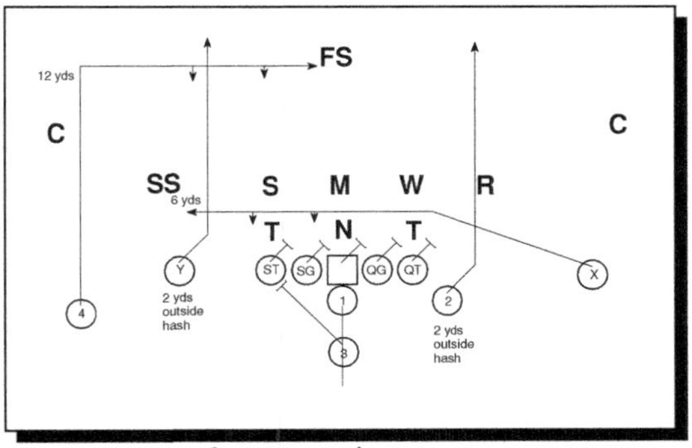

Figure 6-6. Left 864 Utah

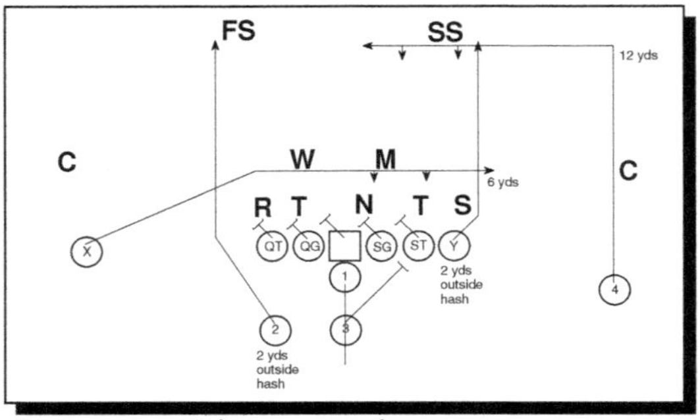

Figure 6-7. Right 764 Utah

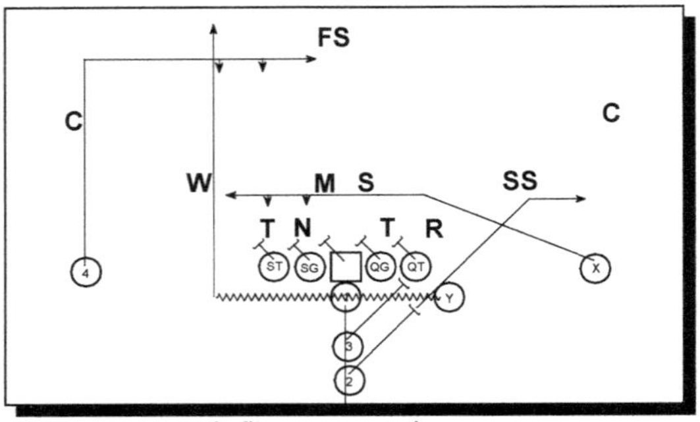

Figure 6-8. Left flip 654 Utah

Read progression for the quarterback is the under route by receiver #3 first and then the in route by the #1 receiver. This progression is a high flow read on the Mike linebacker. Receivers #1 and #3 will reduce their splits so that they may get to the desired positions more quickly.

Read patterns 5 through 9 each employ at least one deep route. This route is referred to as a blink read. The quarterback always takes a quick glance at the receiver first and will throw to him if he is open. This concept means that every pattern has the possibility of the home-run throw.

5 Pattern

Figures 6-9 through 6-12 show examples of the 5 pattern. The 5 pattern is a crossing concept that is used for dropback, play-action, or bootleg passes. Y- and X-receivers always execute the crossing action. Y releases upfield for about four yards and then drags across the formation to the quickside. He aims for a depth of 12 to 15 yards. Y is responsible for setting the depth of the mesh point with X. Y's depth will change in goal line situations. To execute the 5 pattern, Y must always start his route from the strongside of the formation. When the I formation is used, Y must always use flip motion to reach the strongside.

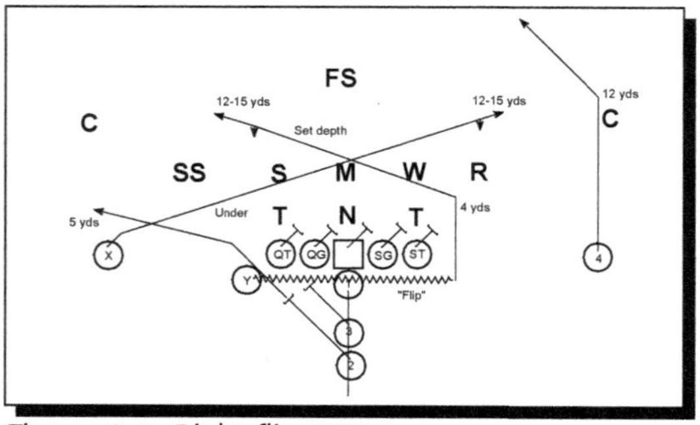

Figure 6-9. Right flip 655

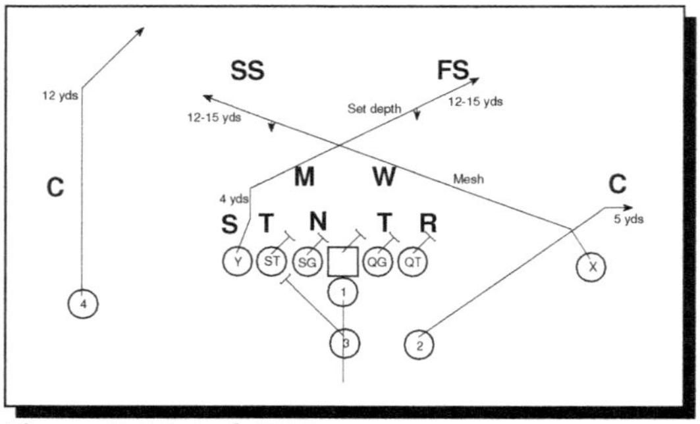

Figure 6-10. Left 765

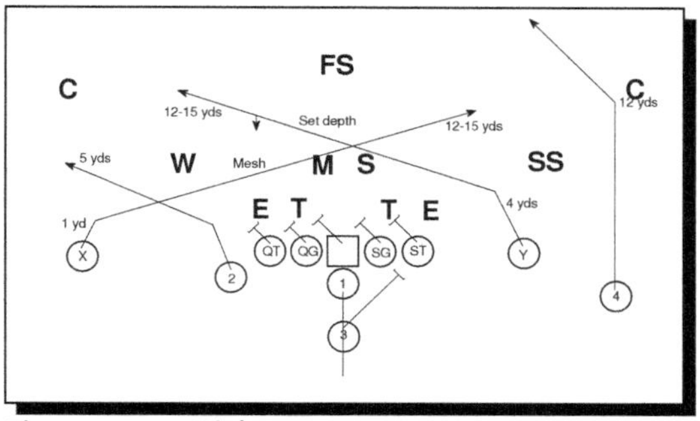

Figure 6-11. Right 865

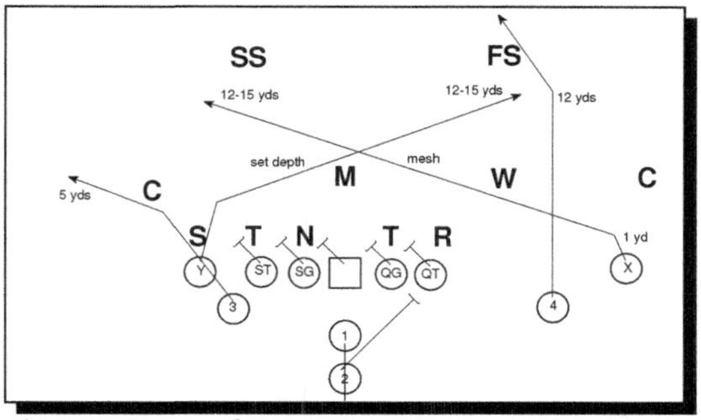

Figure 6-12. Left 955

Receiver #3, the X-receiver, releases upfield one yard and then crosses to the strongside under Y's route. X is responsible for creating the mesh as closely as possible with Y. Normal aiming depth for X is 12 to 15 yards on the strongside.

After the mesh is executed, Y- and X-receivers may settle down in voids in zones. If no voids occur or man-to-man coverage is faced, they continue across the field. The X- receiver may reduce his split for the 5 pattern.

The 4-back runs a 12-yard post route that serves as the blink read. One of two tags may be applied to his route. Ohio tag (Figure 6-13) has the 4-back run a comeback route at a depth of 12 yards. Iowa (Figure 6-14) is a post corner cut at 15 yards of depth by the 4-back.

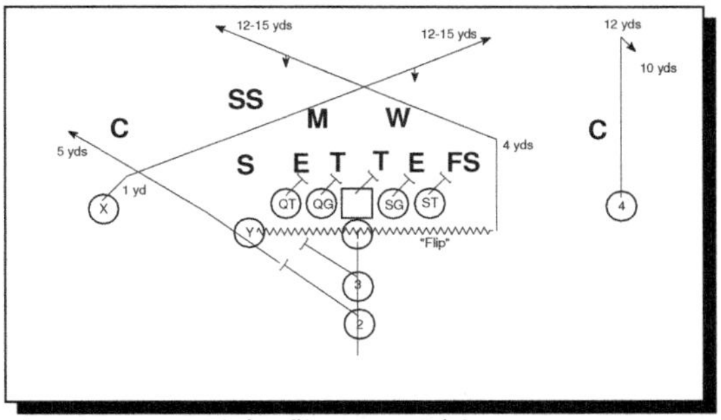

Figure 6-13. Right flip 656 Ohio

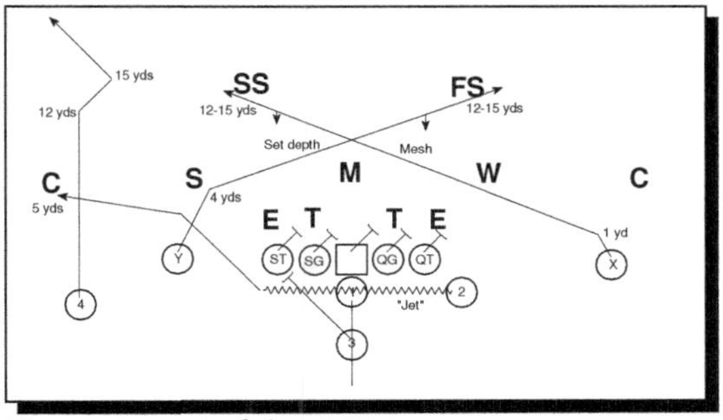

Figure 6-14. Left jet 865 Iowa

The 2-back runs a five-yard flat route. This route may be run to either the quickside or strongside flat, depending on the formation or motion called. From the pistol alignment, the 2-back blocks opposite the offensive line's slide.

Blocking opposite the offensive line's slide is the 3-back's assignment in all formations except the pistol. From the pistol, the 3-back runs a five-yard flat route to the strongside.

The quarterback's read progression for the 5 pattern is the blink read to the 4-back #1. He then reads the mesh point between Y and the X-receiver and throws to whichever receiver breaks open. The five-yard flat route by the running back is his checkdown receiver.

This pattern is very effective versus man-to-man coverages and is also effective against zone coverage. Because of its effectiveness against man-to-man, the 5 pattern is the best single pattern in the goal line offensive attack.

6 Pattern

A 6 pattern (Figures 6-15 through 6-18) is a strongside flood concept. It may be thrown from dropback, play-action, or bootlegs.

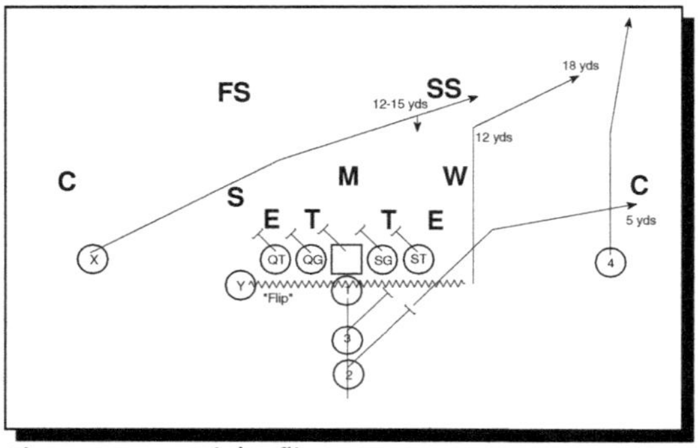

Figure 6-15. Right flip 666

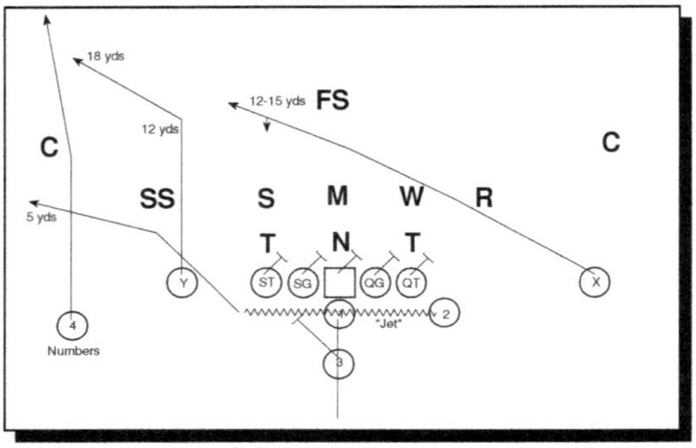

Figure 6-16. Left jet 866

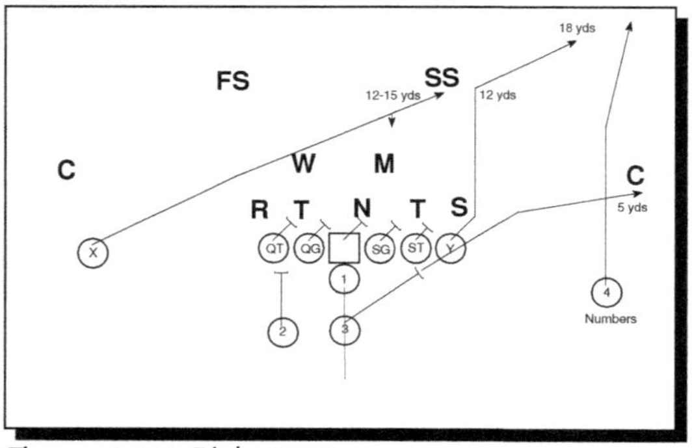

Figure 6-17. Right 756

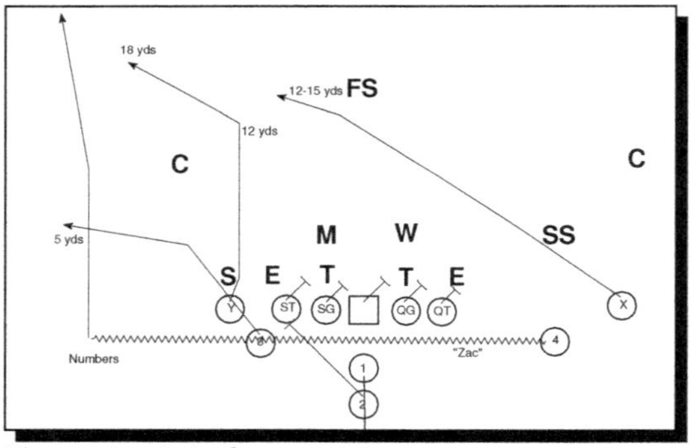

Figure 6-18. Left zac 966

The 4-back runs a go route from whatever position he is in. If he is the #1 receiver, his route is run on the numbers. When he is the #2 receiver, his route is two yards outside the hash mark. When the 4-back is strongside, the go route is the quarterback's blink read.

Y needs to be on the strongside to use the 6 route. He will motion to the strongside from the I formation or run a sneak route behind the line from the I on the 6 route if a Detroit tag is added. Y's basic pass route is a corner cut at 12 yards of depth. He should aim for a position 18 to 20 yards deep. Versus a two-safety defense, Y should flatten his route as he breaks for the sideline.

X runs a drag route to the strongside aiming for 12 to 15 yards depth. He should look for a hole in the zone defense on the strongside into which he can settle. X should never cross the strongside hash mark.

When pistol or wing formations are used, the 3-back runs a five-yard strongside flat route. From I or doubles, he blocks opposite the offensive line slide.

The two-back jet motions and runs the five-yard flat route strongside from doubles formation; he runs the five-yard flat from the I formation. In pistol or wing, he blocks opposite the offensive line slide.

Read progression for the quarterback starts with the blink read to the go route. Y's corner cut is his next choice and the flat route is his third choice. The drag route by X is his fourth choice. Motion by the 4-back to the quickside or a 6 route without motion changes the read progression. Y is now the first choice, with the flat route #2 and the drag cut #3. Figure 6-19 is an example of wing zac 756.

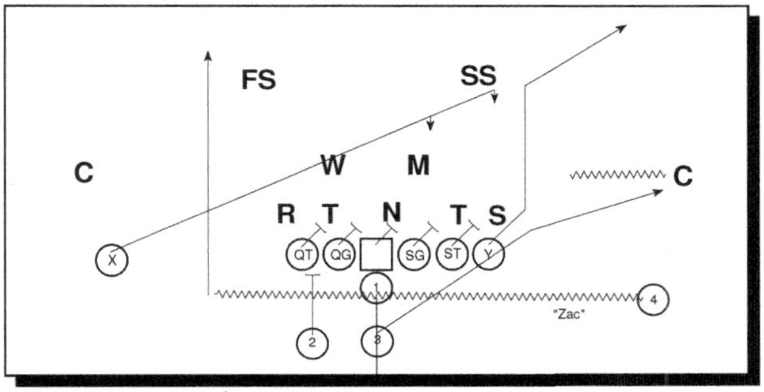

Figure 6-19. Right zac 756

Two tags are used for the 6 pattern. The first of these is Detroit. From pistol formation, this tag has Y or the 3-back run a five-yard flat route. This tag is only used for west 626, a bootleg pass off of the outside zone to the quickside. Figure 6-20 is deep route #1, flat #2, and drag #3.

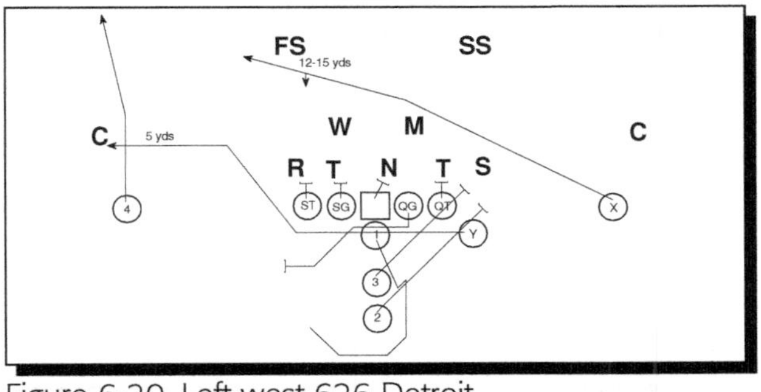

Figure 6-20. Left west 626 Detroit

The second tag, whip, is run from wing or pistol formations as shown in Figures 6-21 and 6-22. Whip affects only the 4-back's pass route. The routes for Y, X, and the five-yard flat cut remain the same. From the pistol formation, zac motion is used to send the 4-back to the strongside. The ball is snapped when he is two to four yards outside of Y. The 4-back executes the whip cut by starting inside on an angle for six to eight yards of depth. He should push inside behind Y to a point over the strong tackle. The 4-back reverse pivots and runs a sideline cut at six to eight yards of depth. If a wing formation is used, zin motion sends the 4-back into position as a tight wing. The whip route is then run from the alignment.

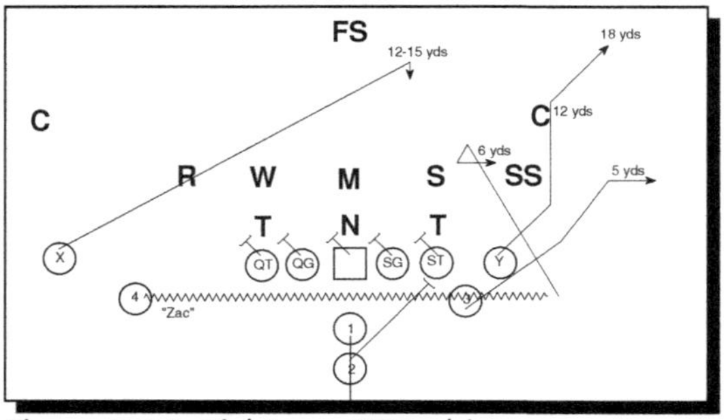

Figure 6-21. Right zac 966 whip

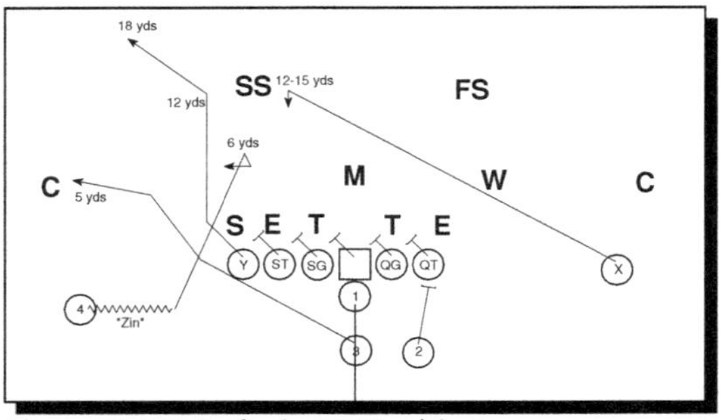

Figure 6-22. Left zin 756 whip

Read progression for the quarterback is the corner route by Y #1 and the flat route by the 3-back #2. The whip cut becomes his third choice, with the drag route by the X-receiver as his fourth choice. This pattern is effective versus man-to-man coverage. The crossing of the receivers from the bunch look may cause confusion for the defense. Other pass patterns are also run from the bunch adjustment.

7 Pattern

The 7 route (Figures 6-23 through 6-26) is a quickside flood pattern. It is important for the offense to flood both the strongside and quickside of the formation. If flood patterns are only run to the strongside of the alignment, secondary coverage will always align or roll to the strongside. The flood patterns are especially useful with bootleg or sprint-out pass actions.

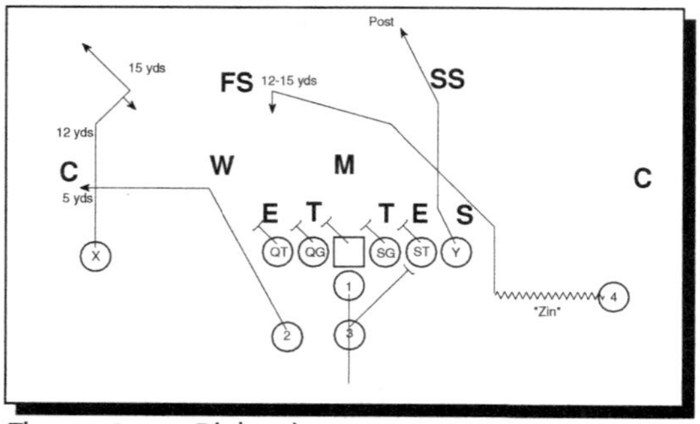

Figure 6-23. Right zin 767

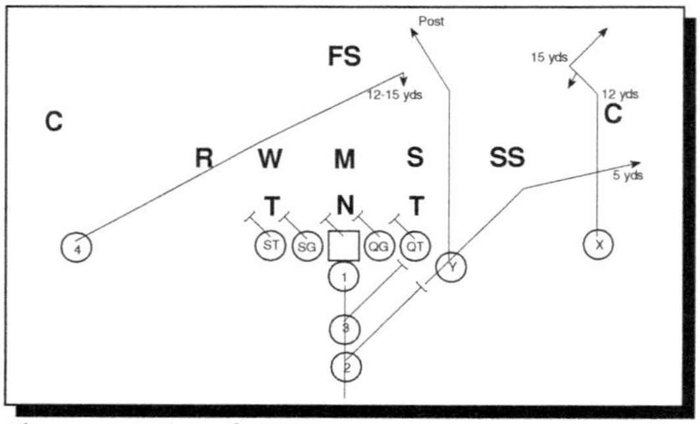

Figure 6-24. Left 657

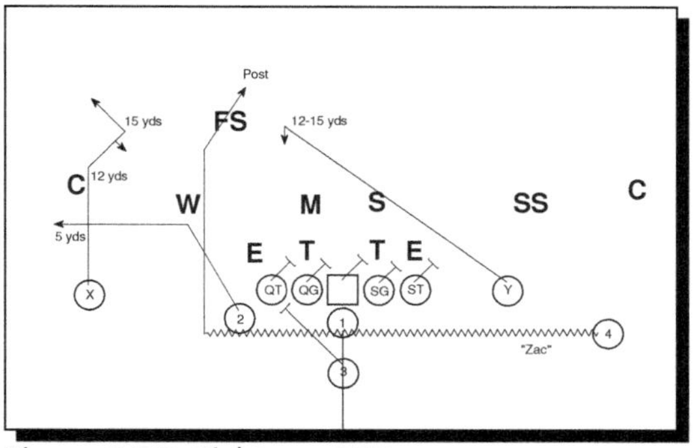

Figure 6-25. Right zac 857

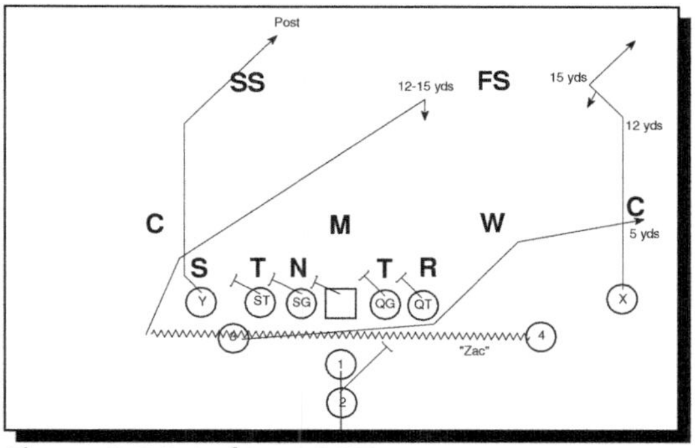

Figure 6-26. Left zac 967

The X-receiver runs a read route on the 7 pattern, reading the single high safety or the double high safeties. Versus a single high safety, X will break toward the near goalpost at a depth of 12 yards. On his second step toward the post, X plants his outside foot and runs a comeback curl. This break is about 14 yards deep. He continues to come back toward the quarterback until he catches the ball. Against two high safeties, X starts his post cut at 12 yards. On his third step, he plants his inside foot and runs the corner route. The X-receiver reads the safeties on the move. He is the primary receiver for the 7 pattern.

Receiver #2 runs a skinny post route, aiming for the near goalpost. Receiver #1 has a drag route to the quickside. He aims for a point 12 to 15 yards in depth. The drag route must never cross the hash mark because of the read route potentially being a curl. Receiver #1 settles in any open area in the secondary once he reaches the quickside of the formation.

From I, wing, or doubles formations, the 2-back runs a five-yard deep flat route to the quickside. He blocks from the pistol alignment. The 3-back blocks from I, wing, or doubles; he will run a five-yard flat to the quickside from the pistol. This sneak route has the 3-back slide quickside on the offensive side of the line of scrimmage. He will often be lost by the secondary as a potential receiver. Read progression for the quarterback is the X-receiver #1, the flat route #2, and the drag as his third choice.

One tag, Peoria, may be used with the 7 pattern. Peoria changes the pass routes for receivers #2 and #3. To use Peoria, the #2 receiver must be on the quickside of the formation. He may be aligned there, as is the case for Y in the I formation. Zac motion by the 4-back is used from the wing and doubles formations to get receiver #2 on the quickside. From pistol, the 4-back is aligned quickside as receiver #2.

Receiver #3, X, runs a 12-yard deep post cut, and receiver #2 runs a post corner cut. Receiver #2 breaks toward the post at 12 yards of depth, plants his inside foot after three steps, and breaks for the corner. Receiver #2 runs his route behind X's postcut.

The #1 receiver runs his drag route to the quickside as he normally does for a 7 pattern. He finds an open area in the zone to the quickside and never crosses the hash mark. The 2-back and 3-back have their normal 7 pattern five-yard flat cuts to the quickside.

The quarterback's progression is receiver #2 as the first choice. The flat route is second choice, and the drag route becomes the quarterback's third choice. The post corner route has a good chance to break open. This route is the blink read for the quarterback. Figures 6-27 through 6-30 show 7 Peoria pass patterns from various formations.

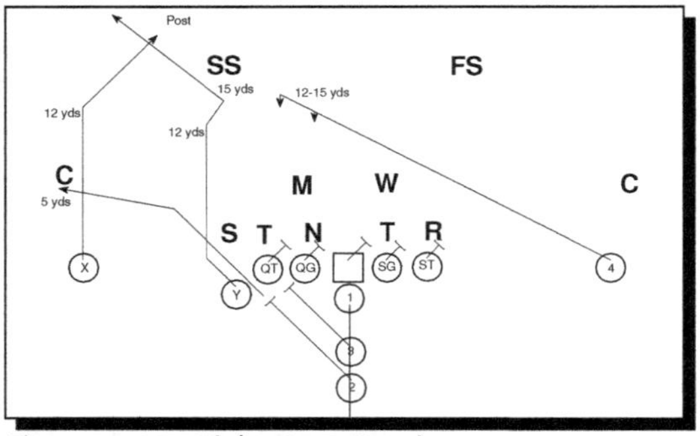

Figure 6-27. Right 657 Peoria

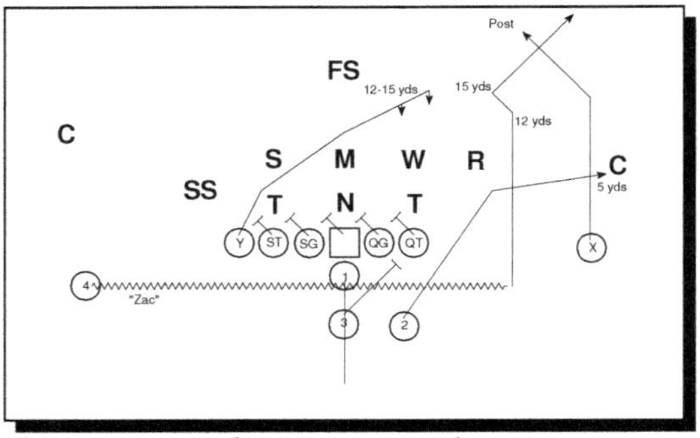

Figure 6-28. Left zac 757 Peoria

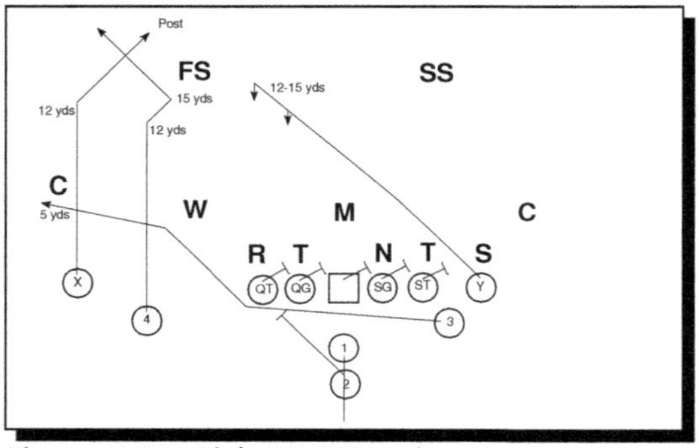

Figure 6-29. Right 957 Peoria

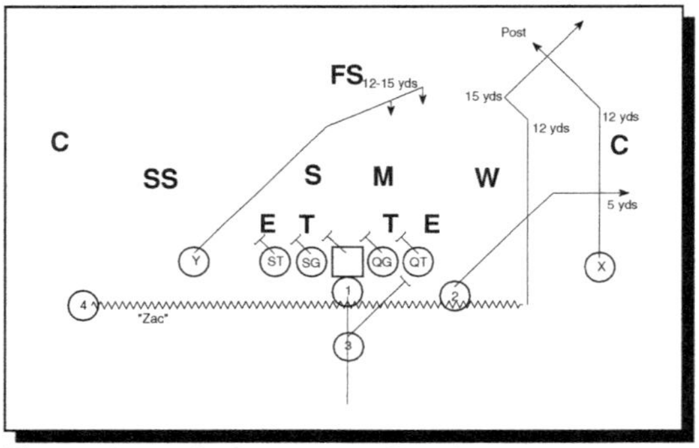

Figure 6-30. Left zac 857 Peoria

8 Pattern

The 8 pattern (Figures 6-31 through 6-34) is also referred to as base pass. It is the most used and most flexible pass pattern in the five-step drop passing attack. All three numbered pass receivers run some form of read route. Their final cuts are determined by the secondary coverage they face.

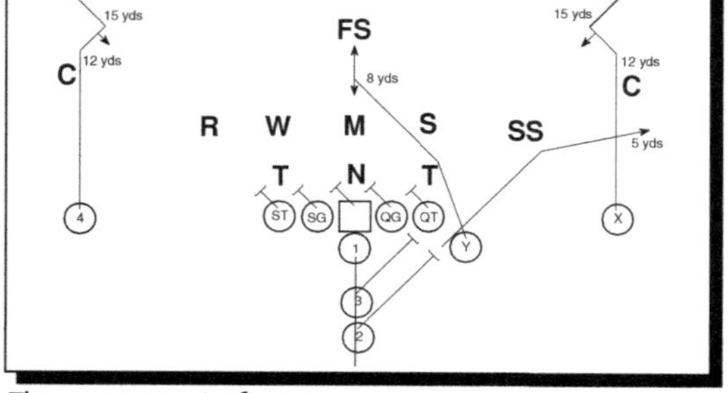

Figure 6-31. Left 658

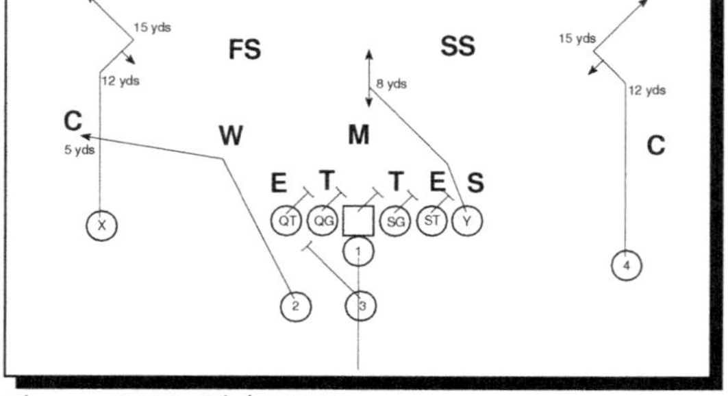

Figure 6-32. Right 758

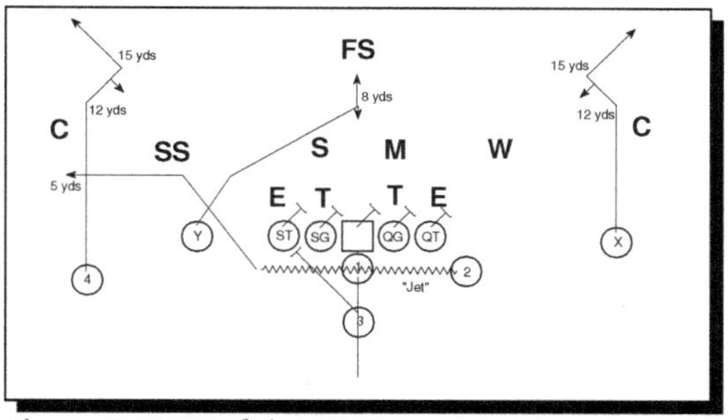

Figure 6-33. Left jet 868

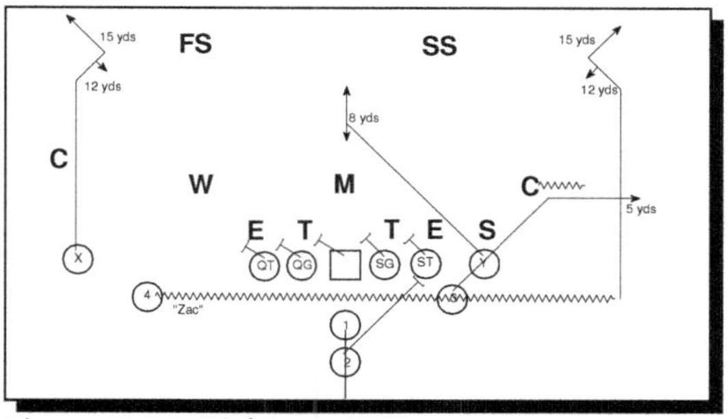

Figure 6-34. Right zac 968

Both the #1 and #3 receivers run breaks for the near goalpost at 12 yards of depth. If they face a single high safety, they take two more steps toward the post, plant the outside foot, and come back toward the quarterback on a curl route. Versus two high safeties or man-to-man coverage, the receivers take three steps toward the post, plant the inside foot, and run a post corner cut.

Receiver #2, usually Y, runs an eight-yard hook route over the center of the formation against a single high safety. With two high safeties or if he faces man-to-man coverage, receiver #2 runs a route directly between the two goalposts.

The 2-back runs a flat route from I, wing, or doubles. From wing formation, his route is always to the quickside flat. In a doubles formation the 2-back can run a quickside flat cut, or he may be sent in jet motion to the strongside to run the strongside flat cut. If the I formation is used, the 2-back runs the five-yard flat route to the same side that the 3-back blocks. In the case of 60 protection, this route will be a strongside flat cut. If 50 protection is used, the route will be run to the quickside of the formation.

In a pistol formation the 3-back runs a five-yard flat cut to the strongside. Zac motion is normally used from the pistol to have the 4-back become the #1 receiver to the strongside.

The quarterback has the route of receiver #2 as his blink read and first choice in his progression. His second choice will be one of the read routes by either receivers #1 or #3. He normally throws to the side of the formation where the flat route is being run. He does not have to throw to that side versus two high safeties, but it is a distinct advantage to have a flat receiver to influence underneath coverage. The third choice in his read progression is the back in the flat.

One tag is used with the 8 pattern. It is Texas and affects the routes of multiple receivers as shown in Figures 6-35 through and 6-37.

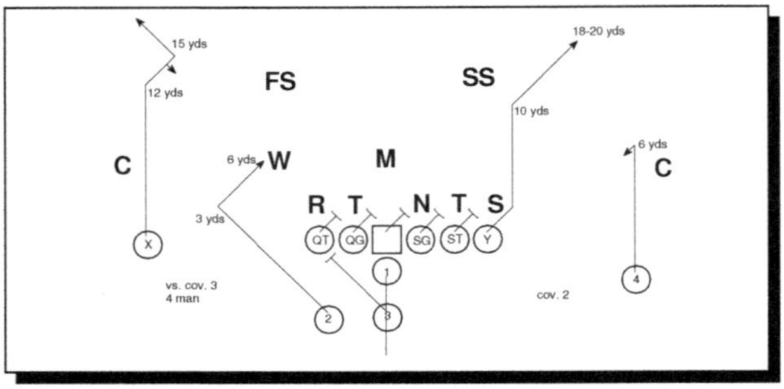

Figure 6-35. Right 758 Texas

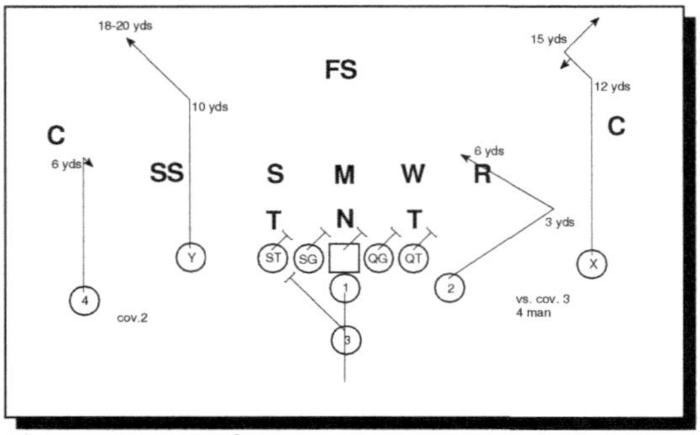

Figure 6-36. Left 868 Texas

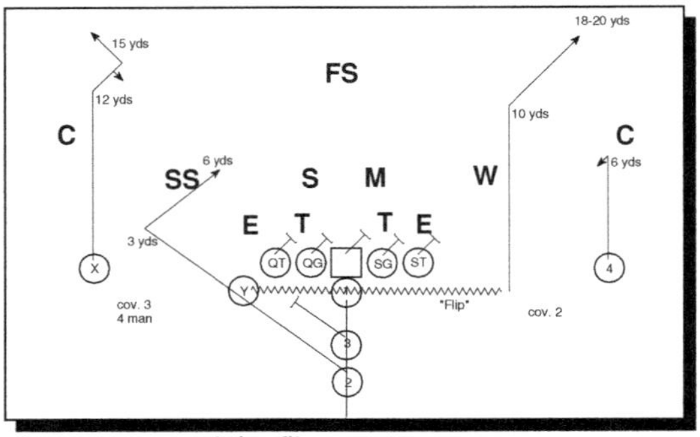

Figure 6-37. Right flip 658 Texas

A smash pattern is created to the strongside of the formation to beat cover 2. Receiver #1, from wing, I, and doubles, runs a six-yard deep hitch cut. The #2 receiver has a 10-yard deep corner route.

On the quickside of the alignment, X-receiver or #3 receiver runs his normal read route for the 8 pattern. A tex or angle cut is the assignment for the 2-back. He begins an initial arrow route, aiming for three yards of depth, but after five steps toward the sideline, he plants his outside foot and breaks inside at an angle, aiming for six yards of depth. If the X-receiver has curled, this creates a high-low read on the curl defender. Versus man-to-man coverage, the quarterback checks the post corner first and the tex cut second.

Versus cover 2 on the strongside, the quarterback's read progression is hitch #1 and corner route #2. When faced with two high safeties, he will work strongside; with one safety, the quarterback throws quickside.

9 Pattern

A 9 pattern is a middle read for the quarterback. Figures 6-38 through 6-41 show 9 patterns.

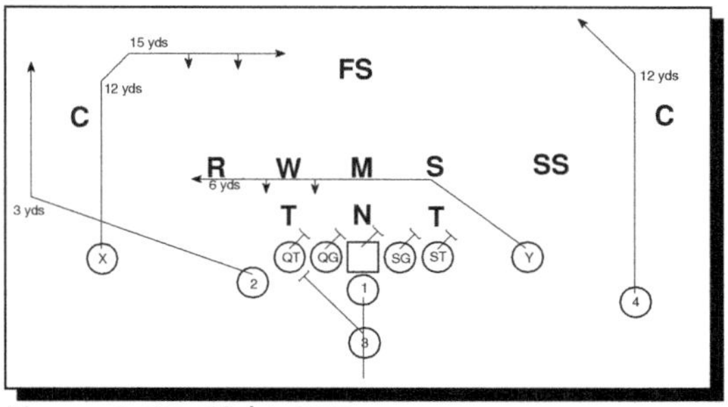

Figure 6-38. Right 859

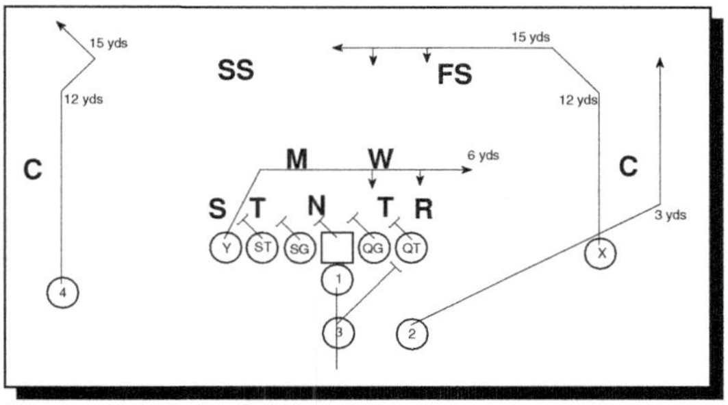

Figure 6-39. Left 759 Iowa

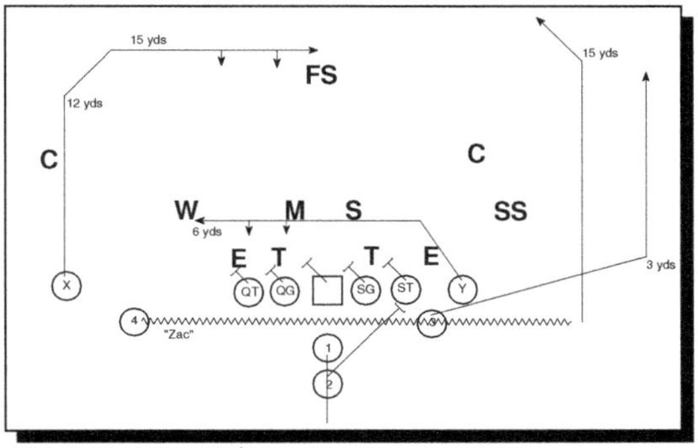

Figure 6-40. Right zac 969

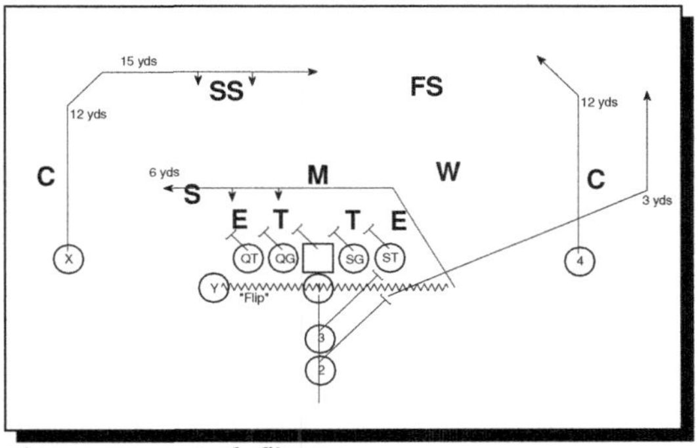

Figure 6-41. Left flip 669

The NCAA route, as it is known, has receiver #1 run a skinny post cut to 12 yards of depth. He is the quarterback's blink read and #1 in his progression. An Iowa tag may be applied to this receiver's route, as shown in Figure 6-39. For Iowa, receiver #1 executes a post corner cut at 15 yards of depth.

Receiver #2 runs a drag route to the quickside of the formation. He attempts to get to a depth of six yards when he reaches the quick tackle's position. Once receiver #2 reaches the quickside, he can settle in any dead spot in the zone coverage. Versus man-to-man, receiver #2 continues to the flat quickside. This route is the third choice in the quarterback's read progression.

X, the #3 receiver, is responsible for a 14- to 15-yard dig cut. He breaks to the post at 12 yards of depth and plants his outside foot after two steps and comes flat to the inside. X looks for holes in zone coverage and settles in the first hole available. Against man-to-man secondary coverage, X continues across the formation to the strongside. The dig route is the quarterback's #2 choice.

If wing, doubles, or I are used as the formation, the 2-back executes an arrow route aiming for three yards of depth. Once he reaches the numbers, the 2-back turns upfield on a wheel cut. Doubles or wing has the 2-back running his route quickside. From I, if 50 protection is called, the flat route is run to the quickside; 60 protection sends the 2-back to the strongside flat. From a pistol alignment, the 3-back is responsible for the flat and wheel cut to the strongside.

The quarterback may throw the three-yard arrow as a checkdown or blitz-beater route. If the corner locks on to the wide receiver, the quarterback throws to the wheel route at a depth of 5 to 15 yards of depth. This route has potential for a big play.

The quarterback must make a pre-snap read based on the following:

- One high safety may indicate cover 3 or man-free coverage.
- Two high safeties may be cover 4, cover 2, or cover 2 man-to-man.
- Loose alignment of corners may indicate cover 3 or cover 4.
- Tight corner alignment may indicate man-to-man coverage or cover 2.
- Inside alignment by a corner could indicate man-to-man.
- Outside alignment by a corner usually indicates zone pass coverage.

When the ball is snapped, the quarterback keys secondary movement to determine possible coverage. The quickside or weak safety is the player whom the quarterback keys. With one high safety, the quarterback keys that safety. The quarterback reads the safety movement as follows:

- Safety settles on hash: If the safety settles in position, this indicates cover 4 secondary coverage.
- Safety rotates deep middle: A rotation to the deep middle of the secondary is either cover 3 or cover 1 man.
- Safety rotates quickside: When the quickside safety rotates up to the quickside, it is cover 3 or man-to-man.

The final play in the dropback pass series is the dropback screen pass thrown to the 2-back. Denver is the tag applied to 80 pass protection that indicates dropback screen. Chapter 4 details the blocking assignments for the dropback screen pass. The strong guard and strong tackle man block the #1 and #2 defenders on the line of scrimmage strongside. The center, quick guard, and quick tackle slide protect to the quickside. The quick guard, center, and strong guard block their assignment for two counts and release into the screen. The quick guard kicks out on the corner, the center blocks in the alley, and the strong guard seals strongside pursuit.

Y blocks the #3 defender on the line. With no number three defensive man, Y blocks the strong safety.

The 3-back double reads the strongside from an inside linebacker to the outside. X-receiver crack blocks the safety on the quickside, and the 4-back crack blocks the first second-level defender to his side.

A pass block to the quickside is simulated by the 2-back. He steps up quickside and keys the quick guard's release. When the guard releases to kick out the corner, the 2-back releases behind the quick tackle's pass set and curls back behind the offensive side of the line of scrimmage. He will set and turn his body back to the quarterback. After catching the ball, the 2-back calls "go" to alert the offensive lineman that he has started to run.

A five-step dropback is made by the quarterback. He looks off the defense to the strongside. After five steps, he hesitates and then drifts back two more steps before turning and throwing the ball to the 2-back. In the case of the screen pass and all other passes, the quarterback must use his eyes to influence the secondary defenders. They will attempt to read the quarterback's eyes to anticipate where he will throw. By looking defenders off, the quarterback will improve the chances of his throwing a pass completion. Figures 6-42 through 6-45 show examples of dropback screen passes.

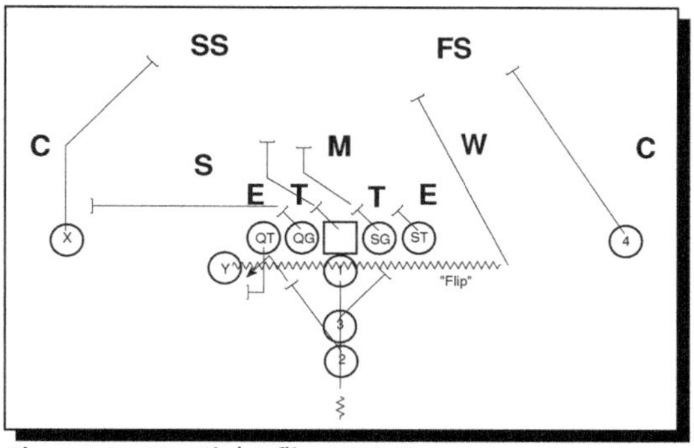

Figure 6-42. Right flip 680 Denver

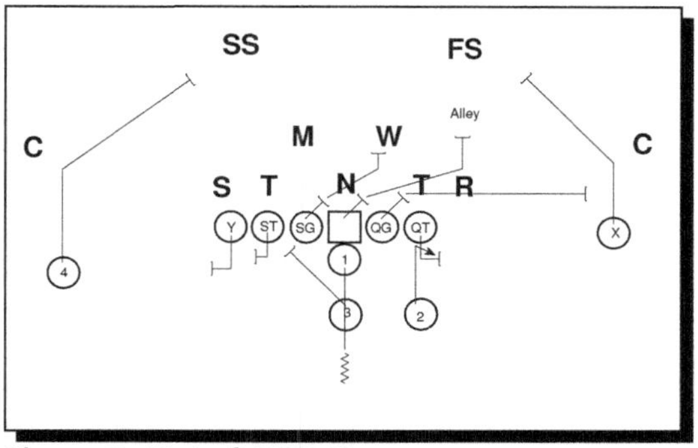

Figure 6-43. Left 780 Denver

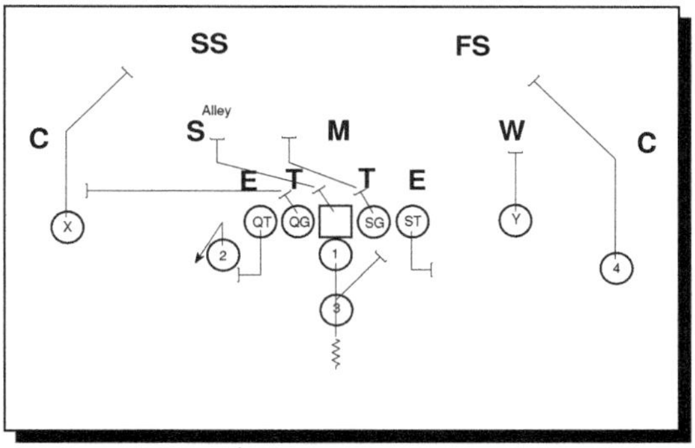

Figure 6-44. Right 880 Denver

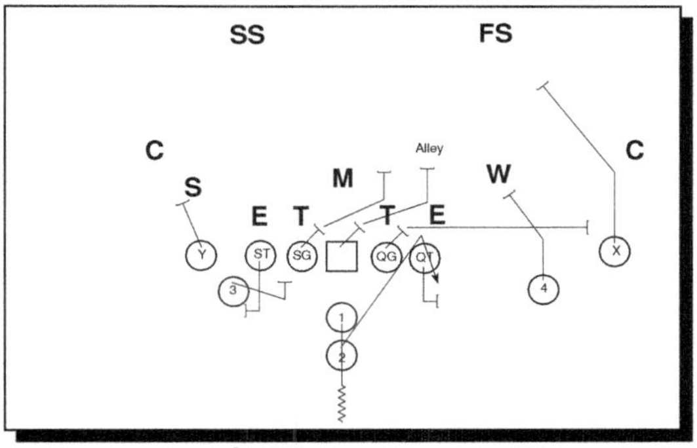

Figure 6-45. Left 980 Denver

CHAPTER 7

The Veer Series

Every offense is built around a basic series of plays. In the case of the no-huddle multiple offense, this series is the veer or triple option. Any coach wishing to implement this offense should start with the veer series. Not every play in the series needs to be included, but it is wise to do so since they complement each other and are designed to attack the three basic areas of the defense: the outside, the inside, and the middle of the defense.

Running an option offense offers many advantages. These advantages include, but are not limited to, the following:

- It teaches players to be physical on both sides of the ball. This attack requires that offensive linemen fire off the ball and attack defenders. Playing against this style of offense in practice requires the defense to be physical.
- It is a ball-control series. It keeps the defense off the field and wears down the opponent's defense.
- The disadvantage of having better players on defense than on offense is decreased. Defensive linemen who are very difficult to block can be neutralized by leaving them unblocked and reading them.
- An offensive line does not have to be huge to be effective since it doesn't have to overpower opponents.
- The option attack forces the defense to play assignment football. Failure to stay with a defensive responsibility can result in big runs.
- The fullback aspects of the attack hit quickly, helping to negate pursuit by the defense.
- The same offense can be used from goal line to goal line. Red zone and goal line defenses often play man-to-man coverages and this is very problematic against option offenses.
- Option football reduces the number of defensive fronts and blitzes normally seen because of the need to play assignment football.
- Option football presents a different challenge to defenses since not a lot of teams are running a wide variety of option plays with the quarterback under the center. Because of this lack of familiarity with the option, defensive teams find it difficult to prepare to face this offense.
- The number of 1-on-1 pass coverage opportunities for receivers increases dramatically because of the need to assign specific phases of the option to defenders.
- The outside veer play, 38, is extremely effective versus 3-3-5 defenses, which have become increasingly popular against the proliferation of spread offenses.
- The midline option, 11, is deadly against over defenses that employ a 3 technique defensive tackle.
- Inside veer plays, 13 and 14, attack the defensive tackles and ends with quick hitting plays.

Because the offense has other types of series such as power, buck, zone, and belly, the defense cannot prepare just to stop the option attack. It is the option concepts, however, that make the total offense so effective.

Any offense that has a single receiver to one side of the formation, such as a pro set, may have a difficult time running the ball toward that side of the formation. An unblocked defender, such as a cover 4 safety, is usually located to that side of the formation. The most consistent way to attack that side is with option football since, by doing so, some defenders are deliberately left unblocked to be read by the quarterback. Chapter 14 will cover practice plans, but it is important to understand that time must be devoted to practice option football if a coach hopes to be successful in running it.

Ten minutes per day should be provided in group work, where offensive backs and quarterbacks work option reads without offensive linemen or wide receivers in the picture. Coaches should play the defenders who are being read, since they can give the exact reads a quarterback needs to see. At first, the reads can be simple and very clear, but as skill improves, the reads are made more difficult. During this group period, the coach should insist on exact steps and paths for the quarterback and running backs so that sound habits are established. Various reads should be given that result in handoffs to the 3-back, keeps for the quarterback, and pitches to the 2-back. The coaches providing the reads watch the quarterback's eyes to ensure that he is watching the read man and not looking at his fullback. A distinct advantage of the no-huddle multiple offense becomes apparent during this period. The 3-back is normally the dive read, and the 2-back is usually the pitchman.

A 9-on-9 period is always a part of the Tuesday and Wednesday practice plans. During this practice period, the #1 defense faces the #1 offense for 10 minutes. Only option plays are run during this period. Wide receivers run one-man patterns versus corner backs in another area during this period. Quarterbacks rotate between 9-on-9 and the passing drill. This period enables the offense to work the option game against a quality defense at a thud tempo. At the same time, the defense is reviewing their option responsibilities.

Scout team personnel provide a 5- or 10-minute period Tuesday through Thursday for a team option review. Defensive scripts should be prepared to ensure that the quarterback sees the reads he can expect for the upcoming game. At least one day a week, this team option period should be one-half line drills to increase the number of repetitions being executed. Additional team option work can be used in goal line and red zone periods. These periods have the #1 offense versus the #1 defense. Option plays are mixed with other plays according to the game plan. Being consistent about scheduling the option practice daily is more important than having longer periods on sporadic days.

Success with the option attack will come if it is practiced correctly and regularly. The coach must understand that when practice first begins there will be misreads, fumbles, and errant pitches. These problems will be eliminated with consistent practice repetitions.

The inside veer plays, 13 and 14, have similar actions and reads. For each play, the quarterback takes a deep 45-degree step with the playside foot and extends the football back to the 3-back as he eyes the read man. The first defender from head-up over the offensive tackle to his outside is the give or keep read. The quarterback rides the 3-back to the quarterback's front hip while reading the action of his first read. If the quarterback sees the defender close on the fullback, he will keep the ball. As the keep is executed, the quarterback pulls the ball with both hands and runs the keep or pitch off the next unblocked defensive player. When read one does not close on the fullback, the ball is given to him. In executing the give, the quarterback pulls out the hand closest to the 3-back and pressures the ball into the fullback's stomach with his front hand. If the quarterback has doubt as to the read man's reaction, the ball is handed off.

If the quarterback decides to keep the ball, he plants the foot deepest into the offensive backfield and drives upfield off of it. When he gets a pitch read from the second read man, the quarterback executes a one-handed end-over-end basketball type pitch to the 2-back. This pitch should be made as far out in front of the quarterback as possible.

Offensive line splits between the guards and center are maintained at two feet. These splits must not vary when the inside veer plays are being run, since the aiming point for the 3-back is the outside hip of the playside guard. A change in the guard's split would force the quarterback to change his steps to mesh with the 3-back.

Splits for the tackles are normally three feet from the guards, but the splits may be increased when the inside veer or midline option plays are used. Varying these splits will not tip the plays as long as the tackles sometimes widen their splits when other plays are run away from them. If a defender aligned over the tackle widens with him, the tackle should split four to five feet from his guard. Wider splits force the first read man wider and create more time for the quarterback's first decision. In order to tackle the 3-back on the dive, the defender has to close hard at once. Figures 7-1 through 7-5 show 14, the inside veer play to the strongside.

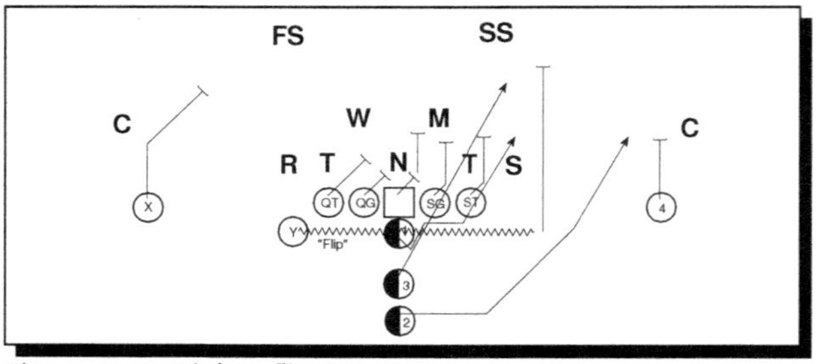

Figure 7-1. Rights flip 614

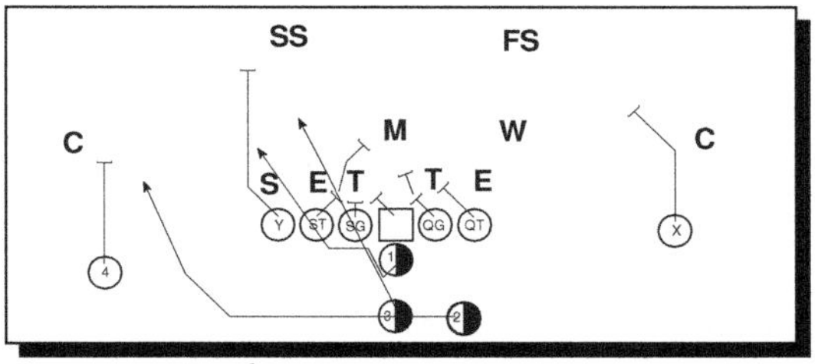

Figure 7-2. Left 714

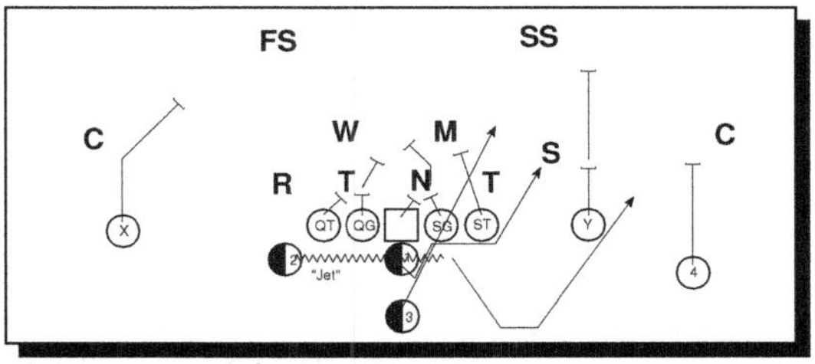

Figure 7-3. Right jet 814

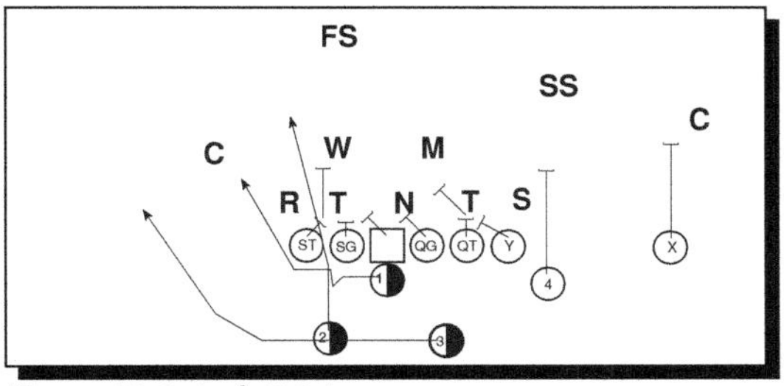

Figure 7-4. Left 514

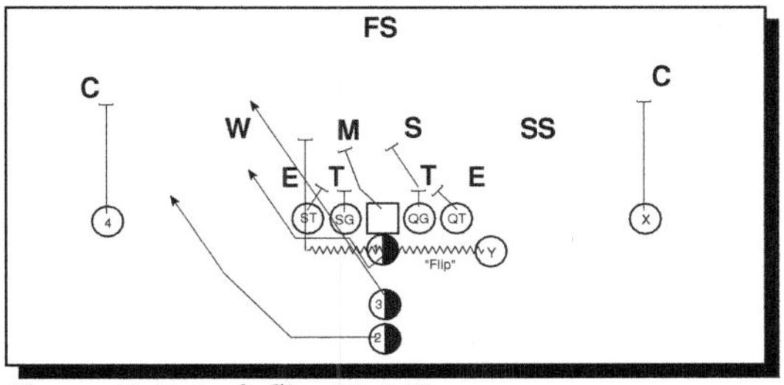

Figure 7-5. Left flip 614 Doug

Blocking assignments for 14 are as follows:

- Y-Receiver: If he is aligned tight on the strongside, Y arc blocks the safety or outside linebacker. When split out strongside, he blocks the man covering him. From a quickside alignment, he attempts to block the near safety. A Doug call on 14 has Y block the inside linebacker strongside.
- Strong Tackle: Versus odd defenses, the strong tackle releases outside a 5 technique defender and seals the inside linebacker. Against an even or gap front, he blocks gap, inside linebacker, or outside linebacker. A Doug call by the strong guard has the tackle double-team a defender over the strong guard.
- Strong Guard: If the defense is an odd look, the strong guard blocks the inside linebacker. Versus a gap or even defense, he zones strongside to a middle linebacker. The strong guard may make a Doug call to his strong tackle when an I formation with flip motion is used. In this case, the strong guard and strong tackle double-team a defender over the strong guard and Y blocks an inside linebacker.
- Center: Against an odd defense the center zones strongside with the quick guard to a middle linebacker or inside linebacker quickside. Versus an even or gap alignment the center zones strongside with the strong guard to a middle linebacker or the inside linebacker from the quickside.
- Quick Guard: The quick guard zone blocks to the strongside.
- Quick Tackle: Regardless of the defensive alignment, the quick tackle always zone blocks to the strongside.
- 4-Back and X-Receiver: The 4-back and the X-receiver are assigned to block the defensive men covering them.

The 3-back aims for the strong guard's outside hip for 14. He makes a soft pocket with his inside elbow up high. The 3-back must allow the quarterback to execute the read and not grab the ball. He clamps on to the ball when he feels the quarterback pressure it into his stomach. If the quarterback pulls the ball out, the 3-back rolls his arms over an imaginary ball and looks to block the first second-level defender in his path.

The 2-back is the pitchman for 14. His ideal relationship with the quarterback is to be five yards deeper than him and two yards in front of him. From an I alignment, he can achieve this relationship by sprinting hard on the snap. If he is in the dive back position, it may be necessary to start him in short motion toward the strongside. This motion is started by the quarterback raising his heel. Jet motion can be used by the 2-back to cross flat to the strongside. This motion is used for 18, the jet sweep. If used for 14, the 2-back backpedals three steps off the line of scrimmage when he reaches the position of the strong tackle's outside foot. As the quarterback turns upfield, the 2-back also turns upfield. At this point, the 2-back must maintain a pitch relationship with the quarterback.

The use of jet motion by the 2-back when running 14 puts the defense in an unusual position. The threat of the jet sweep, 18, forces strongside defenders to initially anticipate the need to get to the outside. This may open the dive path for the 3-back on 14.

If 14 is run from strong (as in Figure 7-4), the 2-back is the dive back, and the 3-back becomes the pitchman. Steps change for the quarterback on 14 from strong formation. He steps flat down the line of scrimmage with his strongside foot. His second step is into the line of scrimmage as he reaches the ball back to the 2-back and executes the ride and read.

It may be advisable to run 14 give or 14 keep from the strong alignment since the 2-back and quarterback read and exchange differ from those between the quarterback and 3-back. When a strong formation is used, the quick tackle takes a maximum split.

Backfield motion for 13 mirrors that of 14. The aiming point for the 3-back is the outside hip of the quick guard, and the 2-back is the pitchman from whatever formation is used. If aligned in a wing position, the 2-back executes a three-step backpedal to get into a pitch position. From the I formation or wing set, the 2-back sprints quickside to be in position for the pitch.

A 45-degree open step to the quickside starts the quarterback's action for 13. The rest of his steps are just opposite those for 14. The thought process for the quarterback on 13 and 14 is give first and react second to the keep or pitch read. A general rule of thumb is that if the read man's numbers are facing the quarterback, it is a give read.

The 13 is diagrammed from several formations in Figures 7-6 through 7-9. The 13 is a very effective option play to the quickside of the formation.

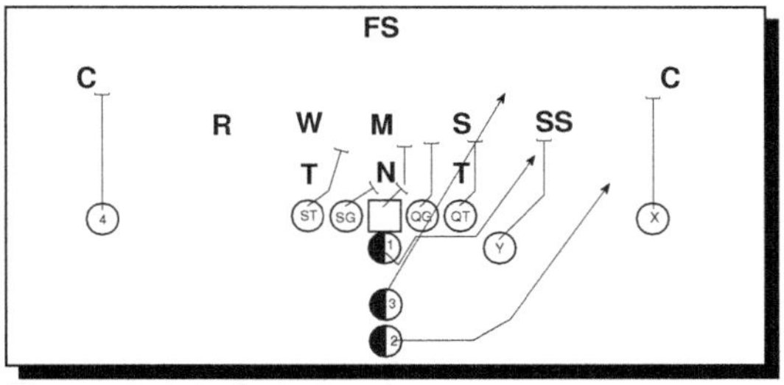

Figure 7-6. Left 613

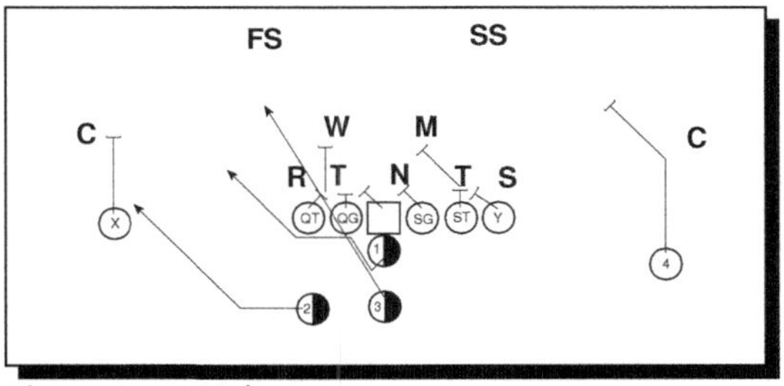

Figure 7-7. Right 713

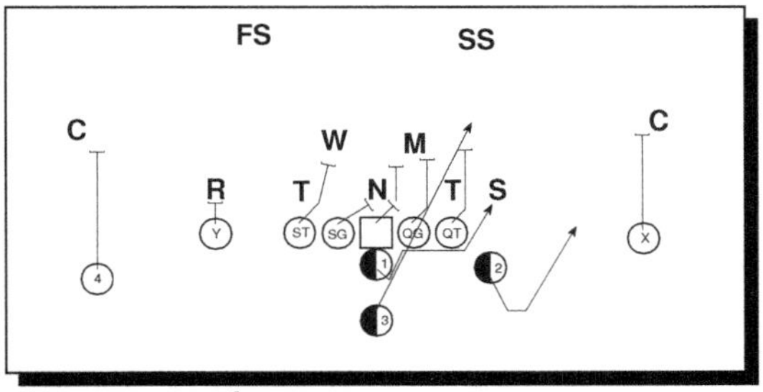

Figure 7-8. Left 813

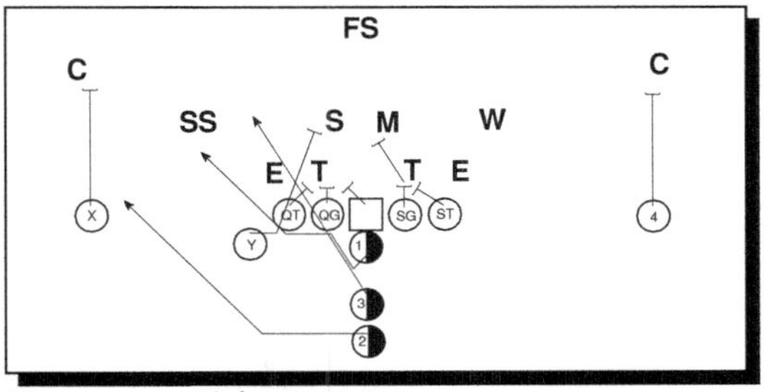

Figure 7-9. Right 613 Doug

Blocking assignments for 13 are as follows:

- Y-Receiver: If aligned quickside, Y arc blocks the force defender, which is usually an outside linebacker or near safety. When he is on the strongside, Y blocks the near safety. If a Doug call is made on 13 and Y is on the quickside, he blocks the first linebacker to the inside.
- Strong Tackle: The strong tackle zone blocks to the quickside.
- Strong Guard: The strong guard zone blocks quickside.
- Center: Versus an odd defense, the center zone blocks to the quickside with the strong guard to a middle linebacker or inside linebacker strongside. When facing an even or gap defense, the center zone blocks quickside with the quick guard to a middle linebacker or inside linebacker quickside.
- Quick Guard: Against an odd defense, the quick guard blocks the inside linebacker. If faced with an even or gap defense, he zones quickside with the center to a middle linebacker or inside linebacker quickside.
- Quick Tackle: If the defense is an odd front, the quick tackle releases outside a 5 technique defensive tackle and seals the first linebacker to the inside. When the defense is a gap or even front, the quick tackle blocks gap, inside linebacker, or outside linebacker.
- 4-Back and X-Receiver: The 4-back and X-receiver block the defenders who are covering them.

Figures 7-10 through 7-12 show the outside veer. This play is run to the strongside. Y must be aligned to the strongside or motion to that position. The 38 hits the off-tackle area or outside. The interior linemen zone block to the strongside, and Y seals the off-tackle hole. The 38 is the best goal line play in the offense. It is really difficult to defend for a 50 defense or the popular 3-5 stack alignment.

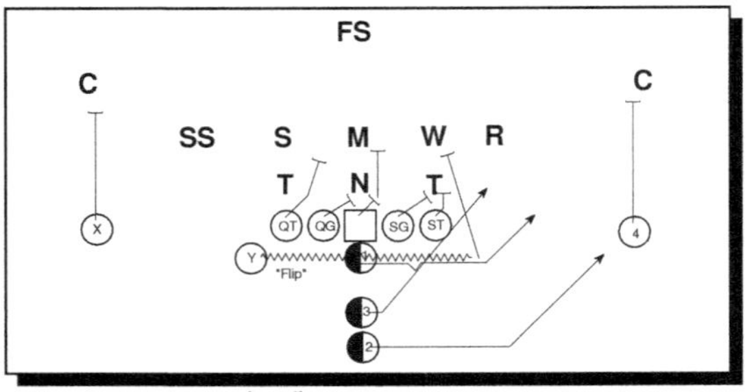

Figure 7-10. Right flip 638

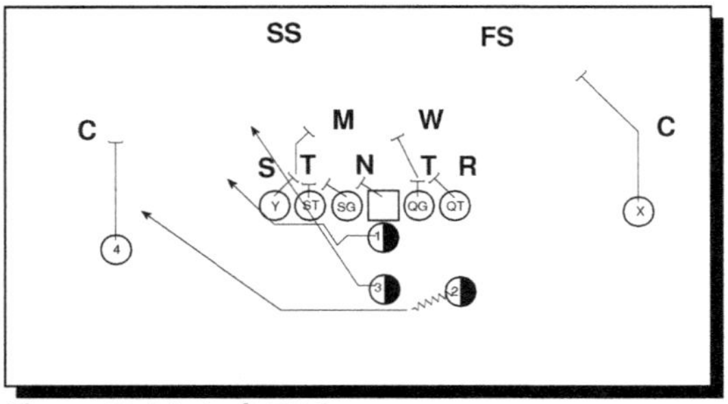

Figure 7-11. Left 738

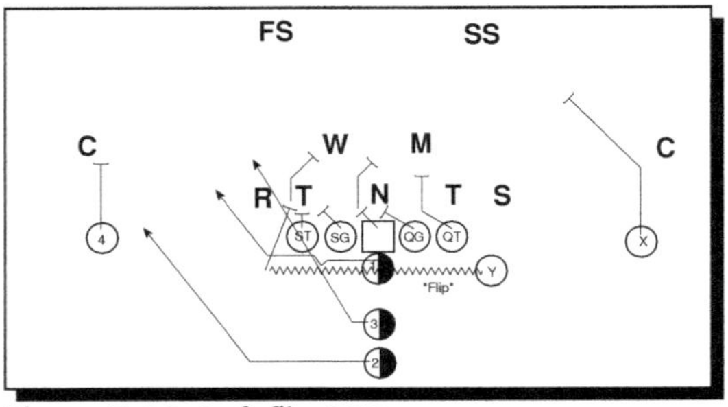

Figure 7-12. Left flip 638

Y zone blocks a 7 or 8 technique defensive end. Versus an over front, he blocks the outside linebacker. If faced with a 5 technique defensive tackle, Y combos with the strong tackle to the inside linebacker. Combined with the zone blocking by the rest of the offensive line, this allows the offense to seal the defenders to the inside of the read man.

Blocking rules for 38 are as follows:

- Y-Receiver: Y zone blocks a 7 or 8 technique defensive end. Versus a 5 technique defensive tackle, he combos the 5 technique with the strong tackle to the inside linebacker. Against an over front, Y blocks the outside linebacker.
- Strong Tackle: The strong tackle zone blocks a 5 technique, 7 technique, or 8 technique defender. Against an over defense, he combos with the strong guard to the first linebacker to the inside.
- Strong Guard, Center, Quick Guard, and Quick Tackle: These interior linemen zone block to the strongside. The technique used is that for outside zone blocking.

The quarterback opens flat down the line of scrimmage. His initial read is the first defensive player outside Y's block. As he approaches the hole, the quarterback reaches the ball back to the 3-back and rides him to the quarterback's front hip. It is essential for the quarterback to sprint to the mesh point so that a ride can be executed. A second read for pitch or keep comes from the next unblocked defender, which may be a linebacker or secondary player. If he reads keep, the quarterback must stick his back foot into the ground and immediately get north or south. The 2-back turns upfield when the quarterback does this to maintain proper pitch relationship.

The outside veer plays provide the easiest reads of any of the triple option plays. The first and second reads are slower than they are for the inside veer or midline option. A high school coach, implementing the offense, would be wise to teach the outside veer and make it the basis for his triple option attack at lower levels of his program.

The aiming point for the 3-back on 38 is the outside foot of the strong tackle. His first step should be a flat lead step with his strongside foot. He will then run a slant at the outside foot of the strong tackle. An attempt should be made to square his shoulders to the line as he reaches the hole. The ride by the quarterback and the give or keep procedure is the same for 38 as it is for the inside veer.

For 38, the 2-back is always the pitchman. He must sprint strongside to establish the proper pitch relationship with the quarterback. From a wing formation, the 2-back may be put in short motion. An ideal pitch relationship is the same for 38 as it is for 14.

A coach must be aware of the most common method of disrupting the outside veer. The defender assigned to the dive will crash immediately for the mesh point to try to blow up the quarterback and 3-back mesh. Since the no-huddle multiple offense's philosophy is one of creating defensive conflicts and taking advantage of those conflicts, there are answers for this problem. The 38 may be run as 38 load, as shown in Figure 7-13. The 3-back runs his normal path, but cuts the defender who crashes and the quarterback takes the ball outside without actually meshing with the 3-back. This play now becomes a two-way option on the next unblocked defensive player.

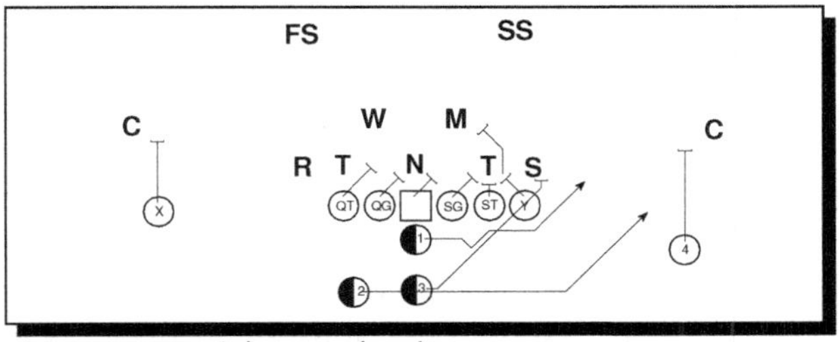

Figure 7-13. Right 738 load

Another way to handle the crashing defender is to run 36 (Figures 7-14 through 7-17). This play traps the defender who is the first read man for 38, the outside veer. The 3-back, 2-back, and quarterback run the same paths as on 38, but the ball is handed to the 3-back running behind the trap block by the strong guard.

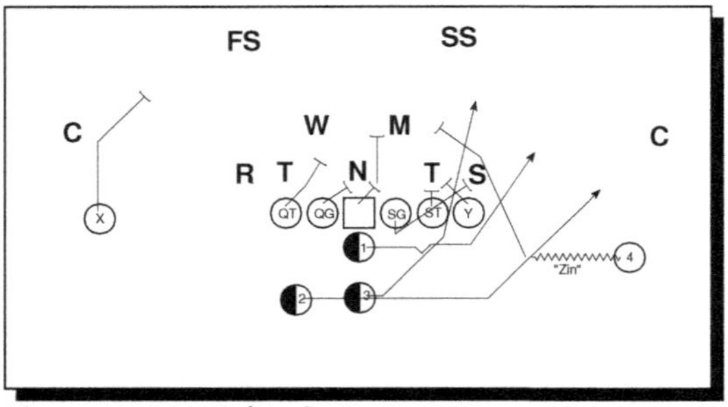

Figure 7-14. Right zin 736

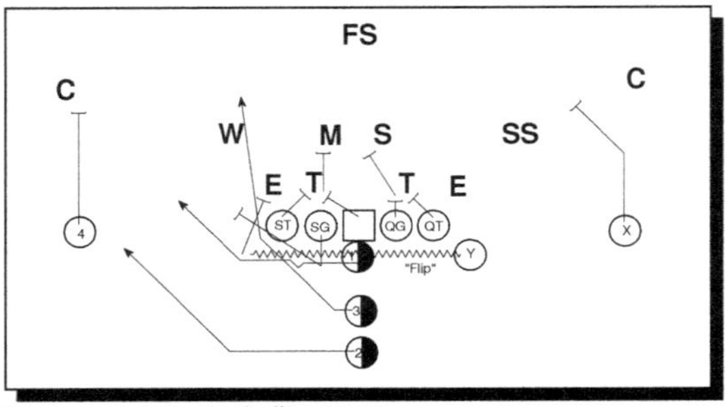

Figure 7-15. Left flip 636

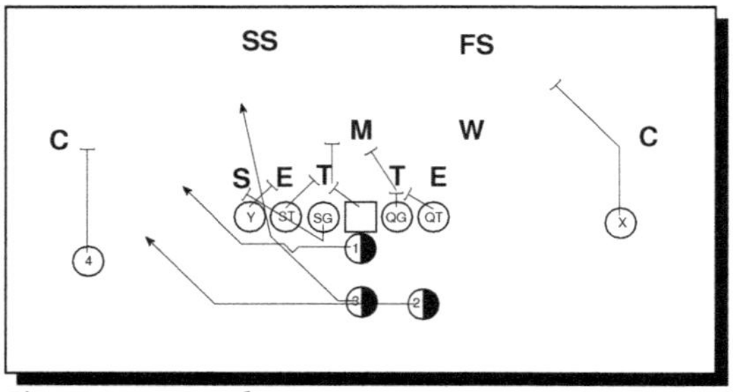

Figure 7-16. Left 735

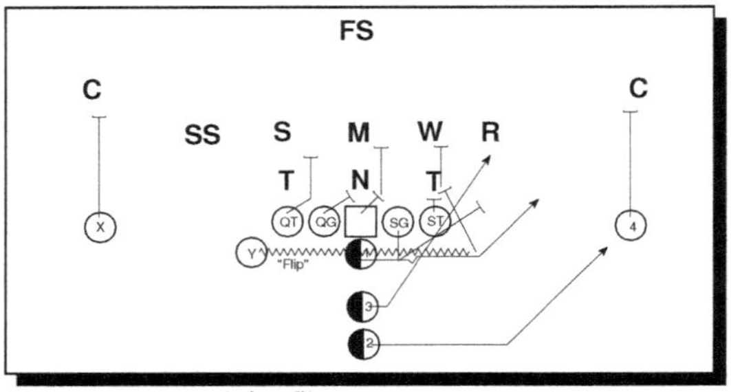

Figure 7-17. Right flip 636

Blocking rules for 36 are as follows:

- Y-Receiver: Gap, down, or the first linebacker inside is Y's blocking assignment. This block is a combo block with the strong tackle if he blocks a man over him.
- Strong Tackle: The strong tackle blocks gap, down, over, or the first linebacker inside.
- Strong Guard: The strong guard pulls strongside and traps the first defender outside Y's down block.
- Center, Quick Guard, and Quick Tackle: The center, quick guard, and quick tackle zone block to the strongside.
- 4-Back: The 4-back blocks the strong safety. If he is put in zin motion, the 4-back blocks the first linebacker to his inside.
- X-Receiver: The X-receiver blocks the defensive man covering him.

The outside veer quickside, 39, may be run from strong or I formations only. This play is the exact opposite of 38. Figures 7-18 through 7-20 show 39. The quarterback opens flat down the line to the quickside. He reads the first defensive player outside Y's block for give to the 3-back or keep. A defensive back or outside linebacker will become the pitch or keep read. Techniques for the quarterback and 3-back for 39 from the I are the same as those for 38. When the play is executed from a strong formation, the 3-back takes a short step forward with his inside foot before running a path for the outside foot of the quick tackle.

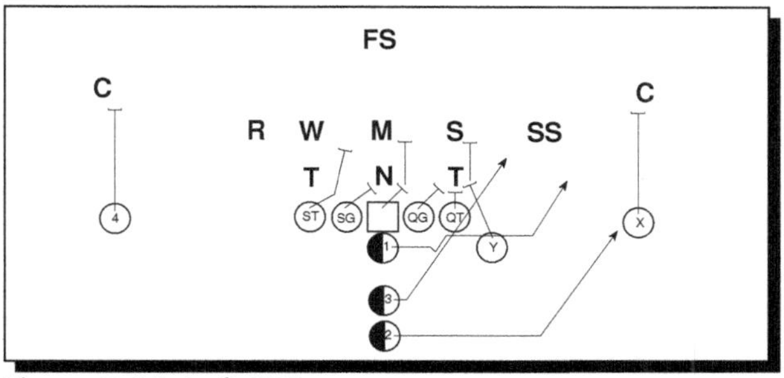

Figure 7-18. Left 639

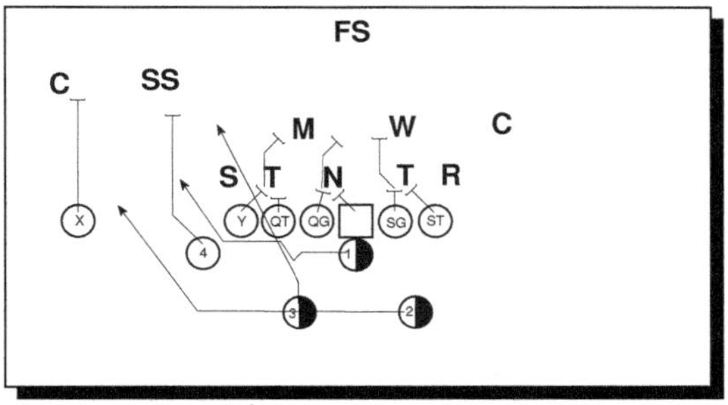

Figure 7-19. Right 539

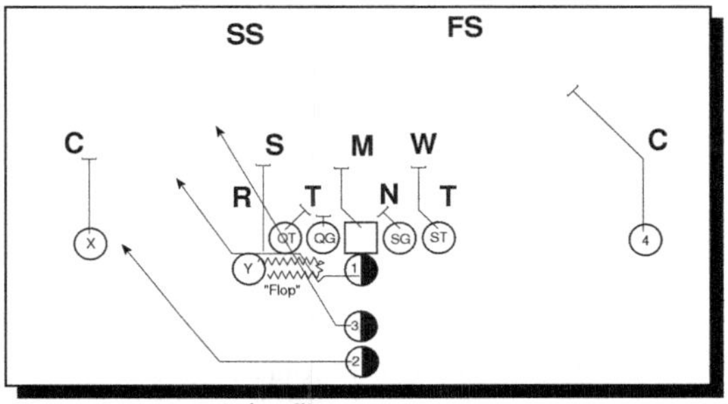

Figure 7-20. Right flip 639

The 2-back is always the pitchman for 39. He sprints to the quickside to establish the proper pitch relationship with the quarterback. This position should be at least five yards deeper than the quarterback and at least two yards in front of him. Blocking assignments for 39 are as follows:

- Y-Receiver: Y zone blocks a 7 or 8 technique defender. Against a 5 technique defensive man, he combos the 5 technique with the quick tackle to the first linebacker inside. Versus an over front, Y blocks the outside linebacker.
- Quick Tackle: The quick tackle zone blocks a 5, 7, or 8 technique defender. Against an over defense, the quick tackle combo blocks with the quick guard to the first linebacker to the inside.
- Quick Guard, Center, Strong Guard, and Strong Tackle: All of these offensive linemen zone block to the quickside.
- X-Receiver: The X-receiver blocks the man covering him.
- 4-Back: The 4-back blocks the #2 secondary defender counting from the outside in.

The 39 may be run as 39 load (Figure 7-21) if the read man for the give is crashing hard. It is probable that the quarterback will not even fake to the 3-back. The 3-back must cut the crashing defender to allow the quarterback to get outside and execute a two-way option on the next defender. When run from strong formation, 39 is an excellent goal line and short-yardage play.

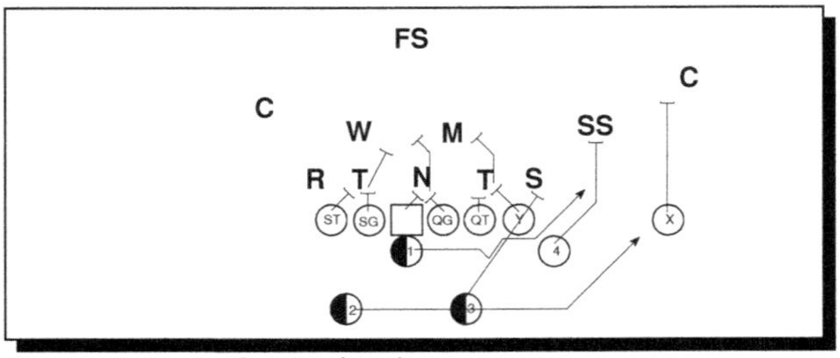

Figure 7-21. Left 539 load

The midline option play, 11, is a great complement to 13, the inside veer quickside, and 31, the fullback trap run to the quickside. The play is based on the principle of constricting the defense by forcing it to concentrate its efforts on stopping the 3-back hitting up the middle of the defense. This tight dive action forces the defense to react to the midline threat and reduces flow to the outside. It enhances the offense's ability to strike along the defensive front with the inside and outside veer plays.

Footwork for the quarterback starts with a step back with the strongside foot at a slight angle to the strongside. The second step is back with the quickside foot slightly to the strongside of the midline. As he reaches the ball back to the 3-back, the quarterback pivots on his strongside toe so that he faces the quickside of the formation. He reads the first down defensive lineman from head-up on the quick guard to the outside for a give or a keep by the quarterback. While reading this defender, the quarterback rides the ball to the 3-back to the quarterback's front hip. If in doubt about the read, the quarterback hands off the ball. When the ball is kept by the quarterback, he runs inside the out block by the quick tackle and follows the lead block in the hole. The 11 is a two-way option, and the ball will not be pitched.

Figures 7-22 through 7-25 show 11 run from I, wing, and doubles formations. If a defensive lineman is aligned in the A gap quickside, 11 should be checked to 13, the inside veer play.

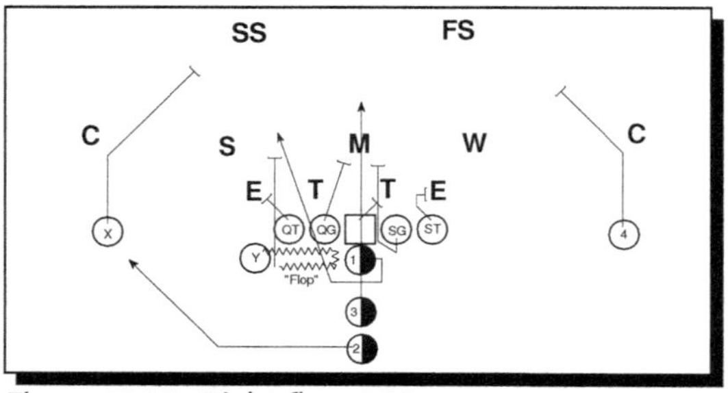

Figure 7-22. Right flop 611

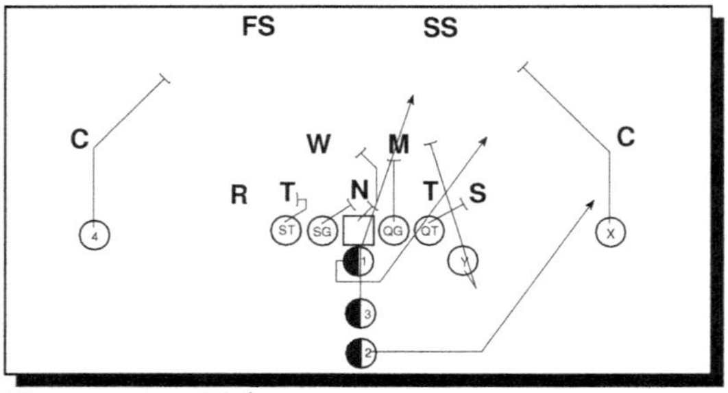

Figure 7-23. Right 611

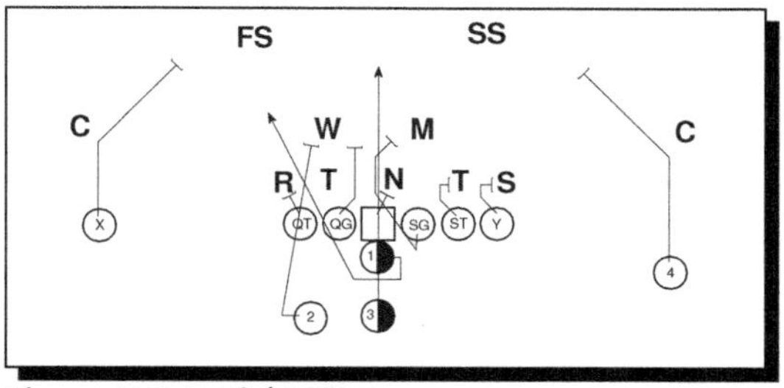

Figure 7-24. Right 711

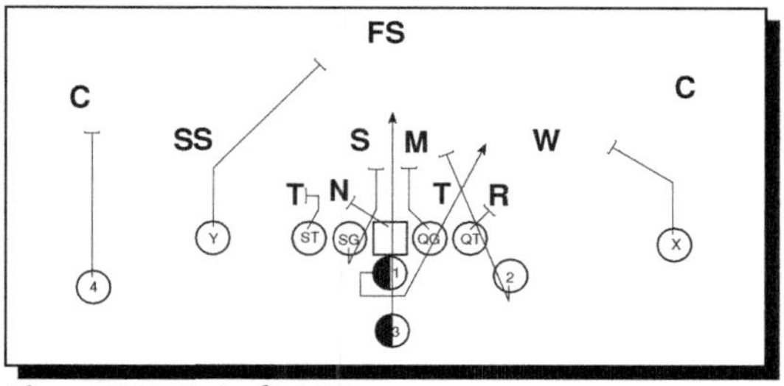

Figure 7-25. Left 811

Blocking rules for 11 are as follows:

- Y-Receiver: From an I alignment, Y is the lead blocker for the quarterback. He leads inside the out block by the quick tackle on the inside or outside linebacker. When 11 is run from other formations, Y blocks the middle or strongside safety.
- Quick Tackle: The quick tackle always blocks out.
- Quick Guard: Versus an even defense, the quick guard releases inside the defensive tackle and blocks a middle linebacker or the inside linebacker quickside. Against an odd defense, he blocks the inside linebacker quickside.
- Center: Against an odd defense, the center zone blocks to the quickside with the strong guard to a middle linebacker or inside linebacker strongside. When facing an even or gap defense, he will block the #1 defensive lineman to the strongside.
- Strong Guard: If the defense is an odd front, the strong guard zone blocks to the quickside with the center. Versus an even or gap assignment, he fold blocks with the center to an inside linebacker strongside.
- Strong Tackle: The strong tackle blocks gap, over, or outside.
- 4-Back: The 4-back blocks the defender covering him.
- X-Receiver: The X-receiver blocks the middle or quickside safety.
- 2-Back: From the I formation, the 2-back runs a path to the quickside as a pitchman for the option. If wing or doubles alignments are used, the 2-back lead blocks on the inside or outside linebacker quickside.

In the no-huddle multiple offense, the midline option is only run to the quickside of the formation. The 11 is another in a series of plays that creates conflicts for defensive players. The defensive tackle aligned to the quickside must respect the 3-back's dive action on 13, the inside veer. This naturally causes him to favor the B gap. When 11, the midline option, is run, this player is left unblocked and must react to stop the 3-back's dive over the center. Because the play hits fast, this defender must react quickly to tackle the 3-back. His reaction becomes predictable and, as a result, creates an easier read for the quarterback. When the defender being read is a 2 or 3 technique tackle, he is asked to react to being unblocked, which is something he normally doesn't experience versus the option.

Figures 7-26 through 7-28 show a variation blocking scheme for 11. It is termed 11G. The blocking rules change only for the quick tackle and quick guard. The quick guard pulls quickside and trap blocks the defensive player, who would normally be blocked by the quick tackle. The quick tackle blocks the first linebacker to his inside. This scheme may result in the defender who is being read reacting outward to the pull by the quick guard. As a result, the read man may not react rapidly to the dive by the 3-back.

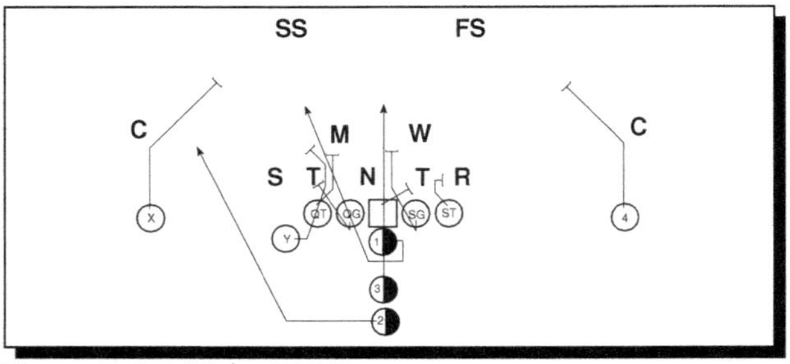

Figure 7-26. Right 611G

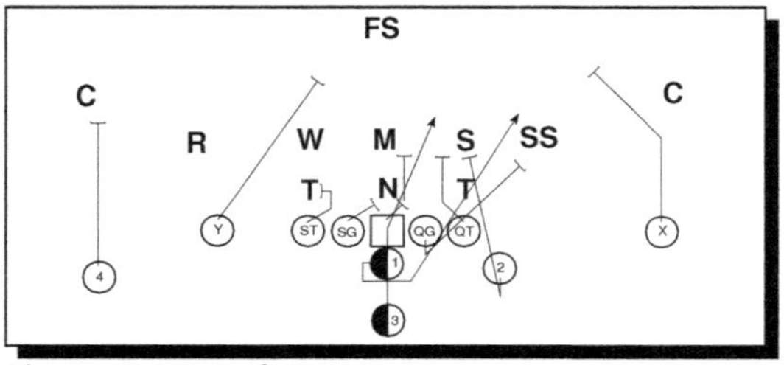

Figure 7-27. Left 811G

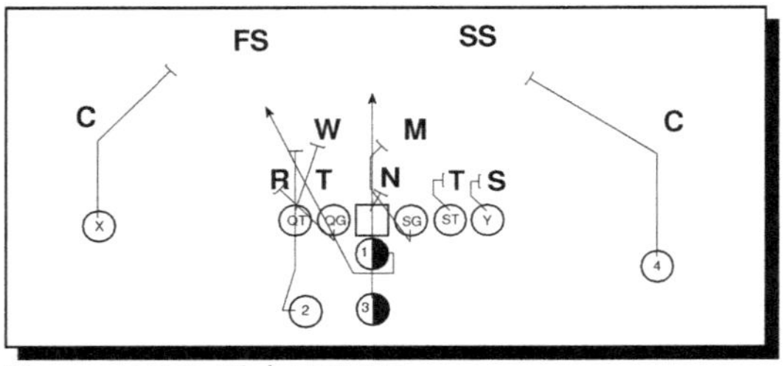

Figure 7-28. Right 711G

The 17 and 16 are option plays that are only run from the pistol formation. The first of these, 17, is a shovel option (Figures 7-29 and 7-30). This play attacks the quickside of the formation and is a form of triple option.

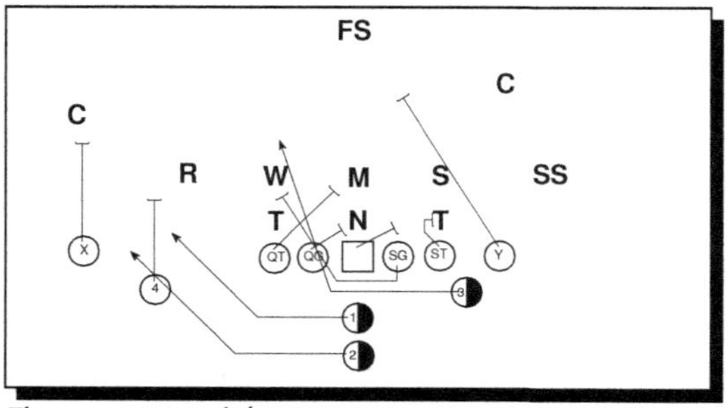

Figure 7-29. Right 917

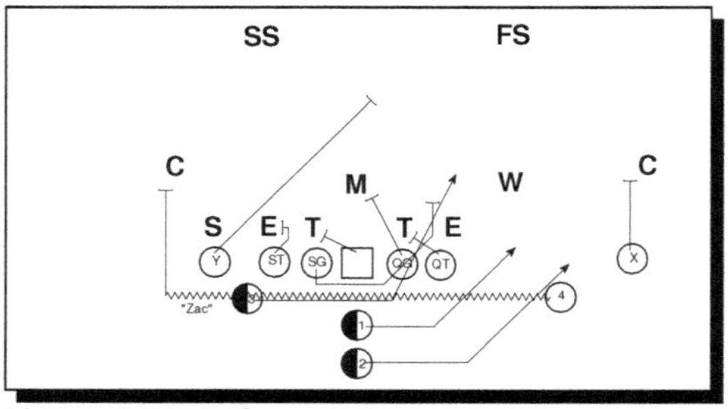

Figure 7-30. Left zac 917

After taking the snap, the quarterback goes flat toward the quickside. His initial read, the first defender from head up with the quick tackle to the outside, determines whether he throws the shovel pass to the 3-back or keeps the ball. If this defender reacts toward the quarterback, the ball is thrown underhanded to the 3-back. This is a forward pass and is an incomplete pass if dropped. When the first read closes on the 3-back, the quarterback turns upfield and executes a two-way option of pitch or keep on the next defensive man he encounters. It is vitally important that the quarterback stays on a flat path to the outside of the first read before turning upfield. This path allows for separation from the 3-back for the shovel pass and forces the first read to make a commitment to either the 3-back or the quarterback.

The 3-back sprints quickside flat behind the line of scrimmage. He follows the strong guard as the guard pulls and turns upfield through the 5 hole. The 3-back must be alert to catch the shovel pass from the quarterback.

Sprinting to the quickside, the 2-back becomes the pitchman for the second phase of the option. He attempts to be in a position five yards deeper than the quarterback and two yards in front of him. The 2-back turns upfield when the quarterback turns up. It is important for the 2-back to remain alert for the pitch at any time after turning upfield since the quarterback's second read may occur in the defensive secondary.

Blocking rules for 17 are as follows:

- Y-Receiver: Y releases crossfield aiming to block a free safety or quickside safety.
- Strong Tackle: Gap, over, or outside is the strong tackle's blocking assignment.
- Strong Guard: Pulling to the quickside, the strong guard turns downfield in the 5 hole. He blocks the inside linebacker or outside linebacker quickside.
- Center: The #1 defender aligned strongside is blocked by the center.
- Quick Guard: Gap, down, middle linebacker or inside linebacker to the strongside is the quick guard's blocking rule.
- Quick Tackle: The quick tackle blocks gap, down, or inside linebacker.
- 4-Back and X-Receiver: The 4-back and X-receiver block the defensive players covering them. If executed properly, 17 is very difficult to defend. It has the potential to break for big plays.

The 16 is a read option play run to the strongside of the formation. If the ball is handed to the 2-back, the play becomes a power off-tackle. When the quarterback keeps the ball, it becomes a quarterback sweep. Interior offensive linemen block 24, the off-tackle play. Complete blocking rules for 16 are as follows:

- Y-Receiver: Y blocks the #1 defender from the outside unless zac motion is employed. In that case, Y blocks #2 defensive man from the outside.
- 3-Back: The 3-back blocks the #2 defensive man counting from the outside. If zac motion is used, the 3-back blocks the #3 defender counting from the outside to the inside.
- 4-Back: The 4-back blocks the defensive player covering him. When zac motion is used, this will be the #1 defensive player counting from the outside.
- X-Receiver: The X-receiver blocks the defender covering him.

- Strong Tackle: Gap, down, or the first linebacker inside is the strong tackle's blocking assignment.
- Strong Guard: Gap, down, middle linebacker or the inside linebacker quickside is the strong guard's blocking assignment.
- Center: The center blocks the #1 defensive player quickside.
- Quick Guard: The quick guard pulls strongside and turns up through the 4 hole. He blocks the inside linebacker to the outside linebacker.
- Quick Tackle: Gap, over, outside is the quick tackle's blocking rule.

The 2-back lead steps to the strongside. He then hits straight ahead over the strong guard. The quarterback places the football into a pocket formed by the 2-back. The 2-back's inside elbow is up and the thumb of his inside hand points down, ensuring that the elbow is kept high. The ball is placed against the 2-back's belly button, and the quarterback makes a ride step forward. If he wants to hand off, he pressures the football against the 2-back's belly button. At this point, the 2-back closes the pocket and grasps the football. If he does not feel pressure, the 2-back rolls his arms loosely and fakes hard into the 4 hole. When the handoff is made, the 2-back keys the quick guard's path and follows him into the hole.

Footwork for the quarterback has him pivot on his strongside toe and reach the ball back to the 2-back. He brings his quickside foot even with the strongside foot. A step forward is taken with the quickside foot as the ride is executed. The quarterback reads the first defensive player from head-up on the strong tackle to his outside. If the read man closes on the 2-back, the quarterback pulls the ball out of the pocket formed by the 2-back and sprints to the outside. If the read man hesitates or moves toward the quarterback, the quarterback pressures the ball into the 2-back and hands it off to him. He then sprints hard strongside, faking the keep.

The 16 is a two-way option play and does not have a pitchman for the quarterback. Figures 7-31 and 7-32 show 16.

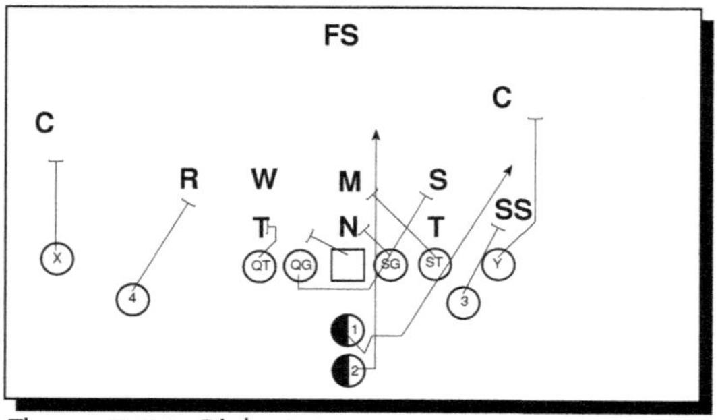

Figure 7-31. Right 916

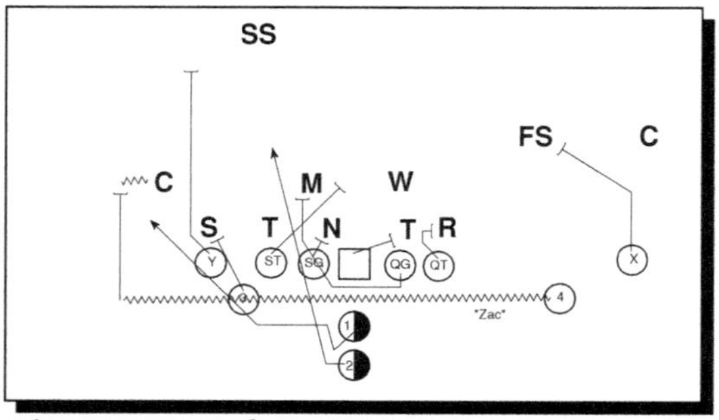

Figure 7-32. Left zac 916

Play-action passes from the veer series are based on a fake of 14, the inside veer to the strongside. The 80 pass protection is used for these passes. Chapter 4 details the pass blocking assignments. The strongside is man-to-man blocking with the strong tackle responsible for #2 on the line of scrimmage and the strong guard blocking #1 on the line. Quickside blocking is slide protection toward the quickside. When patterns 1 through 3 are thrown, line blocking is aggressive cut blocks. Dropback pass techniques are used for patterns 4 through 9.

The 14 is run by the 3-back. He blocks any linebacker blitz in the area. If no blitz occurs, the 3-back runs a six-yard deep hook out route. This route is the checkdown route for the quarterback.

Play-action passes in the veer series are only run from doubles, wing, or I formations. The 2-back always blocks the first defensive player who appears outside the strong tackle's block. If no one shows and patterns 4 through 9 are used, the 2-back runs a five-yard flat cut to the strongside. From a doubles alignment, jet motion is used to get the 2-back to the strongside.

Footwork for the quarterback varies with the pattern called. In the case of quick patterns (Figures 7-33 through 7-35) the quarterback rides the ball to the 3-back and after completing the fake, he moves down the line of scrimmage to throw the football. Moving to his right, he steps first with his right foot and executes the throw as he steps with his left foot. Going to the left, the first step is with the left foot, the second is with the right foot, and he throws as he takes a third step with his left foot.

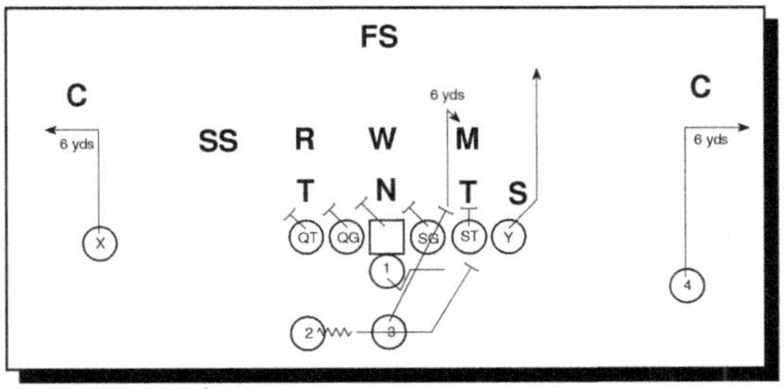

Figure 7-33. Right 781

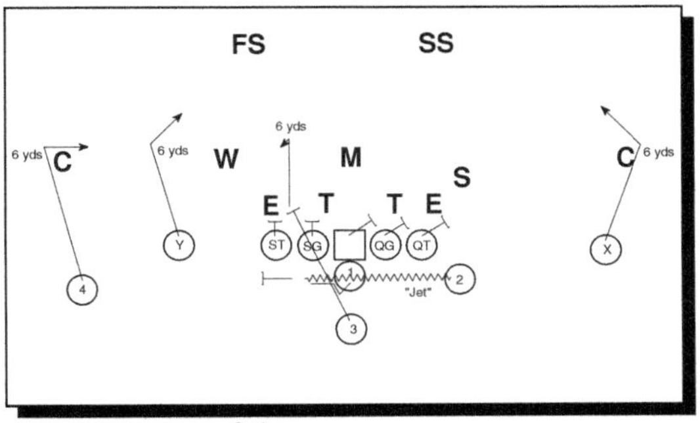

Figure 7-34. Left jet 882

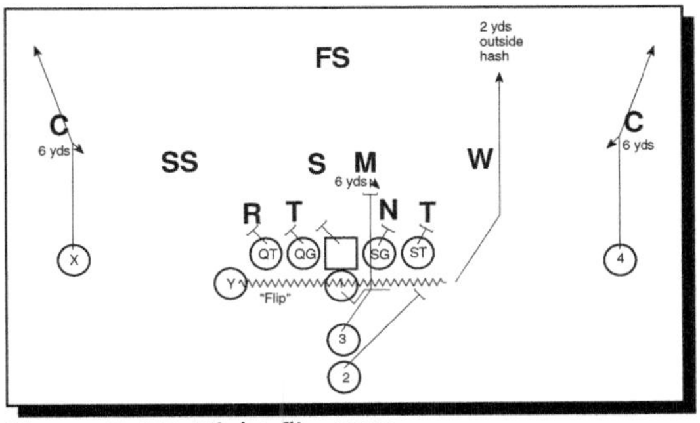

Figure 7-35. Right flip 683

When pass patterns 4 through 9 are used (Figures 7-36 through 7-41) the quarterback makes a ride to the 3-back and executes a five-step drop before throwing the football.

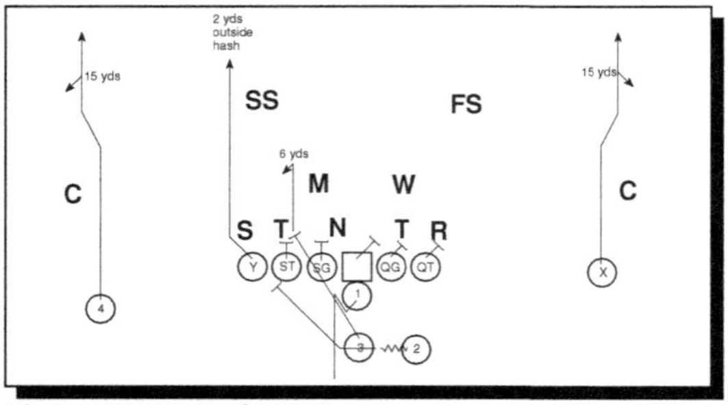

Figure 7-36. Left 784

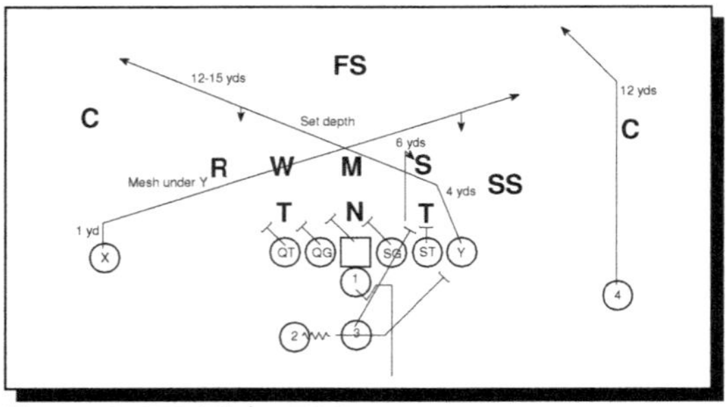

Figure 7-37. Right 785

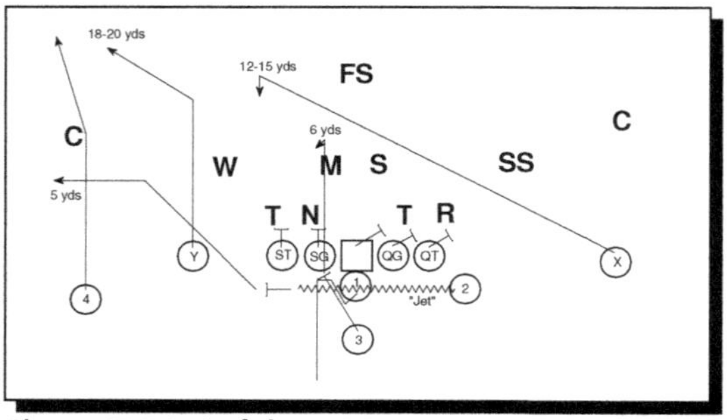

Figure 7-38. Left jet 886

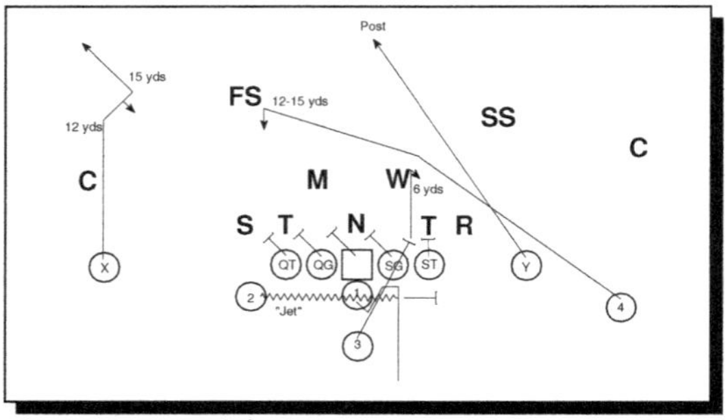

Figure 7-39. Right jet 887

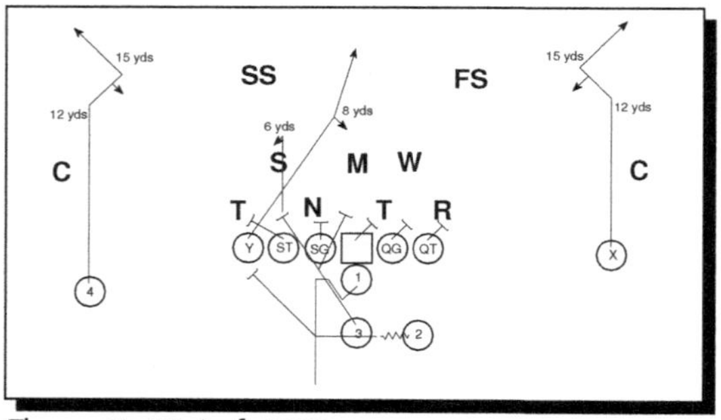

Figure 7-40. Left 788

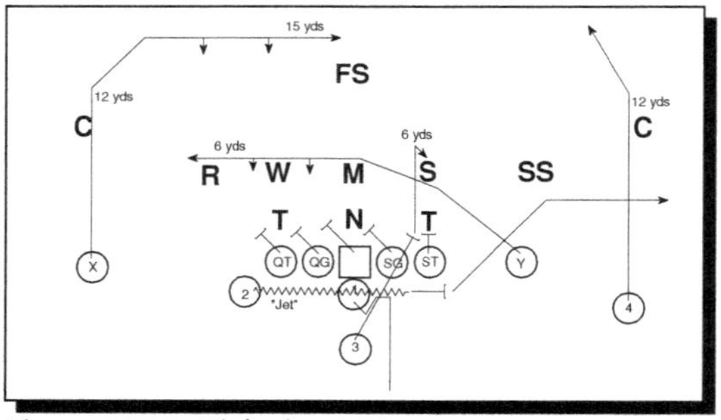

Figure 7-41. Right jet 889

CHAPTER 8

The Buck Sweep Series

The buck sweep series is classic wing-T football. When Dave Nelson created the wing-T offense, one of the first series incorporated was the buck sweep. Its immediate predecessor was the single-wing buck lateral series. In the no-huddle multiple offense, the buck sweep series plays an important role in the running and play-action passing game. This series threatens the entire defensive front. The 3-back trap attacks the middle of the defense, and the buck sweep threatens the strongside perimeter. An off-tackle play is run strongside, and the counter crisscross, quarterback sweep, and bootleg passes are run to the quickside of the formation. The last three plays serve as misdirection parts of the series.

The 28 is the buck sweep play (Figures 8-1 through 8-5). This play is designed to be an outside run to the strongside. Gap blocking is the basis for this play, which helps to negate the effectiveness of inside stunts and blitzes. The threat of the 3-back trap in the middle of the defense and the bootleg action by the quarterback help to slow fast flow defenses.

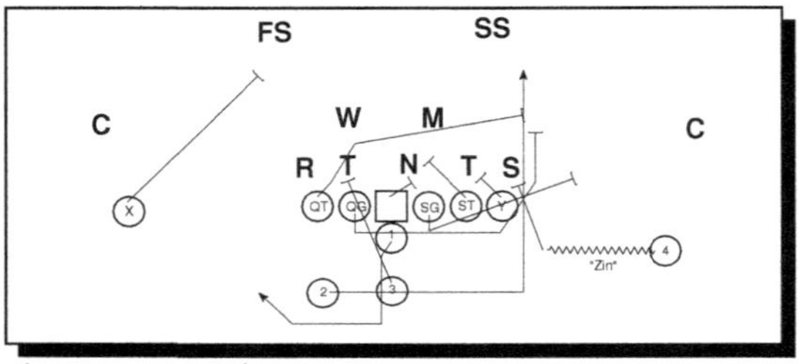

Figure 8-1. Right zin 728

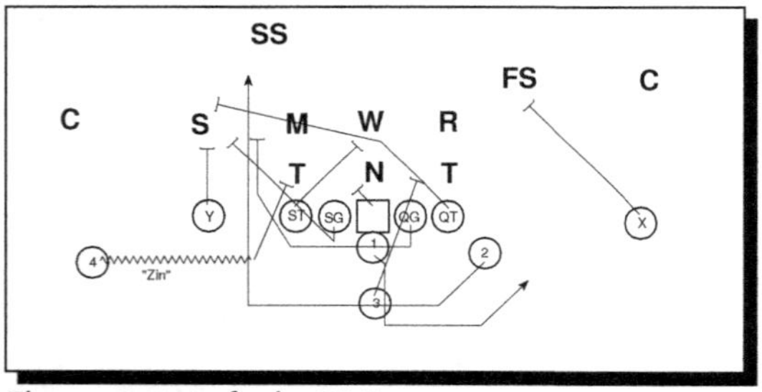

Figure 8-2. Left zin 828

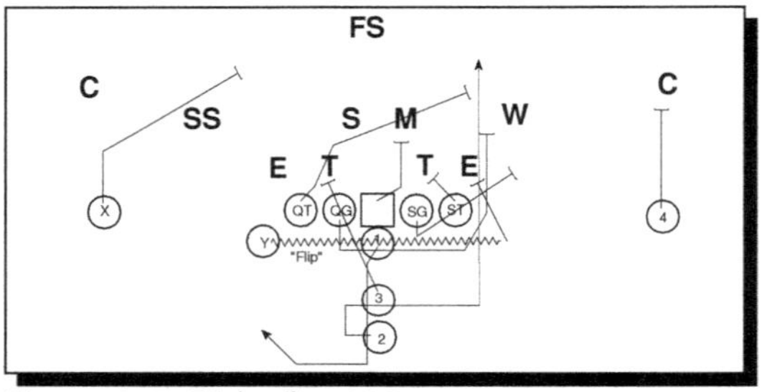

Figure 8-3. Right flip 628

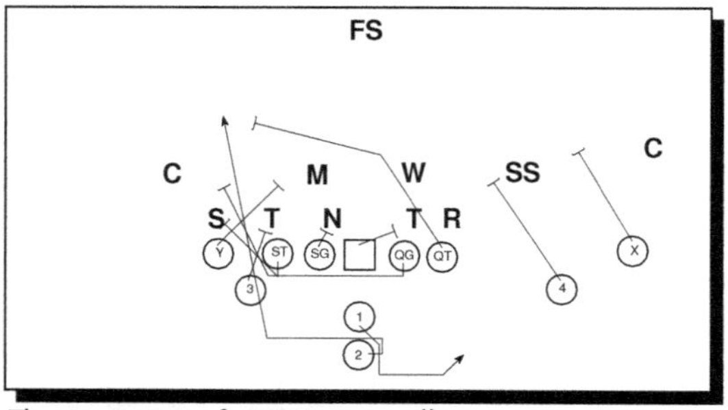

Figure 8-4. Left 928 gap call

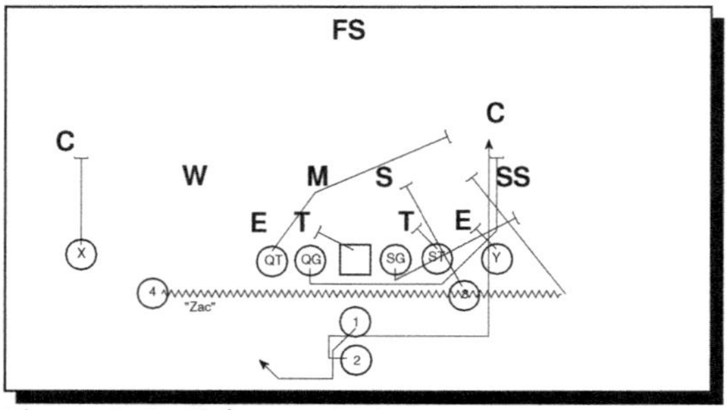

Figure 8-5. Right zac 928

The 28 is run from any formation in the no-huddle multiple offense except the strong alignment. A conventional wing-T offense has a wingback blocking down on the end man on the line of scrimmage. In the no-huddle multiple offense, this down block may come from the Y-receiver aligned or motioned to the strongside, or the down block may be made by the 4-back motioning into a tight wing position or motioning across the pistol formation to a tight wing.

The quarterback opens quickside at 90 degrees on the midline. He does not fake to the 3-back, but a proximity fake occurs by the 3-back's path as he fakes 30. The quarterback hides the ball from the defense, keeping it on his belly button as he comes away from the line of scrimmage. He executes a one-handed handoff to the 2-back on his third step along the midline. After handing off, the quarterback places both of his hands on his belt buckle as he continues for two additional steps straight back on the midline. After his fifth step, the quarterback bootlegs to the quickside as he slides both of his hands to his back hip, hiding them from the defense. At this point, he should be seven yards deep. If he continues to fake the bootleg aggressively, it may affect the reaction of quickside defenders, including secondary players.

The 2-back is the ballcarrier for 28. He may be aligned in the I, wing, or dive back position. If he is in the I tailback position, the 2-back lead steps quickside. He then steps forward with the strongside foot and follows that with a step forward with the quickside foot. A pivot to the strongside is made on the quickside toe. From a starting depth of seven yards, these steps should put the 2-back at the desired depth of five yards. At this point, he flattens his path to the strongside. From a dive back position, the 2-back comes flat to the strongside. If aligned in the wing, the 2-back takes three steps on a 45-degree angle for the foot of the 3-back. He then flattens his path at five yards of depth. Motion is not used by the 3-back for these steps since the 4-back will be running zin motion to acquire a tight wing alignment.

After receiving a handoff from the quarterback, the 2-back runs flat to the strongside. He keys the kick-out block. If the offensive lineman kicks out, the 2-back plants his back foot and executes an L cut, which is a 90-degree cut toward the line of scrimmage inside the kick-out block. If the lead blocker log blocks a defender, the 2-back makes his L cut off the kick-out block coming from the quick guard. To make this cut, the tailback must remain under control. The flat path he runs helps set up the kick-out block as the force defender must come straight upfield to contain the sweep. If the ballcarrier angles toward the line of scrimmage, the force man closes on an angle that forces a much more difficult kick-out block.

The 30 is faked by the 3-back. He aims for the center's butt and rolls his arms on a fake. His blocking assignment is to fill for the pulling quick guard. To do this, he must be prepared to cut off any defender in the quickside A gap. In college football, this fill is usually a cut block.

Blocks by the strong tackle or Y aligned tight strongside or motioning to the strongside are down blocks. If a gap call is made from the pistol formation, the strong guard down blocks, and the strong tackle pulls and kicks out the force defender. These blocks are reverse shoulder blocks with the linemen taking a flat lead step to the inside and aiming to get their heads across the front of any defensive player they are blocking. The primary objective is to stop penetration by the defense and pin defenders to the inside.

If the 4-back is sent in zin motion, or zac motion in the case of a pistol alignment, he moves when the quarterback lifts his heel. Motion should be timed so that the 4-back ends up in a wing position on the strongside. From this position, he blocks the first defensive man to his inside on or off the line of scrimmage. This block is a reverse shoulder block, but it must be made above the defender's waist. When 28 is run from the I formation, the 4-back blocks the defensive man covering him.

Blocking rules for 28 are as follows:

- Y-Receiver: Gap, down, or first linebacker inside is Y's blocking rule. If he is split in doubles, Y blocks the man covering him.
- Strong Tackle: The strong tackle blocks gap, down, or the first linebacker to the inside. If a gap call is made from the pistol formation, the strong tackle pulls strongside and kicks out or log blocks the first defender outside the last down block.
- Strong Guard: The strong guard pulls strongside and kicks out or log blocks the first defensive player outside the last down block. If a defender is in the A gap and the team is aligned in the pistol formation, the strong guard calls "gap" and blocks down on the man in the A gap.
- Center: The center blocks A gap strongside, over, middle linebacker, or inside linebacker quickside. From the pistol formation, the center blocks over or the #1 defensive man to the quickside.
- Quick Guard: After pulling flat to the strongside until he clears the center, the quick guard bows back to two yards of depth to avoid any defensive penetration. He reads the kick-out blocker. If the lead blocker kicks out, the quick guard turns up inside the kick-out block and seals inside on the first second-level defender who appears. When the lead blocker executes a log block, the quick guard will kick out the next defensive man to the outside.
- Quick Tackle: The quick tackle blocks gap first. With no gap defender, the quick tackle goes crossfield to the strongside. He is aiming for about six yards of depth, and the quick tackle kicks out on the first defensive player he encounters.
- X-Receiver: The X-receiver blocks the man covering him.

The 28 is a play that requires multiple repetitions in practice and must be run frequently in games if it is to be successful. The timing and reaction between the pulling linemen and the 2-back can only be developed through many repetitions. A coach cannot be discouraged by the initial failure of the play to be successful. If the coach continues to call the play, it will eventually become an outstanding running play and a signature of the offense.

The 30 is the 3-back trap to the strongside. It is important for the offense to establish 30 as a threat. It sets up the other plays in the buck series. Because of the threat of the 3-back's play in the middle of the defense, the defensive players cannot flow as rapidly to the outside. The 30 and variations of the play are diagrammed in Figures 8-6 through 8-9.

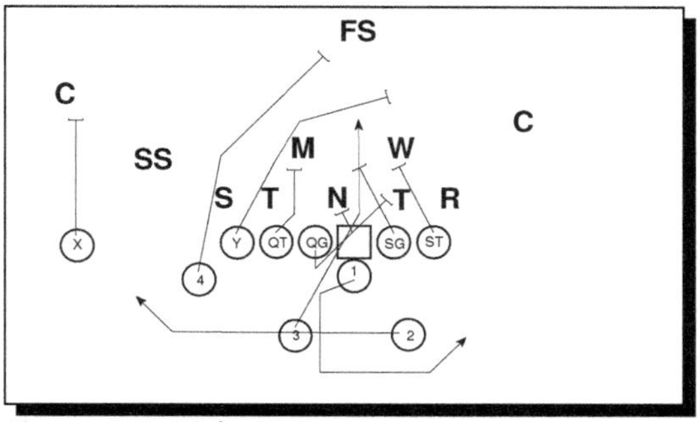

Figure 8-6. Right 530

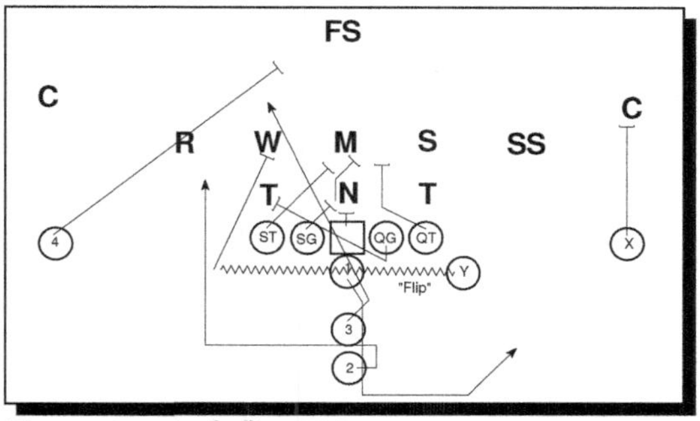

Figure 8-7. Left flip 630

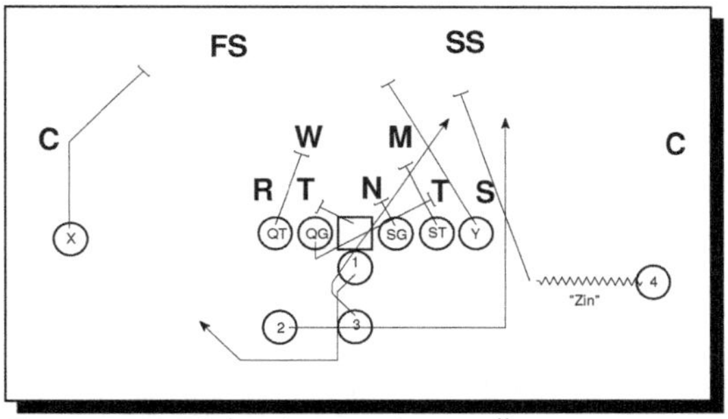

Figure 8-8. Right zin 730 Lou call

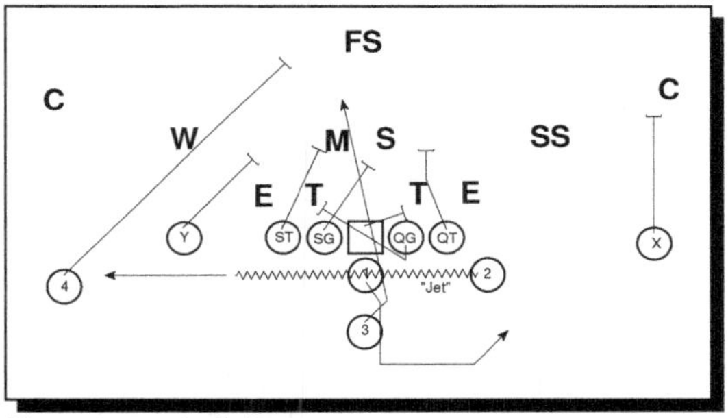

Figure 8-9. Left jet 830

Footwork for the 3-back starts with a step with the quickside foot just to the quickside of the midline. His aiming point is the center's butt, and from this point he reads the trap block by the quick guard. If 30 is run from a strong set, the 3-back lead steps at the center with his strongside foot.

Steps for the 2-back may vary according to the formation used or motion used by him. From I, wing, and doubles, his footwork is the same as used on 28. The tailback should roll his arms and dip his inside shoulder as he receives the fake from the quarterback. After the fake, the 2-back continues to run 28. If a strong formation is used, the 2-back comes flat across the formation to the quickside faking 19, the quickside power sweep. From a doubles formation, jet motion could be run. The 2-back runs fast, flat motion across the formation to the strongside. He fakes 18, the jet sweep to the strongside.

Normally, the quarterback opens to the quickside at a 90-degree angle from the line of scrimmage. He operates on the midline as he makes a one-handed handoff to the 3-back while keeping his other hand on his belt buckle. The handoff to the 3-back should be made on the quarterback's second step. He must be moving on the midline to give the 3-back room to make a cut to the strongside. After handing off, the quarterback continues back on the midline. The quarterback makes a one-handed fake to the 2-back on his third step. Following the fake, the quarterback brings both hands to his belt buckle as he continues for two more steps straight back. At this point, both of his hands are brought to his backside hip as he bootlegs to the quickside.

From the strong formation, the quarterback opens at a 45-degree angle to the quickside. He still makes the handoff to the 3-back on his third step. The quarterback then goes straight back to fake to the 2-back. He takes two additional steps straight back before executing a bootleg action to the strongside of the formation. When jet motion is used from a doubles set, the quarterback lifts his heel to bring the 2-back in motion as on 18. The quarterback does not fake to the 2-back. He opens on the midline and executes the handoff and following steps as he normally does. No fake is made to the 2-back, but the quarterback continues on the midline for five steps before he bootlegs to the quickside of the formation.

Blocking rules for 30 trap are as follows:

- Y-Receiver: Y blocks an outside linebacker or safety to his side of the formation.
- Strong Tackle: The inside linebacker to the outside linebacker is the strong tackle's blocking assignment.
- Strong Guard: Versus an odd defense, the strong guard combo blocks with the center on the nose man to a middle linebacker or quickside inside linebacker. Against an even front, he blocks the middle linebacker or inside linebacker to the quickside. If the defense has a man in the strongside A gap, the strong guard calls Lou for long and blocks the gap defender.
- Center: Against an odd defense the center combo blocks with the strong guard on a nose man to a middle linebacker or inside linebacker quickside. Against an even or gap defense, he blocks the #1 defender to the quickside.
- Quick Guard: The quick guard pulls strongside and traps the first defensive player outside the last down block. If a Lou call is made by the strong guard, this indicates a long trap. The quick guard must get up into the hole and dig the defender out. If he pulls to the right, he uses a right shoulder block; he blocks with his left shoulder when he pulls left.
- Quick Tackle: B gap is the quick tackle's first blocking responsibility. If no defender is in the B gap, the quick tackle blocks the first linebacker to the inside.
- 4-Back: The nearest safety is the 4-back's blocking assignment.
- X- Receiver: The X-receiver blocks the defensive player covering him.

Two variations of 30 are used. The first of these, 30 gut, is shown in Figures 8-10 and 8-11. Gut is used versus even defenses when the strong guard is having trouble releasing inside of the defensive man aligned over him. This play works very well versus a good defensive tackle who reads well. The strong guard pulls strongside and traps the first defensive player he encounters. Instead of trapping, the quick guard fold-blocks with the center on a middle linebacker or inside linebacker quickside. The strong tackle blocks the first linebacker to the inside. The influence pull by the strong guard is used to get the defender playing him to react to the strongside, and he is left unblocked.

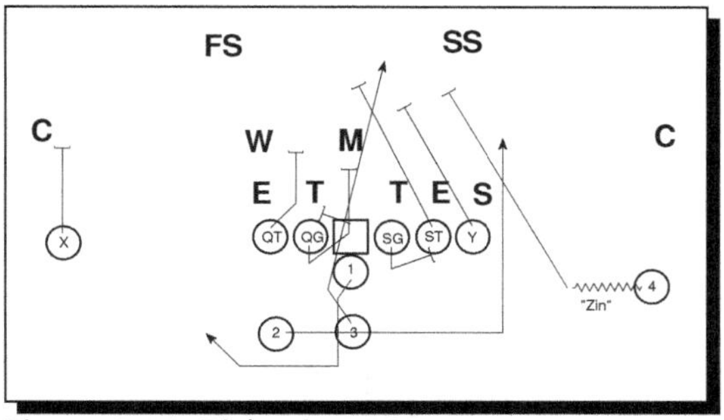

Figure 8-10. Right zin 730 gut

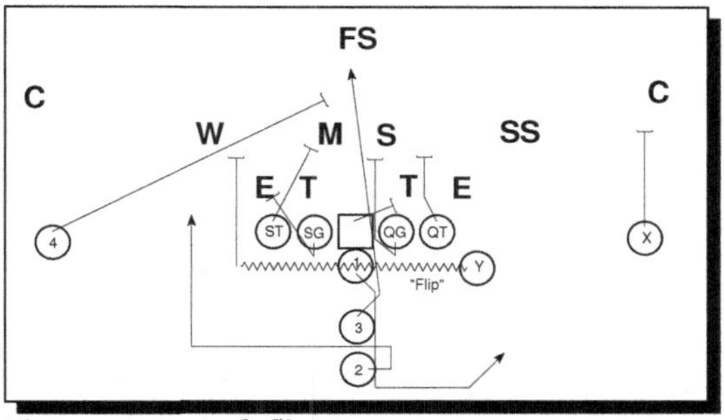

Figure 8-11. Left flip 630 gut

The 30 base is a second variation that is used against a 5-2 defensive alignment. The center blocks the nose man whichever way he wants to go. The guards block the inside linebackers, and the tackles cut off the defensive men aligned over them. The play is man blocked, and the 3-back reads the block of the center on the nose and cuts opposite it. Figure 8-12 shows 30 base.

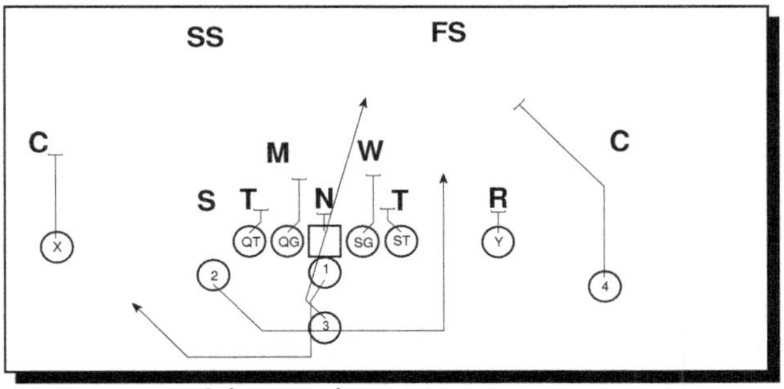

Figure 8-12. Right 830 base

The 26 (Figures 8-13 through 8-15) is the strongside off-tackle play in the buck series. This counter gap play features counter trey blocking. Gap blocking on the strongside seals the seams inside the 6 hole against blitzes and line stunts. This versatile play can be run in all formations except the strong set. When run from the pistol formation, it combines the off-tackle play, bubble screen, and read option into one play.

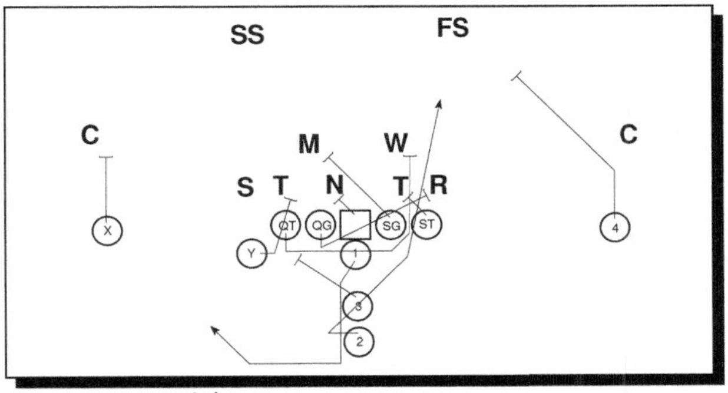

Figure 8-13. Right 626

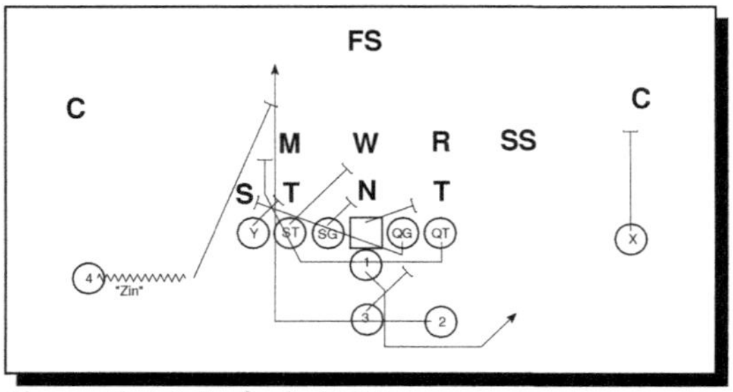

Figure 8-14. Left zin 726

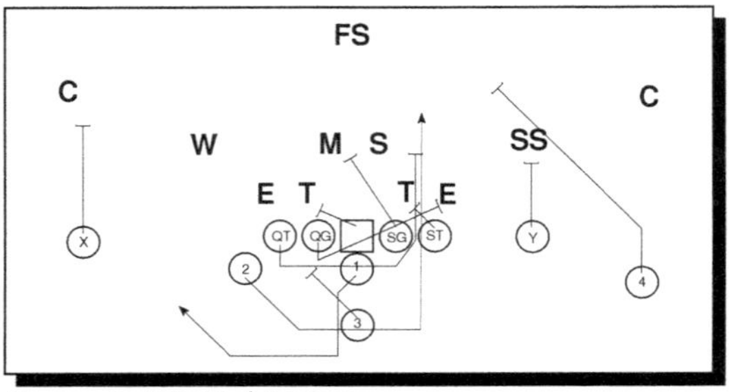

Figure 8-15. Right 826

Quarterback action from I, wing, or doubles has him open to the quickside of the formation at a 90-degree angle, placing him on the midline. He conceals the ball on his belly button as he comes back to execute the handoff to the 2-back. This handoff should occur on the quarterback's third step. After handing off, the quarterback stays on the midline for two steps. He then slides his hand to his back hip and bootlegs quickside. From the pistol formation, the quarterback secures the snap and steps back with his quickside foot as he opens quickside. He reaches the ball back to the 2-back and executes a ride as he keys the first defender from head-up with the quick tackle to the outside. If this defensive player closes hard with the pulling quick tackle, the quarterback executes his option steps and pulls the ball out of the 2-back's belly. He then attacks the quickside as he keys the defensive man covering the 4-back. If this player covers the 4-back on his bubble screen route, the quarterback keeps the ball and turns upfield. When the defender does not cover the 4-back, the quarterback throws the bubble screen pass to him. Figure 8-16 shows this variation of 26. If the defender over or outside the quick tackle does not chase his pull, the quarterback rides the ball to the 2-back and hands off to him. The quarterback will then attack the quickside of the formation as though he has kept the ball.

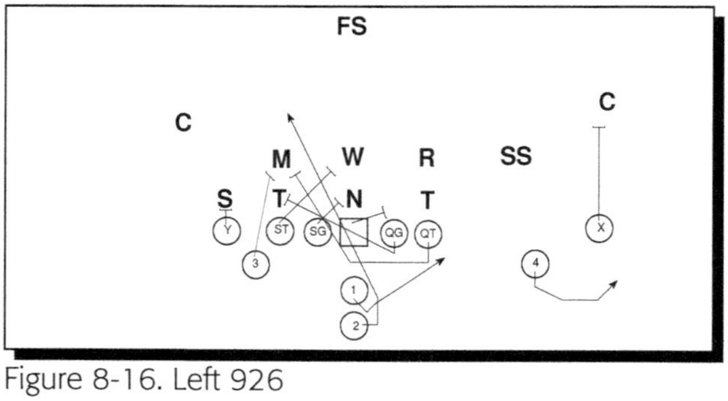

Figure 8-16. Left 926

From an I alignment, the 2-back lead steps quickside. He then aims to hit downhill at the hip of the second offensive lineman in from the outside. This may be either the strong tackle or the strong guard. If the 2-back is in the dive back position in a wing alignment, he lead steps flat strongside and continues on this path until he receives the handoff. At this point, the 2-back aims for the same point that he did from the I tailback position. For a doubles formation, the 2-back lead steps at the 3-back with his strongside foot. He takes three steps at a 45-degree angle and flattens out at five yards of depth. From this point, he does what he did when he was in the dive back alignment. In a pistol formation, the 2-back lead steps quickside and then takes two steps straight toward the line of scrimmage. He gives the quarterback a pocket by raising his strongside elbow. If the quarterback pressures the football into the 2-back's stomach, he clamps on to it. He should plant his quickside foot, break under the quarterback, and follow the quick tackle into the hole. When no pressure is applied, the quarterback pulls the football out of the pocket after finishing the ride. The 2-back rolls his arms and closes the pocket as though he has the ball. The 2-back fakes 26 by running hard and following the block of the quick tackle.

The 3-back fills the B gap to the quickside from I, wing, or doubles formations. He fills for the pulling quick tackle and must be very aggressive. The 3-back does not chase specific defenders, but instead blocks an area. If the pistol formation is used, the 3-back blocks the first linebacker at the second level to his inside.

Blocking rules for 26 include the following:

- Y-Receiver: Y blocks gap, down, or the first linebacker to the inside. Versus a 7 technique defender, Y blocks out. If he is split, Y blocks the defensive player covering him.
- Strong Tackle: The strong tackle's blocking assignment is gap, down, or the first linebacker inside.
- Strong Guard: Gap, down, middle linebacker, or the inside linebacker to the quickside is the strong guard's blocking rule.
- Center: The center blocks the #1 defender to the quickside.
- Quick Guard: The quick guard pulls flat strongside and traps the first defensive man past the last down block. When he pulls right, he traps with his right shoulder. If he pulls left, he blocks with his left shoulder.
- Quick Tackle: The quick tackle pulls strongside and reads the quick guard's block. When the guard traps, the quick tackle turns up into the hole and seals inside out on the linebackers.
- 4-Back: The 4-back blocks the nearest safety from I, wing, or doubles. In a pistol formation, he runs the bubble screen route.
- X-Receiver: The X-receiver blocks the defensive man covering him.

Figures 8-17 through 8-20 show 47. The 47 is the counter crisscross play common to the wing-T. It is only run from wing or doubles formations. The 4-back is always sent in zin motion so that he ends up in a tight wing position on the strongside.

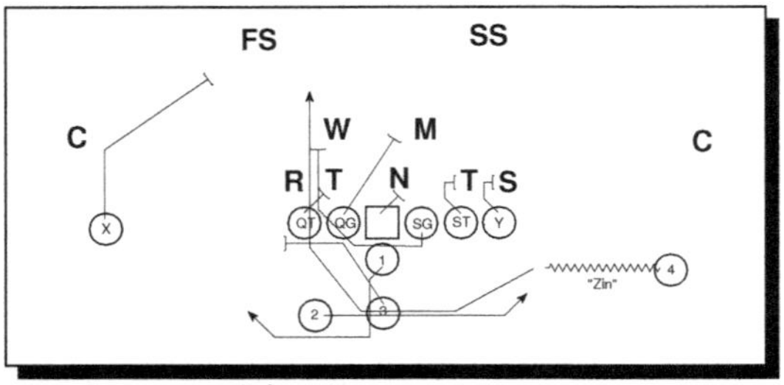

Figure 8-17. Right zin 747

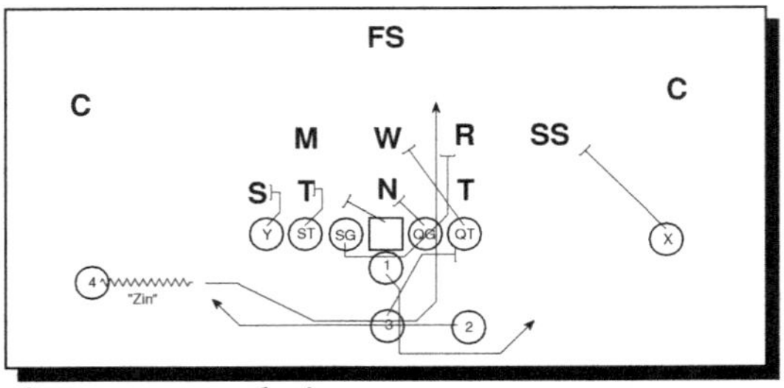

Figure 8-18. Left zin 747

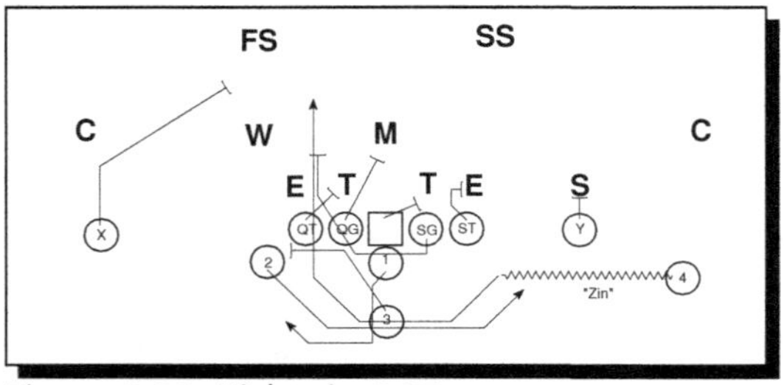

Figure 8-19. Right zin 847

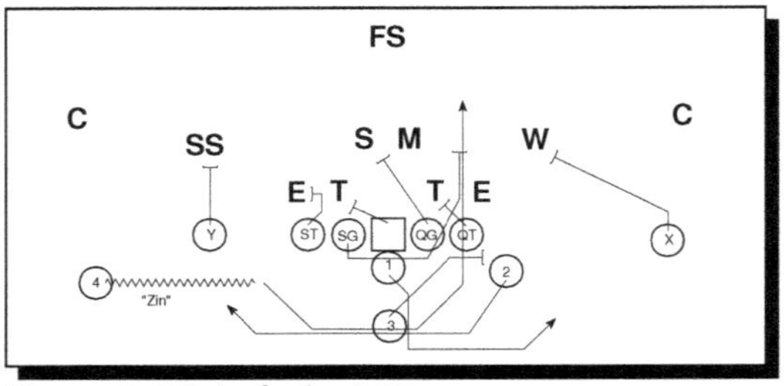

Figure 8-20. Left zin 847

The quarterback footwork is identical to that used for 28, the buck sweep. The handoff to the 2-back is made by placing the football point first into his hands that are held on his inside hip. This technique is done so that the 2-back can more easily make the inside handoff to the 4-back. After handing off, the quarterback goes two additional steps back on the midline and executes a bootleg fake with his hands on his backside hip. This fake is important as it may influence the reaction of the defender on or outside the quick tackle. If the defender can be influenced to hesitate before closing inside, he becomes easier for the 3-back to kick-out on 47. When this defender chases the quick tackle as he blocks down, it is time to run the quarterback sweep off bootleg action.

The 2-back follows the same path as he does for 28. He places his hands on his inside hip with the little fingers together. The quarterback places the ball point-first into his hands. The 2-back continues on a flat path and hands the football inside to the 4-back. The ball is handed off one-handed with the hand closest to the quickside of the formation. After the handoff, the 2-back continues to fake 28.

Zin motion by the 4-back should place him in position as a tight wing to the strongside of the formation. It is his responsibility to get to the proper depth for the handoff made by the 2-back. He forms a pocket by lifting his backside elbow high. The 4-back is responsible for timing his path so that the 2-back makes the inside handoff to him at the proper time. After receiving the handoff from the 2-back, the 4-back follows the strong guard who is pulling through the hole quickside.

The 3-back takes two steps forward slightly to the quickside of the midline. He then goes to an inside-out position to block the first defensive player from head-up on the quick tackle to the outside. He makes a kick-out block similar to the one the 3-back uses for the power off-tackle play, 24. If he is going left, he blocks with the left shoulder; going right, he blocks with the right shoulder.

Blocking rules for 47 are as follows:

- Y-Receiver: Y blocks gap, over, or outside. If he is split, Y blocks the man covering him.
- Strong Tackle: The strong tackle blocks gap, over, or the first defensive player to the outside.
- Strong Guard: Pulling flat to the quickside, the strong guard reads the 3-back's kick-out block. He turns up inside this block and blocks inside to outside on a linebacker.
- Center: The #1 defender to the strongside is blocked by the center.
- Quick Guard: Gap, down, middle linebacker, or inside linebacker to the strongside is the quick guard's blocking rule.
- Quick Tackle: The quick tackle blocks gap, down, or the first linebacker to the inside.
- X-Receiver: The X-receiver blocks the safety to the quickside.

The 47 serves as a counter or misdirection play for the buck series. The gap blocking used for the play helps prevent defensive penetration that might disrupt it. If timed properly, the play hits quickly. Because the ball is handed to the 2-back, the defense reacts by flowing strongside, which creates the possibility of a big play for the offense when the ball is reversed to the 4-back. The 47 is a play that helps create a conflict for the defender head-up or outside the quick tackle. This player may be responsible for containing the quarterback on the bootleg to his outside and also closing the off-tackle hole to stop the counter crisscross play.

Figures 8-21 through 8-24 illustrate the quarterback sweep play 09. This play comes off bootleg action. The quarterback opens quickside on the midline. He fakes to the 2-back on his third step. After executing the fake, the quarterback takes two more steps on the midline and bootlegs to the quickside. He follows the block by the strong guard as he attempts to kick out the first unblocked defender on the quickside.

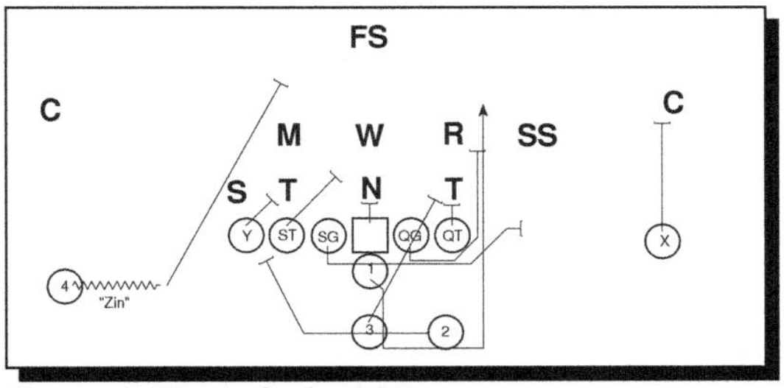

Figure 8-21. Left zin 709

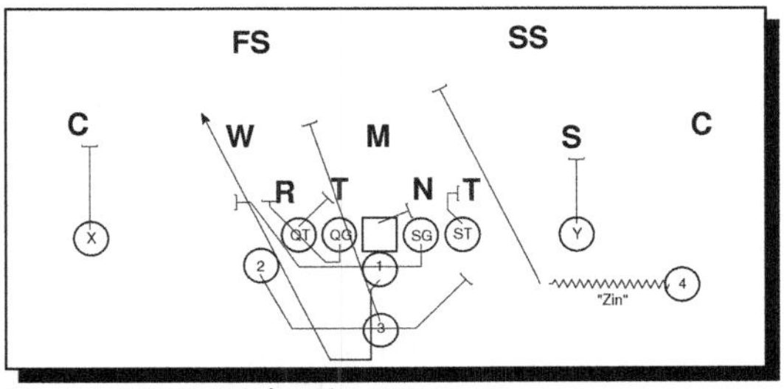

Figure 8-22. Right zin 809

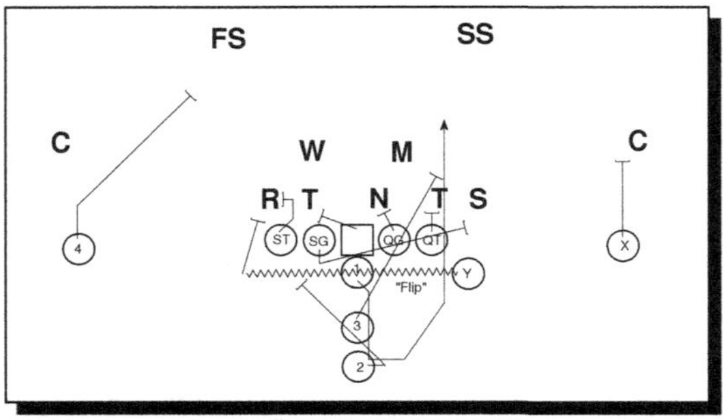

Figure 8-23. Left flip 609

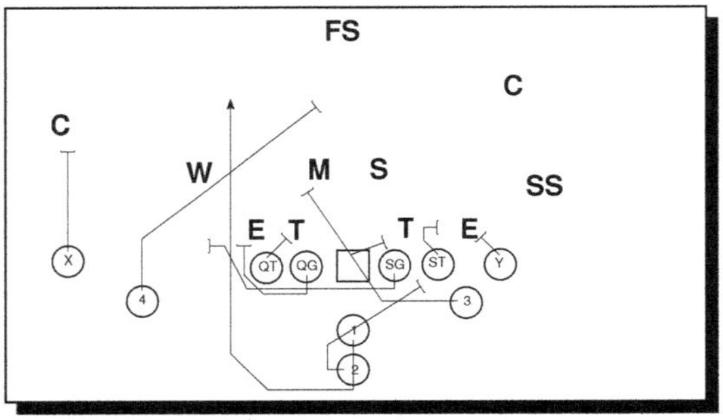

Figure 8-24. Right 909

The 26 is faked by the 2-back. After faking, the 2-back blocks the first defensive player who shows on the strongside. The 3-back goes through the B gap on the quickside and seals the first linebacker from head-up to the inside.

Blocking rules for 09 are as follows:

- Y-Receiver: Y blocks gap, down, or the nearest linebacker. If he is split, Y blocks the man covering him.
- Strong Tackle: The strong tackle blocks gap, down, or the first linebacker inside.
- Strong Guard: The strong guard pulls quickside and kicks out the first unblocked defender on the quickside.
- Center: The center blocks a man over or the #1 defensive man on the strongside.
- Quick Guard: The quick guard blocks gap. If no defender is in A gap, the quick guard pulls quickside and logs the first defender past the quick tackle's block.
- Quick Tackle: The quick tackle blocks #2 on the line of scrimmage.
- 4-Back: The 4-back blocks the nearest safety.
- X-Receiver: The X-receiver blocks the defensive man who covers him.

East is the pass protection scheme and play-action used for bootleg passes run to the quickside of the formation in the buck series. The 26 is the running play that is faked.

Pass patterns 4, 5, 7, and 7 Peoria are used for east passes. These excellent play-action passes serve as the primary misdirection play from the buck series.

The quarterback's footwork is the same as that used for 26. He opens quickside at 90 degrees on the midline. On his third step, he fakes to the 2-back and continues straight back for two more steps. He then executes a bootleg to the quickside. Because east passes are bootlegs into a split end, the quarterback usually has to pull up inside the kick-out by the pulling strong guard.

The 3-back slides through the quickside B gap. Versus a blitz, he blocks it. With no blitz, the 3-back runs a five-yard deep route into the quickside flat. The 3-back is the quarterback's second choice for all east passes. Blocking for east passes was covered in Chapter 4. The assignments are as follows:

- Y-Receiver: Y will always be a pass receiver for east passes. He will be either the #2 or #1 receiver.
- Strong Tackle: The strong tackle blocks gap, over, and outside.
- Strong Guard: The strong guard pulls quickside and blocks the first defender to show outside the quick tackle's block.
- Center: The #1 defender strongside is blocked by the center.
- Quick Guard: The quick guard blocks the #1 defensive player on the quickside.
- Quick Tackle: The quick tackle blocks #2 on the line of scrimmage.
- 2-Back: The 2-back fakes 26 and blocks the first defensive player who shows on the strongside.

Figures 8-25 through 8-28 are east passes with a 7 pattern. For a 7 pattern, X, the #3 receiver, runs a read route. He breaks his route to the post at 12 yards of depth. With a single high safety, X plants his outside foot after two steps to the post and runs a comeback curl cut. Versus two high safeties or man-to-man, X plants his inside foot at 15 yards and runs the post corner route. He is the quarterback's #1 choice.

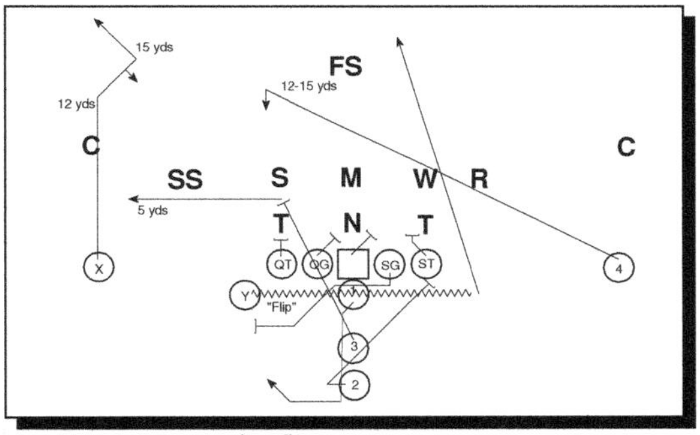

Figure 8-25. Right flip east 627

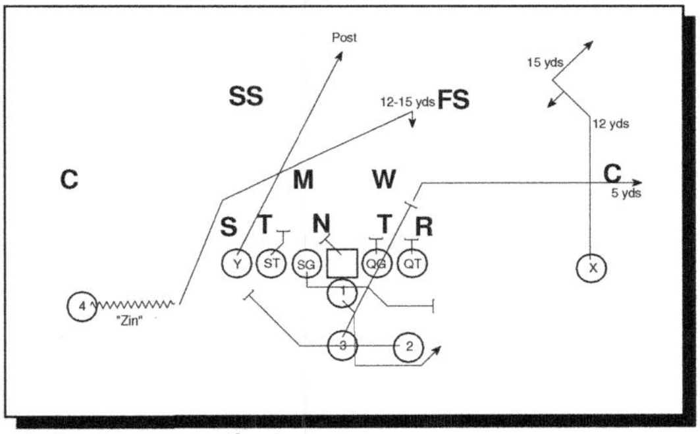

Figure 8-26. Left zin east 727

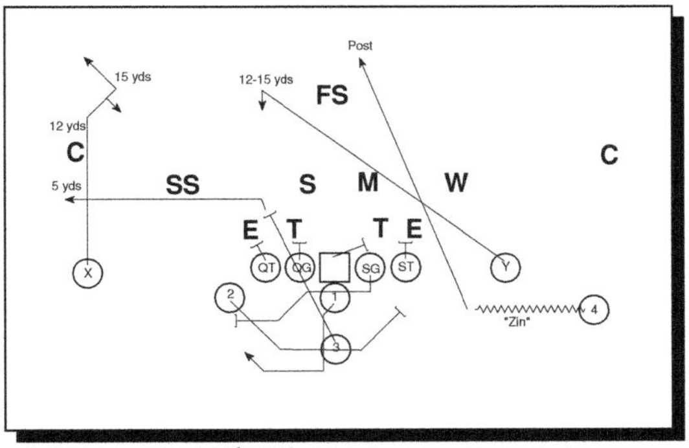

Figure 8-27. Right zin east 827

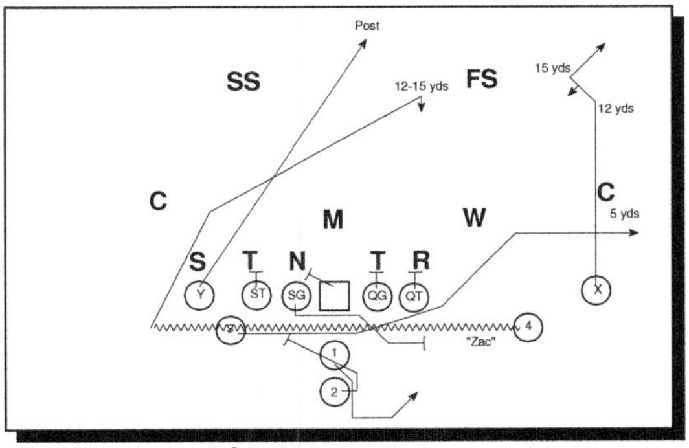

Figure 8-28. Left zac east 927

Receiver #2 runs a post route. Versus two high safeties, he will try to split them. Normally, receiver #2 is not thrown the ball, but is running a clearing route.

The #1 receiver has a drag route to the quickside of the formation. He aims for a depth of 12 to 15 yards. If he finds an open hole in the zone after passing the center, receiver #1 will set down and face the quarterback. This receiver never passes the hash mark on the quickside of the formation. Receiver #1 is the quarterback's third choice.

A Peoria tag may be used with the 7 pattern. This tag changes the routes for the #2 and #3 receivers. As seen in Figures 8-29 through 8-32, the X-receiver, or #3, runs a post cut at 12 yards of depth. The #2 receiver must be on the quickside of the formation for this pattern. He may be aligned there, or he may motion to the quickside. Receiver #2 runs a post corner cut behind the post route run by the X-receiver. He breaks to the corner at 15 yards of depth. This route becomes the quarterback's #1 choice. Receiver #1 and the 3-back run the routes for a 7 pattern, and the 3-back remains the quarterback's #2 choice. The #1 receiver is the third choice for the quarterback.

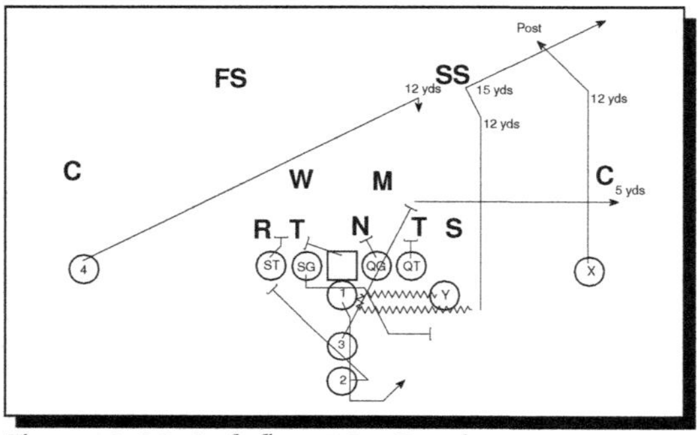

Figure 8-29. Left flop 627 Peoria

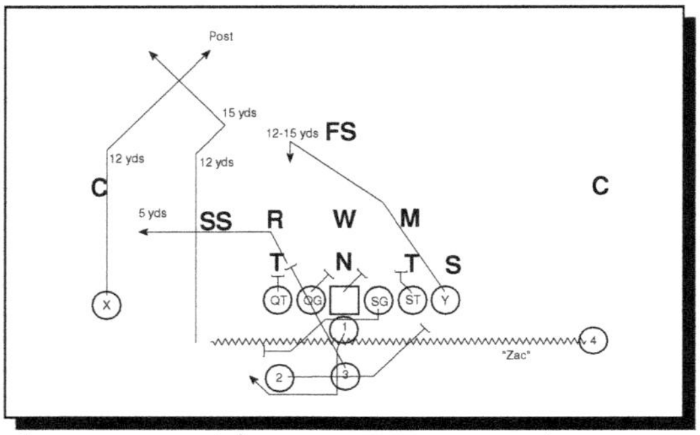

Figure 8-30. Right zac east 727 Peoria

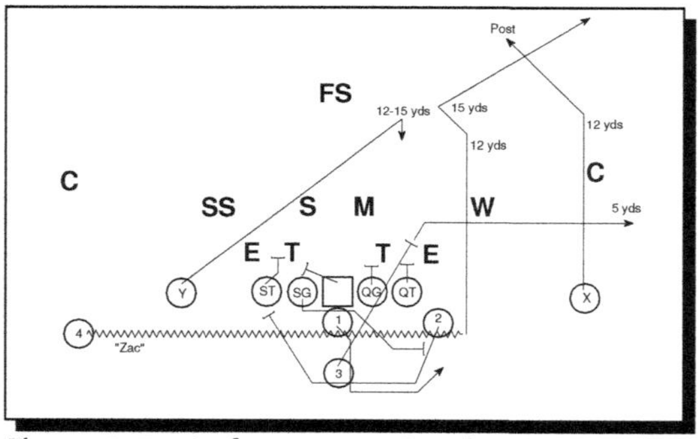

Figure 8-31. Left east 927 Peoria

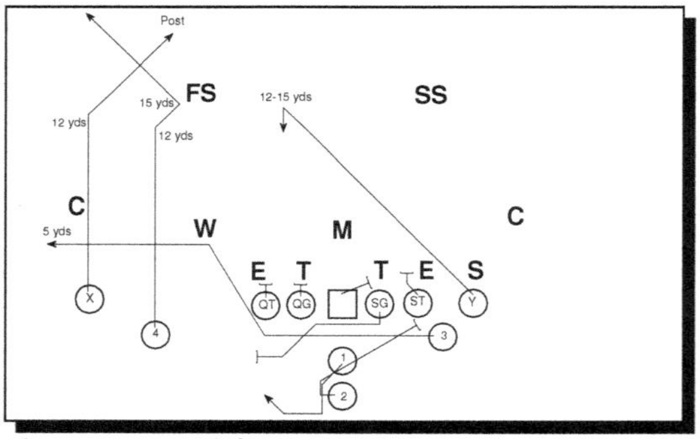

Figure 8-32. Right east 927 Peoria

Figures 8-33 through 8-36 are examples of east passes using the 4 pattern. This pattern becomes a throwback pass off the quickside bootleg action. Both the #1 and #2 receivers must be aligned to the strongside.

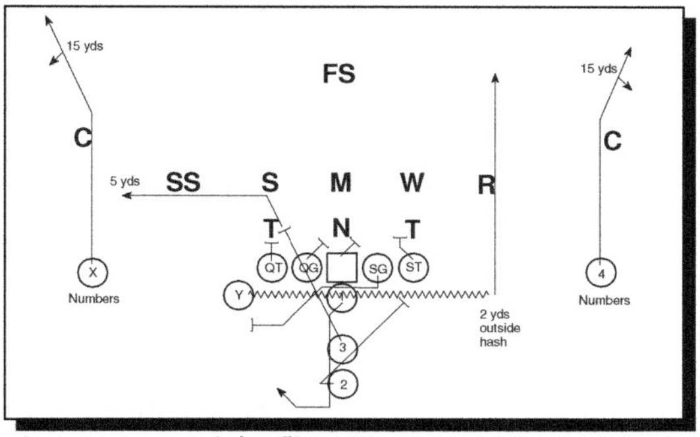

Figure 8-33. Right flip east 624

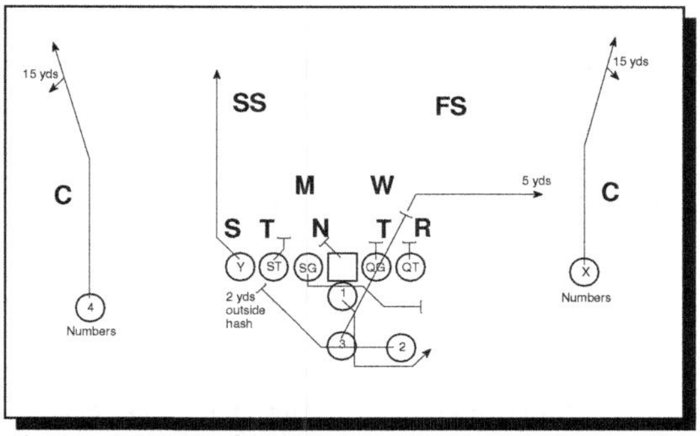

Figure 8-34. Left east 724

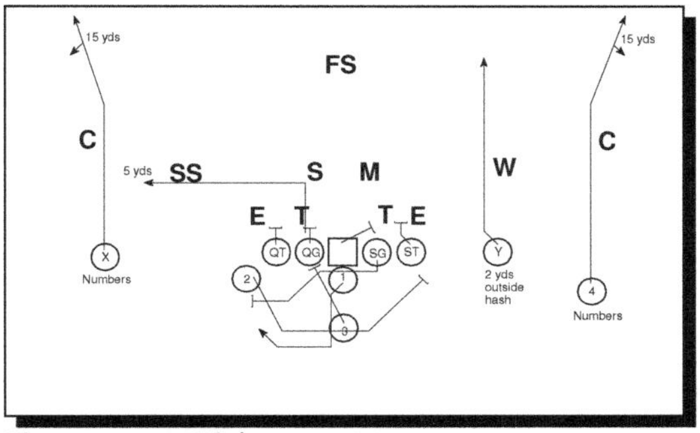

Figure 8-35. Right east 824

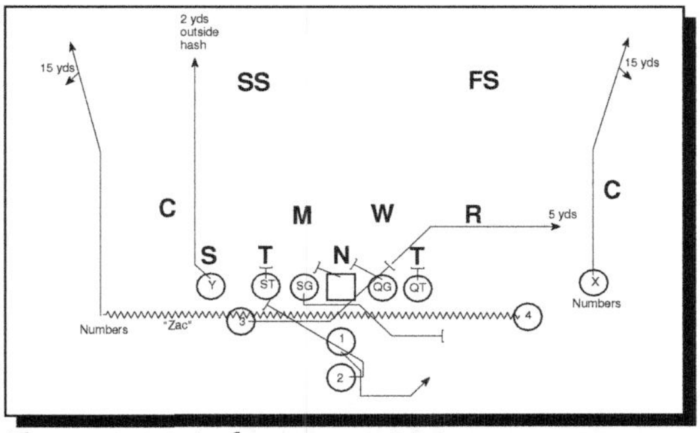

Figure 8-36. Left zac east 924

Receiver #1 runs a vertical route on the numbers to the strongside of the formation. He may convert this cut to a comeback route at 15 yards of depth if the man covering him stays deep. The #1 receiver is the quarterback's first read.

A seam route two yards outside the hash mark is the cut for receiver #2. Receiver #2 is the quarterback's second choice.

The #3 receiver runs a vertical route on the numbers to the quickside of the formation. When the defender covering him remains deep, receiver #3 can convert the vertical to a 15-yard comeback.

A five-yard quickside flat route is run by the 3-back. He is the quarterback's third choice.

East pass action has the quarterback fake 26 and bootleg to the quickside. He pulls up inside the kick-out block by the strong guard. In order to throw back to the strongside, the quarterback must set his feet. He cannot make this throw on the run. This pass is very difficult to defend and may result in a big offensive play.

The 5 pattern is used for east passes in the red zone or versus man-to-man coverage. This crossing pattern is most effective against man-to-man, but is still very effective against zone pass defenses.

Y must be on the strongside of the formation to execute the 5 pattern. Y releases upfield for four yards and drags to the quickside. He sets the depth for the mesh with the X-receiver. The aiming point is 12 to 15 yards in depth. This depth may be varied, depending on field position. In a goal line situation, Y's depth may be 8 to 10 yards. Against zone pass coverage, Y may find an open area and set down in the zone after he reaches the position of the quick tackle. Versus man-to-man coverage, he continues across the field. This route is the quarterback's #1 choice.

The X-receiver releases upfield one yard and runs a crossing route to the strongside of the formation. He is responsible for creating the mesh under Y. X tries to make the mesh as close to Y as possible. His responsibility is to reach 12 to 15 yards of depth on the strongside. Versus zone coverage, he can find a hole in the zone and set in it once he reaches the strong tackle's position. As with Y, X continues across the field against man-to-man coverage.

A post cut is made by the 4-back at a depth of 12 yards. This route is designed to occupy a single safety and to split a two-safety secondary. This receiver is not part of the quarterback's read progression, but if the secondary fails to cover him, an east pass with the 5 route can be called. The first read for the quarterback then becomes the post cut by the 4-back.

The 3-back has a five-yard flat route to the quickside. This route is the quarterback's second choice for this pass.

Figures 8-37 through 8-40 show east passes with the 5 pattern. The quarterback executes his fake of 26 before bootlegging to the quickside.

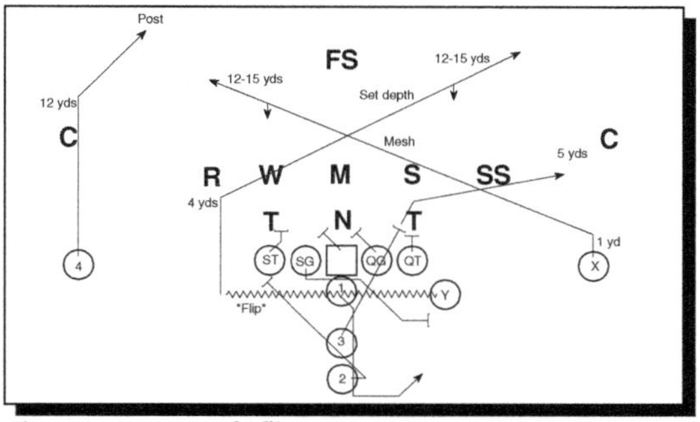

Figure 8-37. Left flip east 625

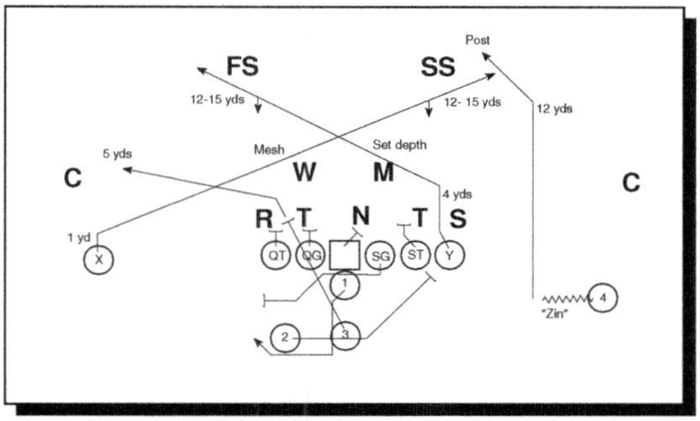

Figure 8-38. Right zin east 725

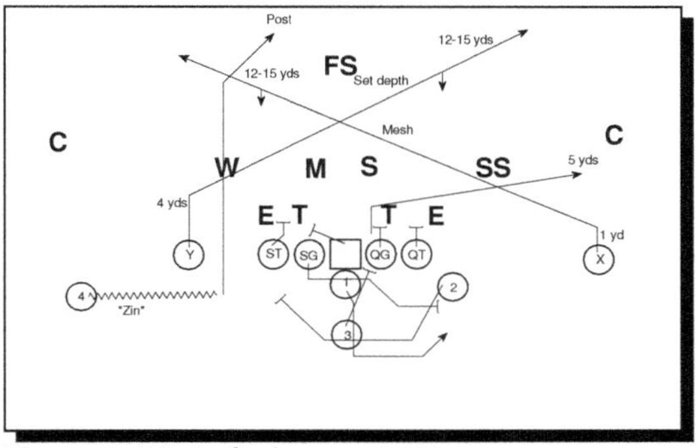

Figure 8-39. Left zin east 825

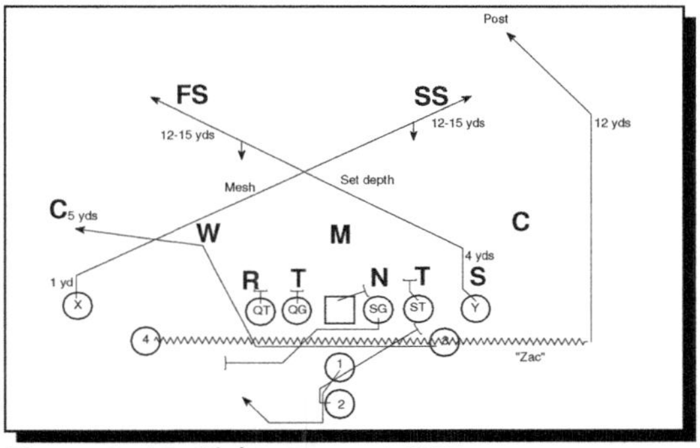

Figure 8-40. Right zac east 825

CHAPTER 9

The Belly Series

The belly series is an example of a wing-T series incorporated into the no-huddle multiple offense. Zac motion in which the 4-back uses fast motion across the formation to the quickside is often used to run or threaten the use of the jet sweep. This motion usually forces some type of defensive reaction. One such reaction could be the secondary rolling to cover 3 to the motion side. The free safety rolls up to become the force man versus the jet sweep. This reaction is countered by running the belly play quickside, the tackle trap to the strongside, or the bootleg pass strongside from the tackle trap action.

Another possible defensive reaction to zac motion is to chase the 4-back across the formation with man-to-man coverage. This could be countered by using zac motion and running veer option or power plays to the strongside.

Adjustments by the defensive front such as slants to motion or fast flow by the linebackers to motion may be countered by use of the belly play, tackle trap counter, bootleg pass strongside from tackle trap action, veer option strongside, or power off-tackle to the strongside. The jet sweep action tends to soften the defensive interior, which facilitates the 3-back belly play, 35.

The jet sweep run by the 4-back, 49, is the first play in the belly series. It is an excellent way to attack the quickside perimeter. It uses zone blocking similar to that used for 29, the outside zone play, but it hits much faster. Handing the ball to the 4-back when he is running at top speed allows him to get outside rapidly. Even if the 4-back is not an exceptionally fast player, he will outrun defenders who are starting from a stationary position. Because of this, the defense normally must move players in reaction to the jet motion, which is a desirable outcome because it creates other opportunities.

From wing or doubles formation, the 4-back runs zac motion across the formation to the quickside. He becomes the ballcarrier on 49. This play is relatively easy to run. It can be installed quickly and doesn't need to be practiced extensively to be successful.

The quarterback lifts his heel to start the 4-back in motion. He must use his cadence to get the ball snapped when the 4-back reaches the strong guard's outside foot. After taking the snap, the quarterback seats the ball on his belt buckle and makes a 180-degree pivot on his quickside toe. His back should be to the defense with the ball hidden by his body. The handoff to the 4-back is made in the quickside A gap. After handing off, the quarterback fakes 35, the fullback belly play, and continues quickside faking the belly option, 15.

As shown in Figures 9-1 through 9-4, zac motion starts with the quarterback's heel raise. The 4-back accelerates so that he is at full speed when he receives the handoff. The 4-back should be one yard deeper than the quarterback when he gets the handoff. After securing the ball, he bows back one more yard, which is done for two reasons. It allows the quickside guard to have room to pull around the quickside tackle's zone block and the 4-back has enough depth to cut inside or outside based on the defense's reaction. The 4-back should be trying to get outside to the numbers, but he must be prepared to cut upfield under overly aggressive defensive pursuit. Faking inside before going outside or faking outside before cutting inside will help set the blocks for the play.

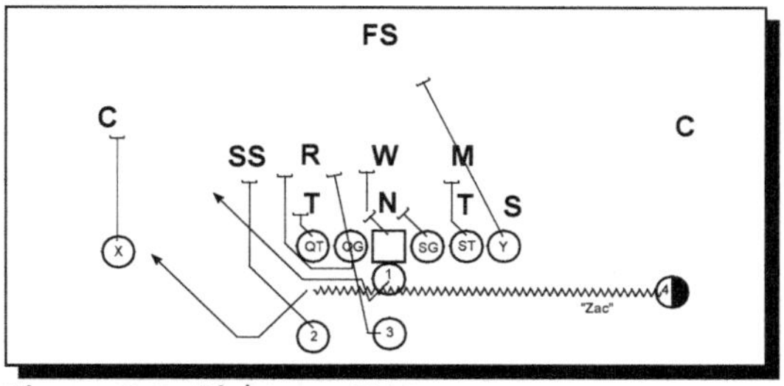

Figure 9-1. Right zac 749

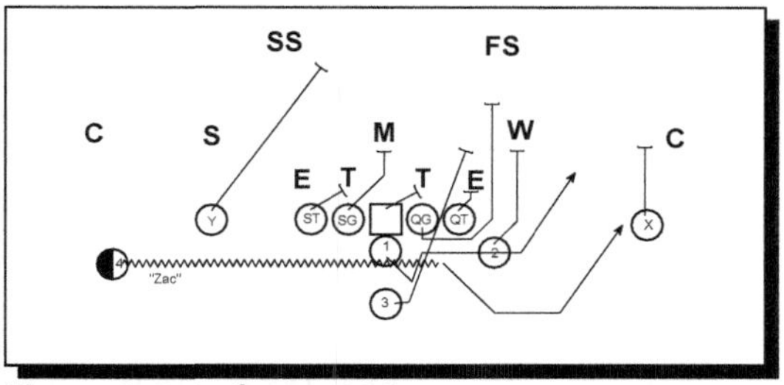

Figure 9-2. Left zac 849

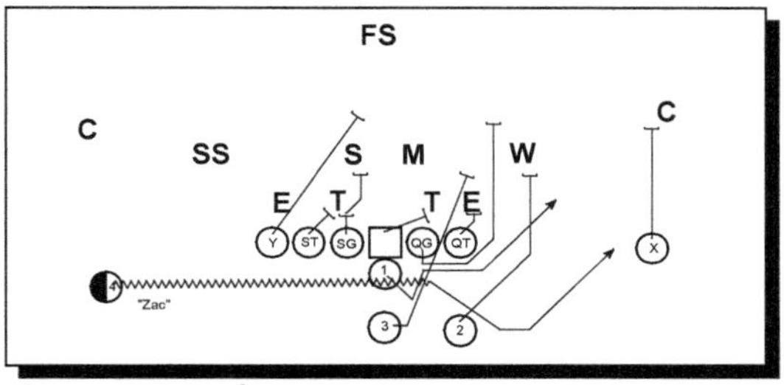

Figure 9-3. Left zac 749

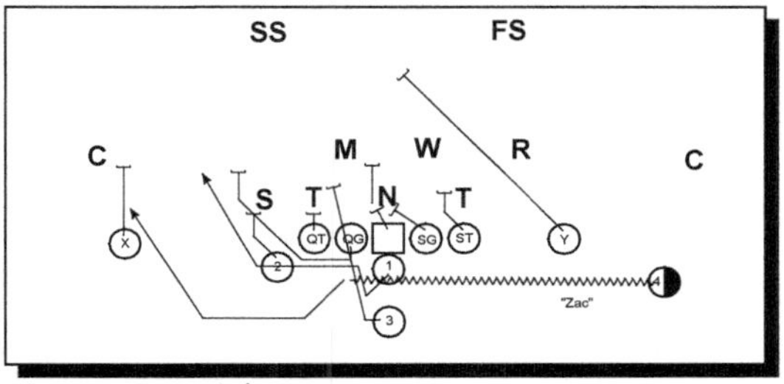

Figure 9-4. Right zac 849

The 2-back zone blocks to the outside on the first defender outside the quick tackle's block. He attempts to hook this player, but if the defensive man fights outside, he can be kicked out. This block is the key for the success of 49. Maintaining contact with the defender is the most important factor. Because 49 hits so quickly, this block need not be sustained for a long period of time.

A crossover step and then a lead step to the quickside is taken by the 3-back, which are the same steps he uses for 35, the belly play. He runs 35 and blocks the first linebacker or second level player he sees to his inside.

Defensive players aligned on the line in the A gap quickside, over the quick guard, or in the quickside B gap are not blocked on 49. If the play is run at full speed, these players have no chance of making the tackle on the four-back.

Blocking assignments for 49 are as follows:

- Y-Receiver: Y blocks the free safety or the strong safety.
- Quick Tackle: The quick tackle zone blocks to his outside. He must hook a defender who is head up or to his outside. Although this defensive man does not have to be blown off the line, he must be stalemated on the line of scrimmage so that he cannot pursue to the outside.
- Quick Guard: The quick guard pulls flat to the quickside. He turns downfield after clearing the quick tackle's block and seals the first defender to his inside.

- Center, Strong Guard, and Strong Tackle: Zone blocking to the quickside is the responsibility of the center, the strong guard, and the strong tackle.
- X-Receiver: The X-receiver blocks the defensive man who covers him.

Using zin motion by the 4-back to create a tight wing position strongside and running strongside plays such as the buck sweep (28), the belly down (36), or the outside veer (38) keeps the defenders from reacting quickside as soon as the 4-back starts in motion. The defense must respect the threat of the strongside attack. When the 4-back continues across the formation in zac motion, there is limited time for reaction to the quickside.

The 35 is the belly play run by the 3-back to the quickside of the formation. It is extremely effective when run with zac motion by the 4-back. The threat of the jet sweep causes defensive players to react to the outside to contain it. This softens the interior defense and creates great opportunities to run the 3-back on the belly play into those areas. An excellent play even without zac motion, 35 becomes an even bigger threat when used with zac motion.

Figures 9-5 through 9-8 show 35. The 3-back takes a crossover step and lead-steps to the quickside. He aims for the outside hip of the guard, but he reads the block on the first defensive man from head-up on the quickside guard to the outside.

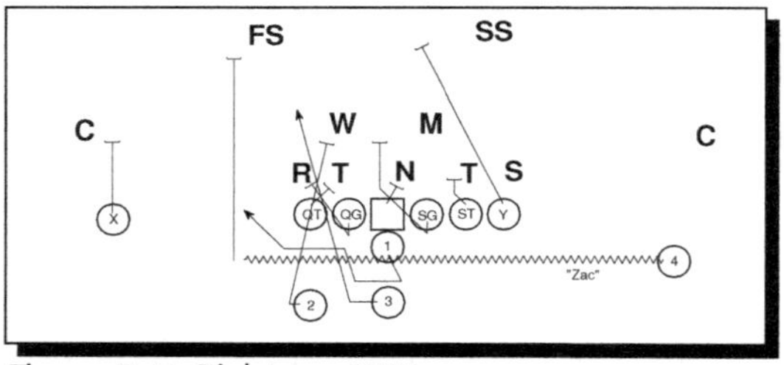

Figure 9-5. Right zac 735

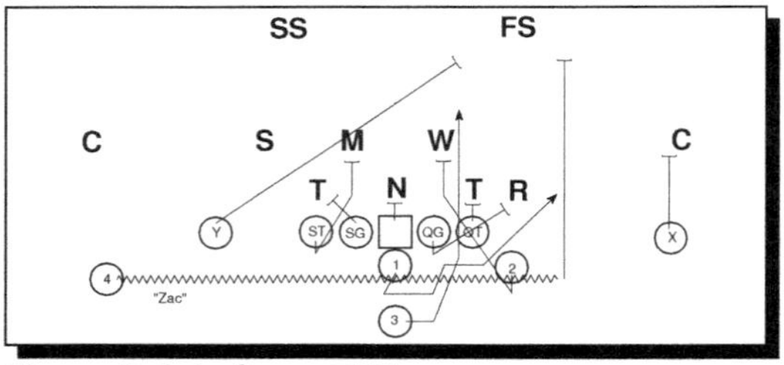

Figure 9-6. Left zac 835

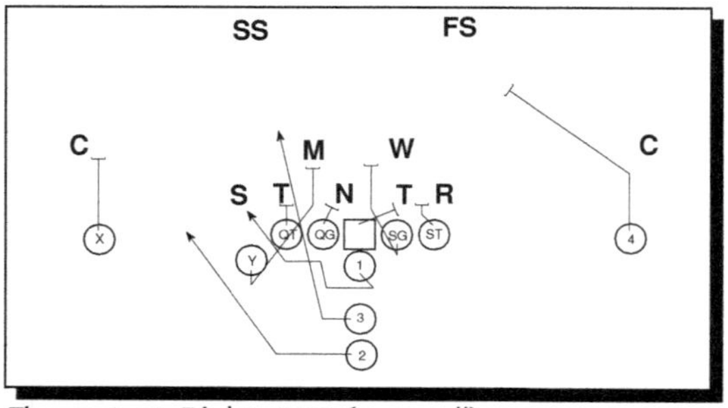

Figure 9-7. Right 635 (gap call)

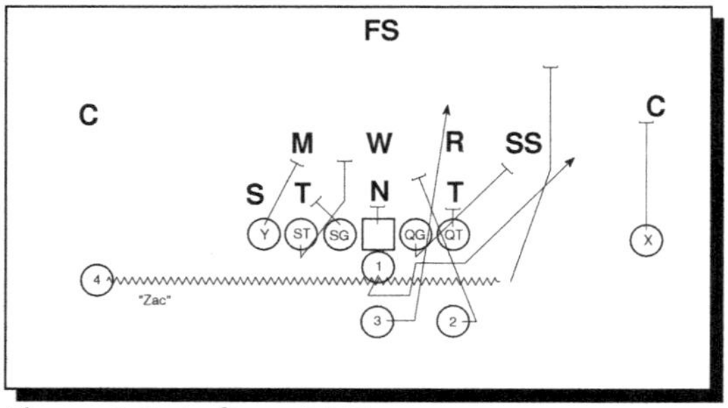

Figure 9-8. Left zac 735

Footwork for the quarterback starts with a pivot quickside at a 45-degree angle. He reaches the ball back to the 3-back and rides him one step forward before completing the handoff. Following the handoff, the quarterback runs the option path used for 15, the belly option play.

When 35 is run from the I alignment, the 2-back runs the path for the pitchman for 15. If a wing formation is used, the 2-back jab steps quickside and reads the block on the first defender from head-up on the quick guard to his outside. He blocks the first linebacker from head-up to the inside. In a doubles set, the 2-back takes two steps back as he reads the block on the same defender as in wing formation. He then blocks the first linebacker from head-up to the inside.

If Y is aligned quickside, he takes two steps back and reads the block on the first defensive man from head-up on the quick guard to his outside. Y then lead blocks on the first linebacker from head-up to the inside. From the strongside, Y releases to block a single high safety or the strong safety.

The blocking rules for 35 include the following:

- Quick Tackle: Versus an odd defense, the quick tackle blocks a man over him. Against an even front, he blocks down. When a gap defense is used, he blocks gap or over.
- Quick Guard: Against a gap defense, the quick guard blocks the defender in the A gap. Versus an even or odd front, he pulls quickside and traps the first defensive man past the quick tackle's block.
- Center: When the defense is odd, the center blocks the defender over him. Against a gap or even front, he blocks back on the #1 defensive man strongside.
- Strong Guard: Versus an even or gap defense, the strong guard fold blocks with the center on a middle linebacker or the inside linebacker strongside. He blocks out versus an odd front.
- Strong Tackle: If the defense is odd, the strong tackle fold blocks with the strong guard on an inside linebacker. With an even or gap front, the tackle blocks gap, over, or near linebacker.
- X-Receiver: The X-receiver blocks the defensive man covering him.
- 4-Back: The 4-back blocks the nearest safety.

The belly play to the split end side has always been one of the very best plays in the wing-T offense. It is no different in the no-huddle multiple offense. It is a good play in short-yardage and goal line situations as well as in the open field. The threat of the jet sweep makes it even more difficult to defend.

The belly option, 15, is diagramed in Figures 9-9 through 9-11. The belly option is a two-way option with a fake of the belly play, 35, and a pitch or keep executed by the quarterback. This play may be run from I, wing, or doubles. Zac motion may or may not be used from wing or doubles.

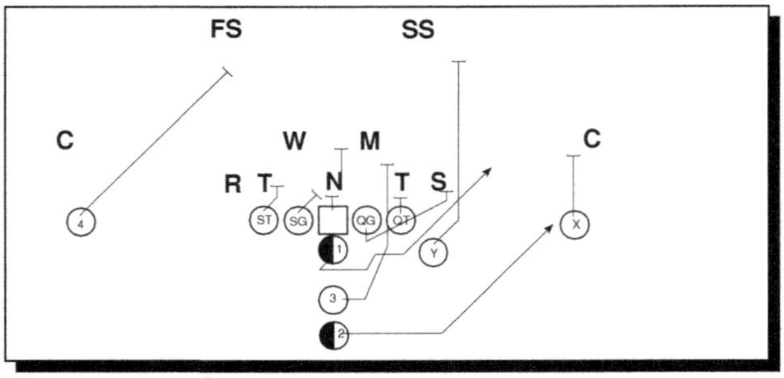

Figure 9-9. Left 615

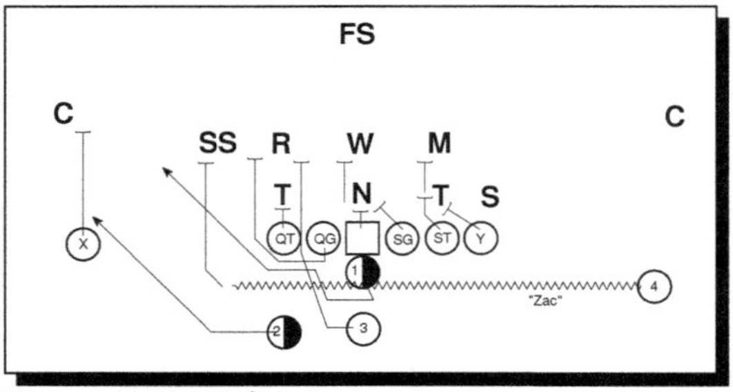

Figure 9-10. Right zac 715

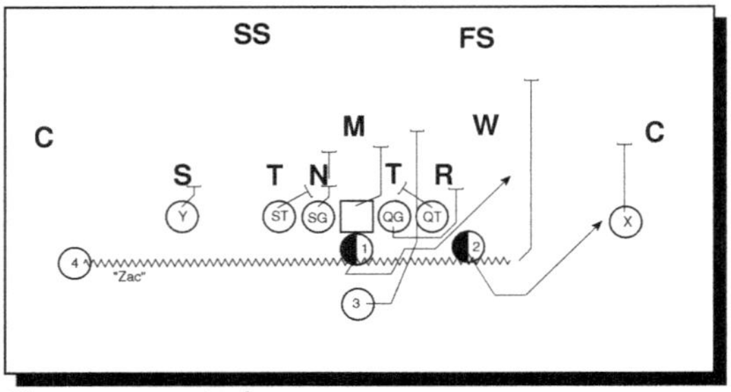

Figure 9-11. Left zac 815

A reverse pivot at a 45-degree angle is made to the quickside by the quarterback. He reaches the ball back to the 3-back and executes a ride with the 3-back before pulling the ball out and attacking the inside shoulder of the first unblocked defender quickside. The quarterback reads this defensive man for pitch or keep.

The 2-back is always the pitchman for 15. From a doubles alignment, he takes three steps back at a 45-degree angle and then delays to achieve a pitch relationship with the quarterback. If a wing set is used, the 2-back opens flat to the quickside to achieve a pitch relationship with his quarterback. In an I formation, the 2-back sprints quickside to gain the pitch position of five yards deeper than the quarterback and at least one yard in front of him.

A crossover step followed by a lead step quickside is made by the 3-back. He then attacks the B gap as he makes a good fake of 35. The 3-back blocks any linebacker from head up to the inside.

Blocking responsibilities for 15 are as follows:

- Y-receiver: From the quickside Y blocks the safety. If aligned strongside, he zone blocks to the quickside. When he is split, he blocks the man covering him.
- Quick tackle: Versus an odd defense, the quick tackle blocks a man over him. Against a gap or even front, he blocks gap, down, or over.
- Quick guard: The quick guard pulls quickside and log blocks the first defensive player past the quick tackle's block.

- Center, strong guard, and strong tackle: The center, the strong guard, and the strong tackle zone block to the quickside of the formation.
- X-receiver: The X-receiver blocks the man covering him.
- 4-back: The 4-back blocks the nearest safety.

The tackle trap counter play is 22. This play may be run from I, wing, or doubles alignments. Figures 9-12 through 9-15 show examples of 22 run from different formations.

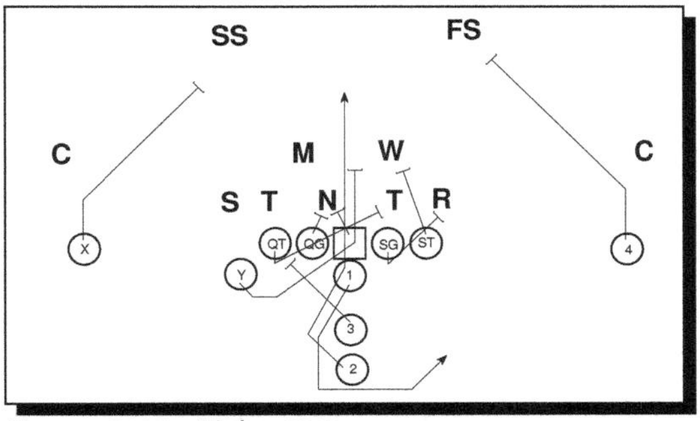

Figure 9-12. Right 622

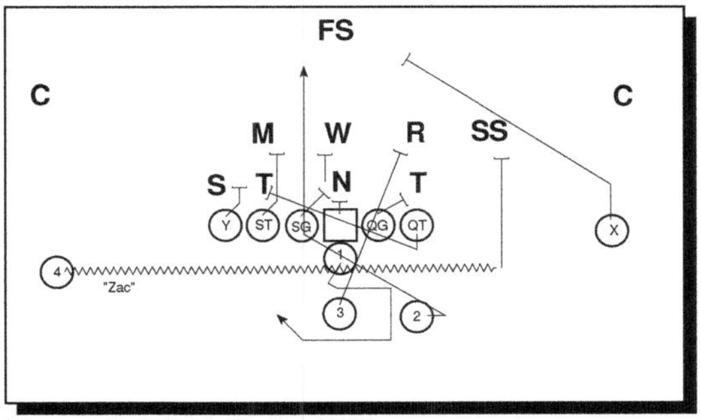

Figure 9-13. Left zac 722

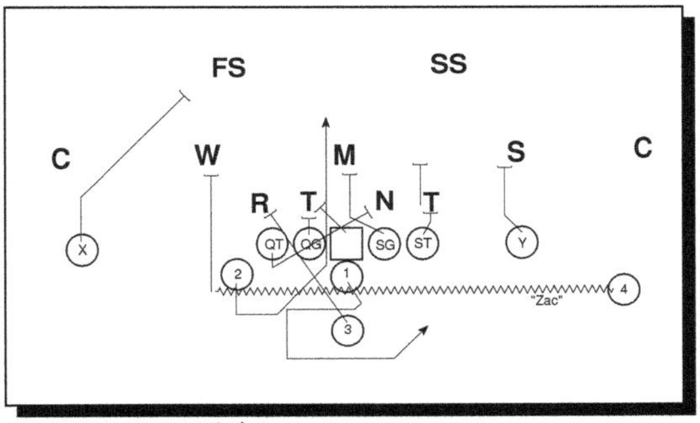

Figure 9-14. Right zac 822

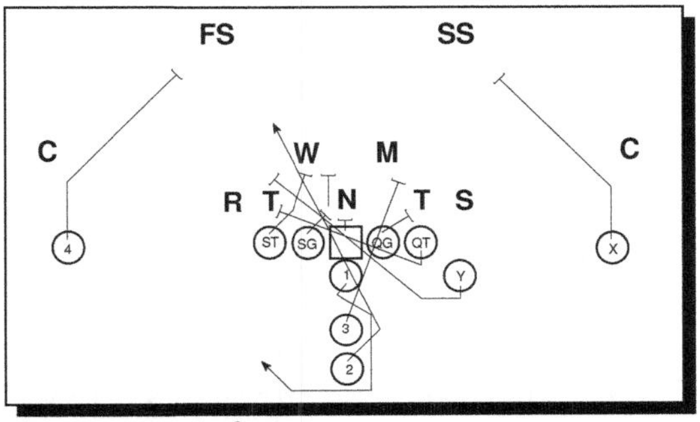

Figure 9-15. Left 622

For 22 the 2-back is the ballcarrier. His footwork changes according to the formation used, but he always receives an inside handoff from the quarterback. When aligned in the I, the 2-back takes three steps on a 45-degree angle, aiming for the outside hip of the quick tackle. He plants his quickside foot and breaks inside, aiming for the center's butt. He gets the inside handoff on the quarterback's third step. From the I formation, the 2-back follows Y's block, who goes inside the quick tackle's trap block and blocks a second-level defender. If the 2-back is in the dive back position from a wing alignment, he jab steps quickside and then aims for the center as he comes forward to receive an inside handoff. A doubles formation has the 2-back backpedal for two steps and then take a path, aiming for the center's butt. Regardless of his starting position, the 2-back must stay on a path at the center. He should hit the hole full-speed just behind the quick tackle's trap block. At times it may seem that there is no hole, but there will be a small crease. The 2-back should never bounce the play to the outside since there will be unblocked defenders strongside. After breaking the line of scrimmage, the 2-back should go straight upfield until he clears linebacker depth. He then runs to daylight.

Footwork for the quarterback starts with a 45-degree reverse pivot to the quickside of the formation. The depth of the pivot varies by the position of the 2-back. In any case, the quarterback must allow the back to take a path, aiming for the center and allowing for an inside handoff from the quarterback. After making his pivot, the quarterback takes the ball to the 2-back. Ideally, the handoff is made on the quarterback's third step. If he were to pivot and wait for the 2-back, the linebackers would not flow and would become more difficult to block. There is no fake to the 3-back, as he fills the quickside B gap.

After executing a one-handed inside handoff to the running back, the quarterback goes straight back from the line of scrimmage at a 90-degree angle until he reaches seven yards of depth. At this point, the quarterback bootlegs strongside, faking the counter bootleg pass. Once he hands off to the 2-back, the quarterback brings both hands to his belt until he starts the bootleg action. He then slides both hands to his backside hip.

Filling for the pulling quick tackle is the responsibility of the 3-back. If the defense is an even or gap front, he aims for the B gap quickside. Versus an odd defense, the fill is over the quick guard since the guard blocks out against odd fronts. The 3-back should not chase defenders; he fills an area. When a defensive lineman follows the pulling tackle or a linebacker blitzes the B gap, the 3-back blocks him. The 3-back may cheat up in his alignment if he is slow on the fill block. A cut block is used by the 3-back on any defender he encounters.

Blocking assignments for 22 are as follows:

- Y-Receiver: From the I formation with Y aligned quickside, he pulls strongside through the hole and seals the first linebacker he sees. He checks strongside and then quickside. If aligned strongside, Y blocks the outside linebacker or strong safety.
- Strong Tackle: The strong tackle blocks the outside linebacker or strong safety.
- Strong Guard: Versus an odd defense, the strong guard combo blocks with the center on the nose man to a middle linebacker or inside linebacker quickside. When the defense is even or gap, he blocks a middle linebacker or inside linebacker quickside. If 22 is run from an I formation, the strong guard pulls strongside and blocks the first defensive player he encounters. This pulling action acts as an influence for the defender being trapped and slows his reaction to the inside. It also prevents the next strongside defensive lineman from slanting inside and stopping the play.
- Center: Against an odd defense, the center combo blocks with the strong guard on the nose man to a middle linebacker or inside linebacker to the quickside. If the front is even or gap, the center blocks the #1 defensive player to the quickside.
- Quick Guard: The quick guard blocks out versus an odd defense. When the defense is even or gap, the guard blocks B gap, over, or A gap. This block may end up as a double-team block with the center.

- Quick Tackle: Pulling to the strongside, the quick tackle trap blocks the first defender past the center. The tackle pulls flat along the line of scrimmage, but must get across the line of scrimmage to dig out the defender being trapped. This trap man will be closing to the inside. If the quick tackle pulls to the right, he traps with his right shoulder; when he pulls to the left, the trap block is made with the left shoulder. The quick tackle must stay low to get under the defensive man's pad.
- X-Receiver: The X-receiver blocks the near safety.
- 4-Back: When zac motion is used for 22, the 4-back motions full-speed across the formation and fakes the jet sweep, 49. After passing the end defender on the line of scrimmage quickside, he turns downfield and blocks the first defensive player he encounters. If no zac motion is used, the 4-back blocks the strongside safety.

The 22 is a great football play. It features misdirection, a double-team at the hole, trap blocking, plus possible influence blocking. The 22 may or may not be run with zac motion, but it becomes a more effective play with zac motion. This play has as much big-play potential as any play in the offense. To be effective, 22 must be run often in practice and should be run several times each game. This play is effective in any down-and-distance situation, including obvious passing downs. The 22 may be used from any field position.

The 31 is a 3-back trap run to the quickside of the formation. It is a complement to 11, the midline option play. The defender being read for 11 is trapped on 31. Dive action by the 3-back is the same for both plays. The 31 is always run with zac motion when wing or doubles alignments are used. The threat of the jet sweep can make the 3-back trap a more effective play. Zac motion with the fake of 31 is used to set up west bootleg passes.

Figures 9-16 through 9-18 show 31. This play may be run from I, wing, or doubles. The 2-back blocks the first man from head-up with the quick tackle to the outside. This block is similar to what the 2-back does for 49, the jet sweep.

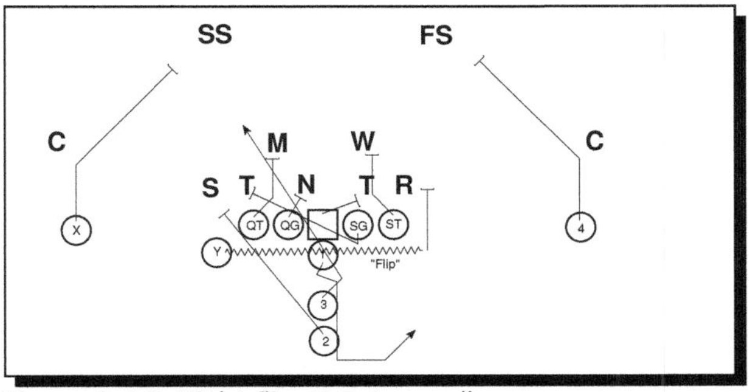

Figure 9-16. Right flip 631 Lou call

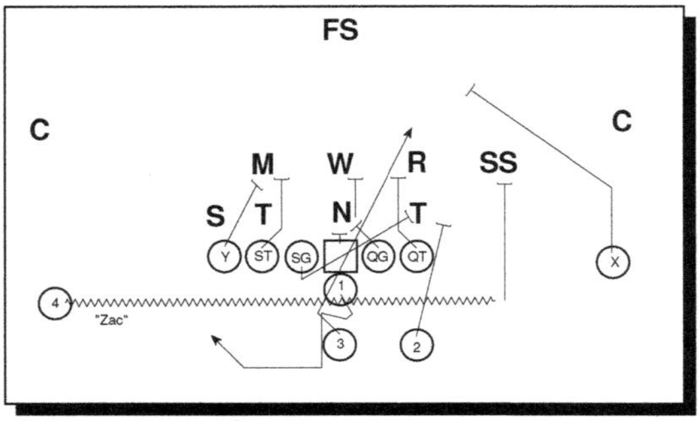

Figure 9-17. Left zac 731

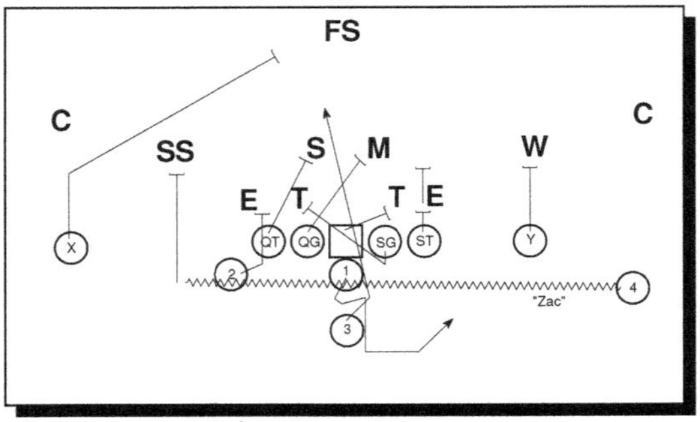

Figure 9-18. Right zac 831

The 31 has the 3-back take his first step with the strongside foot just to the strongside of the midline. His aiming point is the center's butt. He reads the trap block by the strong guard.

The quarterback opens to the strongside at a 90-degree angle from the line of scrimmage. He stays on the midline and makes a one-handed handoff to the 3-back on the quarterback's second step. After handing off, the quarterback brings both hands to his belt buckle as he continues on the midline to seven yards of depth. At seven yards, he brings both hands to his backside hip as he bootlegs to the strongside.

Blocking responsibilities for 31 are as follows:

- Y-Receiver: Y blocks an outside linebacker or safety to his side of the formation.
- Strong Tackle: The strong tackle blocks B gap. If no defensive man is in the B gap, he blocks the first linebacker to the inside.
- Strong Guard: The strong guard pulls quickside and traps the first defensive player outside the last down block. If the quick guard makes a Lou call, this becomes a long trap. The strong guard must get up across the line of scrimmage and dig the defensive man out. If he pulls left, he traps with his left shoulder; if he pulls right, the right shoulder is used.
- Center: Versus an odd front, the center combo blocks with the quick guard on a nose man to a middle linebacker or inside linebacker strongside. Against an even or gap defense, the center blocks the #1 defender strongside.
- Quick Guard: When the defense is an odd front, the quick guard combo blocks with the center on a nose man to a middle linebacker or inside linebacker strongside. Versus an even front, the quick guard blocks a middle linebacker or the inside linebacker strongside. If a defender is in the A gap quickside, the guard calls Lou and blocks down.
- Quick Tackle: The quick tackle blocks an inside linebacker to an outside linebacker.
- X-Receiver: The X-receiver blocks the defensive man covering him.
- 4-Back: The 4-back blocks the nearest safety, whether he has been in zac motion or not.

Three different play-action passes are used in the belly series. The first of these is south, which is a split-flow bootleg pass run from a fake of 49, the jet sweep to the quickside. This pass is only run from wing or doubles formations and always has the 4-back running a zac motion. The 6 pass route is normally used as the pattern.

Figures 9-19 and 9-20 show south 746 and south 846 run from wing and doubles alignments. Zac motion sends the 4-back across the formation to fake 49. After he clears the last defensive player on the line of scrimmage to the quickside, the 4-back turns downfield and runs a seam route two yards outside the hash marks. He is not part of the quarterback's read progression. His pass route is designed to force a single safety or quickside safety to cover him.

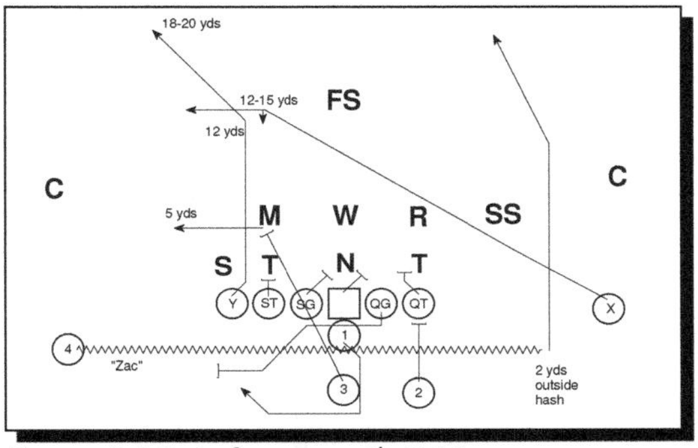

Figure 9-19. Left zac south 746

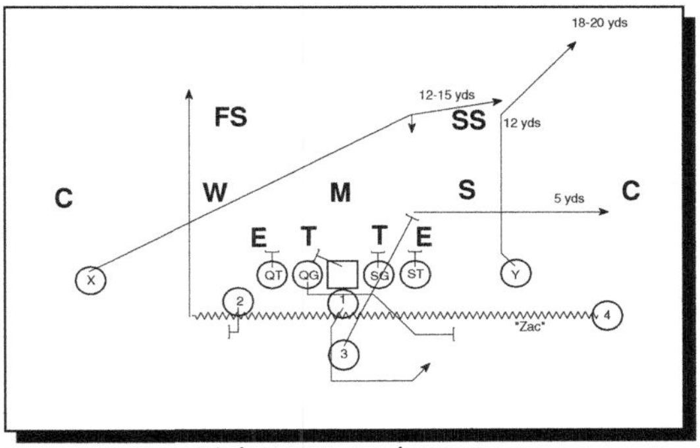

Figure 9-20. Right zac south 846

The 31 is faked by the 3-back. He slides through the 2 or 4 hole. If a linebacker blitzes that area, the 3-back blocks him. Versus no blitz, the 3-back runs a five-yard deep flat route to the strongside.

Y is responsible for running a 12-yard deep corner route. After making his cut at 12 yards, he aims for a depth of 18 to 20 yards. For a south pass, Y is the quarterback's first choice in his read progression.

The X-receiver runs a drag route to the strongside aiming for a depth of 12 to 15 yards. After passing the center, X looks for a hole in the defense into which he can settle. He should never cross the strongside hash mark. This receiver is the quarterback's third choice in his progression.

The quarterback opens to the strongside at a 90-degree angle. He stays on the midline for five steps before bootlegging to the strongside. The football should be kept on his belt buckle until he begins the bootleg action. A proximity fake should occur between the quarterback and the 4-back as he motions across the formation. The read progression for the quarterback is Y as #1, the 3-back as #2, and the X-receiver as #3.

Whether aligned in wing or doubles, the 2-back blocks the first defensive player outside the quick tackle's block for south passes. This block is crucial in protecting the quarterback's backside.

Blocking rules for interior offensive linemen on south, north, and 70 passes are all the same and were covered in Chapter 4. They are as follows:

- Strong Tackle: The strong tackle blocks the #2 defensive player on the strongside line of scrimmage.
- Strong Guard: The #1 defender on the line to the strongside is the strong guard's responsibility.
- Center: The center blocks the #1 defender to the quickside.
- Quick Guard: The quick guard pulls strongside and blocks the first defensive player he encounters.
- Quick Tackle: Gap, over, or outside is the quick tackle's blocking rule.

North 625, north 725, and north 825 (Figures 9-21 through 9-23) are bootleg passes thrown from a fake of 22, the tackle trap. North passes have the quarterback reverse pivot to the quickside at a 45-degree angle. He continues on a path to fake 22 to the 2-back. This fake should occur on the quarterback's third step. The quarterback then goes straight back to seven yards of depth and executes a bootleg to the strongside of the formation.

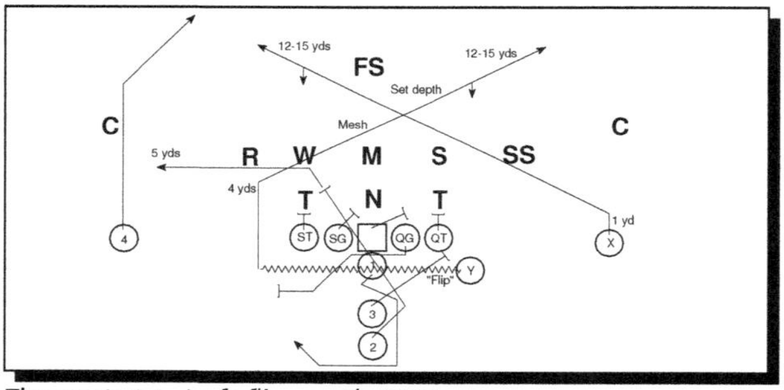

Figure 9-21. Left flip north 625

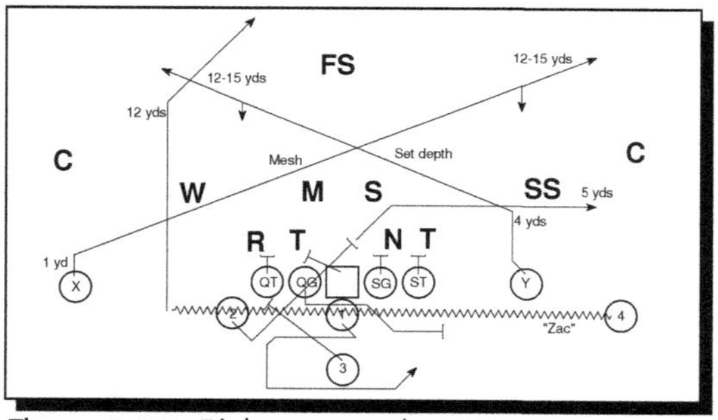

Figure 9-22. Right zac north 825

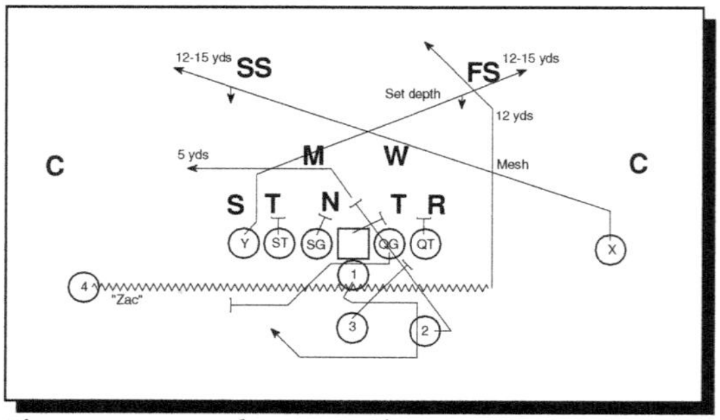

Figure 9-23. Left zac north 725

A 5 route is normally used for north passes. This crossing pattern takes some time to develop. The play-action for north results in the quarterback being slower to get into his bootleg action. As a result, the 5 pattern times well for north passes.

Y needs to be on the strongside for this pattern, which means that when the I formation is employed, Y has to be put into flip motion. Y goes upfield about four yards and then crosses to the quickside, aiming for a depth of 12 to 15 yards. Versus zone coverage, he may set down in a hole in the zone once he reaches the position of the quick tackle. Against man-to-man, he continues across the field. Y is not a primary receiver for north passes. He is, however, responsible for setting the depth of the mesh.

Zac motion is normally used by the 4-back when north passes are run from wing or doubles. He motions across the formation to the quickside and runs a 12-yard deep post cut to occupy the single safety or the safety on the 4-back's side. From the I alignment, the 4-back runs his post cut on the strongside.

The X-receiver releases downfield for one yard and then runs a drag route to the strongside. His aiming point is 12 to 15 yards of depth. The X-receiver is responsible for creating a tight mesh with Y. Ideally, they would almost brush shoulders. After meshing, X should look for the ball any time. Versus zone coverage, X can set down in an opening after he reaches the strong tackle position. Against man-to-man coverage, he continues across the field. The X-receiver is the quarterback's #2 choice in his read progression. The 4-back's post cut is his #1 or blink read.

The 2-back runs 22 from whatever formation is used. He should make a great fake with the quarterback and run hard through the 2 hole. If he encounters a blitzing linebacker, he blocks him; otherwise, the 2-back runs a five-yard deep flat route to the strongside. The 2-back becomes the third choice in the quarterback's progression.

The 3-back blocks the first defensive man who shows outside the quick tackle's block. The interior offensive linemen block the same pass protection as is used for south passes.

Figures 9-24 through 9-26 show 70 passes. These counter bootleg passes have the quarterback bootlegging to the quickside of the formation after faking 22, the tackle trap play. This pass action is run in wing-T programs. It provides the quarterback with a run-pass option after he fakes the counter play. He reverse pivots quickside and takes the ball to the 2-back, where he makes a bare-hand one-handed fake. The fake should happen on the quarterback's third step. After faking, the quarterback bellies back to five yards of depth. The quarterback then turns downfield behind the lead block by the 3-back. His first choice in his read progression is to throw to the X-receiver. The second choice is the five-yard flat route, and the drag cut is his third selection. A decision to run with the ball should be made as quickly as he turns upfield. Without an unblocked contain defender, the quarterback runs the ball.

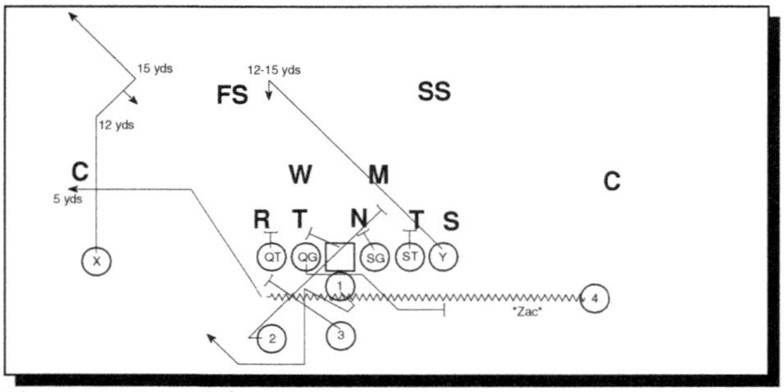

Figure 9-24. Right zac 777

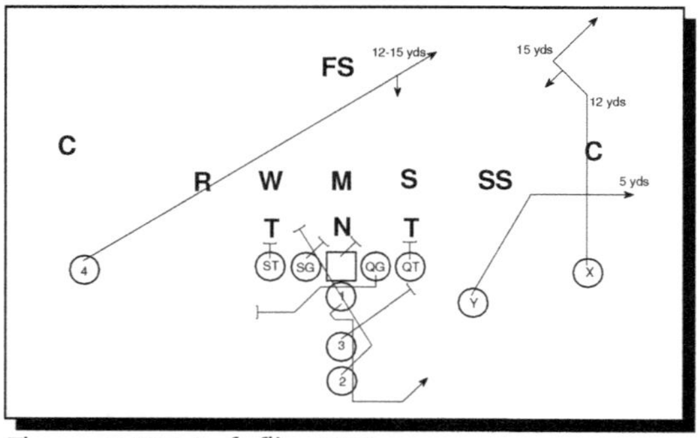

Figure 9-25. Left flip 677

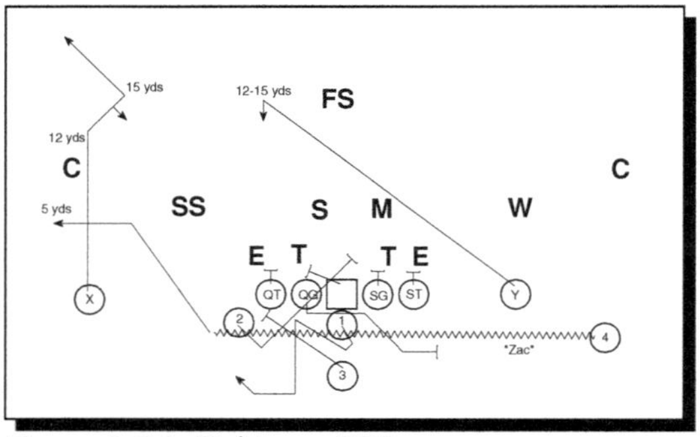

Figure 9-26. Right zac 877

From wing or doubles alignments, the 4-back runs zac motion to the quickside of the formation. Even though a 7 pattern is used for 777 or 877 passes, the 4-back runs a five-yard quickside flat cut. When the I is used, the 4-back executes a drag route to the quickside of the formation. He aims for 12 to 15 yards of depth. After passing the center, the 4-back looks for an area to pull up and face the quarterback. The 4-back must never cross the quickside hash mark.

For 777, 877, and 677 passes, the X-receiver runs a read route. He pushes upfield for 12 yards as he reads the safeties. At 12 yards, he plants his outside foot and breaks for the post. Versus a single high safety, X takes two steps toward the post, plants his outside foot, and breaks inside and back toward the quarterback on a comeback curl cut. Versus two high safeties, he takes three steps toward the post, plants his inside foot, and runs a post corner cut. The X receiver is the quarterback's #1 read.

If an I formation is used, Y runs the five-yard flat route. From wing or doubles alignments, Y executes the drag cut. This route aims for a 12- to 15-yard depth quickside. Y tries to find a void in the secondary coverage where he can set down, but he must not cross the quickside hash mark.

The 2-back runs 22. He should make a great fake and hit the 2 hole at full-speed. His assignment is to block any blitzing linebacker who shows.

The 3-back blocks the first defensive player outside the quick tackle's block. He attempts to hook his man so that the quarterback is able to get to his outside to run the football. The 70 pass protection for the offensive line is the same as south or north protections.

The 70 passes are effective for a number of reasons. The fake of the tackle trap and the pulling action to the strongside by the quick guard cause linebackers to be slow in reacting to the quarterback keep. A 7 route gives the quarterback easy reads, but it is versatile enough to attack any secondary coverage. Many wing-T teams run the belly keep pass, but the counter bootleg is a more difficult play to defend due to the misdirection action.

CHAPTER 10

The Outside Zone Series

Zone blocking is used extensively in the no-huddle multiple offense. Backside offensive linemen are often asked to zone block toward the playside, particularly in the veer series runs. Zone blocking on the playside is used for specific plays such as the outside veer, jet sweep, 3-back dive, and the outside zone.

Two running plays, 29 and 18, make up the outside zone running game. Bootleg passes from outside zone runs include west 626, west 926, and jet east 817. Sprint-out passes to the quickside of the formation are also part of the outside zone series.

Outside zone plays give the offense a way to get the ball to the perimeter of the defense quickly. They provide a contrast to the other ways the offense attacks the outside of the defense, namely option plays and the buck sweep.

One advantage of the outside zone plays is that they can be run successfully when inside line stunts or blitzes are causing offensive problems. Zone techniques allow the offense to seal such stunts inside. These techniques remain constant regardless of the defensive front faced and thus reduce chances for error or confusion. A second advantage of the outside zone plays is that they are relatively easy to run and don't require as many practice repetitions as some other plays that constitute the no-huddle multiple offense running attack.

Techniques for offensive linemen can be reduced to a covered or uncovered technique. An offensive man is considered covered if a defender is aligned on any part of his body. When an offensive lineman is covered, his aiming point is the defender's outside armpit. If a defender is head-up or in an outside shade, the offensive lineman's first step is with the playside foot. It is a flat step with the toes pointed downfield. A second step is made with the foot away from playside. This step is into the crotch of the defensive man. Contact is made with the hand and shoulder away from the playside. The playside hand should go to the outside armpit of the defender. A read is made on the first linebacker from head-up to the inside while the blocker runs his feet with short, choppy steps. He must never cross his feet as he drives the defender. During the drive block, he prepares to come off the defensive lineman to block a linebacker if the uncovered offensive lineman zoning toward him is successful in overtaking the defensive man he is blocking.

An uncovered offensive lineman aims for the near number of the first defensive lineman to his playside. He uses a flat pull step and gets his playside hand on the near number of the defender he pulls toward. Without crossing his feet, the offensive lineman tries to overtake and assume control of this defensive lineman. He watches a linebacker over him or to his outside. If that linebacker fires ahead, the offensive lineman comes off on the linebacker. When overtaking a defensive lineman, the offensive player must get his helmet in front of the defender. If the defensive lineman skates playside, the blocker maintains contact and drives him laterally. He must not allow penetration. If the defense flows laterally, the ballcarrier may cut back into open seams. On the backside of run plays at the college level, the offensive lineman will cut the defensive lineman whenever he can.

A blocking variation used for the outside zone play to the quickside, 29, is to pull an uncovered playside offensive lineman. This could be the center, the quick guard, or the quick tackle. It is the base scheme for 29. If the offense does not want anyone to pull, the word Zorro is added after the play number. Thus 29 Zorro indicates that no offensive linemen will pull.

The jet sweep, 18, always has the strong guard pulling strongside and sealing the first linebacker to the inside. This play is only run from a doubles formation and uses jet motion by the 2-back.

If offensive linemen pull for 29, they stay relatively flat and turn downfield outside the last blocker on the line of scrimmage. Turning upfield, the pulling lineman looks to seal the first defender to the inside.

Figures 10-1 and 10-2 show 29 from the I formation. The quick guard pulls in Figure 10-1 and the center pulls in Figure 10-2. A Zorro call is made in Figure 10-3. This call is 29 from the pistol. No linemen pull because of the Zorro call.

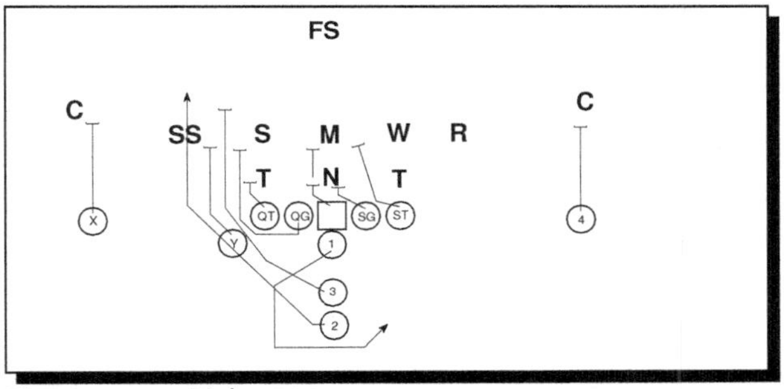

Figure 10-1. Right 629

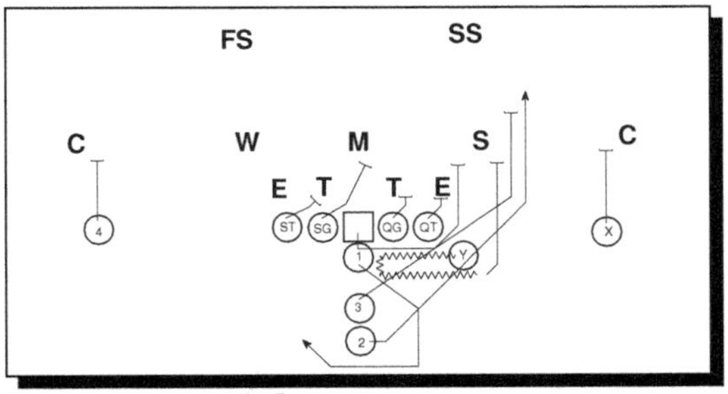

Figure 10-2. Left flop 629

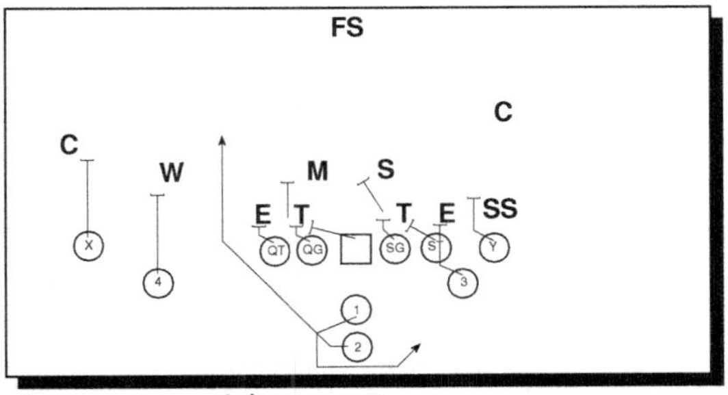

Figure 10-3. Right 929 Zorro

A Ted call is used in Figure 10-4. This call may be used when 29 is run toward the Y-receiver. If the defender over Y is difficult to reach and a defensive lineman is aligned over the quick tackle, Y calls "Ted" and blocks down. The quick tackle pulls quickside and log blocks the man aligned over Y. The defender's normal reaction to Y's down block is to step down aggressively. This move makes it easier to log him to the inside.

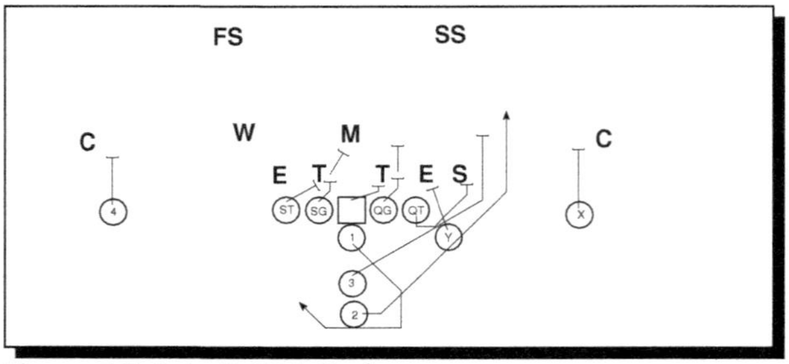

Figure 10-4. Left 629 Ted

The 2-back is aligned in the I tailback position. He takes a lead step quickside followed by a crossover step, aiming one yard outside the quick tackle or Y if he is aligned to the quickside. The 2-back follows the lead block by the 3-back. He may cut back if gaps appear in the defensive pursuit, but ideally he wants to get outside the 3-back's block.

The 3-back will block the first unblocked defensive player to the quickside. This player will be an outside linebacker, safety, or corner, who is usually the force player to the quickside. Normally the 3-back tries to hook him, but he can kick him out and the 2-back cuts upfield under the kick-out block.

An open step to the quickside at a 45-degree angle is made by the quarterback. He must sprint back to get the ball to the 2-back if he is working from under the center. From the pistol alignment, he opens quickside at 45 degrees. Two steps are used for the quarterback to reach the 2-back to execute the handoff. After handing off, the quarterback bootlegs back to the strongside faking west pass action.

Blocking assignments for 29 are as follows:

- Y-Receiver: Y zones quickside. If a Ted call is made, Y blocks gap, down, or the first linebacker inside.
- Quick Tackle: If he is uncovered, the quick tackle pulls quickside outside Y's block and seals the first defender to the inside. When he is covered or Zorro is called, the quick tackle zone blocks quickside. A Ted call has the quick tackle pull quickside and log block the defensive man aligned over Y.
- Quick Guard: When the quick guard is covered, he zone blocks to the quickside. He also does this if 29 Zorro is called. If he is uncovered and no Zorro call is made, the quick guard pulls quickside and seals the first defender to the inside.
- Center: The center zone blocks to the quickside unless he is uncovered. When uncovered he pulls quickside to the outside of the last zone block, turns upfield, and seals the first defensive man to the inside. The 29 Zorro has the center zone block to the quickside.

- Strong Guard and Strong Tackle: Both the strong guard and strong tackle zone block to the quickside.
- 4-Back and X-Receiver: The 4-back and the X-receiver block the defensive players covering them.

A west pass is a full flow bootleg pass that is thrown from a fake of 29. These play-action passes act as a counter for 29, the outside zone play to the quickside. West passes must be run with the 2-back in an I alignment. From this position, he fakes 29 and blocks the first defender outside the last block on the quickside.

The quarterback's footwork begins with an open step quickside at a 45-degree angle exactly the same as that for 29. The quarterback sprints hard to make a fake to the 2-back when he, the quarterback, is under the center. In the pistol formation, he opens quickside and takes two steps at a 45-degree angle to reach the 2-back and fake to him. He then takes two more steps straight back to a depth of seven yards. At this point, he bootlegs back to the strongside of the formation. His blink or first read is the deep route on the strongside run by either the 4-back or Y. The quarterback's second read is the strongside five-yard deep flat route, and his third read is the drag route run by X.

Many offensive systems run a similar bootleg pass as a naked, but the no-huddle multiple offense uses protection involving pulling the quickside guard to the strongside. This same bootleg scheme is used for south, north, western, and 70 passes. An advantage of this protection is that the quick guard pulling strongside protects the quarterback's blind side as he executes a fake of 29 and starts his bootleg action.

The pattern used for a west pass is a 6 pattern with a modification. The 4-back runs a go route. If it is an I formation, this route is run on the strongside numbers. From a pistol set, the 4-back runs the route two yards outside the near hash mark. When the I alignment is used, the 4-back is the quarterback's blink read or #1 choice.

The X-receiver always runs a drag route to the strongside of the formation. His aiming point is 12 to 15 yards of depth. He may set down in a void in a zone coverage after he reaches the strong tackle position, or he may continue his route toward the sideline. The X-receiver is the quarterback's third choice in his read progression.

If Y is on the quickside of an I formation, as in Figure 10-5, he runs a sneak route on the offensive side of the line of scrimmage. Once he reaches a point outside the strong tackle, he runs a five-yard flat cut. When he motions to the strongside, Y blocks down for two counts and then runs the five-yard flat route. In both cases, the five-yard flat cut becomes the quarterback's #2 choice. This is the route most often open. In a pistol alignment, Y runs a 12-yard corner cut. He pushes upfield 12 yards and breaks for the corner. This route becomes the quarterback's blink read and his first choice. Figure 10-6 has Y cross the formation to the strongside and run the five-yard delay cut to the flat. In Figure 10-7, a pistol formation, Y runs the corner route.

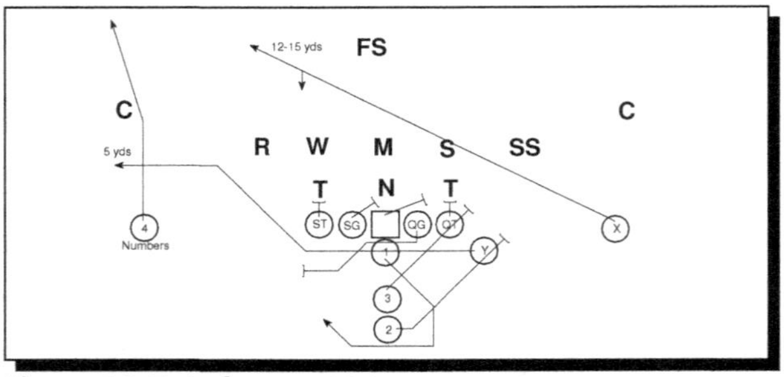

Figure 10-5. Left west 626

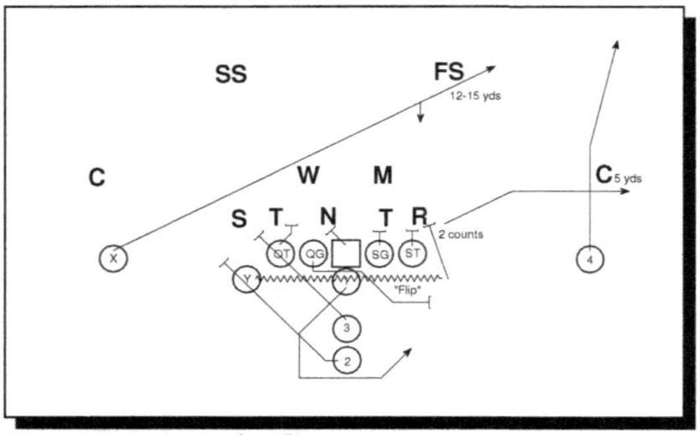

Figure 10-6. Right flip west 626

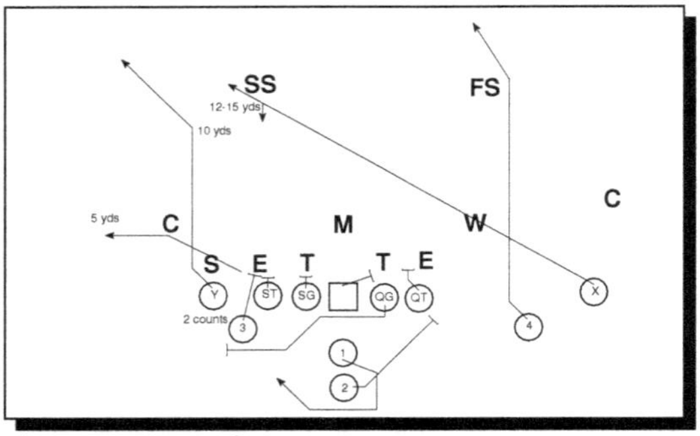

Figure 10-7. Left west 926

The 3-back, when in an I formation, blocks the first defensive man outside the quick tackle's block (Figures 10-5 and 10-6). From the pistol alignment, as in Figure 10-7, the 3-back blocks down for two counts and he runs a five-yard strongside flat route. He then becomes the quarterback's #2 choice.

Blocking assignments for west pass protection are covered in Chapter 4. They are as follows:

- Strong Tackle: The strong tackle blocks #2 on the line of scrimmage.
- Strong Guard: The strong guard blocks #1 on the line.
- Center: The center blocks the first defender quickside.
- Quick Guard: The quick guard pulls strongside and blocks the first defensive player he encounters.
- Quick Tackle: The quick tackle blocks gap, over, or outside.

The 90 passes are semi-sprint-out passes to the quickside of the formation. With the 2-back in an I alignment, the outside zone play, 29, is faked. No play fake occurs when 90 passes are run from other formations. These passes are used to move the pocket and shorten the throw for the quarterback. Some form of flood pattern is normally used for 90 passes.

Blocking rules for 90 pass protection are as follows:

- Y-Receiver: Y is a pass receiver unless a stay call is made or a strong formation is used. If aligned quickside and stay is called, Y zone blocks aggressively to the quickside. When he is on the strongside and stay is called, Y blocks gap, over, or the first defender to the outside.
- Quick Tackle: The quick tackle blocks a man over him or the first defender to the outside. This defensive player must be pinned on the line of scrimmage.
- Quick Guard: The quick guard blocks aggressively on a defensive man in the B gap or over him.
- Center: The center blocks a man in the quickside A gap or over him. If no defender is in these positions, the center steps quickside and hinges strongside. He blocks the first man who appears.
- Strong Guard: The strong guard blocks A gap, over, or steps quickside and hinges to the strongside where he blocks the first defender he sees.
- Strong Tackle: Any defender in the B gap or over him is blocked by the strong tackle. If no defensive player is in these spots, the strong tackle steps quickside and hinges strongside. He blocks the first man who shows.

Figure 10-8 shows 697 Peoria stay. The quarterback opens at a 45-degree angle and sprints back to fake 29 to the 2-back. After faking to the 2-back, the quarterback continues back two more steps before pulling up behind the quick tackle position. His read progression has the X-receiver running a skinny post as his first choice. The second choice is the flat route and the drag is his third selection.

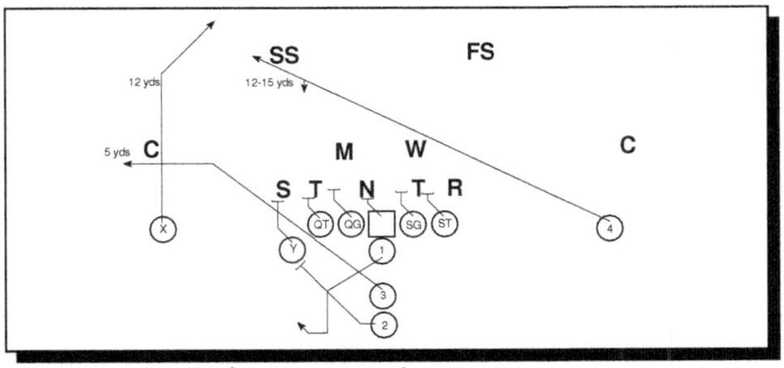

Figure 10-8. Right 697 Peoria stay

The X-receiver runs a skinny post aiming for the near goalpost. If the safety quickside reacts to the play fake, the ball is thrown to X. This play has a chance to be a big play for the offense.

The 3-back runs the five-yard quickside flat route. After faking 29, the 2-back blocks the first defensive player to show outside Y's block.

A drag route to the quickside is run by the 4-back. He aims for 12 to 15 yards of depth. If he finds a void in the secondary coverage after passing the center position, the 4-back may settle in the hole. This route is the quarterback's third choice.

Left 994 (Figure 10-9) is run from a pistol formation. The X-receiver runs a go route on the numbers. If the secondary stays deep, he runs a 15-yard comeback cut. This receiver is the first choice. The 4-back has a seam cut two yards outside the hash mark. He may run a 15-yard comeback if the defense is deep. The 4-back is the second choice for the quarterback.

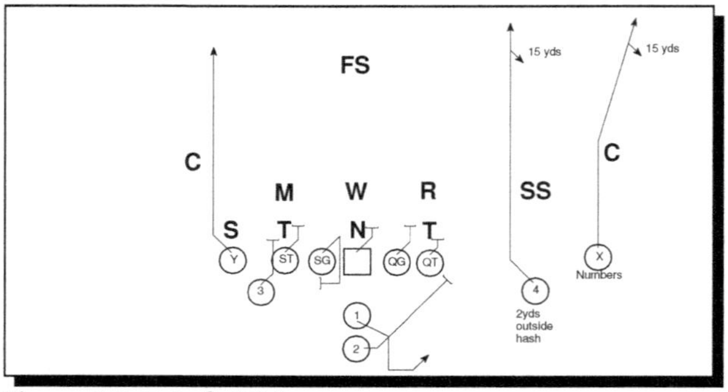

Figure 10-9. Left 994

Y runs a seam route on the strongside. The 3-back blocks gap, over, or outside. The quarterback fakes 29. After pulling up behind the quick tackle, he throws to the X-receiver first and the 4-back second.

An I formation with flip motion is used to run 697 (Figure 10-10). Y motions across the formation and executes a post cut at 12 yards of depth. The X-receiver runs his read route. Versus a single safety, this route becomes a post curl cut. Against two high safeties or man-to-man, X runs a post corner. The 4-back has a drag route to the quickside, aiming for 12 to 15 yards of depth. He must never cross the hash mark to the quickside, and looks for a void in the coverage where he can pull up. A five-yard flat cut to the quickside is the 3-back's responsibility. The 2-back fakes 29 and blocks the first defensive player who shows outside the quick tackle's block.

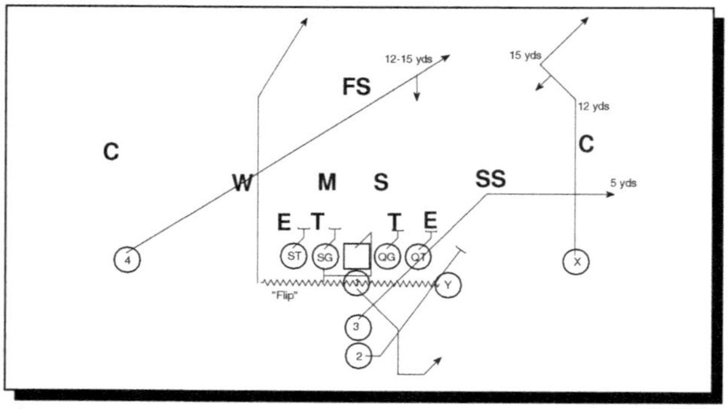

Figure 10-10. Left flip 697

The quarterback fakes 29. He then pulls up behind the quick tackle and goes through his read progression. The X-receiver is the #1 choice, the 3-back his second choice, and the 4-back becomes the third selection.

In Figure 10-11, 597 Peoria is run from the strong formation. Y is an ineligible receiver in a strong alignment and zone blocks to the quickside. The X-receiver has a post cut at 12 yards of depth. The 4-back runs a post corner route, breaking behind X. A five-yard quickside flat route is run by the 3-back, and the 2-back crosses the formation to the quickside and blocks any defender who appears outside Y's block.

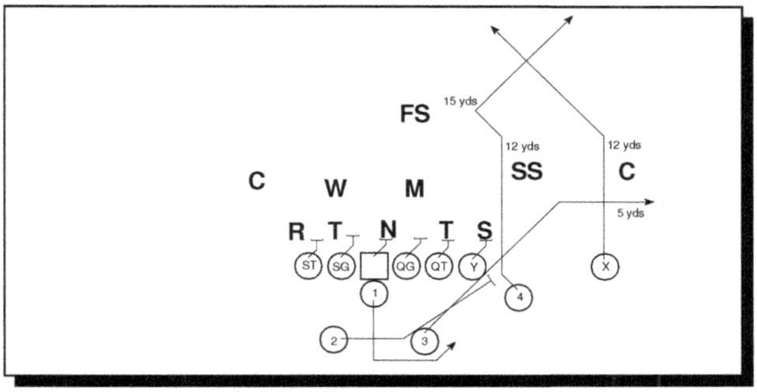

Figure 10-11. Left 597 Peoria

Because of the 2-back's path, the quarterback must open quickside at a 90-degree angle. He comes straight back for five steps to a depth of seven yards before rolling behind the 2-back and pulling up behind the quick tackle. The 4-back running the post corner is #1 in the quarterback's read progression, and the 3-back in the flat is #2.

When wing or doubles formations are used for 90 passes, no play fake is used. The quarterback opens quickside at a 45-degree angle and sprints for five steps to a depth of seven yards. He then sets up behind the quick tackle. The 3-back blocks the first defender outside the quick tackle's block.

Figure 10-12 shows 795 with zac motion by the 4-back. He crosses the formation and has a 12-yard post cut designed to occupy the quickside or single high safety. The Y-receiver goes upfield about four yards and crosses to the quickside, aiming for 12 to 15 yards of depth. He may settle in a void in the secondary after he reaches the quickside tackle's position, or he may continue across the field. Y sets the depth of the mesh. The X-receiver goes upfield one yard and crosses to the strongside, meshing under the route by Y. The X-receiver is responsible for creating as tight a mesh as possible. A five-yard flat route is run by the 2-back into the quickside.

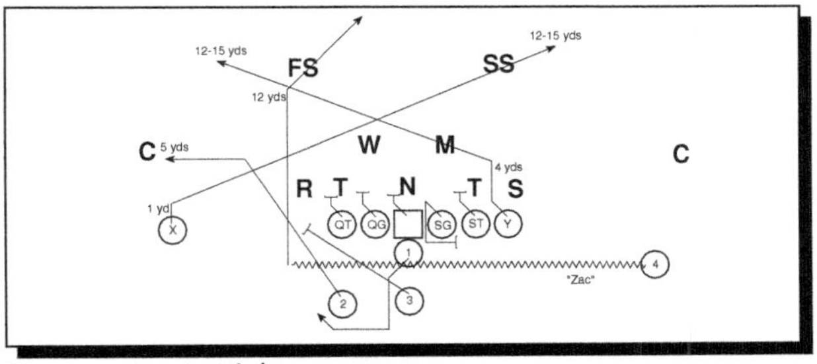

Figure 10-12. Right zac 795

Read progression for the quarterback is Y as #1 on the drag cut. His #2 choice is the 2-back in the quickside flat.

A doubles formation is used to run 899 (Figure 10-13). Zin motion by the four-back brings him inside of Y. He runs a 12-yard post cut to occupy a single safety or the strongside safety if two high safeties are used. The X-receiver has a dig route at 15 yards of depth. After breaking inside, he hunts for a void in the secondary coverage where he can settle. Y runs a shallow drag cut in front of the dropping linebackers. His depth should be no more than six yards. He can settle in a hole in the coverage once he reaches the quickside of the formation. The patterns by X and Y create a high/low read on the linebackers' quickside. The 2-back runs an arrow three yards deep to the numbers on the quickside. He then turns upfield on a wheel route.

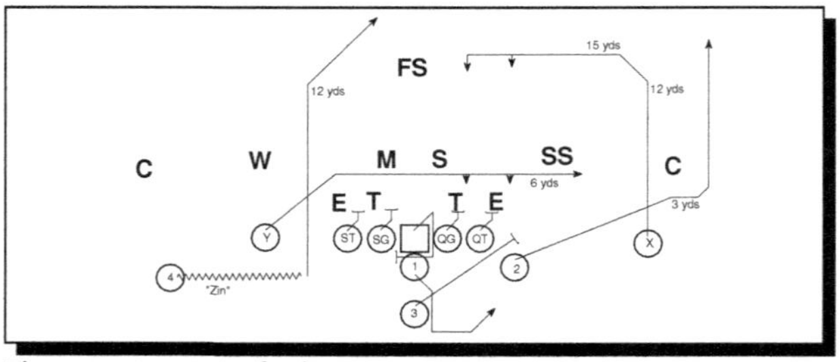

Figure 10-13. Left zin 899

The quarterback sets up behind the quick tackle at seven yards of depth. He looks for X first, Y second, and the 2-back third.

As can be seen in Figures 10-8 through 10-13, a variety of pass patterns may be used with 90 action and protection. This makes the 90 passes a very flexible portion of the no-huddle multiple offense.

The jet sweep play to the strongside, 18, is shown in Figures 10-14 through 10-16. The 18 is a form of the outside zone play, but it is only run from doubles and uses jet motion by the 2-back. This play hits the strongside of the defense with speed. Jet motion can be used for a number of plays including the inside veer (14), the outside veer (38), the belly down (36), the three-back trap (30), and the bootleg pass to the quickside of the formation (east 817). Because of this, the defense cannot react immediately to the flat motion as though it were always going to be the jet sweep.

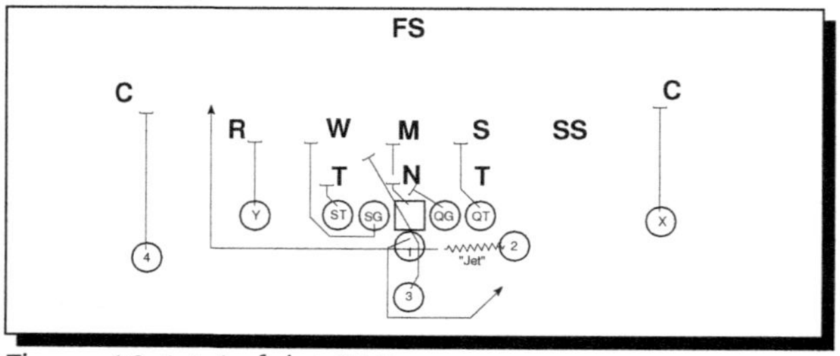

Figure 10-14. Left jet 818

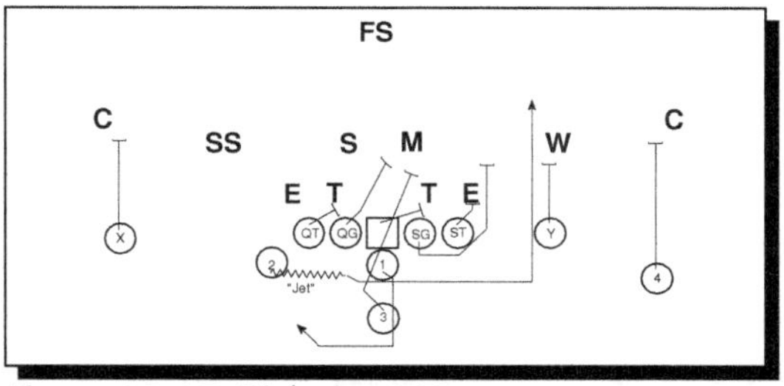

Figure 10-15. Right jet 818

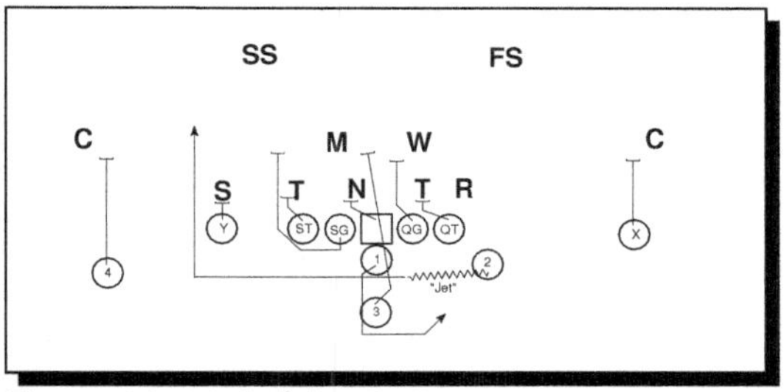

Figure 10-16. Left jet 818

Blocking rules for 18 are as follows:

- Y-Receiver: Y blocks the defensive man covering him.
- Strong Tackle: The strong tackle always zone blocks to the strongside.
- Strong Guard: The strong guard always pulls flat to the strongside. He turns upfield after passing the strong tackle's block. The strong guard blocks the first defender to the inside.
- Center, Quick Guard, and Quick Tackle: The center, quick guard, and quick tackle all zone block to the strongside.
- X-Receiver and 4-Back: Both the X-receiver and the 4-back block the defensive player covering them.

Jet motion by the 2-back starts on the rise of the quarterback's heel. The jet is full-speed flat motion passing directly behind the quarterback. He receives the handoff in the strongside A gap. After he has the ball, he may belly back slightly to allow the strong guard to get around the strong tackle's block. The 2-back aims to get to the numbers, but he may cut upfield if daylight shows.

The quarterback makes a 180-degree pivot to the strongside so that his back is to the line of scrimmage. He hands the ball to the 2-back in the strongside A gap. After executing the handoff, the quarterback goes straight back on the midline to seven yards of depth. He then bootlegs to the quickside faking the east 817 pass.

The 30 is faked by the 3-back. He blocks any linebacker or safety he encounters.

The 18 is a relatively easy play to execute. Once the handoff from the quarterback to the two-back is perfected, the play can be run without a high number of repetitions. It is a quick method of attacking the strongside flank of the defense.

The 30 (Figures 10-17 through 10-19) is part of the zone series when run from doubles with jet motion by the 2-back. The 3-back fakes 30 when the jet sweep is used. As a natural progression, 30 is sometimes run with jet motion. Figure 10-17 is 30 trap, Figure 10-18 is 30 gut, and Figure 10-19 is 30 base. Chapter 8 covers the blocking rules for the 3-back trap and the variations of it. Although 30 may be run any of these ways, the most effective version with jet motion is 30 gut. The strong guard pulls for this play as he does on 18.

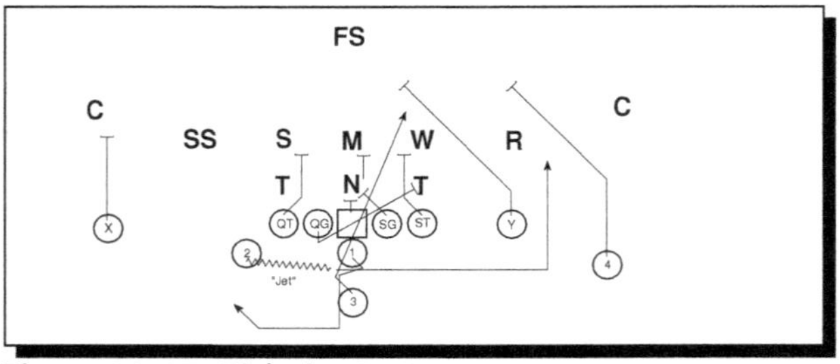

Figure 10-17. Right jet 830

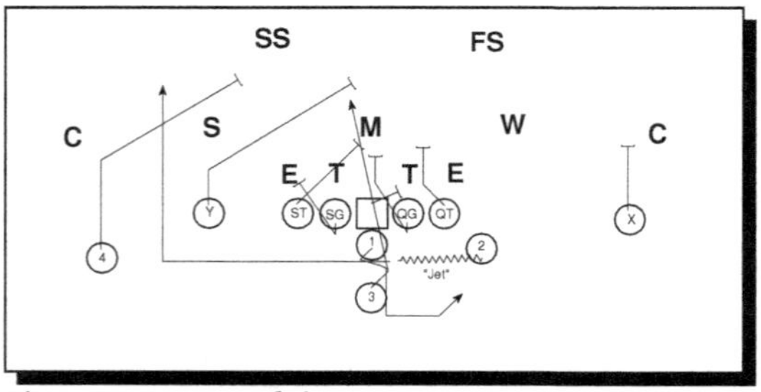

Figure 10-18. Left jet 830 gut

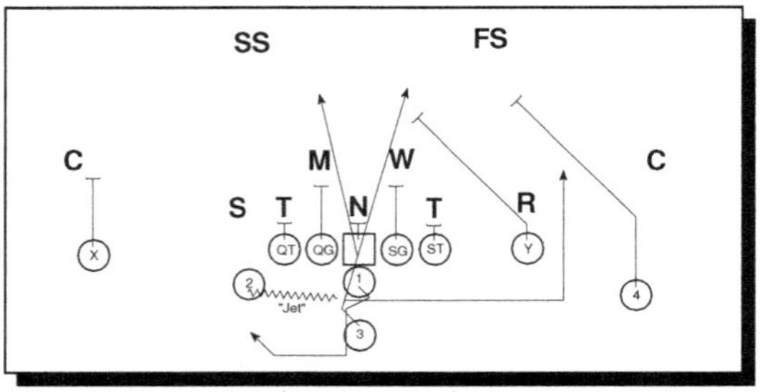

Figure 10-19. Right jet 830 base

The quarterback starts the jet motion by the 2-back with a heel lift. He will not fake to the 2-back. Opening at 90 degrees on the midline, the quarterback goes straight back and executes a one-handed handoff on his second step. After three more steps straight back, he executes a bootleg action to the quickside.

Footwork for the 3-back is the same whenever 30 is run. The jet motion should not affect anything he does.

The final play in the outside zone series is jet east 817 (Figures 10-20 and 10-21). Jet east 817 is a bootleg pass to the quickside of the formation off the jet sweep action. This play is run only from doubles and jet motion by the 2-back. After motioning to the strongside, the 2-back will block the first defensive player who appears outside the strong tackle's block.

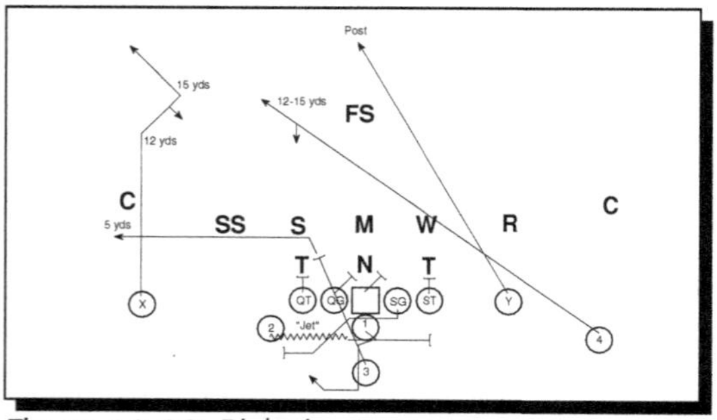

Figure 10-20. Right jet 817

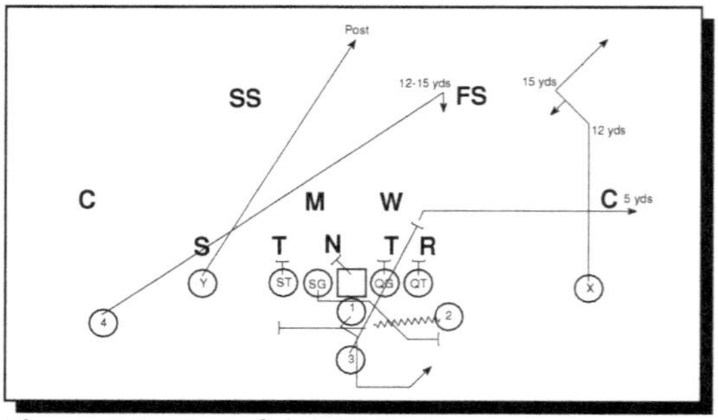

Figure 10-21. Left jet 817

The 4-back has a drag cut to the quickside of the formation. He works to a depth of 12 to 15 yards. Once he reaches the quick tackle position, the 4-back looks to find a void in the coverage where he settles down. He must never cross the hash mark on the quickside.

A post cut at 12 yards in depth is run by Y. His aiming point is the goalpost on the strongside of the formation. This route is designed to occupy a single safety or the strong safety in a two safety alignment.

The X-receiver runs a read route. He reads the secondary coverage as he runs his route and adjusts his cut based on coverage. Versus a single high safety, X makes a post cut at 12 yards of depth. After two steps on the post route, he plants his outside foot and breaks back on a comeback curl route. If faced with two high safeties or man coverage, X executes the 12-yard post cut. After three steps, he plants his inside foot and converts his route to a post corner cut.

The 3-back fakes 30. If he does not need to block a blitzing linebacker in the quickside B gap, the 3-back runs a five-yard flat route to the quickside of the formation.

The quarterback opens quickside at a 90-degree angle. He goes straight back on the midline for five steps. At seven yards of depth he bootlegs to the quickside. His read progression for east 817 is the X-receiver #1, flat route #2, and the drag cut by the 4-back #3.

This pass uses east blocking, and its rules are as follows:

- Strong Tackle: Gap, over, or outside is the strong tackle's blocking assignment.
- Strong Guard: The strong guard pulls quickside and blocks the first defensive man to show outside the quick tackle's block.
- Center: The center blocks the #1 defender to the strongside.
- Quick Guard: The quick guard blocks the #1 defensive player to the quickside on the line of scrimmage. A nose man is counted as #1.
- Quick Tackle: The quick tackle's blocking rule is to block the #2 defensive man on the line of scrimmage quickside.

CHAPTER 11

The Power Series

The power series in the no-huddle multiple offense places emphasis on the off-tackle attack and complementary running plays and play-action passes. The power series is designed as a group of physical running plays and counters to them. They provide a method of attacking off-tackle areas without using the option game.

Strong formation is used for a number of these plays. Since strong formation is an unbalanced alignment to the quickside, the defense is forced to set its strength to the quickside. Failure to do so would result in an inability to stop the power runs to the quickside of the formation. When the offense shifts from strong to other formations, the defense is forced to change its strength as well.

Figures 11-1 through 11-6 illustrate 33, the fullback dive play in the power series. This play is intended to be run primarily from a strong formation, but it can be used from I, wing, or doubles as well. The 3-back aims for the butt of the quick guard and will read his block. His first step is with the quickside foot; he then dives straight ahead as fast as he can hit the hole.

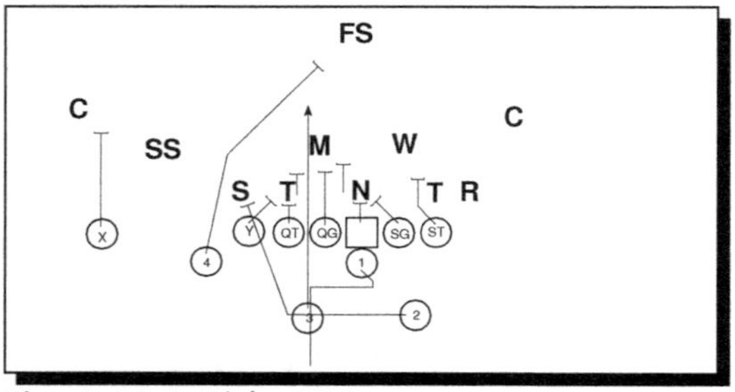

Figure 11-1. Right 533

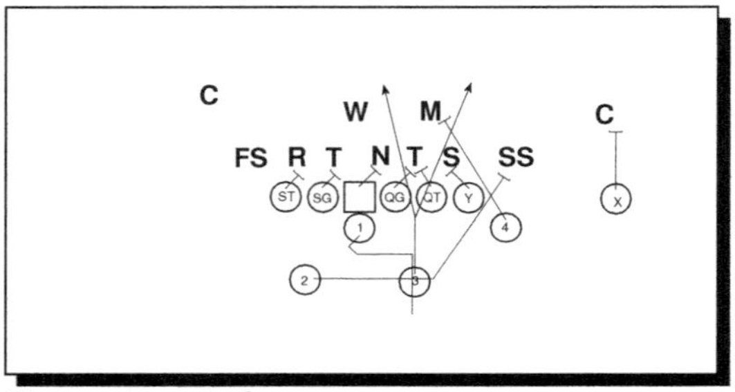

Figure 11-2. Left 533

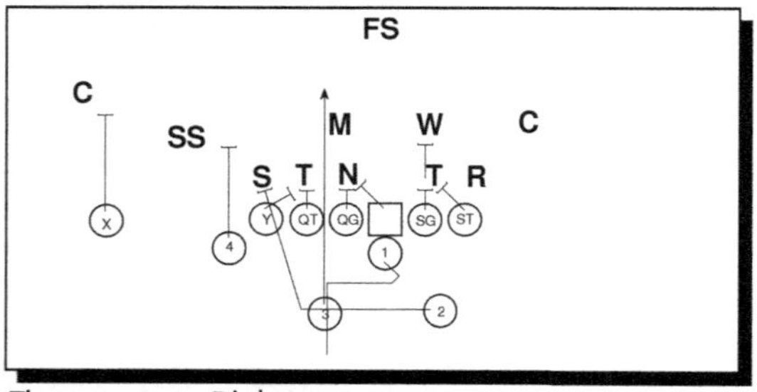

Figure 11-3. Right 533

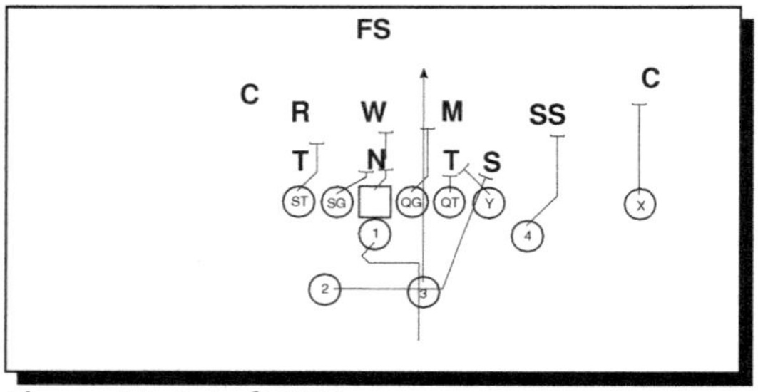

Figure 11-4. Left 533

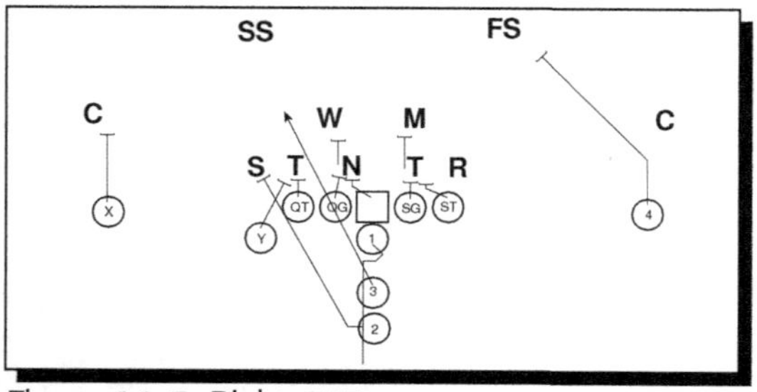

Figure 11-5. Right 633

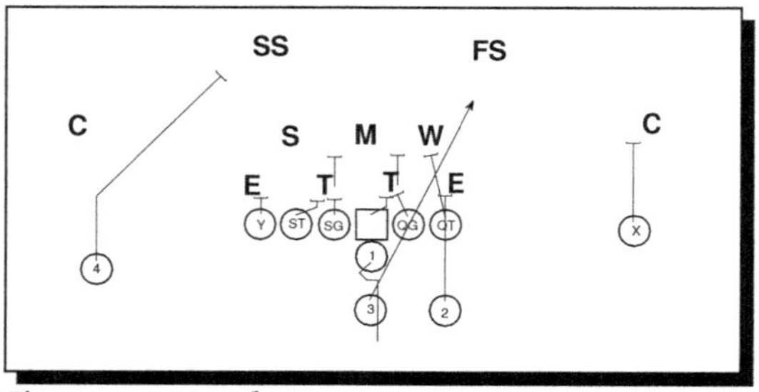

Figure 11-6. Left 733

A 180-degree pivot is made by the quarterback so that his back is to the line of scrimmage. This same pivot is made when 49, the jet sweep to the quickside of the formation, is run. After pivoting, the quarterback makes a one-handed handoff to the 3-back. He then comes back at a 45-degree quickside angle to fake to the 2-back running off-tackle. Following this fake, the quarterback sets up at seven yards of depth as for a 90 pass.

The 2-back fakes 25. When in a strong set, he comes flat across the formation until he reaches the B gap quickside. At this point, the 2-back aims for the quickside tackle's outside hip and runs a slant off-tackle. From an I alignment, the 2-back lead-steps quickside and aims for the quick tackle's outside hip as he fakes 25. If wing or doubles formations are used, the 2-back blocks a defensive man head up or outside the quick tackle.

Blocking rules for 33 are as follows:

- Y-Receiver: Y zone blocks to the strongside.
- Quick Tackle: The quick tackle zone blocks to the strongside.
- X-Receiver: The X-receiver blocks the defender covering him.
- Quick Guard: The quick guard's blocking rule is B gap, over, A gap, or inside linebacker to the quickside.
- Center, Strong Guard, and Strong Tackle: The center, strong guard, and strong tackle all zone block to the quickside.
- 4-Back: The 4-back blocks the nearest safety.

Figures 11-7 through 11-12 show 25, the #1 play run to the quickside in the power series. It is a very effective play for the following reasons:

- Y and the quick tackle almost always double-team block at the inside of the hole.
- The defender outside of the double-team is trapped by the pulling quick guard. This player is threatened by a down block from the 4-back.
- The dive action of the 3-back faking 33 creates an inside run threat.
- A seal block is made on the first linebacker to the inside.
- The X-receiver makes a crack block on the playside safety.

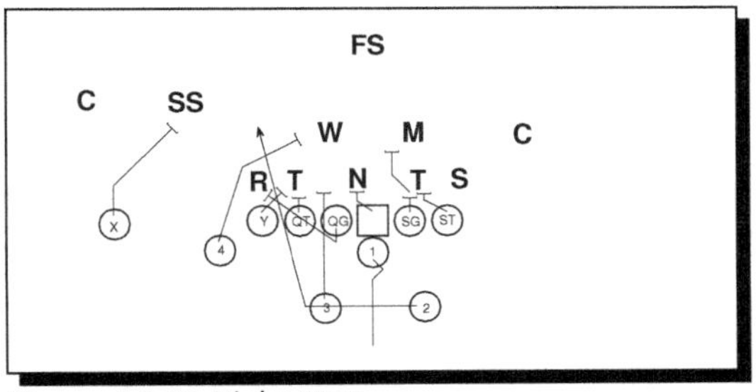

Figure 11-7. Right 525

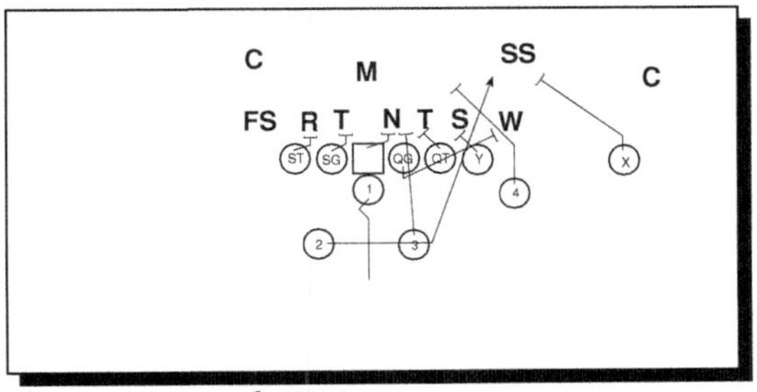

Figure 11-8. Left 525

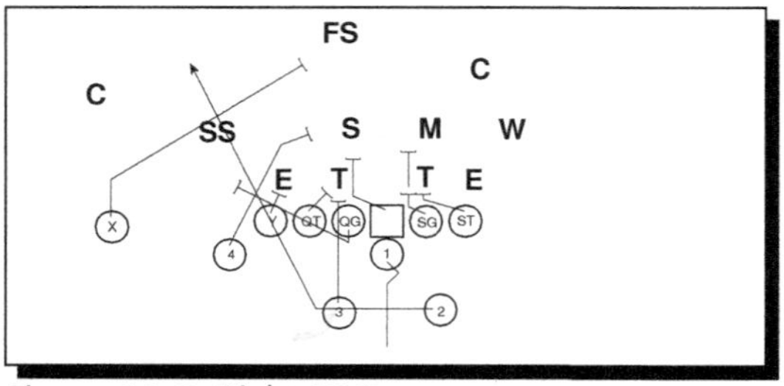

Figure 11-9. Right 525

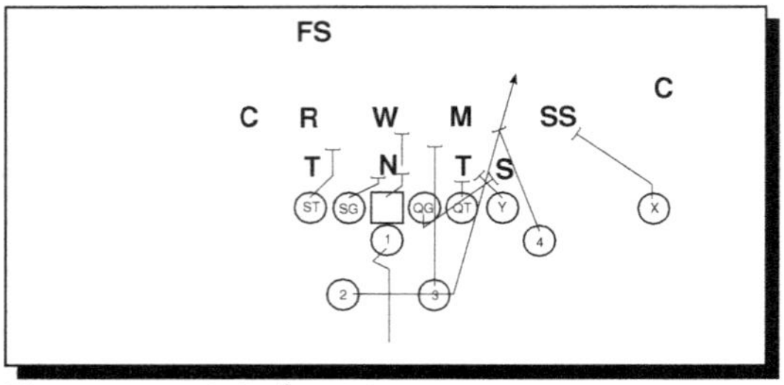

Figure 11-10. Left 525

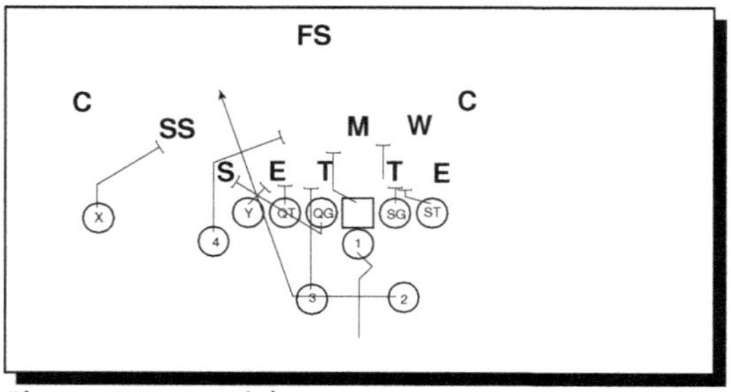

Figure 11-11. Right 525

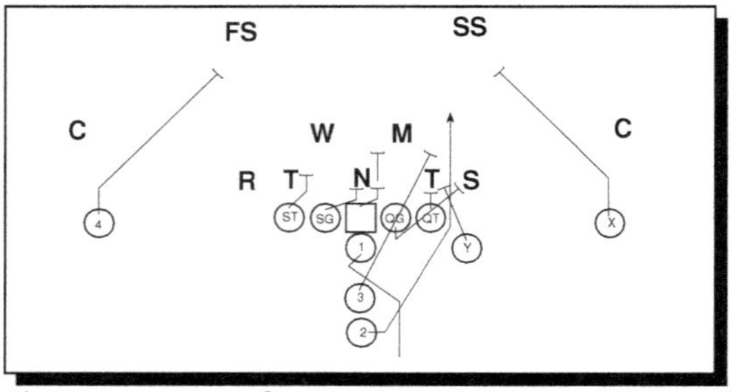

Figure 11-12. Left 625

The quarterback's footwork has him reverse pivot to the quickside at a 45-degree angle. He continues back and hands off to the 2-back. The quarterback then goes straight back to seven yards of depth to fake a 90 pass.

When aligned in the strong formation, the 2-back comes flat across the formation to the quickside B gap. He receives the handoff from the quarterback and aims for the quick tackle's outside hip. The 2-back runs inside the trap block by the quick guard. From the I formation, the 2-back lead steps quickside and aims for the quick tackle's outside hip.

It is the 3-back's responsibility to fill for the quick guard as he pulls. He blocks a defensive lineman head-up with the quick guard or in the A gap quickside. This block is a cut block. If no defensive lineman is in those positions, the 3-back blocks an inside linebacker quickside or the middle linebacker.

Blocking rules for 25 are as follows:

- Y-Receiver: Y blocks gap, down, or outside linebacker.
- Quick Tackle: The quick tackle blocks gap, over, or down.
- Quick Guard: The quick guard pulls flat to the quickside and traps the first defensive man past Y's block. If he pulls to the right, he traps with his right shoulder, and he traps with the left shoulder when pulling left.
- Center: The center blocks A gap quickside, over, middle linebacker, or the inside linebacker strongside.
- Strong Guard and Strong Tackle: The strong guard and strong tackle zone block to the quickside.

The 30 trap, Figures 11-13 and 11-14, is used as an inside counter from the power series if run from a strong formation. Chapter 8 covers 30 as part of the buck series.

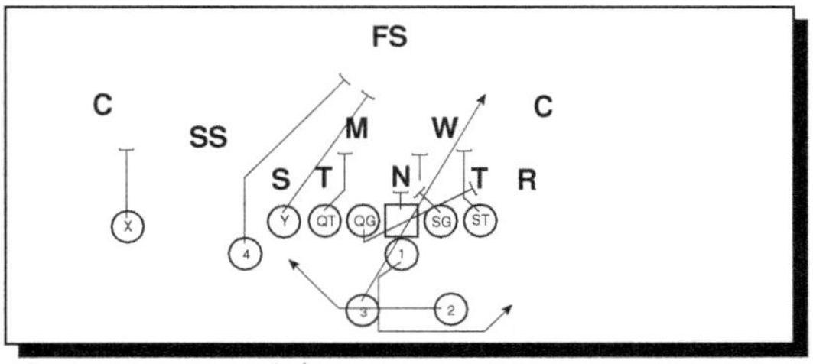

Figure 11-13. Right 530

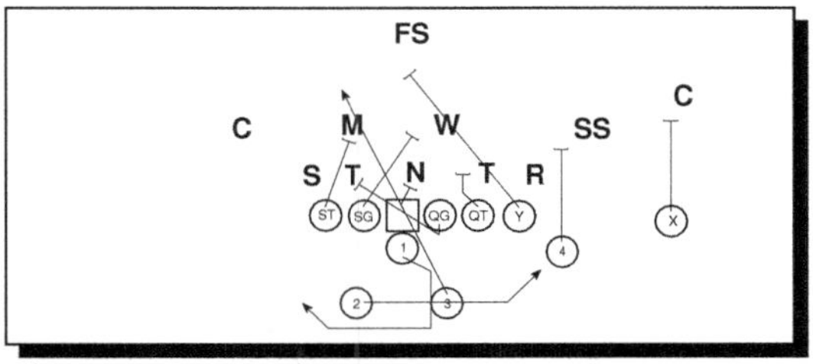

Figure 11-14. Left 530

The 3-back lead steps toward the center with his strongside foot. He aims for the center's butt and receives an inside handoff from the quarterback. From a strong formation the 2-back goes flat across the formation to the quickside. He fakes 19, the quickside power sweep.

When 30 is run from a strong set, the quarterback opens quickside at a 45-degree angle. He takes the ball to the 3-back and hands off on his second step. After handing off, the quarterback goes straight back and fakes to the 2-back. He then goes straight back two more steps and executes a bootleg action to the strongside of the formation.

Blocking rules for 30 trap are as follows:

- Y-Receiver: Y blocks an outside linebacker or safety on his side of the formation.
- Strong Tackle: The inside linebacker to outside linebacker is the strong tackle's blocking assignment.
- Strong Guard: Versus an odd defense, the strong guard combo blocks with the center on a nose man to a middle linebacker or inside linebacker quickside. Against an even front, he blocks the middle linebacker or inside linebacker to the quickside. If a defender is in the strongside A gap, the strong guard calls Lou and blocks the gap player.
- Center: Against an odd defense the center combo blocks with the strong guard on a nose man to middle linebacker or inside linebacker quickside. Versus an even or gap front, the center blocks the #1 defender to the quickside.
- Quick Guard: The quick guard pulls strongside and traps the first defender outside the last down block.
- Quick Tackle: The quick tackle blocks gap or the first linebacker to the inside.

The power sweep, 19, is only run from a strong formation. Figures 11-15 through 11-18 show examples of 19 versus varying formations. This play attacks the perimeter of the defense with speed and power. It forces the defense to shift strength to the quickside to stop the sweep.

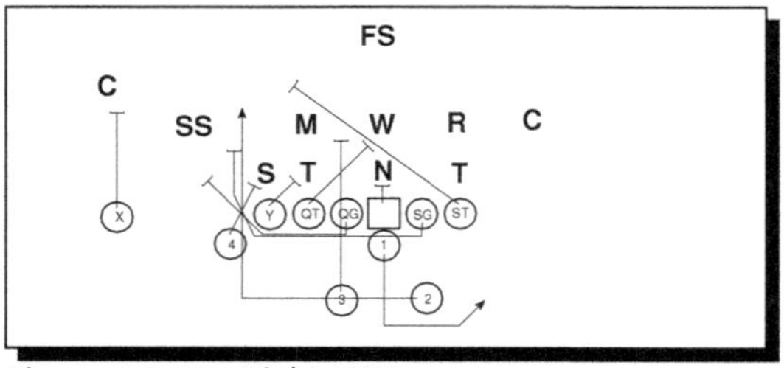

Figure 11-15. Right 519

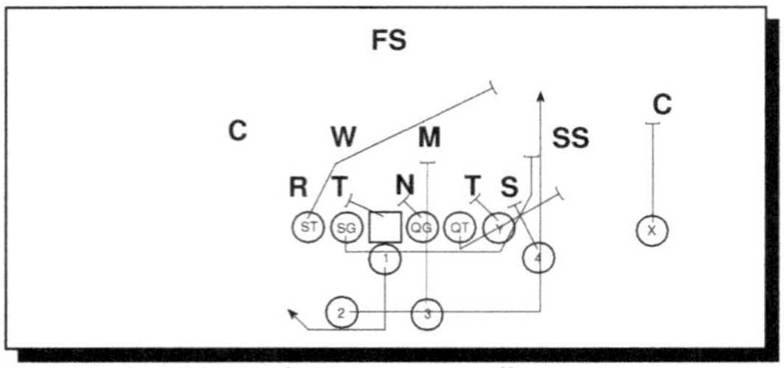

Figure 11-16. Left 519 gap call

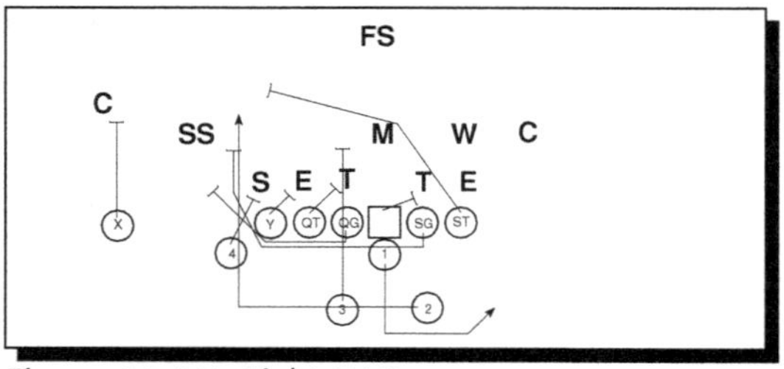

Figure 11-17. Right 519

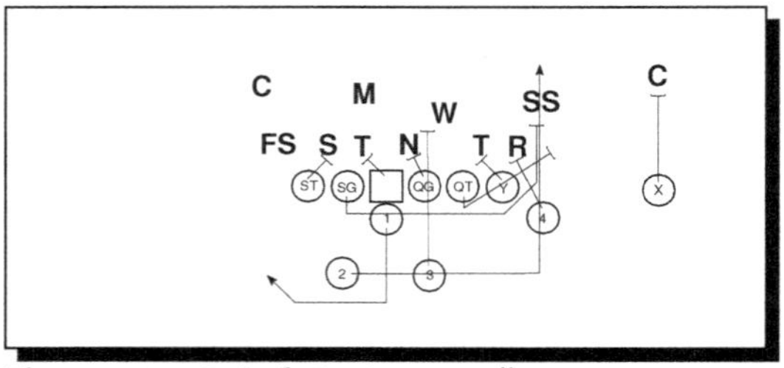

Figure 11-18. Left 519 gap call

The quarterback's footwork starts as he opens to the quickside at a 90-degree angle on the midline. The quarterback goes straight back and hands off to the 2-back on his third step. After handing off, he continues straight back for two more steps to seven yards of depth and then bootlegs to the strongside of the formation.

On the snap of the ball, the 2-back lead steps to the quickside. He comes flat across the formation and takes a handoff from the quarterback. He continues on a flat path and watches the kick-out block on the force defender by the pulling guard or tackle. When the 2-back sees the kick-out, he plants his back foot and L cuts to come straight upfield behind the kick-out block. This same L cut is used by the 2-back for 28, the buck sweep play.

The 3-back goes through the quickside B gap. He seals the first linebacker to his inside.

Blocking assignments for 19 are as follows:

- Y-Receiver: Y blocks gap, down, or the first linebacker to the inside.
- Quick Tackle: Gap, down, or the first linebacker inside is the quick tackle's blocking rule. If the quick guard calls gap, the quick tackle pulls quickside and kicks out the first defender outside the last down block.
- Quick Guard: The quick guard pulls quickside and kicks out the first defensive man past the last down block. If a defender is in the A gap, the quick guard calls gap and blocks down.
- Center: The center blocks a man over or the first defensive man strongside.
- Strong Guard: The strong guard pulls quickside and turns up inside the kick-out block. He seals the first linebacker to the inside.

- Strong Tackle: The strong tackle blocks gap. If no defender is in the B gap, the strong tackle goes crossfield at six yards of depth to kick out any defensive player he encounters.
- 4-Back: The 4-back blocks down on the first defender to his inside on or off the line of scrimmage.
- X-Receiver: The X-receiver blocks the defensive player covering him.

The 46 (Figures 11-19 through 11-22) is a counter crisscross play. The 46 is a counter to the power sweep, 19. The 4-back is the ballcarrier on this play. He jab steps to the outside and then turns inside, coming back to take an inside handoff from the 2-back. He follows the pulling Y. This play is only run from strong formation.

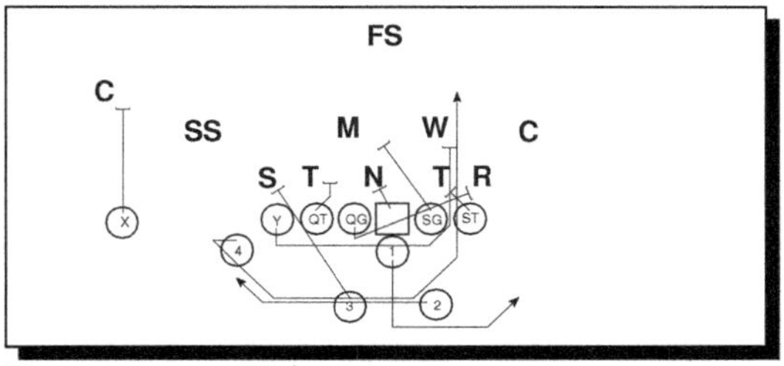

Figure 11-19. Right 546

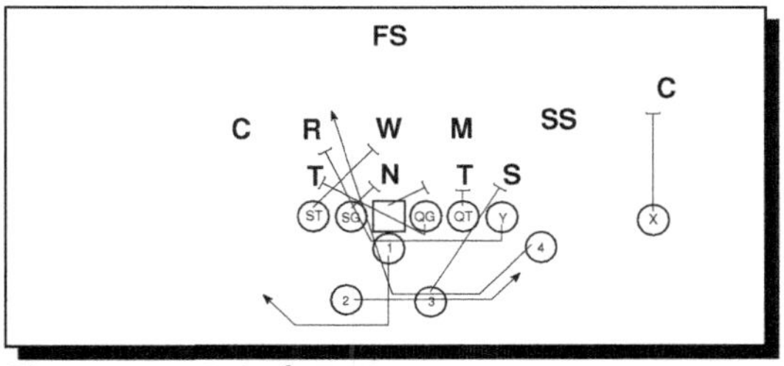

Figure 11-20. Left 546

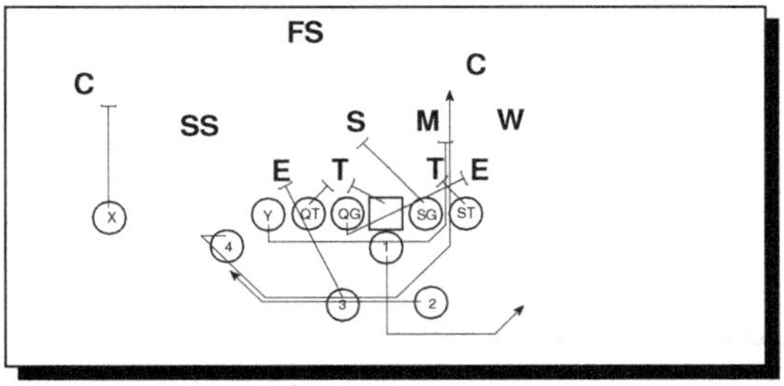

Figure 11-21. Right 546

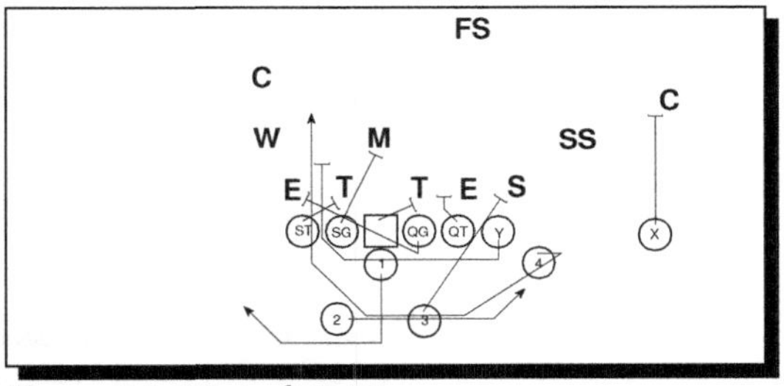

Figure 11-22. Left 546

The quarterback opens quickside at a 90-degree angle on the midline. He hands off to the 2-back on his third step. This handoff is made with the ball placed point-first into the 2-back's hands. After handing off, the quarterback goes two more steps back on the midline before bootlegging to the strongside of the formation.

The 2-back goes flat across the formation toward the quickside. He places his hands on his inside hip with the little fingers together. The ball is placed point-first into his hands. This technique makes it much easier to execute the handoff to the 4-back. The 2-back carries out a fake of 19.

The 3-back takes a path to block the first defensive player outside the quick tackle's block. He aims for the quickside C gap and blocks whomever he encounters.

Blocking responsibilities for 46 are as follows:

- Y-Receiver: Y pulls strongside and goes through the hole behind the quick guard's trap block. Y seals the first defender from the inside to the outside.
- Strong Tackle: The strong tackle blocks gap, down, or the first linebacker to the inside.
- Strong Guard: Gap, down, middle linebacker, or inside linebacker quickside is the strong guard's blocking rule.
- Center: The center blocks the #1 defensive player on the quickside.
- Quick Guard: The quick guard pulls strongside and trap blocks the first defender past the strong tackle's block.
- Quick Tackle: Gap, over, or outside linebacker is the blocking rule for the quick tackle.
- X-Receiver: The X-receiver blocks the defensive man who is covering him.

The 46 is run only when the defense is overpursuing to stop 19, the power sweep to the quickside of the formation. The play can be effective if it is run at the right time.

Western 526 is run only from strong formation. The power off-tackle, 25, is faked, and bootleg action is executed into the strongside of the formation. Figures 11-23 through 11-25 show western 526 versus three different defensive alignments.

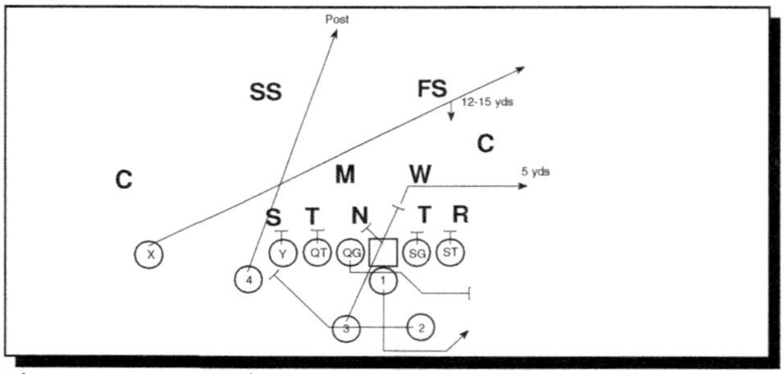

Figure 11-23. Right western 526

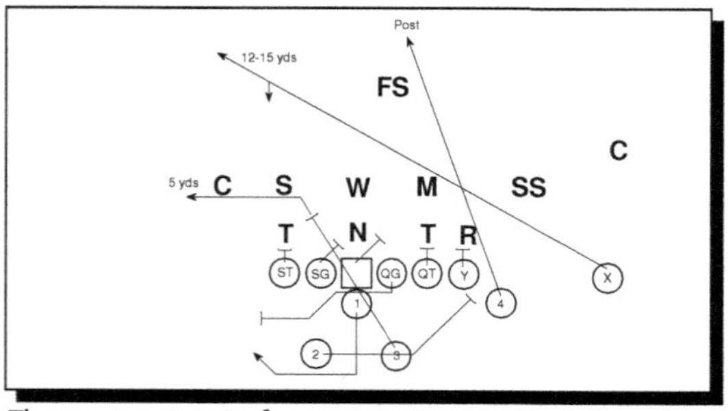

Figure 11-24. Left western 526

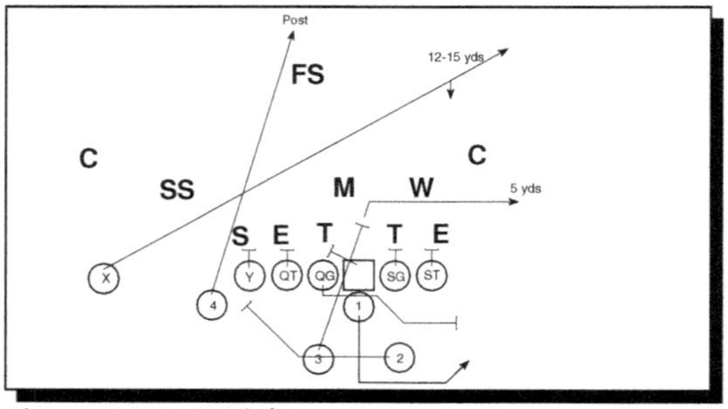

Figure 11-25. Right western 526

The quarterback's footwork has him open at a 90-degree angle to the quickside. He stays on the midline and fakes to the 2-back on his third step. The quarterback then goes two more steps on the midline and bootlegs to the strongside at seven yards of depth. His read progression is the X-receiver running the drag route #1 and the 3-back in the strong flat #2.

Chapter 4 covers blocking rules for western pass protection, but they are as follows:

- Y-Receiver: Y is an ineligible receiver in a strong formation. For strong formation, Y blocks gap, over, or the first defensive player to his outside.
- Quick Tackle: The quick tackle blocks gap, over, or the first defender to the outside.
- Quick Guard: Pulling to the strongside, the quick guard blocks the first defensive man who shows. He pulls flat past the center, then gets depth and attempts to log the defender he is blocking. If this man comes upfield hard, the quick guard kicks him out.
- Center: The center blocks the #1 defensive man to the quickside.
- Strong Guard: The strong guard blocks the #1 defender on the line.
- Strong Tackle: The #2 defensive player on the line of scrimmage strongside is blocked by the strong tackle.

The 2-back comes flat across the formation to the quickside. He fakes 25 and blocks the first defensive player to appear on the quickside. This man could be a blitzing linebacker or secondary player. If no defender appears unblocked, the 2-back can assist any offensive lineman on the quickside.

The 3-back fakes 30. If a linebacker blitzes in the 0 hole, the 3-back blocks him. When the 3-back does not have to block a blitzing linebacker, he runs a five-yard deep cut into the strongside flat. The 3-back becomes the quarterback's second choice in the read progression.

The 4-back is the #2 receiver by his alignment in a strong set. Y is the #1 receiver even though he is ineligible. As the #2 receiver for a six pattern, the 4-back runs a 12-yard post cut. This cut is designed to occupy the single high safety or split two high safeties. The quarterback will only throw to the 4-back if he is specifically instructed to do so.

The X-receiver runs a drag route to the strongside of the formation behind the 4-back's post cut. He aims for a depth of 12 to 15 yards on the strongside. X may set down in a void in a zone coverage once he reaches the strong tackle's position, or he may continue across the field. The X-receiver is the first choice for the quarterback in his read progression.

The 34 is a power off-tackle play run to the strongside of the formation with the 3-back carrying the ball. This play is effective from a strong formation versus a defense that drastically overshifts to the unbalanced side of the formation. It also sets up an effective bootleg pass from 34 action.

Figures 11-26 through 11-29 illustrate 34 run against varying defensive looks. The blocking rules are as follows:

- Y-Receiver: Y goes crossfield at a shallow depth of six yards and kick-out blocks the first defender he encounters at the 4 hole. This defender could be a defensive back or an outside linebacker.

- Strong Tackle: The strong tackle blocks gap, down, or the first linebacker inside.
- Strong Guard: Gap, down, middle linebacker, or inside linebacker quickside is the strong guard's blocking assignment.
- Center: The #1 defender aligned quickside is blocked by the center.
- Quick Guard: The quick guard pulls flat strongside and turns up inside the kick-out block by the 2-back. He seals the first linebacker from inside to the outside. In the case of a log block by the 2-back, he swings outside and kicks out the next defender.
- Quick Tackle: The quick tackle blocks gap, over, or the first defensive player to the outside.
- X-Receiver: The X-receiver blocks the man covering him.
- 4-Back: The 4-back goes crossfield at a depth of 10 to 12 yards and blocks the first defender he encounters.

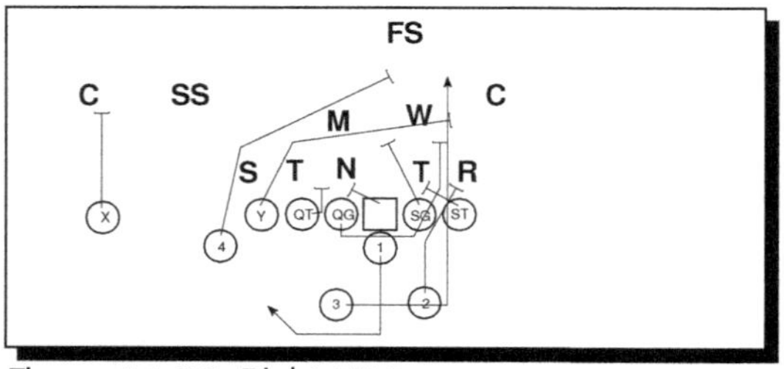

Figure 11-26. Right 534

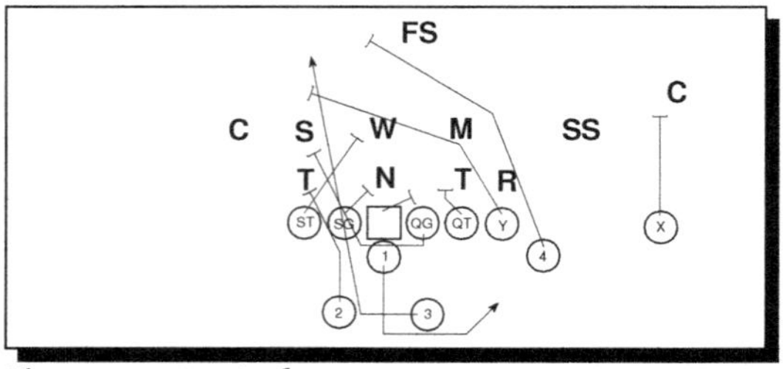

Figure 11-27. Left 534

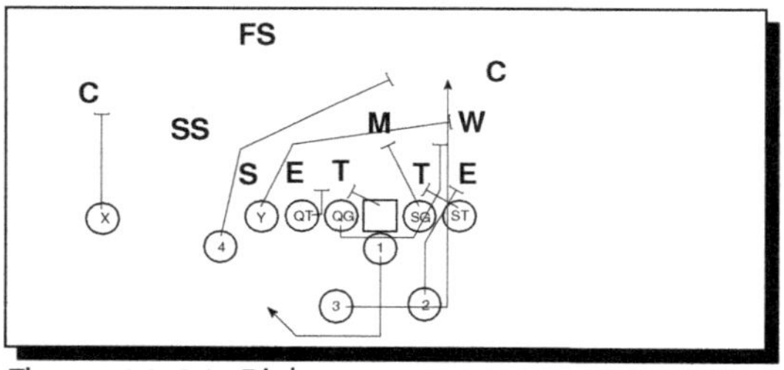

Figure 11-28. Right 534

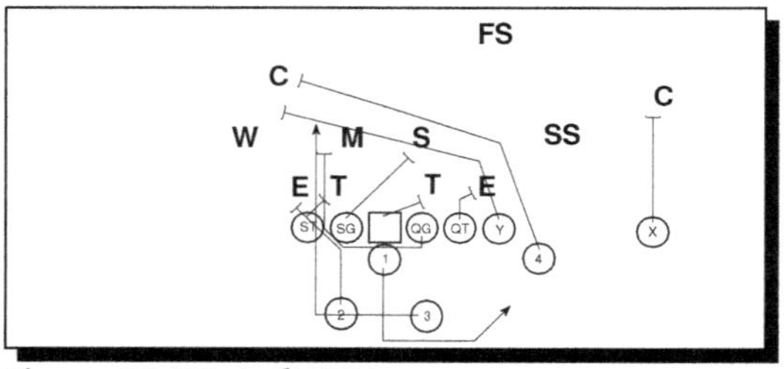

Figure 11-29. Left 534

The quarterback opens quickside at a 90-degree angle on the midline. He goes straight back and hands off to the 3-back on his third step. After taking two additional steps on the midline, he bootlegs to the quickside faking an eastern pass.

An open lead step is taken by the 3-back. He then comes flat across to the strongside reading the block of the 2-back. If the 2-back is able to kick out his defender, the 3-back turns up inside the kick-out block and follows the block of the quick guard. When the 2-back is forced to log block his defensive man, the 3-back breaks outside that block, looking for the block of the quick guard.

The 2-back takes a step straight ahead. This step is taken to help him establish an inside-out angle to block the first defensive player outside the strong tackle's block.

Ideally, the 2-back kicks this man out. But if the defender closes so hard that the kick-out block can't be made, the 2-back logs the defensive man to the inside.

Blocking for 34 is similar to that used for 24, the power off-tackle play. The differences are in the assignments for Y, the 3-back, the 2-back and 4-back, but blocking rules for the five interior offensive linemen are the same.

The 34 may be run from doubles, as in Figures 11-30 and 11-31. Jet motion is used by the 2-back to put him in position to block the first defensive player outside the strong tackle's block. The ball is snapped just after the 2-back passes the quarterback position. This technique allows the 2-back to execute his block at full speed from a great angle.

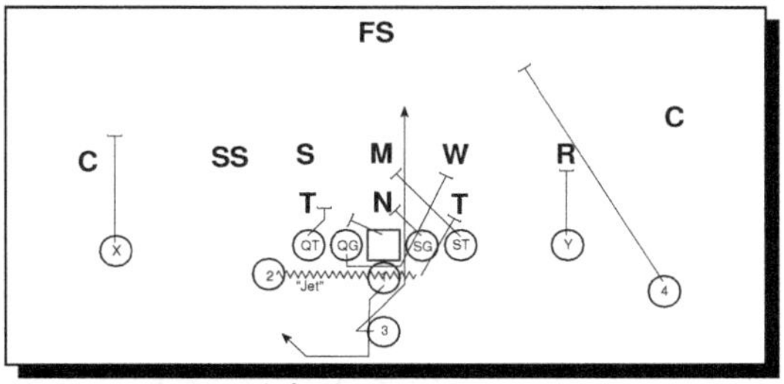

Figure 11-30. Right jet 834

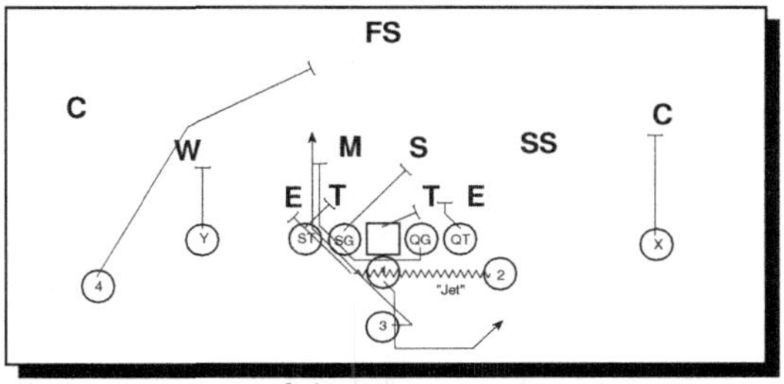

Figure 11-31. Left jet 834

A lead step to the quickside is taken by the 3-back. This step allows the quick guard to get ahead of him to the 4 hole. The 3-back aims for the strong guard's outside hip and hits the hole downhill.

Footwork for the quarterback does not change. He still opens quickside on the midline and hands to the 3-back on his third step. This action is followed by his bootlegging to the quickside. Y blocks the man covering him. The 4-back blocks the safety to his side.

Eastern 534 (Figures 11-32 through 11-34) is a bootleg pass to the quickside of the formation. The run being faked is 34. This pass is only run from a strong formation.

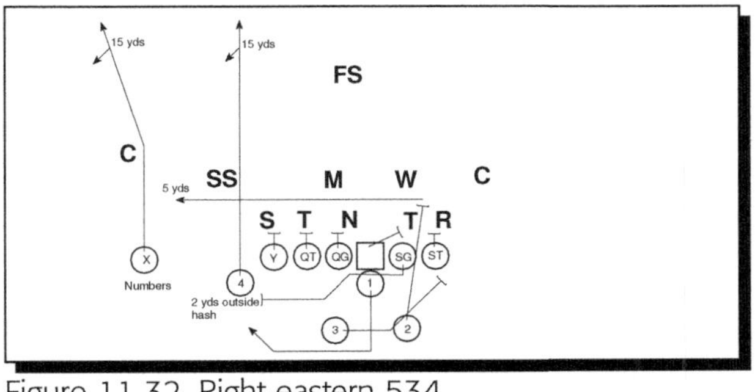

Figure 11-32. Right eastern 534

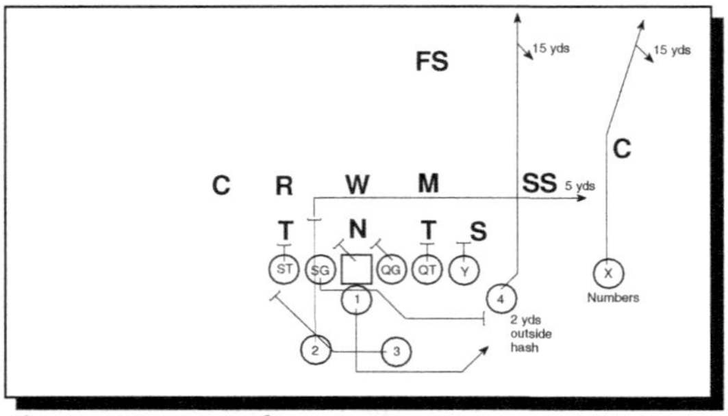

Figure 11-33. Left eastern 534

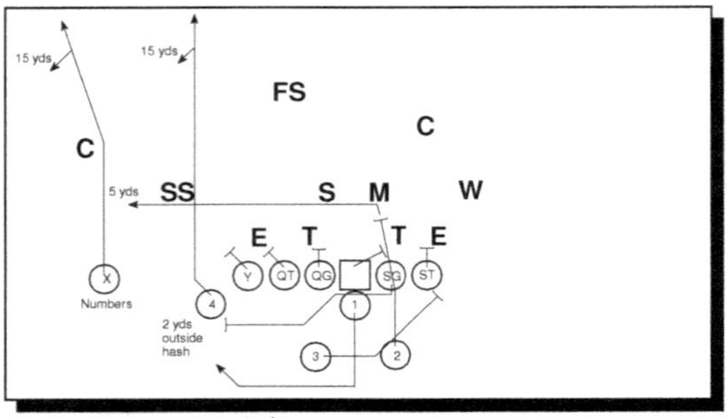

Figure 11-34. Right eastern 534

Eastern pass protection is covered in Chapter 4. The blocking rules are as follows:

- Y-Receiver: Y blocks #3 on the line of scrimmage or the outside linebacker or safety.
- Quick Tackle: The quick tackle blocks the #2 defender on the line of scrimmage.
- Quick Guard: The quick guard blocks #1 on the line of scrimmage.
- Center: The center blocks the first defensive player to the strongside.
- Strong Guard: The strong guard pulls to the quickside and blocks the first defender he encounters. He looks to log block the player, but he can kick him out.
- Strong Tackle: The strong tackle blocks gap, over, or the first defensive player to the outside.

The 3-back fakes 34. He is responsible for blocking the first defensive man outside the strong tackle's block.

The 2-back fills for the pulling strong guard. He blocks any blitz in the A or B gap to the strongside. Versus no blitz, the 2-back crosses to the quickside and runs a delayed five-yard flat cut to the quickside of the formation.

A 4 pass pattern has the X-receiver running a vertical route on the numbers. If the coverage stays deep, he will convert the go cut to a 15-yard deep comeback.

The 4-back runs a go route two yards outside the playside hash mark. As with the X-receiver's route, this route will be converted to a 15-yard deep comeback cut when the coverage player stays deep.

Opening to the quickside at 90 degrees, the quarterback comes straight back on the midline and fakes to the 3-back on his third step. After faking, he continues straight back for two steps to a depth of seven yards before bootlegging to the quickside. Because of the presence of four blockers quickside, including the pulling strongside guard, eastern becomes a true run or pass option for the quarterback. His read progression is the X-receiver #1, the 4-back #2, and the 2-back #3. If the pulling guard comes to the outside with no one to block, the quarterback may call go to him and run the football following the guard downfield.

Eastern is a difficult play to defend because of the vertical pass threat. The additional threat of a run by the quarterback puts great pressure on the defensive perimeter.

The 24 is a physical football running play that attacks the off-tackle hole to the strongside of the formation. This play may be run from I or wing sets. It may be run to a tight end or split end. The 24 allows the offense to attack the defense and serves to develop a tough mental attitude for the offense. It can be run from one goal line to the other, and it is successful against any defensive scheme without major blocking adjustments.

If the 2-back is in an I alignment, the quarterback reverses out at 5 or 7 o'clock. He tries to get the ball to the 2-back as deep as possible in the backfield. A one-handed handoff is made by the quarterback, after which he sets up at seven yards of depth to fake a play-action pass. The reverse action by the quarterback helps hide the football and may cause linebackers to hesitate a split second before flow is established. When the 2-back is in the dive back position, the quarterback reverses out at 90 degrees and takes the ball straight back on the midline to hand off before setting up to fake a pass.

From an I back position, the 2-back lead steps toward the 6 hole. If the play is toward a tight end, the 2-back's aiming point is the outside hip of the strong tackle. When no tight end is present, he aims for the outside hip of the strong guard. In the dive back alignment, he lead steps strongside and stays flat until taking the handoff.

The 2-back reads the 3-back's block on the first defender to the outside of the last down block. This block is supposed to be a kick-out block, but if the defensive man closes hard, the 3-back may have to log him. If the 3-back logs the defensive man, the 2-back may bounce the play to the outside. Versus a cover 4 secondary, the 2-back may have an unblocked safety filling the hole. He must be able to beat this defender 1-on-1 at least some of the time.

A kick-out block on the first defensive man past the last down block strongside is made by the 3-back. To get a good angle for this block, the fullback aims for the outside hip of the second offensive lineman from the end of the line. He then turns out on an inside-out path to attack the first defender who shows. When blocking to the right, the 3-back uses his right shoulder; he uses his left shoulder if he blocks to his left. His pads must be lower than those of the defensive man. Speed and momentum help get movement on the defender. As a last resort, the 3-back can log the defensive man to the inside.

Figures 11-35 through 11-38 show 24. Blocking rules for 24 are as follows:

- Y-Receiver: When he is on the strongside, Y blocks gap, down, or the first linebacker to the inside. If a defender aligns on Y's inside eyes or head-up, he blocks out on the first defensive man to his outside. If he is on the quickside of the formation, Y blocks down.
- Strong Tackle: The blocking responsibility for the strong tackle is to block gap, down, or the first linebacker to the inside.
- Strong Guard: Gap, down, middle linebacker, or the inside linebacker to the quickside is the blocking assignment for the strong guard.

- Center: The blocking assignment for the center is to block the #1 defensive player to the quickside.
- Quick Guard: The quick guard pulls flat to the strongside. After passing the strong guard's position, the quick guard turns his shoulder parallel to the line of scrimmage and shuffles to the hole. He leads through the hole and blocks the first linebacker from the inside out. The shuffle technique allows the guard to turn sharply up in the hole and avoid having defenders scrape under him.
- Quick Tackle: The quick tackle blocks gap, over, or outside.

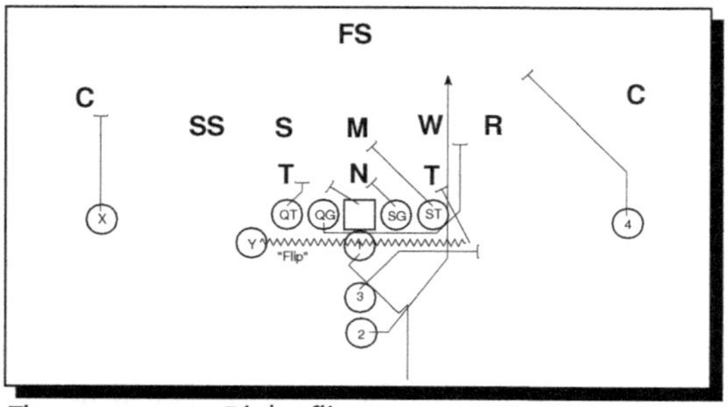

Figure 11-35. Right flip 624

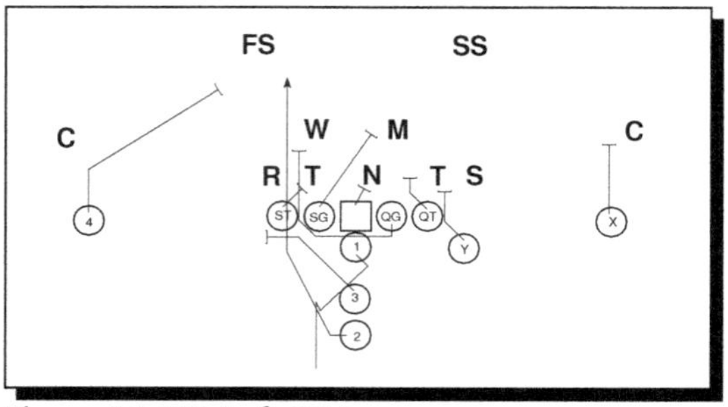

Figure 11-36. Left 624

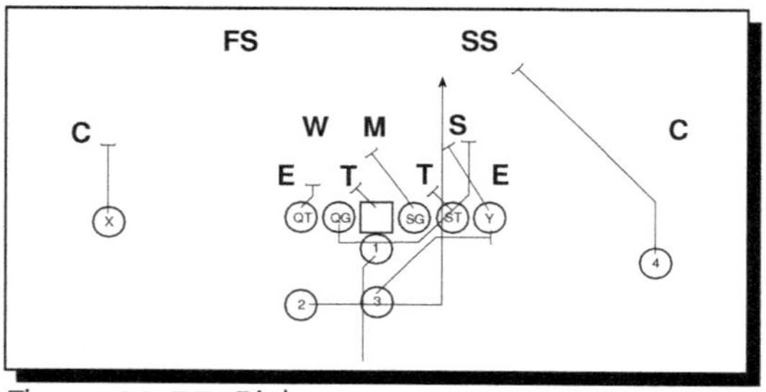

Figure 11-37. Right 724

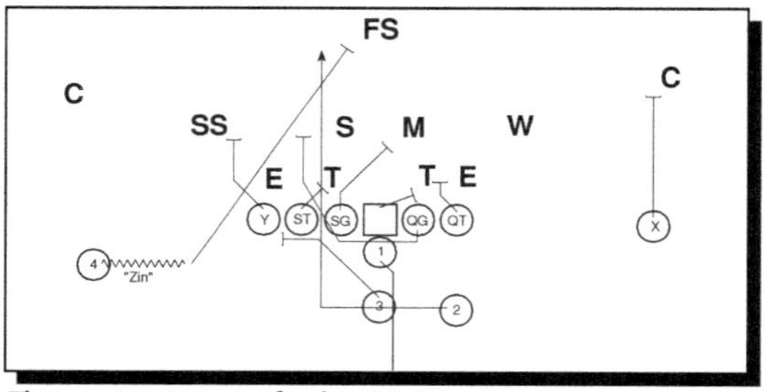

Figure 11-38. Left zin 724

The 27 (Figures 11-39 through 11-42) is a counter play run from I or pistol alignments. This play attacks the off-tackle area to the quickside of the formation.

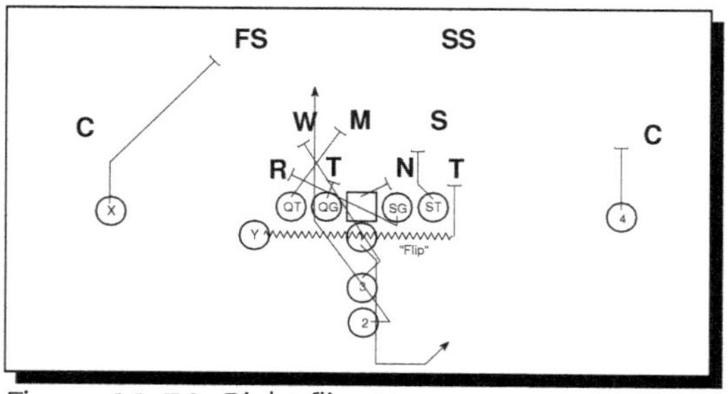

Figure 11-39. Right flip 627

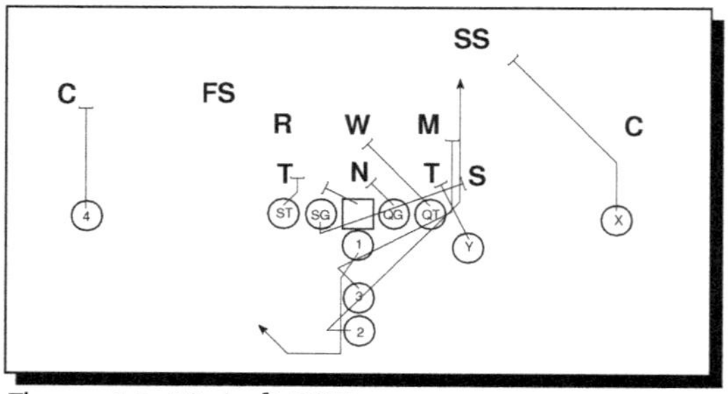

Figure 11-40. Left 627

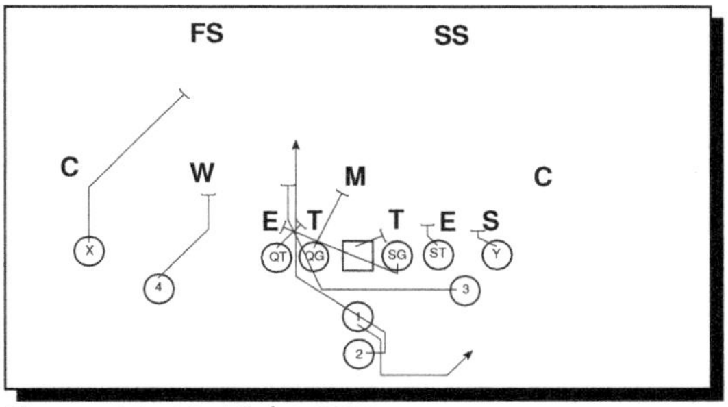

Figure 11-41. Right 927

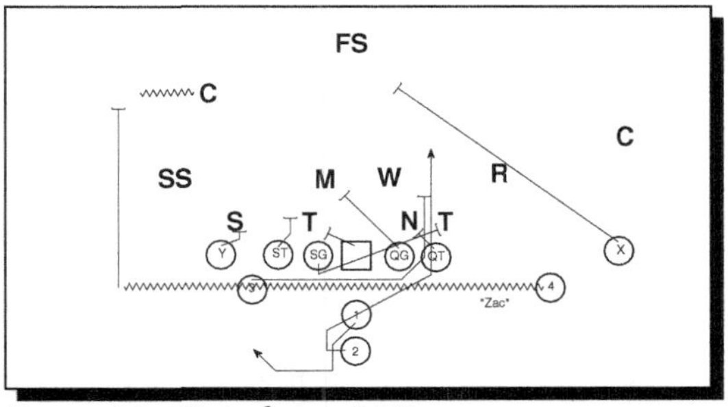

Figure 11-42. Left zac 927

Blocking assignments for 27 are as follows:

- Y-Receiver: Y blocks gap, down, or the first linebacker inside whether he is on the quickside or strongside of the formation.
- Strong Tackle: The strong tackle blocks gap, over, or outside.
- Strong Guard: The strong guard pulls to the quickside and traps the first defensive man outside the last down block. If this defender closes so hard that he can't be trapped, the strong guard logs him to the inside.
- Center: The #1 defensive man on the strongside is the center's responsibility.
- Quick Guard: Gap, down, middle linebacker, or the inside linebacker to the strongside is the quick guard's blocking rule.
- Quick Tackle: The quick tackle blocks gap, down, or first linebacker to the inside.
- X-Receiver: The X-receiver blocks the near safety.
- 4-Back: The 4-back blocks the defensive player covering him.

Footwork for the quarterback from the I on 27 has him open to the strongside at 90 degrees on the midline. He goes straight back and makes a handoff to the 2-back on his third step. After the handoff, the quarterback goes straight back two more steps and then bootlegs to the strongside of the formation. The handoff to the 2-back is made with one hand, while the other hand remains on his belly button. After handing off, both hands of the quarterback are brought to the belt buckle. When the quarterback begins to turn on the bootleg, he slides both his hands to the backside hip to hide the ball. When run from the pistol, the quarterback catches the snap and opens strongside at 90 degrees. He hands off to the 2-back on his first or second step. After continuing straight back until he reaches seven yards of depth, the quarterback then bootlegs to the strongside.

From an I alignment, the 2-back counter steps to the strongside and then aims for the hip of the second offensive lineman to the inside on the quickside of the formation. The 2-back hits the play downhill as he follows the 3-back into the hole. If the 3-back has to bounce outside because the quick guard log blocks, the 2-back will also bounce outside. If a pistol formation is used, the 2-back lead steps strongside and comes straight forward to receive a handoff from the quarterback. Once he secures the handoff, the 2-back cuts under the quarterback and follows the block of the 3-back.

If he is in the I formation, the 3-back takes a crossover step and then a lead step at the outside hip of the strong tackle. He plants his outside foot and turns to the quickside. He follows the strongside guard and goes through the hole behind the guard's trap block. The 3-back looks to the inside first and then the outside for a linebacker to block. If the strong guard has been forced to log his man, the 3-back bounces outside and blocks the first defender he encounters. From the pistol alignment, the 3-back pulls quickside behind the line of scrimmage and reads the strong guard's trap block.

The 80 pass protection and action used from the I or pistol formations fakes 24 and allows a variety of pass patterns to be thrown. As shown in Figures 11-43 through 11-47, the 4, 5, 6, 8, and 9 patterns may all be thrown with 80 pass protection and action. Chapter 4 covers in detail the blocking rules for 80 protection.

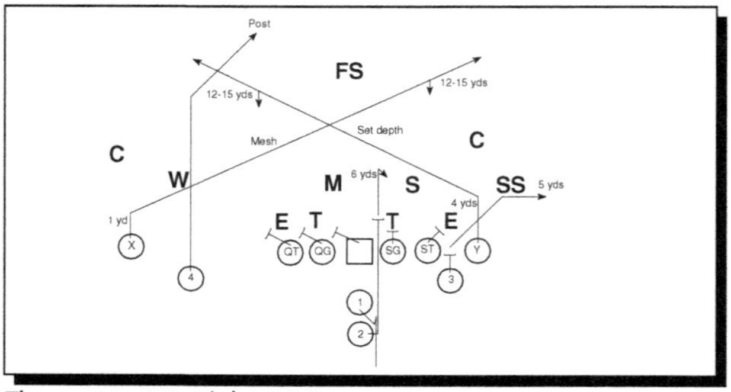

Figure 11-43. Right 985

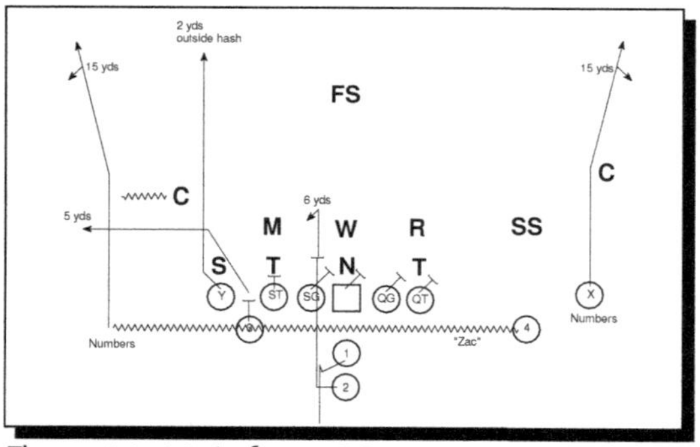

Figure 11-44. Left zac 984

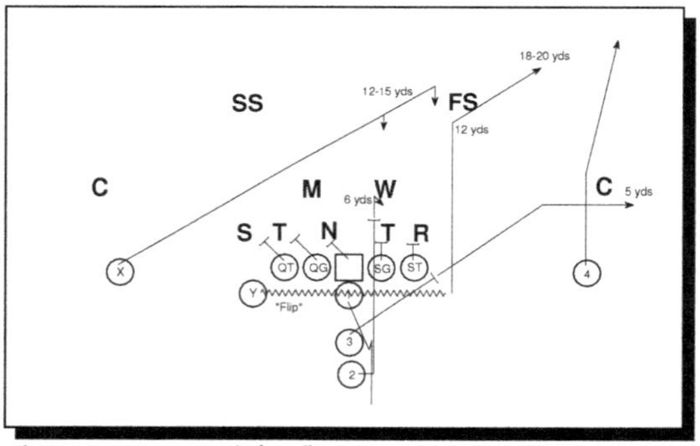

Figure 11-45. Right flip 686

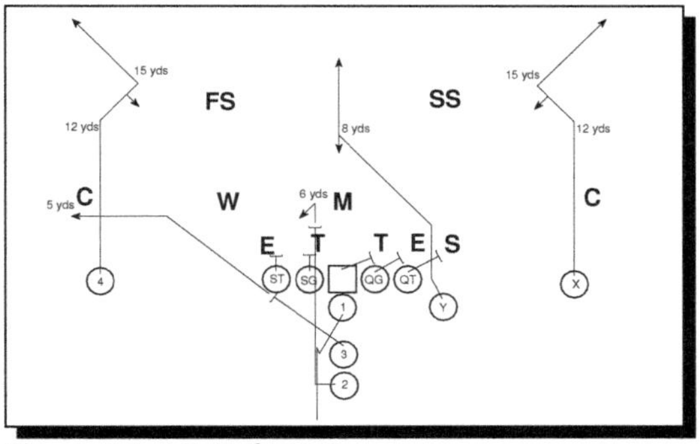

Figure 11-46. Left 688

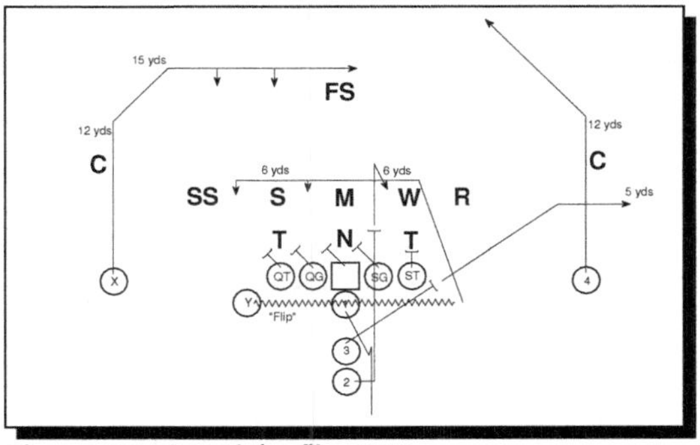

Figure 11-47. Right flip 689

Blocking rules for 80 pass protection are as follows:

- Y-Receiver: Y will be a pass receiver on 80 passes.
- Strong Tackle: The strong tackle blocks the #2 defensive man on the line of scrimmage.
- Strong Guard: The #1 defender on the line is blocked by the strong guard.
- Center: A gap quickside to over the quick guard is the center's blocking assignment.
- Quick Guard: The quick guard blocks B gap to over the quick tackle.
- Quick Tackle: C gap to the first defender to the outside is blocked by the quick tackle.
- 3-Back: The 3-back blocks the first defensive player outside the strong tackle's block. If no defender shows, the 3-back runs a five-yard deep flat route to the strongside.

The 2-back lead steps to the strongside. He comes straight ahead as the quarterback fakes a handoff to him. It is important that he rolls his arms over the ball fake. His aiming point should be the outside hip of the strong guard. The 2-back is responsible for blocking a blitz in either the A or B gap strongside. Versus no blitz, he runs a six-yard deep hook-out checkdown pattern. The 2-back will be the quarterback's final read progression for all patterns. Throwing to the 2-back often results in substantial gains and should be an automatic completion.

The 80 pass protection is a combination man protection strongside with slide protection to the quickside. Four potential blockers are on the strongside. When combined with a good fake of 24, this protection is very sound versus most forms of stunts and blitzes.

When the I formation is used for 80 passes, the quarterback reverse pivots to either 5 or 7 o'clock as he does on 24. He brings the ball back to the 2-back and makes a good fake to him before continuing back to seven yards of depth to set up to pass. This drop should take five steps. From a pistol alignment, the quarterback catches the snap and opens at a 90-degree angle to the strongside of the formation. He starts from a depth of four yards. A fake of 24 is made to the 2-back as the quarterback drops to his seven yards depth. This drop should only take two steps.

Figure 11-43 shows 985. The 5 pattern is a crossing concept. It can be run from I or pistol. The 4-back runs a 12-yard post cut. Y pushes upfield four yards and crosses to the quickside, aiming for 12 to 14 yards of depth. He sets the depth of the mesh. After the mesh occurs, Y may set down in any void in the coverage or continue across the field. The X-receiver pushes upfield for one yard and crosses to the strongside of the formation. He crosses under Y and is responsible for creating the mesh. His aiming point is 12 to 15 yards of depth, and he may set down in a void in the secondary once he reaches the strong tackle's position. The read progression for the quarterback is the 4-back #1, the X-receiver #2, the 3-back in the flat #3, and the 2-back as the checkdown receiver.

Figure 11-44 shows 984. The 4 pattern is a vertical pattern. The X-receiver and the 4-back run go routes on the numbers. If the defensive players covering them stay deep, the X-receiver and the 4-back convert the routes to comeback cuts at 15 yards of depth. Y has a seam route two yards outside the hash mark. The quarterback's read progression is the 4-back #1, Y #2, the strongside flat cut #3, and the six-yard checkdown by the 22-back #4. This pattern may be run from I or pistol. In the case of Figure 11-44, the 4-back is sent in zac motion to create two vertical routes on the strongside of the pistol formation.

Figure 11-45 shows right flip 686, a strongside flood pattern. The 4-back and Y must both end up on the strongside of the formation. This means that flip motion must be used from the I, or zac motion must be run from the pistol. A go route on the number is run by the 4-back. He is the quarterback's #1 choice. Y has a 12-yard deep corner route, aiming for 18 to 20 yards of depth. Y is the quarterback's #2 choice. The X-receiver runs a drag route to the strongside aiming for 12 to 15 yards of depth. He may set down in a void in the secondary once he reaches the strongside of the formation. He should never cross the playside hash mark. The quarterback reads the five-yard flat route by the 3-back as his third choice, the drag route by the X receiver as #4, and the 2-back checkdown as #5.

It is not realistic to expect the quarterback to go through five reads on any one pass. The 6 pattern creates high/low reads on the outside with the 4-back, Y, and the flat route by the 3-back. These three choices are probably all the quarterback will have time for. A high/low read is also created by the X-receiver's drag route and the six-yard checkdown by the 2-back. On any 6 pattern, the quarterback may elect to work that high/low read on a linebacker rather than the outside progression. This particular read results in short throws and a high completion percentage.

The 8 pattern (Figure 11-46) may be thrown from the I formation with or without motion by Y, or from a pistol alignment with zac motion by the 4-back. Figure 11-46 shows 688. This pattern is effective against any secondary coverage because of the read routes for Y, X, and the 4-back. When doubt arises as to what pattern to call, the 8 pattern is used. The X-receiver and the 4-back drive downfield for 12 yards. They plant their outside foot and break for the near goal post. Versus a single high safety, they take two steps toward the post, plant the outside foot, and run a comeback curl cut.

Against two high safeties or man-to-man, they take three steps toward the post, plant the inside foot, and break toward the corner. Y's read route has him run an eight-yard deep hook over the center against a single high safety. Versus two high safeties or man, Y will run a go route directly between them.

Read progression for the quarterback is Y as the #1 choice. The 4-back is his second choice, and the five-yard flat cut by the 3-back is his third choice. The 2-back's six-yard hook-out route is the checkdown for the quarterback. Against a single safety, the 8 pattern creates a horizontal bracket with four receivers versus three defenders. Versus two safeties, a vertical bracket is created by the three deep routes.

Figure 11-47 shows 689. This pattern is run from I with flip motion by Y or from the pistol with or without zac motion by the 4-back. The 9 pattern is a middle read concept. A 12-yard post cut is run by the 4-back. He is the #1 choice for the quarterback. When the strong safety reacts up or freezes on the fake of 24, the post route is thrown. The X-receiver breaks to the near post at 12 yards of depth. He plants his outside foot and takes two steps toward the post before planting the outside foot and coming flat inside on a dig route.

The X-receiver looks for a void in the coverage quickside where he can settle. His route is the quarterback's second choice. Y runs a shallow drag cut to the quickside, getting no more than six yards deep. He looks for a hole in zone coverage quickside into which he can set down. Y becomes the quarterback's third choice. The 2-back runs the six-yard hook out as a checkdown for the quarterback. Versus man coverage Y and X continue their routes across the field.

CHAPTER 12

Specials

Specials are offensive plays or formations that are not part of the normal offense. Specials are sometimes referred to as trick plays. The goal is to prepare to run a different one of these plays each game. A coach does not want to spend a lot of practice time developing any one of these plays or formations, but they have a place in the offense as change-ups or potential big plays. Use of special plays forces the defense to prepare for those they have seen in previous games.

Theories differ about when to call special plays during a game. Some coaches believe that specials should be run early in a game before an opponent runs theirs. Others believe special plays should be saved to be run in crucial game situations and to change momentum.

Figure 12-1 shows 867 ladder. A doubles formation is used. The basic pass pattern is a 7 pattern, and 60 pass protection is utilized. The X-receiver runs a comeback curl against all coverages. He breaks to the post at 12 yards of depth and takes two steps toward the post. His outside foot is planted, and he comes back inside on the curl route. The Y-receiver runs a post cut, and the 4-back drags quickside to a depth of 12 to 15 yards before setting in a void in the coverage on the quickside. The 2-back runs a three-yard deep arrow to the quickside flat. He turns upfield on a wheel route once he is outside the X-receiver. A five-step drop is taken by the quarterback. He throws to X on the curl. If this choice is covered, the quarterback has the option of throwing to the 4-back. The X-receiver catches the pass and pitches the ball to the 2-back running the wheel. The 2-back is responsible for being in the correct position for the pitch.

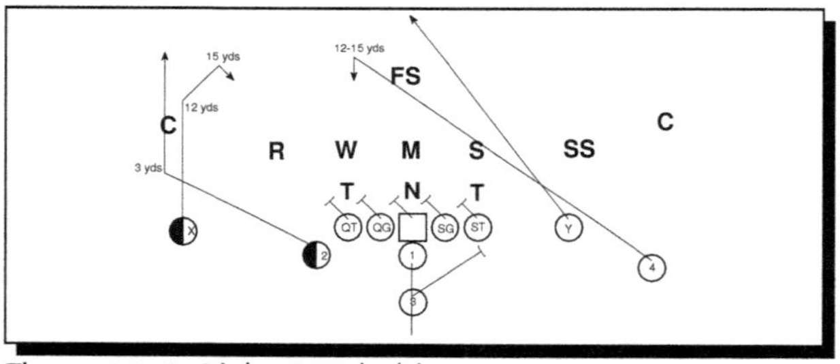

Figure 12-1. Right 867 ladder

Zac 777 ladder is shown in Figure 12-2. The 4-back runs zac motion to the quickside flat at three yards of depth. He then runs the wheel and becomes the pitchman. The

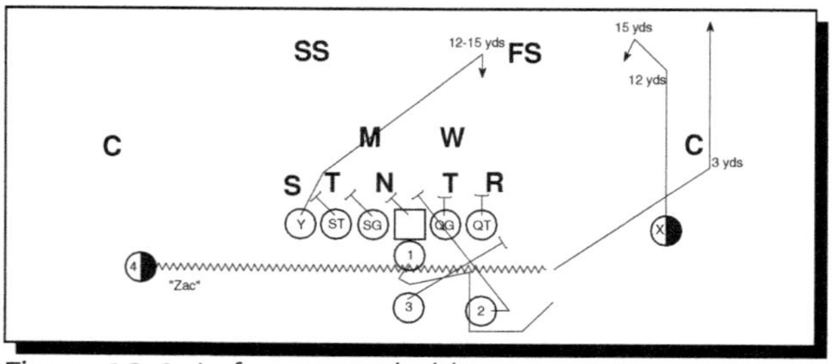

Figure 12-2. Left zac 777 ladder

70 pass protection has the 2-back fake 22. He continues to roll to the quickside and throws to the X-receiver, who pitches to the 4-back after making the catch. X must be careful not to pitch the ball if the pitchman is covered tightly.

The ladder special will often result in a touchdown if run correctly. Timing on the play is crucial for success. One benefit of using the ladder special is that the corner to the quickside may not play the X-receiver curl route as aggressively for fear of the pitch.

Figures 12-3 and 12-4 show the flea flicker special. This play is only run from the I formation, and flip motion for the Y-receiver is used to get him to the strongside. The play designation is 689 flea. The 80 pass protection and action are used. Y motions across the formation and blocks gap, down, or over. He ideally double-teams with the strong tackle on the second defender on the line. Doing so creates a run read for the safety and should cause him to fill, allowing the post route by the 4-back to come open. The quarterback reverses out as on 24 and hands off to the 2-back. He will go to seven yards of depth and turn and wait for the 2-back to toss him the ball. He then tries to hit the post route for a touchdown. If the post route is not open, the quarterback can throw to the X-receiver running a dig cut. The 2-back lead steps strongside and comes straight forward to receive the handoff. He then goes forward to a position two yards from the line of scrimmage and turns and pitches the ball to the quarterback.

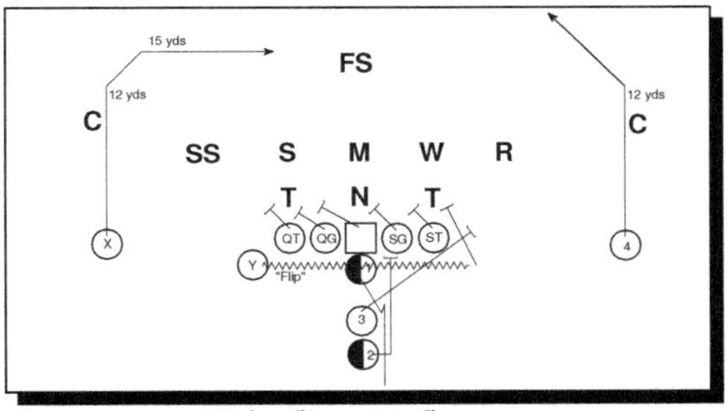

Figure 12-3. Right flip 689 flea

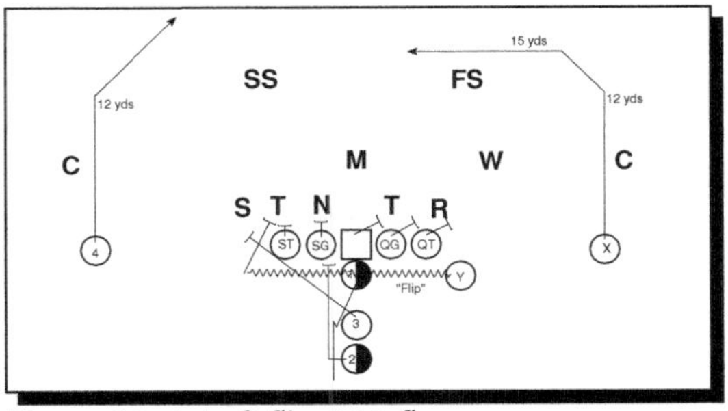

Figure 12-4. Left flip 689 flea

The flea flicker special has a good chance of being successful for a big play. One of the best running plays in the offense is being faked, and the blocking used plus the ball being handed to the 2-back should cause the defense to read run.

The 97 throwback is shown in Figures 12-5 and 12-6. Figures 12-5 and 12-6 show zin 997 throwback. The 4-back is sent in zin motion. He drags across the formation, aiming for a depth of 12 to 15 yards. The X-receiver has a comeback curl route at 14 yards deep. A go route is run by the Y-receiver. His is a clearing route. The 3-back blocks the first defensive man outside the strong tackle's block. He blocks for three counts and releases on a delay route. The route should be no deeper than two yards. The 90 pass protection is covered in Chapter 4. The quarterback opens quickside and sprints to seven yards of depth. He sets up behind the quick tackle and throws back to the strongside. His first choice is the 4-back on the drag route, and the second choice is the delay cut, which will normally be open.

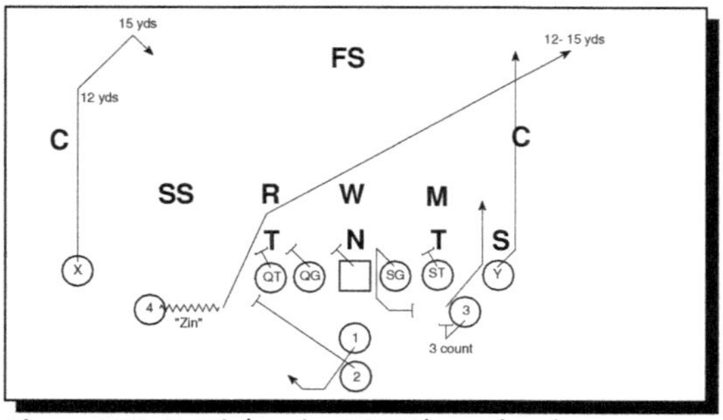

Figure 12-5. Right zin 997 throwback

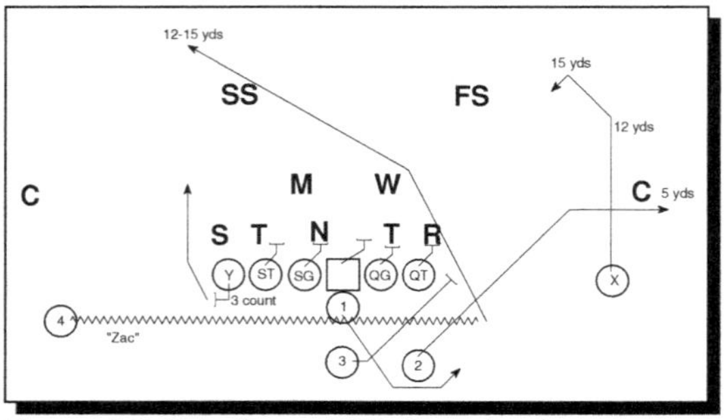

Figure 12-6. Left zac 997 throwback

Figures 12-7 through 12-9 show 13 reverse from various formations. The X-receiver cuts his split from the quick tackle down to six yards. On the snap of the ball, X comes down the line until he is two yards outside the quick tackle. He then veers back, aiming for four yards of depth. The quarterback pitches the ball to the X-receiver. X follows the quick guard to the strongside and turns upfield outside the last block on the line of scrimmage to the strongside.

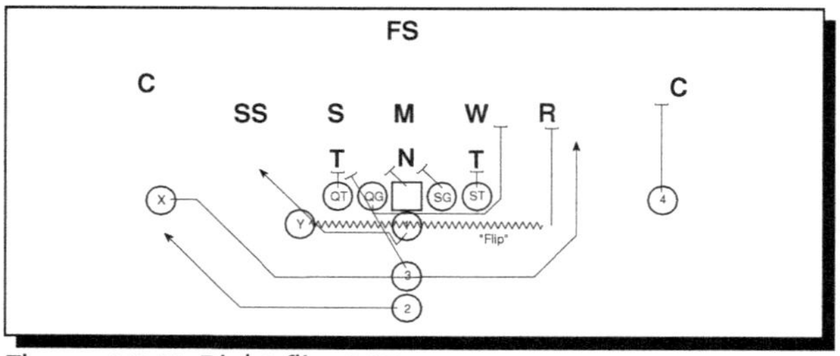

Figure 12-7. Right flip 613 reverse

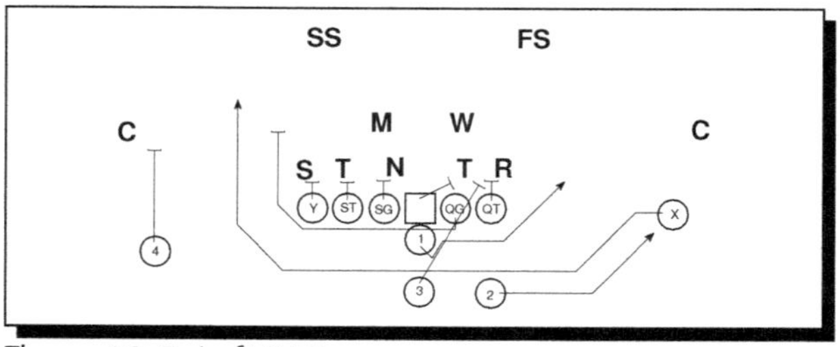

Figure 12-8. Left 713 reverse

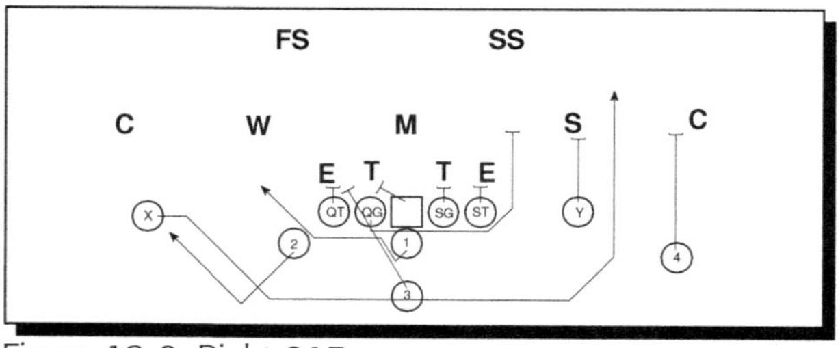

Figure 12-9. Right 813 reverse

The 13 is run by the 3-back. He dives over the outside foot of the quick guard. The 3-back rolls his arms over the ball as the quarterback rides the ball to him. The 3-back blocks any linebacker or other defender he encounters.

The quarterback opens to the quickside as though he is running 13, the inside veer. He reaches the ball back to the 3-back and rides the ball to him as he steps toward the line. After pulling the ball out of the pocket created by the 3-back, the quarterback continues on a path to the quickside. He pitches the football to the X-receiver as their paths cross.

Blocking assignments for 13 reverse are as follows:

- Y-Receiver: Y blocks gap, over, or outside linebacker strongside or the man covering him in doubles.
- Strong Tackle: The strong tackle blocks the #2 defensive player on the line of scrimmage.
- Strong Guard: The #1 defender on the line is blocked by the strong guard.
- Center: The center blocks the first defensive player on the quickside.
- Quick Guard: The quick guard pulls strongside. He turns upfield outside the block of the last offensive lineman on the strongside and blocks the first defender he encounters.
- Quick Tackle: The quick tackle blocks gap, over, or the first defender to the outside.
- 4-Back: The 4-back blocks the defensive man covering him.
- 2-Back: The 2-back runs a pitch path for 13. He must be deeper than the path of the X-receiver.

The 13 reverse pass (Figures 12-10 through 12-12) is a natural extension of 13 reverse. The play is run the same way as 13. The exception is that the 4-back fakes a stalk block on the defender covering him and runs a go route on the numbers. From a doubles alignment, the Y-receiver also fakes a block on the man covering him and runs a seam cut two yards outside the hash mark. These stalk block fakes should be held for at least two counts to allow the reverse to develop. The X-receiver takes the pitch from the quarterback and fakes the reverse before throwing to the 4-back or, in the case of doubles, Y. The success of the play relies on the receiver beating his defender since X will probably not be a great passer. After he pitches the football to X, the quarterback blocks any defender who comes outside the quick tackle's block. The quick guard pulls to the strongside and blocks the first defensive player who shows. He cannot go downfield since this is a forward pass.

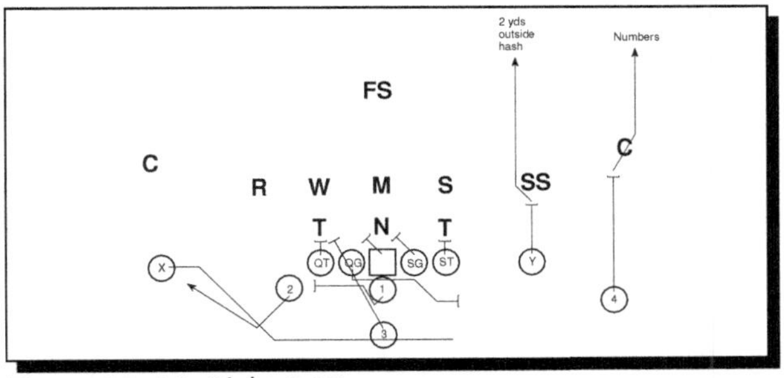

Figure 12-10. Right 813 reverse pass

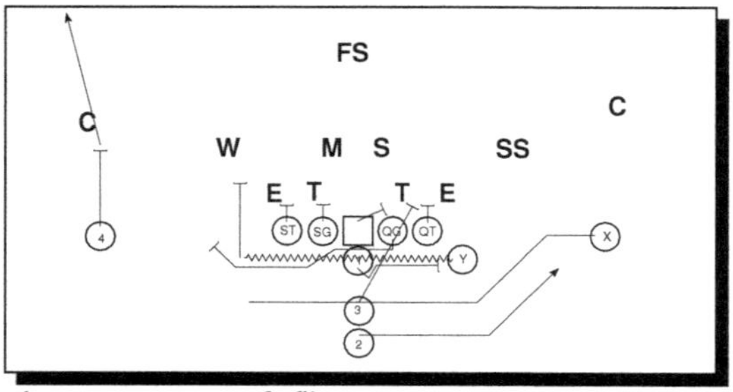

Figure 12-11. Left flip 613 reverse pass

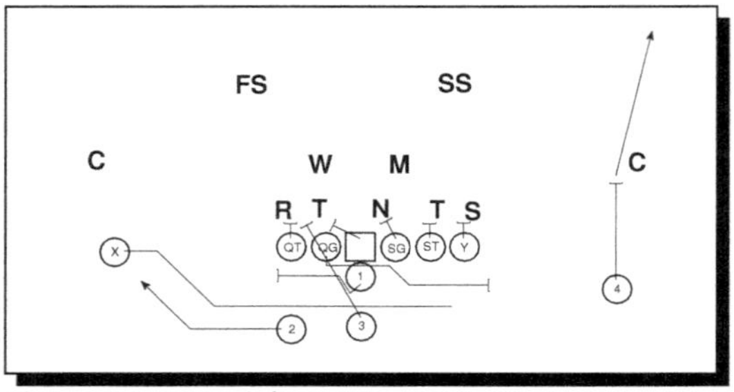

Figure 12-12. Right 713 reverse pass

The 50 boot screen is run off 26 counter trey backfield action. Figures 12-13 through 12-15 show 50 boot screen from three different formations. The 50 pass protection is the basis for the play, which is slide protection toward the strongside of the formation. The 3-back blocks the first defensive player outside the quick tackle's block. The strong guard blocks two counts and releases to block out on the force defender strongside. The center blocks two counts and releases to block the first defensive player in the alley. The quick guard also blocks two counts, releases strongside, and turns back to block the first pursuing linebacker.

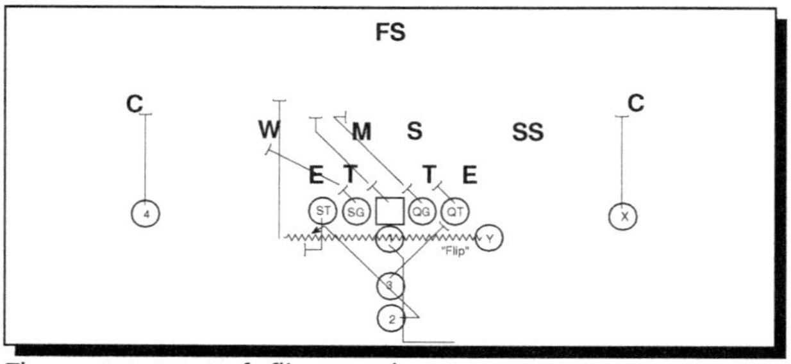

Figure 12-13. Left flip 650 boot screen

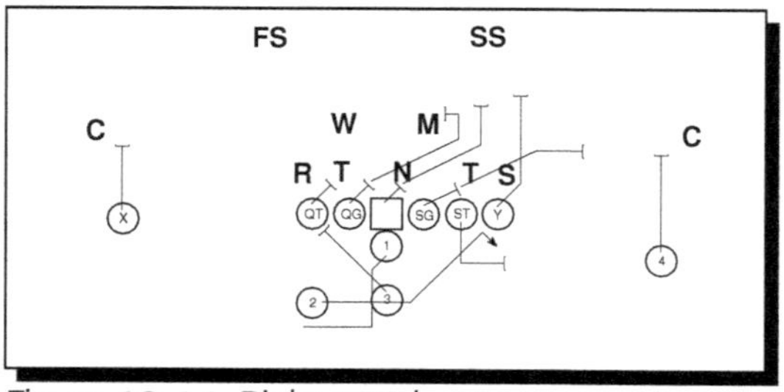

Figure 12-14. Right 750 boot screen

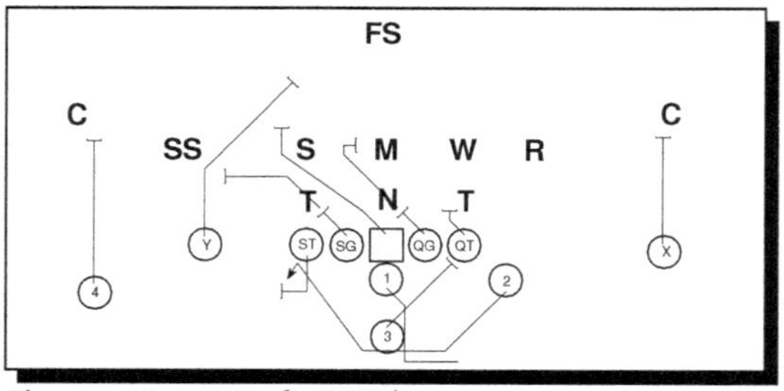

Figure 12-15. Left 850 boot screen

The quarterback opens quickside at a 90-degree angle and comes straight back to fake 26 to the 2-back. He goes straight back two more steps and bootlegs to the quickside for two steps. He pulls up and turns back strongside and throws the screen pass to the 2-back.

The 2-back fakes 26. He continues to run to the 6 hole until he is to the line of scrimmage. He comes back under the strong tackle's block and faces the quarterback. When he catches the pass, the 2-back calls go to his offensive linemen and turns downfield with the ball.

The Y-receiver blocks the safety on the strongside. The 4-back and the X- receiver both block the men who are covering them.

If east passes have been used effectively, the 50 boot screen becomes an excellent play. When the defense reacts to the bootleg action, the boot screen attacks that reaction.

The hitch and waggle play (Figures 12-16 and 12-17) is run from doubles with jet motion or pistol with zac motion. The 50 pass protection, which is slide to the quickside, is the base protection for the hitch and waggle. When doubles is used, the 3-back blocks strongside and attempts to hook the first defender from head-up with the strong tackle to the outside. If a pistol formation is employed, the 2-back makes this block.

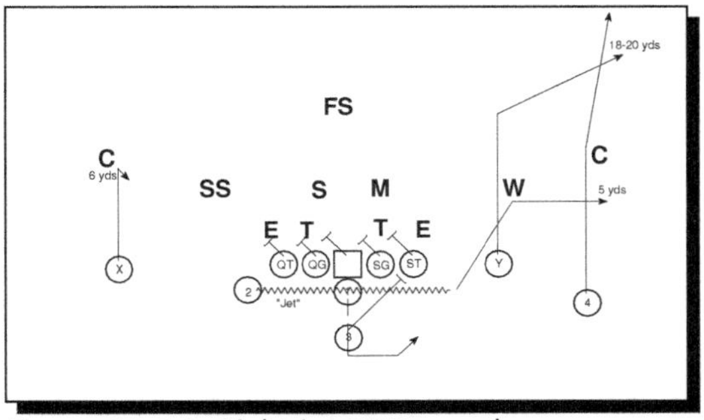

Figure 12-16. Right jet 856 waggle

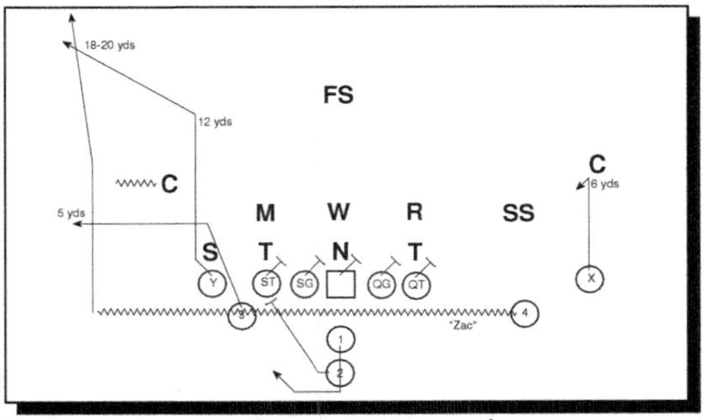

Figure 12-17. Left zac 956 waggle

The X-receiver runs a hitch route and is the #1 receiver in the read progression. The 4-back runs a go route on the strongside numbers. Zac motion is used from the pistol to get the 4-back into position. The Y-receiver has a corner cut. He pushes upfield 12 yards and breaks to the sideline, aiming for 18 to 20 yards of depth. He is the quarterback's #2 choice. If doubles is employed, the 2-back is sent in jet motion across the formation to the strongside. He runs a five-yard flat to the strongside. From the pistol alignment, the 3-back has the five-yard flat cut into the strong flat. The flat route is the quarterback's third choice.

The quarterback takes a three-step drop and looks to throw the hitch to the X-receiver. If X is covered, the quarterback reverses to 90 degrees on the midline. He goes straight back to seven yards of depth and then rolls to the strongside behind either the 3-back's or the 2-back's block. If he waggles strongside, he throws to Y on the corner cut or the five-yard flat cut. The hitch waggle concept is a solid play using the quick game or the flood pattern.

Figures 12-18 through 12-20 show 28 halfback pass. This play is run off of 28, buck sweep action.

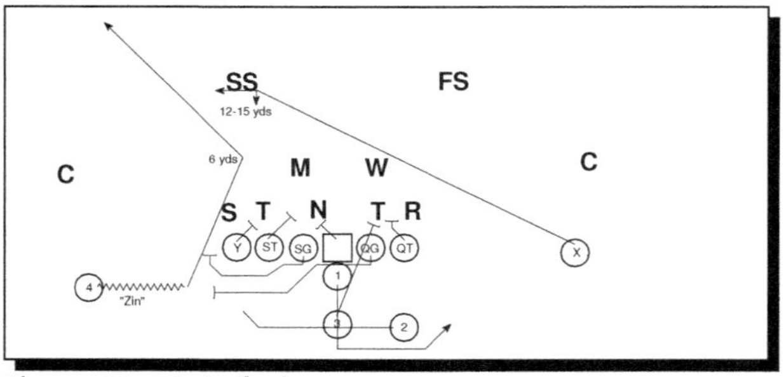

Figure 12-18. Left zin 728 pass

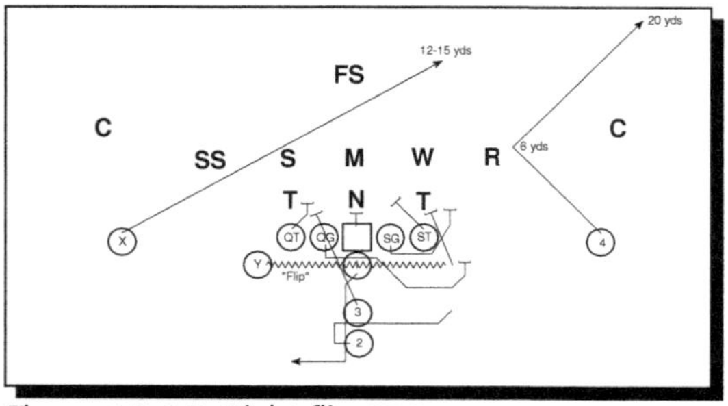

Figure 12-19. Right flip 628 pass

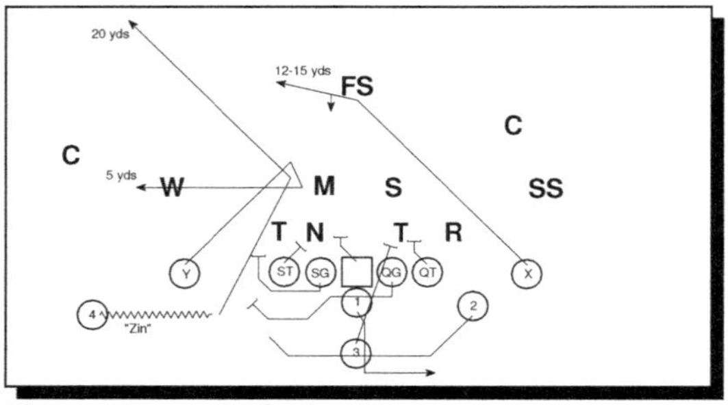

Figure 12-20. Left zin 828 pass

Blocking rules for 28 halfback pass are as follows:

- Y-Receiver: Y blocks gap, down, or over except from doubles. In doubles, he runs a six-yard deep pivot route into the strong flat.
- Strong Tackle: The strong tackle has a blocking rule of gap or down. He comes down on the line to protect for a blitzing linebacker.
- Strong Guard: The strong guard pulls strongside and log blocks the first defender outside the last down block.
- Center: The center blocks strongside A gap or over. If no defensive man is in those positions, he steps to the strong A gap and hinges quickside.
- Quick Guard: The quick guard pulls strongside and attempts to log the first defensive player outside the strong guard's block. He can kick this player out if the defender penetrates upfield.
- Quick Tackle: Gap, over, or outside on the line is the quick tackle's blocking rule.
- 3-Back: The 3-back fakes 30 and blocks any defender in the quickside A gap or over the quick guard. When no defensive man is in those positions, he checks for linebacker blitzes in the A or B gap quickside.

The 4-back comes inside on a 45-degree angle to a depth of six yards. He tries to get inside as far as the Y-receiver's position on the end of the strongside line of scrimmage. From wing or doubles formations, the 4-back is sent in zin motion into a tight wing position. When he reaches the position where Y would have been aligned, the 4-back plants his outside foot and reverse pivots at a 45-degree angle. He then runs a V route, aiming for 20 yards of depth.

The X-receiver has a drag route to the strongside, aiming for 12 to 15 yards, which is the same route he runs for a 6 pattern. Versus man-to-man, he keeps moving, but against a zone coverage he settles in any void in the zone once he reaches the strong tackle's position.

Footwork for the quarterback is the same as for 28. He opens quickside at 90 degrees on the midline. On his third step straight back, he hands off to the 2-back, after which he takes two more steps back on the midline and executes a bootleg toward the quickside.

The 2-back runs 28. After taking the handoff from the quarterback, he tucks the ball away and comes flat strongside faking the buck sweep. He pulls up behind the block of the quick guard and throws to the 4-back running the V cut. If the 2-back is a better-than-average passer, he could be allowed to throw to the X-receiver if the 4-back is covered. The V route should be relatively easy to throw. If the 4-back is covered, the 2-back can call go to his guards and turn upfield, getting whatever yardage he can. The 28 halfback pass is an effective play versus a secondary that is very aggressive in filling for the buck sweep.

A gold call added to the bubble screen plays is shown in Figures 12-21 through 12-23. Figure 12-21 illustrates zac 760 Frank gold. The 4-back goes in zac motion to the quickside as he does for 760 Frank, which is the bubble screen to the 4-back. The X-receiver fakes a stalk block on the man covering him. When the quarterback pump fakes to the 4-back, X converts his route to a fade cut. The quarterback takes a three-step drop and pump fakes the bubble screen to the 4-back. He then throws the fade route to X. The 60 pass protection is used, which is aggressive slide protection toward the quickside. The 3-back and 2-back block strongside. The Y-receiver also gap protects to the quickside unless doubles is used.

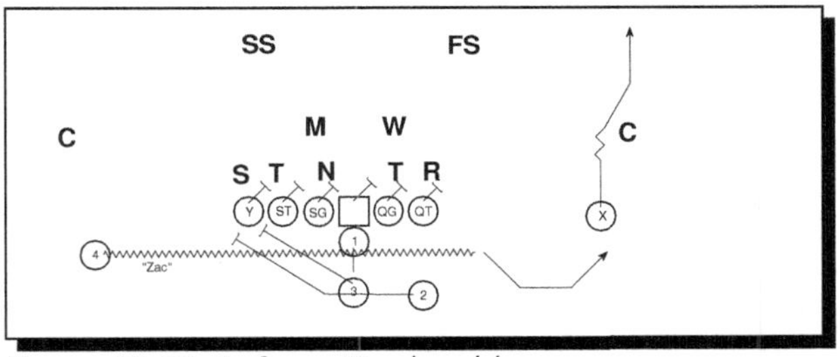

Figure 12-21. Left zac Frank gold

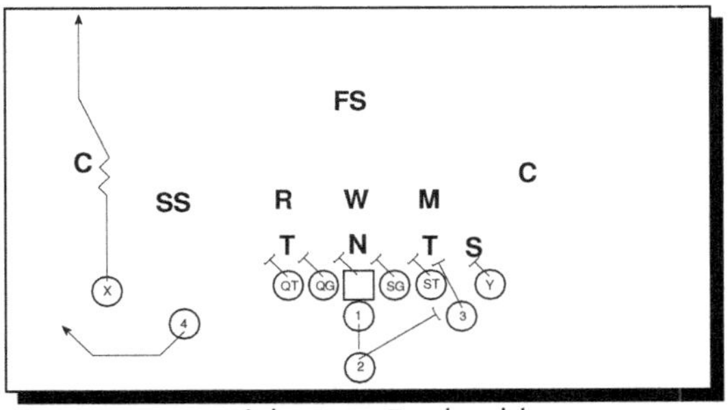

Figure 12-22. Right 960 Fred gold

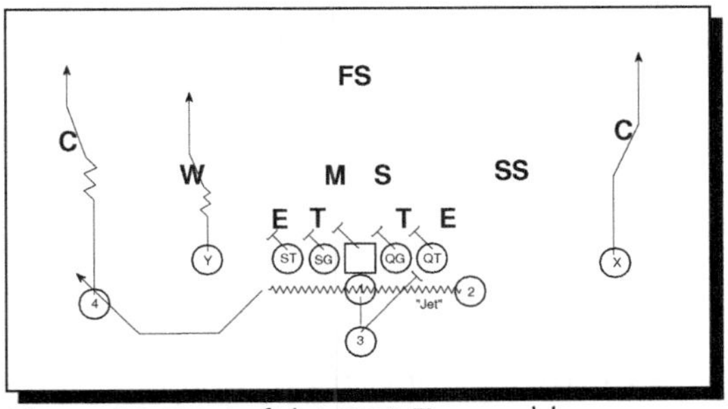

Figure 12-23. Left jet 850 Tom gold

Figure 12-22 is 960 Fred gold. This play is run from a pistol alignment. The quarterback still pump fakes to the 4-back and throws the fade to the X-receiver. Since the pistol has the quarterback at four yards of depth, he does not take any additional drop. It is a catch-and-throw technique for him. The 2-back blocks the first man to show outside the Y-receiver's block. The 3-back and Y both slide protect to the quickside, as does the offensive line.

From doubles formation, 850 Tom gold is used. The 2-back is sent in jet motion to the strongside, and the quarterback fakes the bubble screen to him. The 4-back and Y both fake stalk blocks on the defenders covering them. The 4-back then runs a fade cut, and Y has a seam route two yards outside the hash mark. Read progression for the quarterback has him working inside out from the seam to the fade route. The 50 pass protection is used for this play, which is slide protection toward the strongside of the formation. The 3-back blocks the first defensive player outside the quick tackle's block. The X-receiver runs a fade cut on the quickside.

If the bubble screen passes have been effective, the gold tag can result in a big play, which will often be a touchdown. If the intended receiver is covered, the quarterback is instructed to throw the ball away.

The next special is not a specific play. X-ray is motion across the formation to the strongside by the X-receiver or split end. This motion is only run from the wing formation. The 4-back must be aligned on the line of scrimmage to the strongside. Y becomes an ineligible receiver. X is two yards off the line of scrimmage on the quickside of the formation. When the quarterback raises his heel, X starts his motion across the formation. When he passes the quarterback, X turns his shoulder parallel to the line and shuffles to a position as a tight wingback one yard outside the tight end. An unbalanced alignment has been created.

Plays run to the strongside from this set include the following:

- 30: 3-back trap
- 28: buck sweep
- 36: belly down
- 38: outside veer
- 14: inside veer
- 26: counter trey
- North 724: counter bootleg pass
- 783: fade pass from a fake of 14

To the quickside of the formation, the following plays are used:

- 35: 3-back belly
- 15: belly option
- 13: inside veer
- 11: midline option
- 22: tackle trap counter

Figures 12-24 through 12-27 show examples of plays that can be run from x-ray motion. Because of the unbalanced formation created, the defense is required to make some type of adjustment.

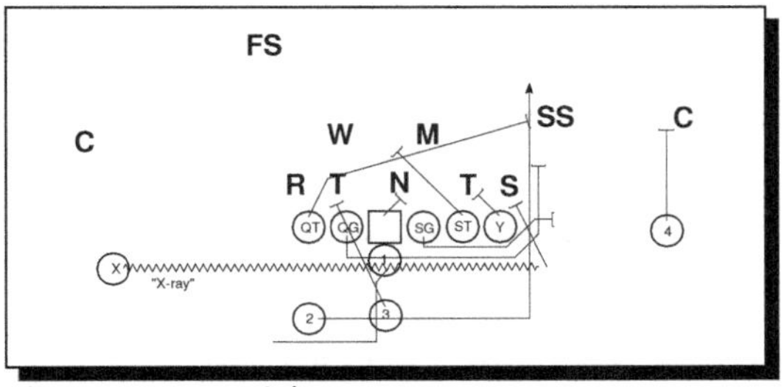

Figure 12-24. Right x-ray 728

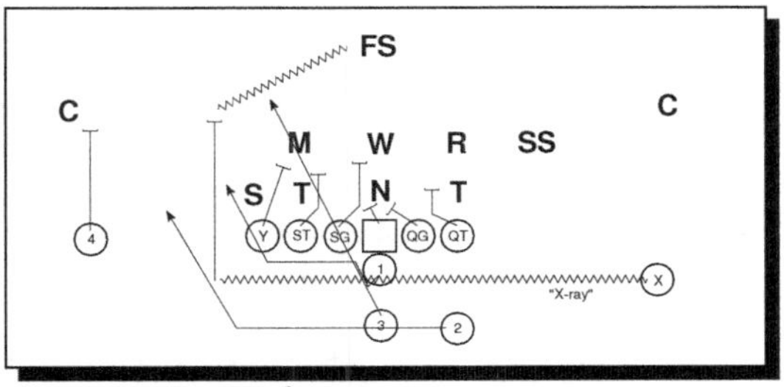

Figure 12-25. Left x-ray 714

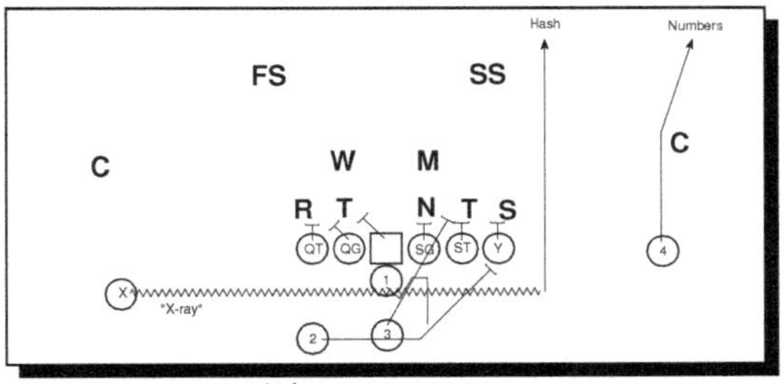

Figure 12-26. Right x-ray 783

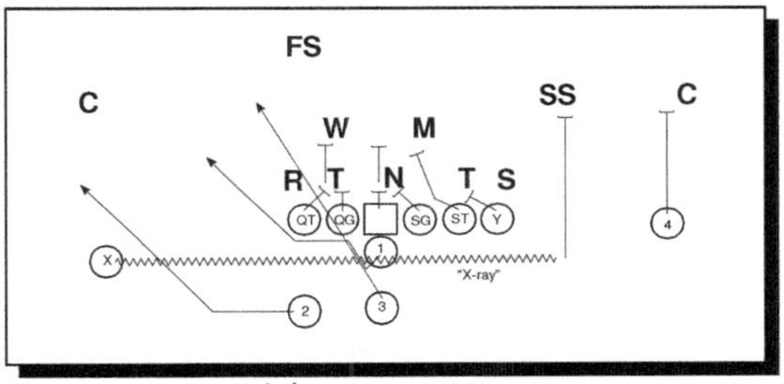

Figure 12-27. Right x-ray 713

Sally Rand (Figures 12-28 through 12-31) is only run from pistol alignment. This play is a form of read option. The quarterback takes the snap and steps back as he opens at 90 degrees to the quickside. Versus an odd defense, he reads the outside linebacker to the quickside. When the defense is an even or gap front, he reads the end man on the line of scrimmage. The quarterback extends the ball back to the 2-back and rides him one step as he reads. If the read man closes, the quarterback pulls the ball and runs the ball to the quickside. If the read man does not close, the quarterback gives the ball to the 2-back and fakes the keep.

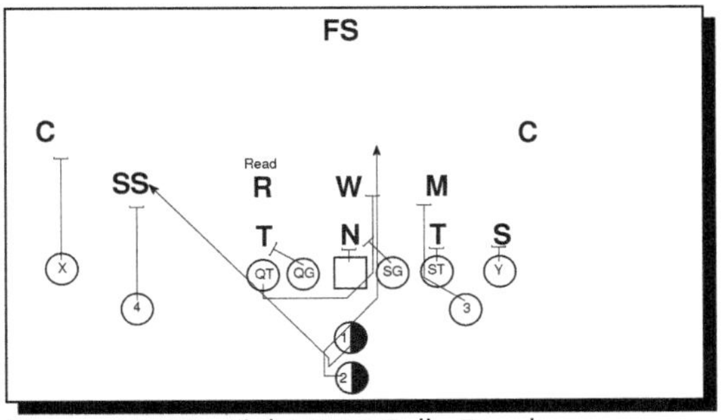

Figure 12-28. Right 900 Sally Rand

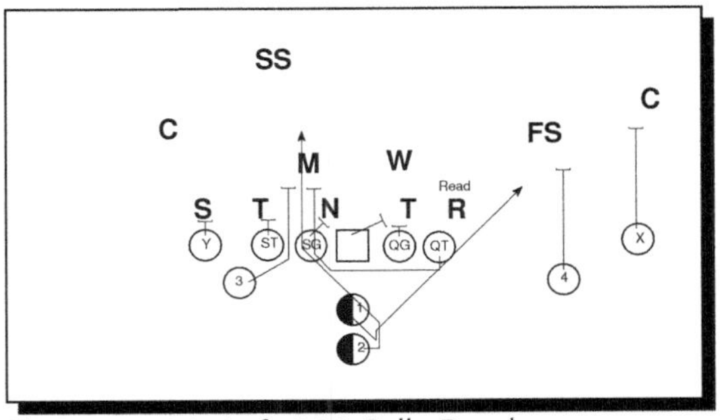

Figure 12-29. Left 900 Sally Rand

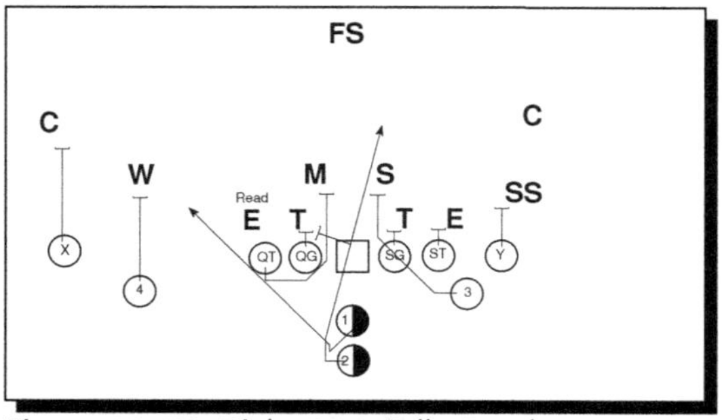

Figure 12-30. Right 900 Sally Rand

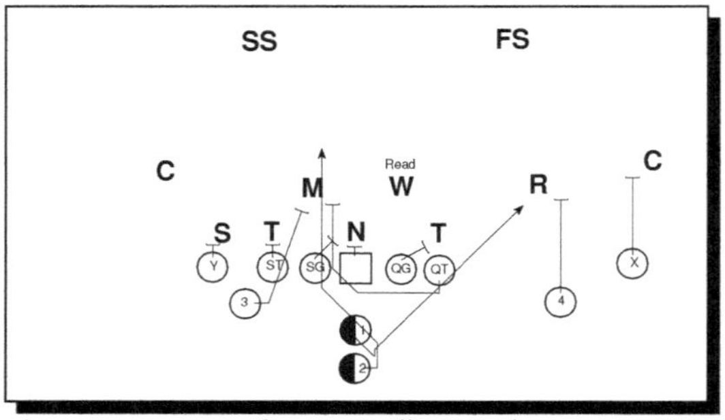

Figure 12-31. Left 900 Sally Rand

The 2-back lead steps quickside and takes two steps straight forward as the quarterback rides the ball to him. He reads the block on the first defensive lineman to the strongside and hits the hole as quickly as possible.

Blocking rules for Sally Rand are as follows:

- Y-Receiver: Y blocks the #3 man on the line strongside or the outside linebacker.
- Strong Tackle: The #2 man on the line of scrimmage is blocked by the strong tackle.
- Strong Guard: The strong guard blocks #1 on the line of scrimmage strongside.
- Center: The center blocks over or the #1 defender to the quickside.
- Quick Guard: A gap, over, or outside is the quick guard's blocking rule.
- Quick Tackle: The quick tackle pulls strongside and leads through the hole. He blocks the middle linebacker or the inside linebacker quickside to the strongside.
- 3-Back: The 3-back reads the block by the strong tackle and blocks the inside linebacker or the outside linebacker strongside.
- 4-Back and X-Receiver: The X-receiver and 4-back block the defenders who are covering them.

CHAPTER 13

Blocking Rules Summary

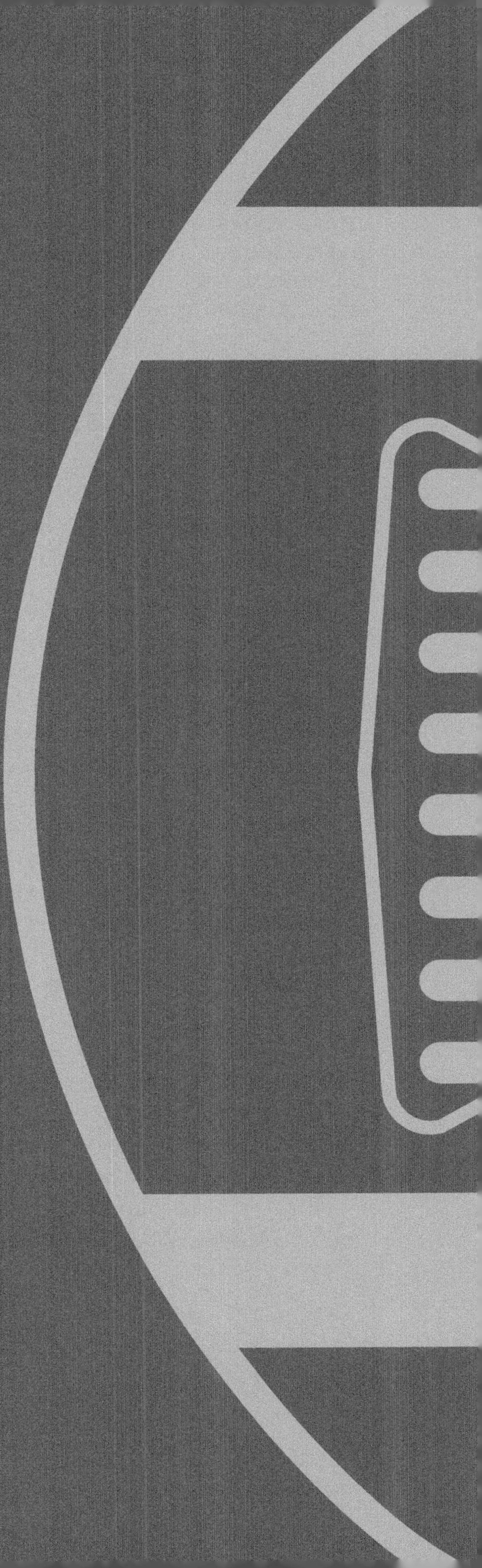

Chapter 13 provides a summary of the blocking rules for each offensive position in the no-huddle multiple offense. This offense is a rule-blocking system. It is essential that all players memorize the rules for their positions. The easiest way to accomplish this goal is to provide each player with a one-page summary of the blocking rules for his position to be memorized. Players should be required to write the rules for each play weekly as a test. When games are played on Saturday, this test should be given on Friday prior to practice. The coach must grade each test and return it to the player on game day. Weekly test scores should be recorded by the coach so that he has a record of the player's progressive understanding of his assignments. Failure to learn his blocking assignments should affect a player's playing time.

Knowing what to do is one step in a player's ability to perform. The second step is to know how to perform the techniques needed to be successful. This step is accomplished through actual drill and practice of proper techniques. The third step is to put the first two steps together to run the individual plays correctly in a competitive environment.

The following terms used in constructing blocking rules are defined as follows:

- *Gap:* The gap refers to the player's gap to his inside.
- *A Gap:* For the center, A gap quickside is the gap between the center and the quick guard. A gap strongside is the gap between the center and the strong guard.
- *B Gap:* B gap is the gap between the guard and the tackle.
- *C Gap:* C gap is the gap between Y and the tackle.
- *D Gap:* D gap is the gap to the outside of Y.
- *Down:* A down call has the offensive lineman blocking a defender aligned over the offensive lineman to his inside.
- *Over:* A defender is considered to be over if he is aligned on the line of scrimmage with any part of his body over the offensive lineman.
- *Middle Linebacker:* A middle linebacker is a single linebacker aligned over the center.
- *Inside Linebacker:* The first linebacker aligned from the inside of the offensive formation to the outside is designated as the inside linebacker.
- *Outside Linebacker:* The first linebacker from the outside of the formation to the inside is the outside linebacker.
- *Odd Defense:* Any defense with a man aligned on the line of scrimmage over the center is designated as an odd defense.
- *Gap Defense:* If a defender is aligned in the guard's A gap, this defense is designated as a gap defense.
- *Even Defense*: When a defender is aligned over the guard, the defense is called an *even defense*.

Figure 13-1 shows the way in which defensive techniques are numbered for the no-huddle multiple offense. Figure 13-2 is the gap lettering for the offense.

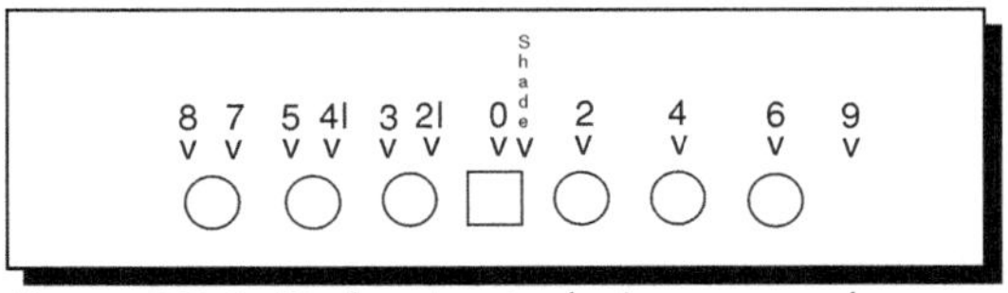

Figure 13-1. Defensive techniques numbers

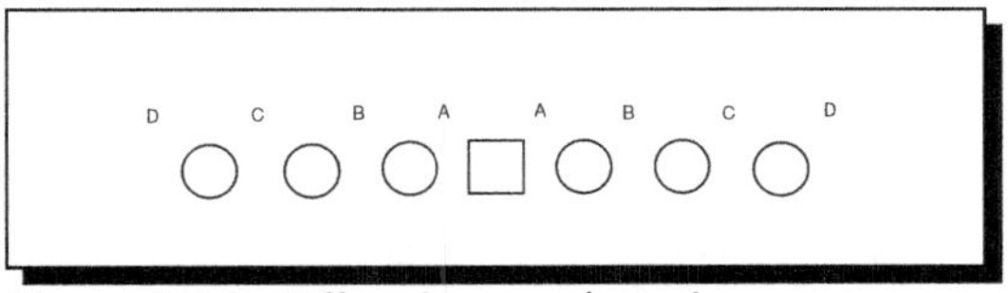

Figure 13-2. Offensive gap lettering

Blocking Rules by Position

Y-Receiver

Run

- *14, 13, 30, 31:* Safety or outside linebacker.
- *29, 33:* Zone quickside; if split out, man covering.
- *38, 39:* Zone 7 or 8 technique; combo 5 technique with tackle, over, outside linebacker.
- *36, 28, 09, 25, 19, 27, 26, 24:* Gap, down, first linebacker inside.
- *11:* I formation, lead blocks for quarterback.
- *11, 49, 15:* Middle or strong safety.
- *17, 34:* Goes crossfield to six yards depth; kicks out first defender encountered.
- *47:* Gap, over, or outside.
- *16:* #1 defender from outside; zac motion, blocks #2 defender from outside.
- *35:* First linebacker from head-up to inside.
- *22:* Outside linebacker, strong safety; from I formation, pulls through 2 hole, seals first linebacker to show strongside.
- *46:* Pulls strongside through hole behind kick-out block by quick guard; seals first defender inside.
- *18:* Zone strongside.

Pass

- *Stay call or any strong formation pass:* Gap, over, outside.
- *80 Denver:* #3 on line of scrimmage; no #3, blocks outside linebacker, safety.
- *80, 90, 50, 60, 70, east, west, north, south:* Pass receiver.

Strong Tackle

Run

- *36, 16, 26, 06, 46, 34, 24:* Gap, down, first linebacker inside.
- *28:* Gap, down, first linebacker inside; from pistol with gap call, pulls strong and kicks out first defender outside last down block.
- *14:* Gap, inside linebacker, outside linebacker.

- *38, 39, 18:* Zone strongside.
- *13, 49, 15, 33, 25, 29:* Zone strongside.
- *11, 17, 47, 27:* Gap, over, outside.
- *16:* Gap down, middle linebacker, inside linebacker quickside.
- *30, 30 gut:* Outside linebacker, inside linebacker.
- *30 base:* Over.
- *22:* First linebacker inside.
- *31:* B gap, first linebacker inside.
- *19:* Gap; goes crossfield at six yards depth, kicks out first defender encountered.
- *35:* Even or gap; *gap:* over, near linebacker; odd: folds with strong guard on inside linebacker.

Pass

- *80, 80 Denver, 70, west, western, north, south:* #2 on line of scrimmage.
- *90:* B gap, over, hinge strongside.
- *60:* B gap.
- *50:* C gap.
- *East, eastern:* Gap, over, outside.

Strong Guard

Run

- *13, 39, 49, 15, 33, 25, 29:* Zone quickside.
- *38, 14:* Zone strongside.
- *24, 16, 26:* Gap, down, middle linebacker, inside linebacker quickside.
- *I 22, 36, 30 gut:* Pulls strongside, traps first man encountered.
- *28:* Pulls strongside, kicks out or log first man outside last down block. From pistol gap call, blocks A gap.
- *17, 47, 19:* Pulls quickside through 7 hole; seals inside linebacker or outside linebacker.
- *31, 09, 27:* Pulls quickside; traps first defender past last down block.
- *11:* Odd: zone quickside; even or *gap:* folds with center on inside linebacker strongside.
- *30 base:* Inside linebacker.
- *35:* Odd: blocks out; even or *gap:* folds with center on middle linebacker, inside linebacker strongside.
- *18:* Pulls strongside, turns upfield outside strong tackle's block, and seals first man inside.
- *22:* Odd: combos with center on nose, middle linebacker, inside linebacker quickside; even or *gap:* middle linebacker, inside linebacker quickside.
- *30 trap:* Odd: combos with center on nose, middle linebacker, inside linebacker quickside; even or *gap:* middle linebacker, inside linebacker quickside.

Pass

- *West, north, south, 80, 70, western:* #1 on line of scrimmage.
- *80 Denver:* #1 on line of scrimmage for two counts, releases quickside, turns back, and blocks first defender who shows.
- *90:* A gap, over, hinge strongside.
- *60:* A gap.
- *50:* B gap.
- *East, eastern:* Pulls quickside; blocks first defender who shows.

Center

Run

- *14, 38, 36, 18:* Zone strongside.
- *13, 39, 49, 15,33:* Zone quickside.
- *17, 16, 47, 27:* #1 defender strongside.
- *26, 46, 34, 24:* #1 defender quickside.
- *09, 19:* Over, #1 defender strongside.
- *28:* A gap strongside, over, middle linebacker, inside linebacker quickside; from pistol: over #1 defender quickside.
- *35: Odd: over; even or gap:* #1 defender strongside.
- *22, 30 trap, 30 gut: Odd:* combos with strong guard on nose, middle linebacker, inside linebacker quickside; even or *gap:* #1 defender quickside.
- *31: Odd:* combos with quick guard on nose, middle linebacker, inside linebacker strongside; even or *gap:* #1 defender strongside.
- *11: Odd:* zone blocks quickside; even or *gap:* #1 defender strongside.
- *30 base:* Over.
- *25:* A gap quickside, over, middle linebacker, inside linebacker strongside
- *29:* Covered or *Zorro call:* zone blocks quickside; *uncovered:* pulls quickside and seals inside.

Pass

- *80, 60:* A gap quickside.
- *80 Denver:* A gap quickside, two counts, releases quickside and blocks in the alley.
- *90:* A gap quickside, over, hinge strongside.
- *50:* A gap strongside.
- *East, eastern:* #1 defender strongside.
- *70, west, western, north, south:* #1 defender quickside.

Quick Guard

Run

- *14, 38, 36, 18:* Zone strongside.
- *17, 47, 27:* Gap, down, middle linebacker, inside linebacker strongside.
- *13, 39:* Zone quickside.
- *34, 16, 24:* Pulls strongside through 4 hole; blocks inside linebacker, outside linebacker.
- *30 trap, 26, 46:* Pulls strongside; traps first defender outside last down block.
- *49:* Pulls quickside, seals first defender inside.
- *11G, 25:* Pulls quickside; traps first defender outside last down block.
- *15, 09:* Pulls quickside; logs first defender past quick tackle's block.
- *19:* Pulls quickside; kicks out first defender past last down block.
- *33:* B gap, over, A gap, inside linebacker quickside.
- *29:* Covered or Zorro call: zone quickside; uncovered: pulls quickside and seals first linebacker inside.
- *28:* Pulls strongside. If lead blocker kicks out, seals first defender inside; if lead blocker logs, kicks out first defender outside log block.
- *35: Gap:* A gap; odd or even: pulls quickside and traps first defender outside quick tackle's block.
- *11:* Odd: inside linebacker; even or *gap:* middle linebacker, inside linebacker strongside.
- *30 gut:* Folds with center on middle linebacker, inside linebacker quickside.
- *30 base:* Inside linebacker quickside.
- *22: Odd:* blocks out; even or *gap:* B gap, over, A gap.
- *31: Odd:* combos with center on nose to middle linebacker, inside linebacker strongside; even: middle linebacker, inside linebacker strongside; *gap:* block A gap.

Pass

- *80, 60:* B gap.
- *80 Denver:* B gap two counts, releases quickside, kicks out corner.
- *90:* B gap, over.
- *50:* A gap.
- *East, eastern:* #1 defender on line of scrimmage.
- *70, west, western, north, south:* Pulls strongside and blocks first defender encountered.

Quick Tackle

Run

- *14, 38, 36, 33, 18:* Zone strongside.
- *16, 46, 34, 24:* Gap, over, outside.

- *17, 47, 27:* Gap, down, inside linebacker.
- *39, 49:* Zone quickside.
- *29:* Zone quickside; if uncovered, pulls quickside and seals first linebacker inside.
- *26:* Pulls strongside; turns up in 6 hole and seals first linebacker inside.
- *13:* Gap, inside linebacker, outside linebacker.
- *19:* Gap, down, first linebacker inside. Gap call pulls quickside and kicks out first defender past last down block.
- *11:* Blocks out.
- *11G, 30 trap:* First linebacker inside.
- *09:* #2 on line of scrimmage.
- *25:* Gap, over, down.
- *30 base:* Over.
- *31:* Inside linebacker, outside linebacker.
- *22:* Pulls strongside, traps first defender past the center.
- *28:* Gap, crossfield six yards deep; kicks out first defender encountered.
- *35, 15:* Odd: over; even or *gap:* down.

Pass

- *80, 80 Denver, 60:* C gap.
- *90:* Over, outside.
- *50:* B gap.
- *East, eastern:* #2 on the line of scrimmage.
- *70, west, western, south, north:* Gap, over, outside.

4-Back

Run

- *18, 29, 14, 13, 38, 39, 11, 17, 16, 27:* Defensive player covering 4-back.
- *36, 30, 09, 24:* Strong safety.
- *26:* Near safety. From pistol, runs bubble screen.
- *28:* Zin motion or zac from pistol; blocks first defender inside on or off the line of scrimmage.
- *47, 49, 46:* Carries ball.
- *35, 15, 31, 33, 34:* Near safety.
- *25:* Seals first linebacker inside.
- *19:* First defender inside on or off the line of scrimmage.
- *22:* Zac motion: blocks first defender encountered; no zac motion: blocks strong safety.

Pass

- *80 Denver:* Crack blocks second level.
- *East, eastern, west, western, north, south:* Pass receiver.

X-Receiver

Run

- *14, 13, 38, 39, 36, 17, 16, 28, 30, 15, 35, 26, 09, 49, 31, 33, 25, 19, 46, 34, 24, 18, 29:* Block man covering X-receiver.
- *11, 47, 22, 27:* Quickside or middle safety.

Pass

- *80 Denver:* Cracks near safety.
- X-receiver runs a pass route on all other pass plays.

3-Back

Run

- *13, 14, 36, 38, 39, 11, 31, 30 trap, 30 gut, 30 base, 33, 34, 35:* Carries ball.
- *24:* Kicks out first defender strongside outside last down block.
- *47, 46:* Kicks out first defender quickside outside quick tackle's block.
- *22, 26:* Fills B gap quickside.
- *28, 18:* Fills A gap quickside.
- *Pistol 28:* Blocks first man inside on or off the line of scrimmage.
- *29:* Blocks first unblocked defender quickside.
- *19, 09:* Goes through quickside B gap; seals first linebacker inside.
- *25:* Fills for quick guard.
- *17:* Shovels pitchman.
- *16:* #2 defender from outside; in zac motion, #3 defender from outside.
- *15, 49:* Fakes 35, blocks inside linebacker.
- *27:* Leads through 7 hole, blocks inside linebacker, outside linebacker.

Pass

- *90:* Strong or I: five-yard flat route quickside; pistol: steps quickside and hinges strongside and blocks first defender who appears; wing or doubles: blocks first defensive man quickside after last reach block on the line of scrimmage.
- *60, eastern:* Blocks first defender outside strong tackle's block; pistol: runs pass route.
- *50:* Blocks first defender outside quick tackle's block; pistol: runs pass route.

- *80:* Wing or doubles: fakes 14 and blocks blitzing linebacker in B gap; if no blitz, runs six-yard hook out. I or pistol: blocks first defender outside strong tackle's block; if no defender appears, runs a five-yard route strongside.
- *East:* Releases through B gap quickside. Blocks blitzing linebacker; if no blitz, runs five-yard flat route quickside.
- *West:* Blocks first defender outside quick tackle's block. Pistol: blocks gap, over, outside two counts and runs five-yard flat route strongside.
- *South:* Fakes 31 and runs five-yard flat route strongside.
- *North, 70:* Blocks first defender outside quick tackle's block.
- *80 Denver:* Double reads inside linebacker to outside linebacker strongside.
- *Western:* Fakes 30, blocks blitzing linebacker; no blitz, runs five-yard flat strongside.

2-Back

Run

- *18, 28, 26, 24, 22, 25, 27, 29, 19:* Carries ball.
- *14, 38, 36:* Pitchman on option strongside.
- *13, 39, 17, I 11, 15, I 35:* Pitchman option quickside.
- *47, 46:* Takes handoff from quarterback with little fingers together and hands off inside to 4-back.
- *33:* Fakes 25.
- *Strong 14, 16:* Dive man over strong guard; quarterback gives or keeps.
- *11:* Wing or doubles: lead blocks on inside or outside linebacker quickside.
- *30 trap, 30 gut, 30 base:* Fakes 28.
- *09:* Fakes 26; blocks first defender who shows strongside.
- *49:* Zone blocks quickside on first defender outside quick tackle's block.
- *35:* Wing or doubles: reads block on first defender from head-up on quick guard to his outside. Blocks first linebacker from head-up to inside.
- *31:* Blocks first man from head-up to inside.
- *Strong 30:* Strong formation, fakes 19.
- *34:* Kicks out first defender outside the strong tackle's block.

Pass

- *90:* I, strong, or pistol: blocks first defensive man quickside after last reach block on line of scrimmage; wing or doubles: pass route.
- *60: I:* blocks first defender outside 3-back's block strongside; if no one shows, runs five-yard flat route. Pistol: blocks first defender outside strong tackle's block; wing or doubles: runs pass route.

- *50: I:* blocks first defender outside 3-back's block quickside; if no one shows, runs five-yard flat route quickside. Pistol: blocks first defender outside quick tackle's block; wing or doubles: runs pass route.
- *80: I or pistol:* fakes 24 and blocks any blitz in A or B gaps; if no blitz, runs six-yard hook out route. Wing or doubles: blocks first defender outside strong tackle's block.
- *East:* Fakes 26; blocks first defender outside strong tackle's block.
- *Eastern:* Fills for strong guard and blocks blitzing linebacker in A or B gaps; if no blitz, runs five-yard flat route quickside.
- *Western:* Fakes 25; blocks first defender who shows quickside.
- *West, South:* Fakes 29; blocks first defender outside quickside.
- *North, 70:* Fakes 22; blocks blitzing linebacker over center. If no blitz, runs five-yard flat route strongside.
- *80 Denver:* Steps up quickside and simulate a pass block. When quick guard releases, goes behind quick tackle's pass block and curls back to offensive side of the line of scrimmage. Calls "Go" after catching the screen pass.

Principles of Run Blocking

Three phases: A. Approach; B. Contact; C. Follow-through

- Stance
  - ✓ Feet shoulder-width.
  - ✓ Foot stagger toe to instep.
  - ✓ Z in knees and ankles.
  - ✓ Flat back.
  - ✓ Down hand inside back knee, weight on fingers. [Raise hand without losing balance.]
  - ✓ Off arm rests across thigh.
  - ✓ Bull neck to see target.
- Eyes on aiming point
  - ✓ You must see what you are hitting.
  - ✓ Eyes take you to the target.
  - ✓ Don't close the eyes.
  - ✓ Don't turn the head.
  - ✓ Look the block in.
- Targets are exact
  - ✓ Head-up: playside number.
  - ✓ Tight reach: playside number
  - ✓ Wide reach: playside armpit
  - ✓ Combo or double-team: near number.
  - ✓ Down block: near hip; put head across front.

- Steps
  - ✓ Stay square; keep feet under and maintain balance.
  - ✓ First step four inches long is position step, based on alignment of defender.
    - ⇨ Must be made before defender moves.
    - ⇨ Never cross over on first step.
  - ✓ Second step is power step through defender's crotch.
    - ⇨ Backside knee through crotch.
    - ⇨ Backside pad through target.
- Initial blow
  - ✓ Initial blow is with shoulder pad under defender's pad; then transfer to hands.
  - ✓ Must be lower than opponent.
  - ✓ Keep elbows in.
  - ✓ Hands inside under defender's pad; thumbs up.
- Vertical leverage decides the outcome.
  - ✓ Point of contact is shoulder pad under defender's breastplate.
  - ✓ Must be lower than defender.
  - ✓ Allows use of levers: legs, hips, knees, back.
  - ✓ Most explosive position is knee under hips.
- Arch back on contact
  - ✓ Helps power to get defender moving.
- Backside knee
  - ✓ Run feet; keep knees under the pads.
  - ✓ Don't allow feet to cross.
  - ✓ Bring backside knee through crotch.
  - ✓ Hit same pad and same pad.
    - ⇨ Right knee: right pad.
    - ⇨ Left knee: left pad.
- Finish block
  - ✓ Extend arms.
- Trap block
  - ✓ First step at 45-degree angle.
  - ✓ Throw elbow on side pulling toward.
  - ✓ Pull right: trap with right shoulder.
  - ✓ Pull left: trap with left shoulder.
  - ✓ Get up in the hole and dig defender out of the hole.
  - ✓ Aiming point is near hip of defender.
  - ✓ Head behind defender.

- Sweep pulls
  - ✓ Lead blocker
    - ⇨ First two steps at 45-degree angle for depth around down blocks.
    - ⇨ Kick out like a trap.
    - ⇨ If defender closes really hard, log him.
  - ✓ Trail blocker
    - ⇨ Stay flat until you clear center.
    - ⇨ Get depth to get around down blocks.
    - ⇨ Look inside, then outside.
    - ⇨ Cut defender when possible.
- Double-team or combo block
  - ✓ Inside blocker's target is inside number of defender.
  - ✓ Outside blocker's target is outside number.
  - ✓ Keep eyes on linebacker.
  - ✓ Don't come off until at linebacker level.
  - ✓ Get helmet across defender when partner goes to linebacker.
- Zone blocking
  - ✓ Keep eyes on linebacker; basically a reach block and pull technique.
  - ✓ Covered lineman: rip and read
    - ⇨ Aim for outside armpit of defender
    - ⇨ First step is with foot toward aim point.
    - ⇨ Second step is in crotch of defender.
    - ⇨ Backside pad under opponent's breastplate.
    - ⇨ Stay on defender until pushed off by uncovered lineman.
  - ✓ Uncovered lineman
    - ⇨ Aim for near number of defender.
    - ⇨ Eye linebacker.
    - ⇨ Get one hand on defender in pulling direction.
    - ⇨ Basically a pull technique to get to defender.

Principles of Pass Blocking

- Must have a target pre-snap.
  - ✓ Target is inside number of defender.
  - ✓ Don't watch defender's head.
- Take a pass set that allows straddling a line from the defender to the quarterback.
  - ✓ Inside foot is post foot that drops first.
  - ✓ Post foot should be forward.

- ✓ If defender is:
  - ⇨ Head up: slide step inside.
  - ⇨ Inside: set heavy inside.
  - ⇨ Outside: one step set.
- Outside knee is in defender's crotch.
- Keep shoulders square to line of scrimmage.
- Get depth and width to line.
- Posture
  - ✓ Chin in, not up or down.
  - ✓ Hands in, thumbs up.
  - ✓ Elbows bent and in ribcage.
  - ✓ Set foot is back; post foot up.
  - ✓ Keep knees bent; strive to keep thighs parallel.
  - ✓ Banana spine.
  - ✓ Feet flat; weight inside of feet.
  - ✓ Punch.
    - ⇨ Hands to numbers inside defender's hands.
    - ⇨ Thumbs up. Grab breastplate of defender.
    - ⇨ Keep elbows in.
    - ⇨ Press defender away.
    - ⇨ If the grab is missed, repunch.
- Feet should keep moving.
  - ✓ Never cross feet.
- Tackles
  - ✓ Must kick/slide vs. wide rusher.
  - ✓ Keep shoulders square.

CHAPTER 14

Practice Planning

Implementing and perfecting specific plays as well as preparing for the next opponent is done through the weekly practice schedule. The entire offense, with the exception of special plays, should be installed in the pre-season. Samples of pre-season practice schedules and a schedule for installing the offense are covered in the latter part of this chapter.

Sunday is a day off for players and coaches. It is essential that they have time away from football to recharge their batteries. The off day allows them the opportunity to spend time with family or friends. They may attend church if they wish, watch NFL football, or just hang out with friends or family.

In-season weight training is done before school on Monday and Thursday. Lifting twice a week should maintain strength and help heal injuries.

Practice schedules presented in this chapter are based on a Saturday game day and assume that the team is a two-platoon program. These practice plans call for an official starting time of 3:45 p.m. Daily classroom meetings are held beginning at 3:15 p.m., with the exception of the Friday meeting that begins at 3:00 p.m. Monday through Thursday, the meetings should not exceed 15 minutes, but the Friday meeting will run until 3:30 p.m. These meetings should ideally be by position groups. Players should come to the meeting room dressed in practice gear, but without helmet, shoulder pads, or football shoes.

Following the daily meeting, specialists including punters, place kickers, holders, long snappers, return men, and quarterbacks have five minutes to get to the practice field for 10 minutes of pre-practice for their special skills. Coaches should be assigned to each skill group. Kick returners may be coached by the wide receiver coach, long snappers are the responsibility of the offensive line coach, a coach is assigned to punters, and a fourth member of the staff coaches place kickers and holders. This 10-minute period should be carefully supervised, and a regular routine should be established.

Quarterbacks, under the direction of the quarterback coach, pair off for a series of drills. The first drill involves execution of the pitch for option plays. Quarterbacks align on the sidelines of the field five yards apart. On the coach's signal, they jog down the yard lines to the middle of the field, pitching the football to each other. After each of the pairs reaches the middle of the field, they come back down the yard lines to the sidelines, executing the option pitch. This drill has each quarterback break down and come under control to execute the pitch. By going one way down the line and then returning to the sideline, each quarterback pitches with both his left and right hands.

After the option pitch drill, quarterbacks pair up for warm-up throwing drills. They kneel on their right knees 10 yards apart, and each quarterback executes five throws to his partner. Then they kneel on their left knees and repeat the process. Coaching emphasis should be on proper follow-through, ball position, and shoulder turn. Following the knee drills, quarterbacks stand with their left shoulders facing each other and, without striding, make five throws to each other. They then stand with their right shoulders facing each other and execute five throws. Points of emphasis are proper shoulder turn, ball position, and follow-through. During whatever time remains, quarterbacks throw to each other using first a three-step drop and next a five-step drop. The coach emphasizes proper footwork for the drops, as well as stride length and direction.

For the first five-minute period of regular practice time, the entire team does agility drills as a warm-up. Players are placed in lines at the goal line facing upfield. The number of lines used varies by the size of the squad, but near equal numbers should be in each line and as few players in each line as possible. A whistle starts each segment of the drill. On the first signal, players do a high knee lift jog for 20 yards. The second segment has players do lunges back to the goal line. They then shuffle to the right for 20 yards and return to the goal line, shuffling to the left. A carioca to the right is done to the 20-yard line, followed by a carioca to the left back to the goal line. Players then run backward to the 20-yard line. The last segment is a 20-yard accelerating stride back to the goal line.

Periods two and three have the 3-backs, 2-backs, Y-receivers, 4-backs, X-receivers, quarterbacks, and centers work on one-man routes. A play strip is used to create proper spacing for the receivers. Right formation is used on Monday and Wednesday; left formation is used on Tuesday and Thursday. Y-receivers align in a line on the strongside of the formation. The 2-backs and 3-backs align in a wing position to the quickside one yard outside the quick tackle position. X-receivers align on the numbers to the quickside of the play strip, and 4-backs line up on the numbers on the formation's strongside. Two quarterbacks line up behind the guard positions to the strongside and quickside of the play strip. Two centers line up over the guard positions. The quarterback to the strongside calls the cadence, and both centers snap the ball on the call of set. The quarterbacks throw to the wide receivers on the first snap. On the second snap, the quarterback aligned quickside throws to the 2-back or 3-back and the quarterback on the strongside throws to Y. Quarterbacks rotate positions after two throws. Figure 14-1 shows this setup in right formation.

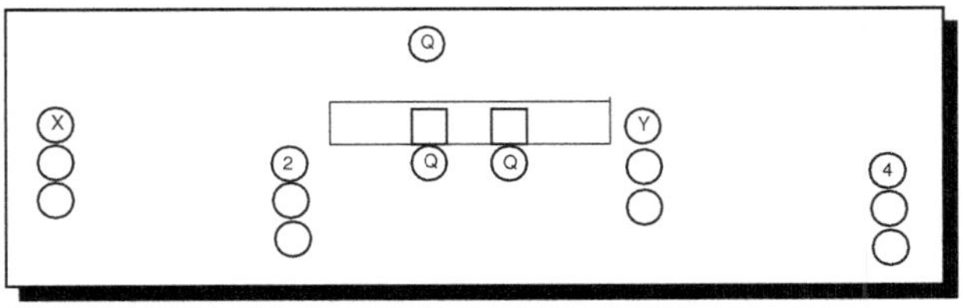

Figure 14-1. One-man pass routes

On Monday, the 4-back and X-receiver run six-yard hitch routes, fades, and six-yard in routes. Y utilizes a six-yard hitch, a seam, and the 0 mesh route. The 2-backs and 3-backs practice hitch, seam, and 0 mesh cuts.

Tuesday has the 4-backs and X-receivers run six-yard slants, fades, and 15-yard comebacks. Y-receivers run slants, seams, and three-yard arrows. The 3-backs and 2-backs practice tex routes, seams, and arrow routes.

On Wednesdays, the 4-backs and X-receivers practice six-yard out routes, six-yard slant cuts, and post corner cuts. Routes for the 2-back and 3-back are six-yard outs, six-yard hitches, and the wheel route. Y runs six-yard outs, three-yard arrow, and six-yard hitch routes.

On Thursdays, the 4-backs and X-receivers practice the post curl route, six-yard out, and six-yard hitch. Y-receivers run the six-yard slant, eight-yard hook over center, and the 0 mesh pattern. The 2-backs and 3-backs run the five-yard flat route, the wheel cut, and the 0 mesh pattern.

This 10-minute period allows for practice of the center-quarterback exchange. The quarterbacks operate under center half of the time and from the pistol the other half. The period provides an opportunity for potential receivers to practice a number of the basic routes in the passing attack and to time them with the quarterbacks. It is important that a fast pace be maintained so that tempo is created and the maximum number of reps are achieved.

Offensive guards and tackles use periods two and three on Monday for footwork drills. Typical drills have them come from their three-point stance and practice the first step with their right foot and then left foot. Steps practiced include a fire-out for base blocks, zone reach, pull right or left, and pass set. Another drill run has the linemen kick slide down a yard line and shuffle right or left on the coach's signal.

The first three periods are maintained Monday through Thursday. Beginning with period four, the practice schedule changes on a daily basis.

Figure 14-2 shows the Monday practice schedule. The 15-minute meeting period is used to review the Saturday game tape. Players dress in helmets and shoulder pads for the Monday practice session.

Period four is devoted to kicking and defending extra points and field goals. All members of the squad participate in this session. Periods five and six are punt and punt return sessions, while period seven and eight are kickoff and kickoff return sessions. The 4-backs, X-receivers, Y-receivers, 3-backs and 2-backs are involved in these special teams.

Quarterbacks work with their coach on a series of drills in periods five through eight. Hash mark drills are the first set of drills. A quarterback is positioned on the right hash mark 15 yards away from a partner on the left hash mark. The quarterback on the right hash mark calls cadence. He takes a three-step drop and throws to his partner on the left hash mark. His partner then calls cadence, executes a three-step drop, and throws back to the quarterback on the right hash mark. Three-step drops are followed by five-step drops, followed by sprint-outs toward the receiver. The 80 play-action is executed from the I and wing alignments and throws are made. Bootleg action toward the receiver is executed throwing on the move, and 70 pass-action faking 22 is practiced. After each action has been executed, the quarterbacks switch hash mark positions and repeat the sequence. The coach concentrates on proper footwork, faking,

Sample Daily Practice Plan for Monday

Meeting Time: 3:15–3:30 p.m. | **Formation:** Right

Specialists: 3:35–3:45 p.m. | **Dress:** Helmets/shoulder pads

Period	2B and 3B	Quarterback	4B and X	Y	Offensive Line
1	Agility: High knee, lunges, shuffles, carioca, backward run, strides				
2, 3	1. Hitch 2. Seam 3. Mesh 0	One-man routes Right formation	1. Hitch 2. Fade 3. 6-yard in	1. Hitch 2. Seam 3. Mesh 0	Footwork drills
4	Kick extra points and field goals.				
5, 6	Punt and punt return	Hash mark drill	Punt and punt return		1. Five-man sled 2. Down-and-fold 3. Down-and-log 4. Set, punch 5. Twists
7, 8	Kickoff and kickoff return		Kickoff and kickoff return		
9, 10	Align and explain scout team defense.				
11, 12	Option reads Right formation: 13, 14, 38, 39, 11, 17, 16		1. Ball security 2. Gauntlet 3. Stalk block 4. Releases	1. Boards 2. Zone blocks	
13, 14	1. Ball security 2. Gauntlet 3. Block two-man sled 4. Pass block shields	Unit pass patterns vs. air Right formation: 8, 5, 4			1. Trap, combo, shuffle 2. Down and sweep
15	Team half-line option: 13, 11, 39, 14, 514, 16				
16	Team half-line option: 13, 11, 39, 14, 514, 16				
17, 18, 19	7-on-7 right formation, defense plays cover 3 Run back-to-back: #1 offense vs. #1 defense #2 offense vs. #2 defense				1-on-1 Pass block vs. defensive line
20, 21	Buck series vs. scout team				
22, 23	Power series and zone series vs. scout team				
24, 25	Belly series right vs. scout team				
26, 27	Two-minute offense #1 offense vs. #1 defense #2 offense vs. #2 defense				

Figure 14-2. Sample daily practice plan for Monday

ball position, stride, shoulder turn, and follow-through. This period is good for intense coaching of these mechanics. Four quarterbacks may be drilled using the hash marks.

Offensive tackles, guards, and centers other than long snappers go with the offensive line coach for drill work. The first drill is takeoff on the five- or seven-man sled. Two takeoffs utilizing each shoulder are done. The offensive line coach calls a variety of snap counts and ends each repetition with a whistle.

The next series of drills has two linemen on offense and two playing defense. The defenders may use shields some days or the drills may be done at a thud pace. Figures 14-3 through 14-7 illustrate these drills. Players are in two lines facing the defenders. The coach calls "Set" to start the drill, and he blows a whistle to end it. Offensive blockers become defenders after each turn and the defenders go to the end of the line. Players go once in each line. Figure 14-3 shows a down block and a fold block. A down block and a log block are shown in Figure 14-4. Sweep blocks with a kick-out block and a seal block are shown in Figure 14-5. A dummy is laid on the ground on the offensive side of the line of scrimmage to force the pulling linemen to get proper depth. Figures 14-6 and 14-7 show two pass blocking drills. For Figure 14-6, on the snap the offensive linemen pass set, punch, and grab the defender. Figure 14-7 is work against defensive line twists. The coach stands behind the offensive linemen and signals the twists he wants the defenders to execute.

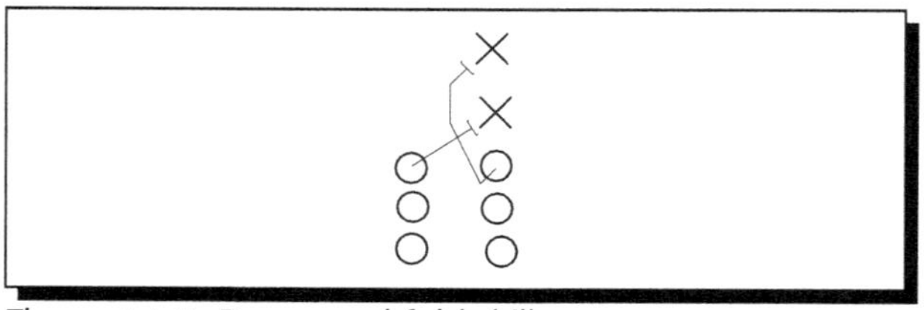
Figure 14-3. Down-and-fold drill

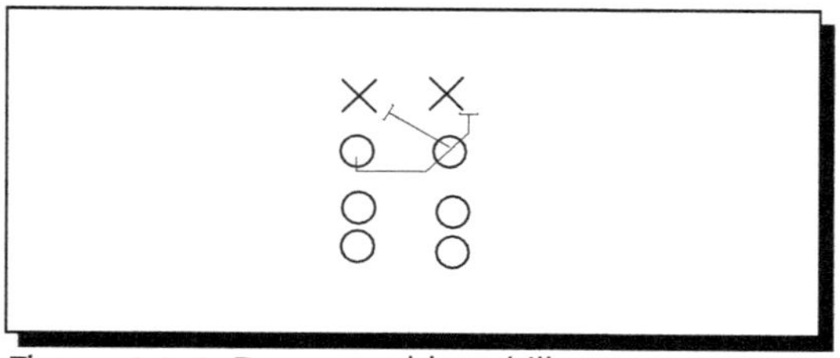
Figure 14-4. Down-and-log drill

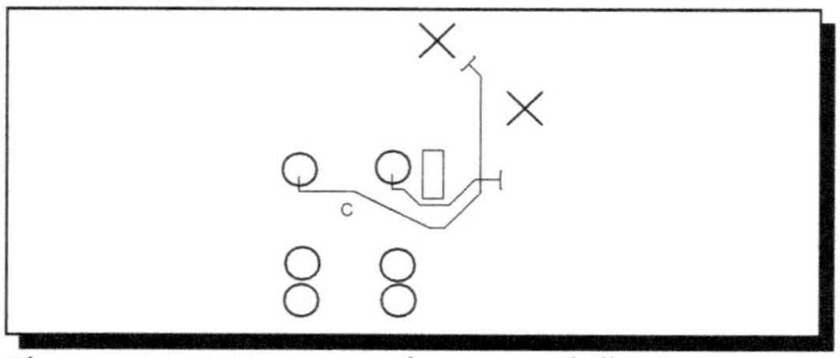

Figure 14-5. Down-and-sweep drill

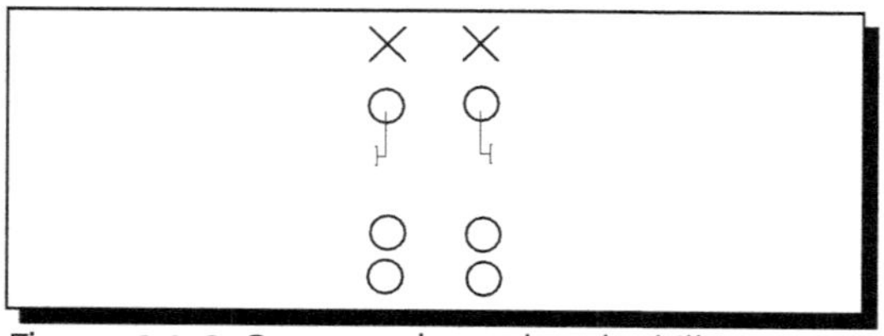
Figure 14-6. Set, punch, and grab drill

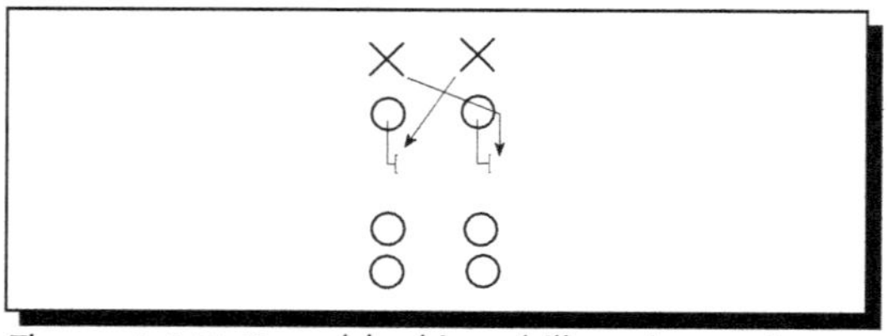
Figure 14-7. Pass blocking drill against twists

The drills should be completed within the 20 minutes that kicking is practiced. Direction of the drills should be changed each day. Players go to the right on Monday and Wednesday and to the left on Tuesday and Thursday.

On Monday periods 9 and 10 are used to align and explain the upcoming opponent's defense for scout team purposes. Scout teams are created by the offensive personnel. Offense #2 acts as the defensive scout team for offense #1, and offense #1 is the defensive scout team for offense #2. Creating effective scout teams is a challenge when players are assigned to only scout teams. By having offensive units act as scout teams, a better effort is given by the scout teams. Morale is maintained, and the offensive players develop a better feel for the opponent's defense if they actually align in it and react to the offense. Normally, the 4-back and the X-receiver play defensive corners. The quarterback and 2-back are safeties. The center plays the nose on an odd front and the middle linebacker for an even front. The guards play defensive tackles for an even front and inside linebackers on an odd alignment. The offensive tackles play defensive ends. Y and the 3-back play the outside linebacker positions. Scout team personnel are aligned by using the technique numbering system by which blocking assignments are created. Shields may be used by the scout team at times, or thud tempo may be used without tackling. Thud tempo must be taught during preseason practice. Alignment to offensive formations and basic stunts are covered during periods 9 and 10 for both the first and second scout team units.

Periods 11 and 12 have the quarterbacks, 3-backs, and 2-backs run option reads with coaches supplying the read men. A play strip is used to create proper spacing. The waiting quarterback simulates a snap to the quarterback running the play. The quarterback coach acts as the dive read so that he can check to see that the quarterback is watching the read and not his running back. The running back coach simulates the keep or pitch read. Offensive units run the same plays back-to-back. They run inside veer (13 and 14) outside veer (38 and 39) midline option (11), shovel option (17), and power option (16). A primary goal is to get as many repetitions as possible for each backfield unit. Right formation is used Monday and Wednesday, and left formation Tuesday and Thursday.

Y and the offensive linemen use periods 11 and 12 for two drills. One of these is a board drill. Four to five boards are used so that repetitions are quickly done. Each blocker gets two repetitions. For the first repetition, he lines up at the end of the board with his right foot in the middle of the board. On the snap count, he must step first with the right foot. For the second repetition, his left foot is in the middle of the board, and he takes his first step with the left foot. Blockers go from their three-point stance. A defensive man is placed on the board in a four-point stance. He must remain low throughout the block. This defender may have a shield some days or be live. He gives resistance as the blocker drives him the length of the board. The points of emphasis are proper footwork straddling the board, aiming point eyes on target, hand placement, and so forth. The blocker becomes the defensive man after his turn and the defender goes to the end of the line of blockers. Figure 14-8 shows the setup for the board drill.

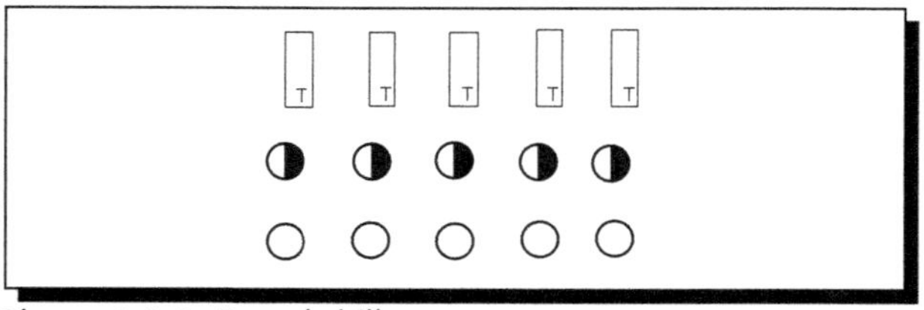

Figure 14-8. Board drill

Following the board drill, the offensive linemen and Y work a zone blocking drill. Figure 14-9 is the zone drill run to the right. The drill is run right one day and left the next. One offensive lineman is covered, and one is uncovered. A down defender is on the offensive lineman in the direction of the zone block. A linebacker is stacked behind him. The coach points the direction for the down defender to go; the linebacker goes in the opposite direction. A snap count is given by the coach, and the offensive players execute the zone block using their covered and uncovered rules and techniques. After one repetition, the defenders go to the end of the line, and the blockers go on defense. Offensive players switch lines so that they have an opportunity to block as both the covered and uncovered blockers. As with other two-man blocking drills, more than one group may go at a time, but it is difficult for a coach to watch more than two groups at one time.

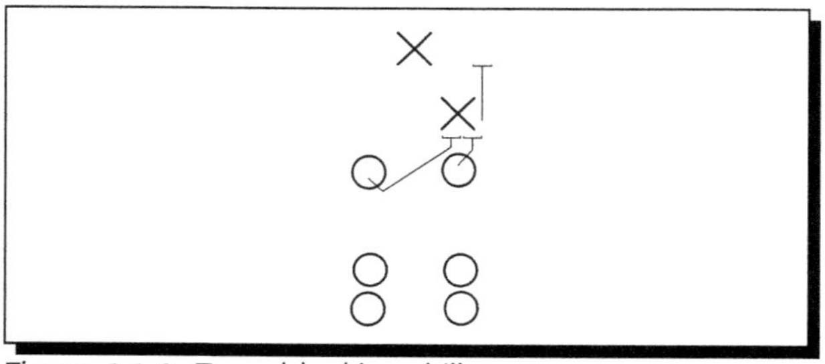

Figure 14-9. Zone blocking drill

The 4-backs and X-receivers work with the wide receiver coach in periods 11 and 12. The first drill they do is a ball security drill. Players pair off with a partner. One player has a football held high and tight with his right hand and arm. His partner places a hand on the ballcarrier's left shoulder. The ballcarrier jogs forward 10 yards. His partner tries to knock the football loose. He chops down on the ball first and then upper cuts on the ball. He repeats this action for 10 yards. After 10 yards, the ballcarrier turns around and places the ball in left hand and arm. He then jogs 10 yards back to his original position as his partner attempts to knock the ball loose. Partners switch places so that the previous defender carries the ball and his partner tries to dislodge it. This drill takes very little time.

The receivers next run the gauntlet drill. Figure 14-10 illustrates this drill. Receivers align to one side of a cone. The coach pats a football, and the first man breaks toward the coach, who throws a pass to the receiver. The receiver should look the ball in, catch it in his hands, and tuck the ball away. He plants his right or back foot and L cuts around the cone. He runs through the blaster, covering the ball with both hands and arms. After coming out of the blaster, he approaches a cone and cuts to the right or left of it, switching the football so that his body is between the ball and the cone. He cuts to the other side of the next cone, switching the ball to the opposite side. Two hand shields are laid on the ground five yards from the last cone. The ballcarrier approaches the middle of the two shields and plants his inside foot and executes a jump cut to the outside of the shield. The jump cut is made to the right if the receivers have started from the left side. When they start from the right, the jump cut is made to the left. A stand-up dummy is held five yards beyond the shields. Receivers contact the dummy with the inside shoulder and forearm and make a spin move to score. Each receiver runs the gauntlet only once. Receivers will be started from the opposite side at the next practice.

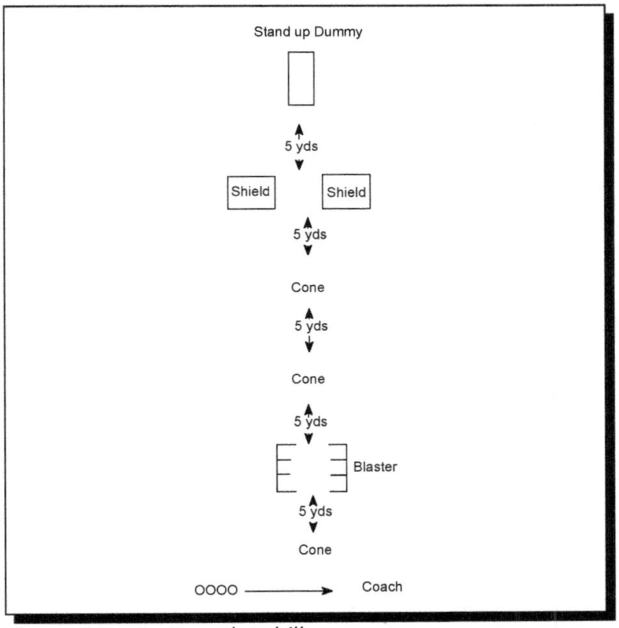

Figure 14-10. Gauntlet drill

Receivers next run a stalk blocking drill or cut block drill. The stalk block is drilled on Monday and Wednesday. Two lines of receivers face players designated as defensive backs. The coach calls cadence, and the receivers fire off the line. Defenders backpedal three steps and break down, and the receivers then execute the stalk block. On Tuesday and Thursday, defenders hold stand-up dummies at five yards of depth. Receivers fire off the line and execute a cut block on the stand-ups. Blockers become defenders for the next receivers, and receivers go to the ends of the lines. Each receiver should go once in each line. It is assumed that the sideline is to the receiver's outside. He should strive to take the defender to the inside when possible. Figure 14-11 shows the drill for stalk blocking.

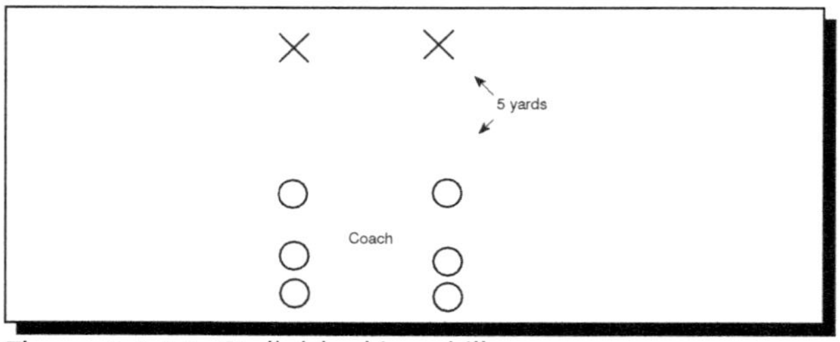

Figure 14-11. Stalk blocking drill

The final drill used with the receivers is a release drill. The same setup is used for this drill as is used for the blocking drill except defenders are placed in a press position on the inside of the receivers. On the snap count, receivers execute a release on the defender. The first release used is a rip under with the forearm and shoulder. The second release is a swim move, and a third release is a rapid feet fire, head fake, and rip move. One release is worked on each day. The fourth day each receiver works on his favorite release.

Quarterbacks, 4-backs, X-receivers, and Y-receivers run unit pass patterns versus air in periods 13 and 14. Right formation is used on Monday and Wednesday, and left formation is used on Tuesday and Thursday. A play strip is utilized to ensure better spacing for Y. Each offensive unit runs the same pattern. Coaching points include proper spacing, depth of route, and timing. Three quarterbacks may go at the same time. They are aligned behind the center and the two guards. The quarterback lined up over center calls the cadence. On the snap of the ball, the quarterbacks take a five-step drop. The quarterback over the strong guard throws to the 4-back, the quarterback over center throws to Y, and the third quarterback throws to the X-receiver. Since each receiver has a ball thrown to him, each tends to work harder running the pattern. After one repetition, the quarterbacks rotate, with the strongside quarterback moving to the quickside, the quickside quarterback going over center, and the center quarterback moving strongside. Each pattern is runs three times so that all quarterbacks throw to all receivers. On Monday, the three patterns run are the 4, 5, and 8 patterns. Figure 14-12 shows the setup for the drill from right formation.

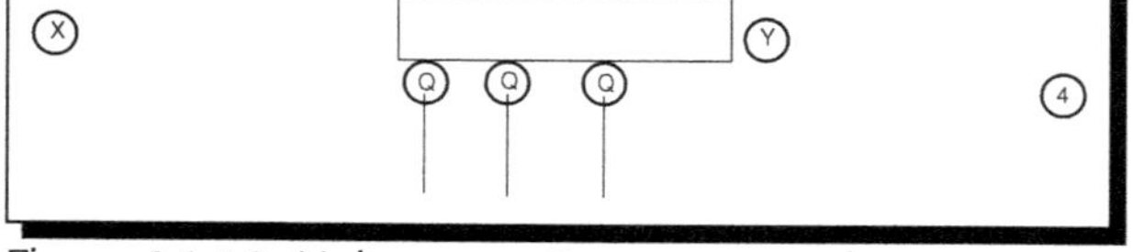

Figure 14-12. Unit pass patterns versus air

Drills run by the 2-back and 3-back during periods 13 and 14 start with the ball security drill used by the 4-back and X-receiver during periods 11 and 12. This drill is followed by the gauntlet drill. The third drill is blocking the two-man sled. Players align in a six-point stance two at a time on the two-man sled. On the call of set, players execute a full extension, contacting the sled with the left or right shoulder and finishing on their bellies. They then assume a three-point stance and execute a full extension on set. The last part of the drill has them in a three-point stance and firing out on set and driving the sled with a right or left shoulder block until the coach blows a whistle. Players switch lines and go to the end of the line. Each back goes once with the left shoulder and once with the right shoulder.

The final drill is pass blocking on shields. Two lines of players set up five yards from the line of scrimmage. Two opponents have shields and on the call of set the shield holders pass rush. The two backs step up and pass block the rushers. The coach is aligned between the two backs simulating a quarterback. He gives the snap count and blows the whistle to end the drill. Pass blockers become shield holders, and the shield holders go to the end of the line of pass blockers. Each back should go one time in each line. This drill is shown in Figure 14-13.

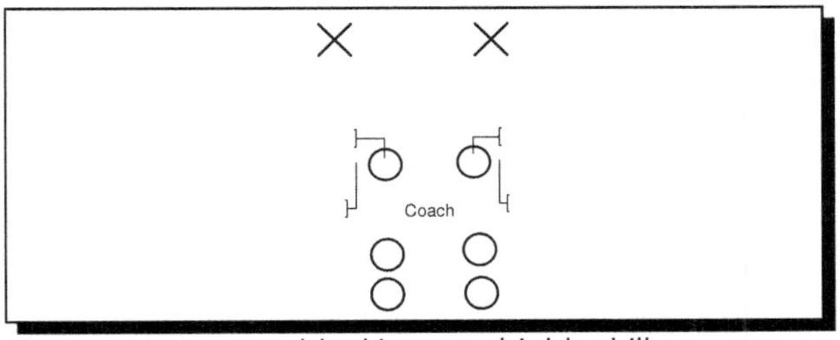

Figure 14-13. Pass blocking on shields drill

As shown in Figure 14-14, offensive linemen work on a drill that includes a trap block, a combo double-team block, and a shuffle pull. Four offensive linemen align on a yard line with two feet between them. They are in three-point stances. On defense, a player aligns head-up on the end offensive player. A second defender is aligned head-up on the second offensive man from the outside. A linebacker is lined up over the third offensive man from the outside, and a second linebacker stacks behind the defender on the end of the line. The coach calls cadence to start the drill and blows a whistle to end it. Offensive man #4 uses a rip release to the inside to double-team the defender over offensive player #3. They combo block this man. The coach has signaled this defender as to which way he should move. The inside linebacker fills opposite him. Offensive player #2 pulls and executes a trap block on the defender on the end. Offensive player #1 executes a shuffle pull through the hole created by the trap block and blocks the outside linebacker. After one repetition, the offensive players rotate so that offensive man #4 becomes #1, #3 becomes #4, and so forth. The drill is run four times so that every offensive player executes each technique. After all offensive players play each position, they switch to defense, and the defenders go to the end of the lines for offensive players. Defenders may carry shields, or the drill can be thud tempo. This drill is run to the right on Monday and Wednesday and to the left on Tuesday and Thursday.

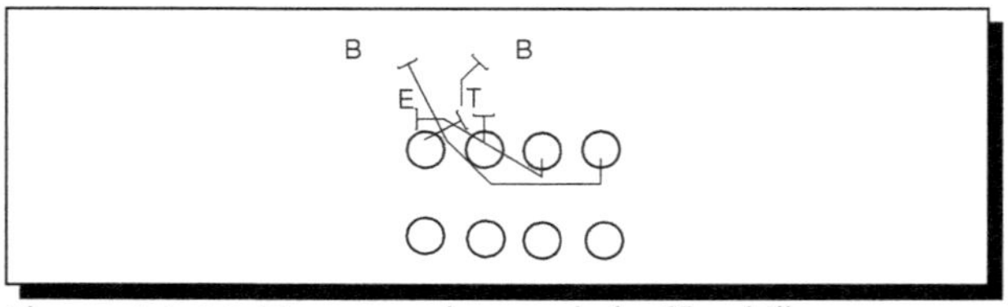

Figure 14-14. Trap, combo, and shuffle drill

Period 15 is devoted to a half-line option activity. Figures 14-15 and 14-16 illustrate the setup for the period. Right formation (Figure 14-15) is used on Monday and Wednesday, and left formation (Figure 14-16) is used on Tuesday and Thursday. The option plays 39, 11, 17, and 13 are run to the quickside, while 14, 38, and 16 are practiced to the strongside. These plays are run in rapid sequence versus scout team personnel. Scout teams as shown in Figure 14-15 consist of the #1 4-back playing strong safety, the #2 Y playing Sam linebacker, the #2 strong tackle playing defensive end, the #2 strong guard playing the defensive tackle, and the second 4-back playing Mike linebacker. Alignment on the quickside has the #2 quick guard aligned as the defensive tackle, the #2 quick tackle is the defensive end, the #2 X-receiver plays linebacker, and the #1 X-receiver is free safety or outside linebacker. Offensive units have the #1 set of backs and center with the strong guard, tackle, and Y on the strongside. A second offensive backfield and center, along with the quick guard and quick tackle, are lined up to the quickside. A coach stands behind each offensive unit to check for correct reads and blocking.

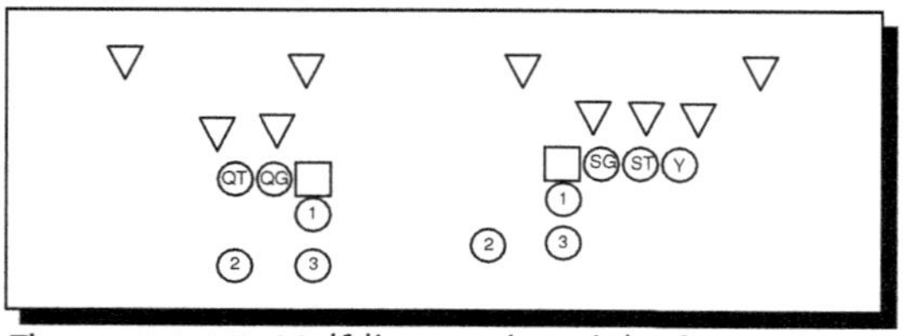

Figure 14-15. Half-line option right formation

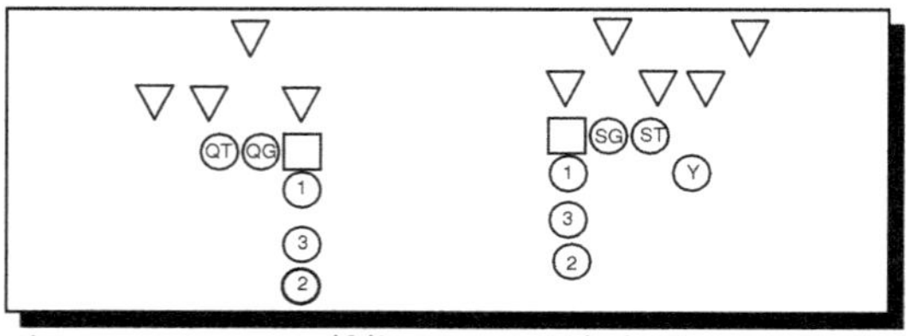

Figure 14-16. Half-line option left formation

The ball is always snapped on the call of set by the quarterback on the strongside. Both units go at the same time and reset as quickly as possible for the next snap. After each play is run twice, the offensive backfields and center switch from the quickside to the strongside and vice versa. After three minutes the #1, offensive guards, tackles, and Y switch to defense, with the #2 offensive linemen switching to offense. Y aligns strongside on Tuesday and Wednesday and quickside on Monday and Thursday. When Y is aligned quickside 39, 13, and 11 are practiced. On Monday, 500 formations are used. On Tuesday, the quickside is a 700 formation, and the strongside is a 600 alignment. On Wednesday, 800 formation is set quickside with the strongside in a 700 alignment. On Thursday, a 600 formation is set quickside with an 800 alignment set on the strongside. Only one defensive stunt is used each day so that the quarterbacks know what to expect and get several repetitions versus that stunt.

Figure 14-16 shows left formation versus a 5-2 defensive look. If it is desirable to work a third set of offensive backs, the third set might wait for the first two reps to be run and then step in on the quickside while the offensive backs from the quickside rotate to the strongside. The offensive backs from the strongside wait on the quickside while the next two reps are run. This drill provides for maximum repetitions of the option game.

Period 16 on Monday is a team drill where screen passes and the week's special plays are practiced against a scout team. Screen passes practiced include 80 Denver, 760 Frank, 960 Fred, 650 Frank, jet 850 Tom, and 850 Frank. The 80 Denver is a screen pass from dropback pass action. The other four plays are bubble screens and wide receiver screens. These plays are run against a scout team holding shields. The primary emphasis is timing between the quarterback, receiver, and blockers. Each week, a special or trick play is selected from those discussed in Chapter 12. This play is practiced during this period. The first offensive unit runs each of the plays one time in the first three minutes of period 16. The second offensive unit has two minutes in which to run plays. They run 80 Denver, one bubble screen, and the week's special play. If time remains, they will work on other quick screens.

On Monday, periods 17 through 19 are a 7-on-7 for quarterbacks, 3-backs, 2-backs, 4-backs, X-receivers, and Y-receivers. The #1 defensive secondary and linebackers work against offense #1. At the same time, offense #2 works versus defense #2. These drills are set up back-to-back with the line of scrimmage the opposite 40-yard lines. Plays run on Monday are 797, eastern 534, north 725, south 846, west 626, 727, 51, 58, 850, 62, 64, 63, 59 Iowa, zin 766 whip, and 864 Utah. The defense plays their normal cover 3, which provides an opportunity for the offense and defense to work against the best competition available. Right formation only is used on Monday. All plays should originate with a simulated snap. Kickers or managers may be used as snappers.

During periods 17 through 19, the offensive linemen work on 1-on-1 pass protection versus the defensive linemen. Figure 14-17 shows the setup for the drill. On Mondays, right formation is used. The offensive line coach stands behind the defense and signals the snap count. He calls cadence. The defensive line coach stands behind the offense and sounds a whistle to end the drill. A large bell-bottomed stand-up dummy is placed seven yards deep behind the center to simulate the quarterback. The dummy is the target for pass rushers. Only one offensive blocker and one defensive lineman go live on each snap. This approach prevents injuries where players fall over each other. Having the entire offensive line in their stance for each repetition creates proper spacing for the offensive linemen and the pass rushers. Starting with the quick tackle position, cadence is called, and the defensive end over him pass rushes. After the whistle sounds to end the drill, the offensive line coach signals the next snap count. Snap counts should be varied. After the #1 tackle goes, the second unit quick tackle replaces him. This rotation allows all offensive linemen to work versus line rushers. The defensive linemen also rotate personnel. A large number of repetitions are possible during this 15-minute period, and chance of injury is minimal. This drill is the best possible drill for development of pass protection and pass rush techniques.

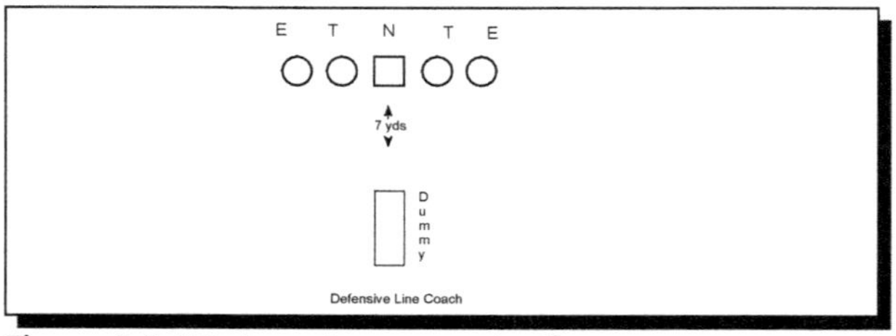

Figure 14-17. 1-on-1 pass protection

Team offense versus a scout defense is practiced in periods 20 through 25. On Monday, the scout players use shields. Anytime scout team defenses are used, one offensive coach is assigned to them to call defenses, ensure proper alignment, and encourage effort. In each 10-minute segment, offense #1 runs the 12 scripted plays first. No-huddle is always used. The plays are signaled to the quarterback by the same coach who is responsible for doing this on game day. The offense aligns on the line of scrimmage as quickly as it can after running each play. The quarterback calls the play at the line as in a game.

After the script for that 10-minute period is completed, offense #1 becomes the scout team and offense #2 runs as many plays from the script as possible in the remaining time period. On Monday, all plays are run from right formation.

Periods 20 and 21 are used to run the buck series primarily, along with some passes. Plays practiced during this period include 28, 30, 47, 26, 19, 09, east 727, 69, 34, 66, 916, and eastern 534.

Power series and zone series are practiced in periods 22 and 23. Plays scripted on Monday are 24, 27, 33, 25, 29, jet 818, 917, west 626, 860, 783, 962, and jet east 817.

Belly series and several passes are used in periods 24 and 25. The script includes 49, 31, 35, 15, 22, 46, 36, 777, north 725, south 846, 51, and western 526.

The final two periods on Monday are used to practice the two-minute offense. Offense #1 practices versus defense #1, while offense #2 goes against defense #2. Chains are used for down-and-distance situations. This segment is at a thud tempo. No player is tackled to the ground, and pass rushers must pull off the quarterback.

Figure 14-18 shows a Tuesday practice plan. The meeting is devoted to a scouting report on the upcoming opponent. Full pads are worn for this practice. Period one is the same agility procedure as on Monday.

Sample Daily Practice Plan for Tuesday

Meeting Time: 3:15–3:30 p.m.	**Formation:** Left
Specialists: 3:35–3:45 p.m.	**Dress:** Full pads

Period	2B and 3B	Quarterback	4B and X	Y	Offensive Line
1	Agility				
2 3	1. Tex 2. Seam 3. Arrow	Left formation	1. Slant 2. Fade 3. 15-yard comeback	1. Slant 2. Seam 3. Arrow	1. Five-man sled 2. Down-and-fold 3. Down-and-log
4	Extra points and field goals				
5 6	Punt and punt return	Hash mark drill	Punt and punt return		1. Down-and sweep 2. Zone blocks
7 8	Option reads: 13, 14, 11, 38, 39, 17, 16		1. Ball security 2. Gauntlet 3. Cut blocks 4. Releases	1. Boards 2. Trap, combo, and shuffle	
9 10	1. Block two-man sled 2. Cut block 3. Gauntlet 4. Pass block shield	Unit passes vs. air Left formation: 6, 4, 9			1. Pass block: set punch 2. Pass block: twists 3. Footwork
11	Half-line option vs. scout team 713, 711, 917, 614, flip 638, 916				
12 13	9-on-9 vs. #1 defense Option: 13, 11, 39, 14, 38, 22, 916, 917, 927		One-man routes vs. corners 4, post, dig, post corner	9-on-9 vs. #1 defense Option	
14 15 16	7-on-7 left formation Defense plays cover 1 man and cover 2 #1 offense vs. #1 defense #2 offense vs. #2 defense				Pass block 1-on-1 vs. defensive line
17	Team offense vs. scout team Option: 539, 514, 639, 917, 738 #1 offense (3 minutes) #2 offense (2 minutes)				
18 19	Buck series vs. scout team #1 offense (6 minutes) #2 offense (4 minutes)				
20 21	Power series and zone series vs. scout team #1 offense (6 minutes) #2 offense (4 minutes)				
22 23	Belly series and dropback series vs. scout team #1 offense (6 minutes) #2 offense (4 minutes)				
24 25	Red zone offense (live) #1 offense vs. #1 defense (6 minutes) #2 offense vs. #2 defense (4 minutes) Script				
26	Goal line offense (live) #1 offense vs. #1 defense (6 minutes)				
27	#2 offense vs. #2 defense (4 minutes) 525, 539, 535, 519, western 526, flip 624, flip 685 Ohio				

Figure 14-18. Sample daily practice plan for Tuesday

During periods two and three, one-man routes are run. The 2-backs and 3-backs practice the tex route, seam, and arrow routes. The 4-back and X-receiver practice the slant, fade, and 15-yard comeback routes. Y runs slant, seam, and arrow cuts. The offensive linemen block the five-man sled and drill the down-and-fold and down-and-log techniques. Centers practice snaps to the quarterbacks while they are throwing one-man routes.

During period four, the team kicks and defends extra points and field goals. Punts and punt returns are practiced during periods five and six. Quarterbacks run the hash mark drill. Offensive linemen drill zone blocks and run the down-and-sweep drill.

Option reads are practiced by quarterbacks, 3-backs, and 2-backs in periods seven and eight. Left formation is used. Offensive linemen and Y block on the boards and do the trap, combo, and shuffle drill.

In periods 9 and 10, quarterbacks, Y-receivers, 4-backs, and X-receivers run unit pass versus air from left formation. Routes practiced are 6, 4, and 9. The 2-backs and 3-backs block the two-man sled, pass block against shields, and run the gauntlet. They also practice cut blocks against stand-up dummies as shown in Figure 14-19. Two lines face stand-up dummies aligned five yards away and two yards to the outside. On the coach's call of set, the two players at the front of the lines attack the stand-up dummies with cut blocks. The right line uses the left shoulder, and the left line blocks with the right shoulder. It is possible to substitute a cross-body block for the shoulder block. Offensive linemen perform footwork drills, pass block twists versus shields, and execute the set and punch pass block drill.

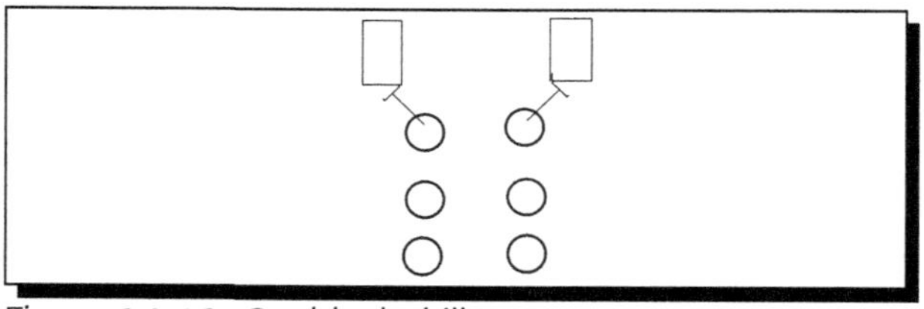

Figure 14-19. Cut block drill

The half-line option is practiced in period 11. Left formation is used. Plays 713, 711, and 917 are run to the quickside of the formation. On the strongside, 614, 916, and flip 638 are practiced.

Defense #1 goes against offense #1 in left formation on a 9-on-9 drill during periods 12 and 13. This period is a live full-contact period for the offensive line, Y, running backs, and one quarterback. Quarterbacks are switched after five minutes between 9-on-9 and a drill that has 4-backs and X-receivers running one-man routes against the cornerbacks. One-man routes practiced on Tuesday are the post, dig, post corner, and the 4 routes. A second team group of running backs, offensive linemen, and Y are substituted into the 9-on-9 drill periodically. This drill is good for both offense and defense. Even if the defense is not facing an option opponent, the option responsibilities are being reviewed.

The 7-on-7 drills in periods 14 through 16 have the #1 offensive skill players working on the passing game versus defense #1. Offense #2 goes against defense #2. The defense plays cover 1 man and cover 2. All passes are run from left formation and are scripted as follows: western 526, 877, zac 797 Peoria, jet east 817, 850, 62, zac 966 whip, 55, 689, 63, 854 Utah, 868, and 61.

Team offense is practiced against a scout team for periods 17 through 23. All plays are scripted and run from left formation. Thud tempo is used for these periods. In period 17, option runs are executed. Offense #1 runs all six option plays listed for three minutes, and offense #2 runs option for two minutes.

The buck series plus some passes are practiced in periods 18 and 19. Power and zone runs are executed in periods 20 and 21, while the belly series and several passes are run during periods 22 and 23. For each 10-minute segment, offense #1 practices for six minutes versus offense #2 as scout team. Offense #2 then runs plays for four minutes against offense #1, playing scout team defense. By using the no-huddle approach, plays may be executed rapidly. Plays are signaled to the quarterback at the line of scrimmage. The pace of these team periods acts as the primary conditioning drill for the football team.

Defense #1 opposes offense #1 for periods 24 through 27. For six of each 10-minute segments, the #1 teams go against each other, and defense #2 practices against offense #2 for four minutes.

Periods 24 and 25 are red zone practice. The ball is placed on the 20-yard line going in to score. This period may be a thud tempo practice segment. Left formation is used, and the ball is moved as each play is run. All plays are scripted.

The final two periods, 26 and 27, are live contact. These goal line plays have the ball placed on the eight-yard line as a starting point. Four downs are allowed for offense #1 to score versus defense #1. Following that, offense #2 gets the ball on the eight-yard line with a first down against defense #2. Offense #1 gets a second four-down series against defense #1. Five hundred formations are emphasized. This series is a great way to finish practice because of the enthusiasm created by the competitive nature of the goal line segment. Following period 27, the entire team gathers around the head coach for final announcements and comments before being dismissed.

Figure 14-20 shows a Wednesday practice plan. It is similar to Tuesday's plan. During the pre-practice meeting, the team watches tape of the upcoming opponent. Full equipment is worn on Wednesday. Period one is the normal agility session. The 2-backs and 3-backs practice the six-yard out, wheel, and hitch routes during periods two and three. Y works on six-yard outs, three-yard arrow, and hitch cuts. The 4-back and X-receiver run the six-yard out, slant, and post corner routes. Offensive linemen block the five-man sled and perform the down-and-log drill.

Sample Daily Practice Plan for Wednesday					
Meeting Time: 3:15–3:30 p.m.			**Formation:** Right		
Specialists: 3:35–3:45 p.m.			**Dress:** Full pads		
Period	**2B and 3B**	**Quarterback**	**4B and X**	**Y**	**Offensive Line**
1	Agility				
2 3	1. 6-yard out 2. Wheel 3. Hitch	Right formation	1. 6-yard out 2. Slant 3. Post corner	1. 6-yard out 2. Arrow 3. Hitch	1. Five-man sled 2. Down-and-log
4	Extra points and field goals				
5 6	Kickoff and kickoff return	Hash mark drill	Kickoff and kickoff return		1. Down-and-fold 2. Down-and-sweep
7 8	Option reads: 13, 14, 38, 39, 11, 16, 17, 514		1. Stalk block 2. Ball security 3. Gauntlet 4. Releases	1. Boards 2. Zone blocks	
9 10	Pass block vs. linebackers	Unit passes vs. air Right formation: 7, 8, 4 Utah			1. Trap, combo, shuffle 2. Footwork
11	Half-line option vs. scout team 713, 711, 917, 614, flip 638, 916				
12 13	9-on-9 vs. #1 defense Option: 13, 11, 39, 38, 14, 916, 917, 22		One-man routes vs. corners 4, post, dig, post corner	9-on-9 vs. #1 defense Option: 13, 11, 39, 14, 38, 916, 917, 2	
14 15 16	7-on-7 right formation Defense plays cover 4 and cover 2 man under #1 offense vs. #1 defense #2 offense vs. #2 defense				Pass block 1-on-1 vs. defensive line
17	Team offense vs. scout team Screen passes and special play of the week				
18 19	Buck series vs. scout team (thud tempo) #1 offense (6 minutes) #2 offense (4 minutes)				
20 21	Power series and zone series vs. scout team (thud tempo) #1 offense (6 minutes) #2 offense (4 minutes)				
22 23	Belly series and dropback series vs. scout team (thud tempo) #1 offense (6 minutes) #2 offense (4 minutes)				
24 25	Third downs (thud tempo) #1 offense vs. #1 defense (6 minutes) #2 offense vs. #2 defense (4 minutes) Script: Third-and-long, third- and-medium., third- and-short				
26	Goal line offense (live)				
27	#1 offense vs. #1 defense #2 offense vs. #2 defense 629, flip 638, flop 639, west 626, 685 Ohio, 630 base, 611, 610				

Figure 14-20. Sample daily practice plan for Wednesday

Period four is for extra points and field goals, while kickoffs and kickoff returns are executed during periods five and six. Quarterbacks practice the hash mark drill, and offensive linemen work on the down-and-sweep and down-and-fold drills.

Right formation is used for option reads in periods 7 and 8. Offensive linemen and Y block on the boards and drill zone blocks. Stalk blocks, the gauntlet, releases, and ball security drills are run by 4-backs and X-receivers.

The 2-backs and 3-backs pass block versus the linebackers in periods 9 and 10. The backs align in the I formation. Two linebackers are aligned on the line of scrimmage 10 yards apart. The coach calls cadence from behind the 2-back. Linebackers rush from the outside as the 3-back steps up to his right to take on one pass rusher, and the 2-back steps left to block the other linebacker. The coach sounds a whistle to end the drill. Running backs use normal pass rush techniques or cut block the blockers when instructed to do so. Offensive linemen practice the trap, shuffle, and combo drills. They then work on the footwork series of drills. Quarterbacks, 4-backs, Y-receivers, and X-receivers practice unit passes versus air from right formation. They execute 7, 8, and 4 Utah patterns.

Half line option plays versus a scout team are run in period 11. These plays are 813, 811, 917, 738, 714, and 916.

Right formation is used for the 9-on-9 line segment in periods 12 and 13. The veer series is run from a script. The 4-backs and X-receivers practice four cuts, post, dig, and post corner routes 1-on-1 versus the cornerbacks.

The 7-on-7 drill is held in periods 14 through 16. Right formation is employed, and offense #1 goes against the #1 defensive secondary and linebackers. Offense #2 performs against defense #2. Secondary coverages used by the defense on Wednesday are cover 4 and two-deep man under. Plays run from a script cover all 10 pass concepts and most pass actions. These plays are 97, eastern 534, north 725, south 846, west 626, east 627, 51, 63, 52, 860, 58, 864, and 689 Iowa.

Screen passes and the special play of the week are practiced versus a scout team with shields in period 17. Right formation is used.

Offense is practiced against a scout team in periods 18 through 23. A thud tempo is employed, and plays are run from right formation. Periods 18 and 19 are for buck series plus passes; periods 20 and 21 are power and zone series and some passes. The belly series and passes are practiced in periods 22 and 23. Plays are scripted and called using the no-huddle approach. Each 10-minute segment should have offense #1 run plays for six minutes and offense #2 for four minutes.

Periods 24 and 25 have the defense go against the offense in a series of third-down situations. Third-and-long situations where seven or more yards are needed to gain a first down and third down with three or fewer yards to go are both practiced. Chains are used. A thud tempo is maintained as scripted plays are run. Offense #1 goes for six minutes and offense #2 for four minutes. The ball is moved from the middle of the field to each hash mark.

Goal line offense is practiced live in periods 26 and 27. These periods are the same as those on Tuesday except that plays are run from right formation and 600 alignments are used.

For Thursday practice (Figure 14-21) players wear helmets and shoulder pads. The 3:15 p.m. meeting is devoted to watching tape on the upcoming opponent. Agilities are performed in period one. In periods two and three, one-man routes for the 2-back and 3-back are a five-yard flat, the wheel, and mesh 0. The 4-backs and X-receivers run hitch, six-yard outs, and post curl cuts. Y-receivers practice slants, eight-yard hooks, and mesh 0 routes. During these periods, the offensive line blocks the five-man sled and performs the down-and-log drill.

Extra points and field goals are kicked in period four, punts and punt returns are practiced in periods five and six, and kickoffs and kickoff returns are worked on in period seven. The offensive linemen block on the boards and run the down-and-sweep and down-and-fold drills. Quarterbacks use the hash mark drills and practice ball security.

Option reads are practiced from left formation in periods eight and nine. The 4-backs and X-receivers cut block, run the gauntlet, practice releases, and drill ball security. Offensive linemen and Y-receivers work on zone blocks and the trap, combo, and shuffle drill.

Left formation is used for unit passes in periods 10 and 11. The patterns reviewed are the 5, 8 smash, and 6 whip. The 2-backs and 3-backs block the two-man sled, practice cut blocks, run the gauntlet, and drill ball security. Offensive linemen perform the set and punch drill, pass block twists, and work footwork.

The half-line option is practiced versus scout team in period 12. Left formation 639, 611, 613, 814, and 916 are practiced.

The 7-on-7 drills are practiced from left formation during periods 13 through 15. The #1 secondary and linebackers play cover 3 and cover 2 against offense #1. Offense #2 goes against defense #2. Plays scripted are western 526, 877, 697 Peoria, jet east 817, 860, 62, 53, 858 smash, 864 Utah, north 725, 759, zac 966 whip, 51, 768, and east 727. Offensive linemen aligned in left formation pass block 1-on-1 versus the defensive line.

Period 16 is a team period versus scout defense. All screen passes and the special play of the week are practiced from left formation.

Periods 17 through 22 are team offense practiced against scout teams. Left formation is used, and thud tempo is employed. The ball is placed on the offense's one-yard line for the black zone segment in period 17. Offensive plays run are 533, 653, flip 624, flip 630 base, and flip 689.

<table>
<tr><th colspan="6">Sample Daily Practice Plan for Thursday</th></tr>
<tr><td colspan="3">Meeting Time: 3:15–3:30 p.m.</td><td colspan="3">Formation: Left</td></tr>
<tr><td colspan="3">Specialists: 3:35–3:45 p.m.</td><td colspan="3">Dress: Helmets/shoulder pads</td></tr>
<tr><th>Period</th><th>2B and 3B</th><th>Quarterback</th><th>4B and X</th><th>Y</th><th>Offensive Line</th></tr>
<tr><td>1</td><td colspan="5">Agility</td></tr>
<tr><td>2</td><td rowspan="2">1. 5-yard flat
2. Wheel
3. Mesh 0</td><td rowspan="2">One-man routes
Left formation</td><td rowspan="2">1. Hitch
2. 6-yard out
3. Post curl</td><td rowspan="2">1. Slant
2. 8-yard hook
3. Mesh 0</td><td rowspan="2">1. Five-man sled
2. Down-and-log</td></tr>
<tr><td>3</td></tr>
<tr><td>4</td><td colspan="5">Extra points and field goals</td></tr>
<tr><td>5</td><td rowspan="2">Punt and punt return</td><td rowspan="2">Hash mark drill</td><td colspan="2" rowspan="2">Punt and punt return</td><td rowspan="3">1. Block boards
2. Down-and-fold
3. Down-and-sweep</td></tr>
<tr><td>6</td></tr>
<tr><td>7</td><td>Kickoff and kickoff return</td><td>Ball security</td><td colspan="2">Kickoff and kickoff return</td></tr>
<tr><td>8</td><td colspan="2" rowspan="2">Option reads: 13, 14, 38, 39, 11, 16, 17</td><td rowspan="2">1. Cut block
2. Gauntlet
3. Releases
4. Ball security</td><td colspan="2" rowspan="2">1. Zone blocks
2. Trap, combo, shuffle</td></tr>
<tr><td>9</td></tr>
<tr><td>10</td><td rowspan="2">1. Block two-man sled
2. Cut block
3. Gauntlet
4. Ball security</td><td colspan="3" rowspan="2">Unit passes vs. air
Left formation: 5, 8 smash, 6 whip</td><td rowspan="2">1. Footwork
2. Set, punch
3. Twists</td></tr>
<tr><td>11</td></tr>
<tr><td>12</td><td colspan="5">Half-line option vs. scout team: 611, 613, 639, 814, 916</td></tr>
<tr><td>13</td><td colspan="4" rowspan="3">7-on-7 left formation
#1 offense vs. #1 defense
#2 offense vs. #2 defense
Defense plays cover 3 and cover 2</td><td rowspan="3">Pass block 1-on-1 vs. defensive line</td></tr>
<tr><td>14</td></tr>
<tr><td>15</td></tr>
<tr><td>16</td><td colspan="5">Team offense vs. scout team
Screen passes and special play of the week</td></tr>
<tr><td>17</td><td colspan="5">Black zone: Ball on 1-yard line vs. scout team
533, 653, flip 624, flip 689</td></tr>
<tr><td>18</td><td colspan="5">Buck series vs. scout team</td></tr>
<tr><td>19</td><td colspan="5">Power series and zone series vs. scout team</td></tr>
<tr><td>20</td><td colspan="5">Belly series vs. scout team</td></tr>
<tr><td>21</td><td colspan="5">Dropback series vs. scout team</td></tr>
<tr><td>22</td><td colspan="5">Quick game vs. scout team</td></tr>
<tr><td>23</td><td colspan="5" rowspan="2">Team offense (thud tempo)
#1 offense vs. #1 defense (6 minutes)
#2 offense vs. #2 defense (4 minutes)
Script: Third-and-long, third-and-short</td></tr>
<tr><td>24</td></tr>
<tr><td>25</td><td colspan="5" rowspan="2">Red zone offense: 20-yard line (thud tempo)
#1 offense vs. #1 defense (6 minutes)
#2 offense vs. #1 defense (4 minutes)</td></tr>
<tr><td>26</td></tr>
<tr><td>27</td><td colspan="5">Goal line offense (live)</td></tr>
</table>

Figure 14-21. Sample daily practice plan for Thursday

Buck series plays scripted for period 18 include 28, 30, 26, 47, 19, and east 827. Power and zone plays practiced in period 19 are jet 818, 629, 927, 916, jet east 817, and west 629. Belly plays scripted for period 20 are 49, 35, 15, 22, 31, and north 825. Period 21 is devoted to dropback passes 864, 755, 658, zac 969, 868 Texas, and 854 Utah. Period 22 is the last scout team sequence. Plays run are 860, 761, 52, 853 two, 917, and 534.

Defense #1 works against offense #1, and defense #2 against offense #2 for periods 23 through 27. Thud tempo is used, and the offense runs left formation. Periods 23 and 24 are third-down situations. Plays are scripted, and chains are used. Third down and seven or more to go and third down with three or fewer yards to go are practiced. The #1 groups work six minutes, and the #2 groups practice four minutes.

The ball is placed on the 20-yard line going in to score for the red zone for periods 25 and 26. Chains are used, and the ball is moved. Offense #1 has six minutes, and offense #2 has four minutes. Plays are scripted.

Goal line offense is run in period 27. Offense #1 runs five plays versus defense #1. Offense #2 then runs five plays against defense #2. Plays run are 525, 514, 530 base, western 526, and 533.

Friday's practice schedule (Figure 14-22) has players wear helmets and sweats or shorts. A meeting is held at 3 p.m. Each offensive player is asked to write the blocking rule for his position for every running play and pass protection. These tests are graded and returned to the players on Saturday. Grades are recorded as an incentive for players to learn their blocking responsibilities. Quarterbacks are asked to diagram each of the basic pass patterns and number their read progression.

Specialists work on the field from 3:35 to 3:45 p.m. Periods one through three are dedicated to performing the pre-game warm-up routine. The first period has the team execute the normal agilities for each practice day. These are followed by a series of stretching activities. The pre-game warm up concludes with 25 jumping jacks.

Extra points and field goals are practiced in period four. Periods five and six are used to perform punts and punt returns, and kickoffs and kickoff returns are executed during periods seven and eight. Contact is restricted to tagging off on return men and no contact is made for blockers or rush men. During these four periods, quarterbacks do the hash mark drill, ball security, and an option pitch drill.

Offensive linemen use periods five through eight to review blocking assignments. The first offensive line aligns in right formation, and the #2 line acts as a scout team. They line up as defensive linemen and linebackers. The offensive line coach calls out the play to be run and on the snap count of set, offensive linemen step to their assignment. Plays are run rapidly with the intent of covering each run play and pass protection. After the first line has covered each play, the #2 offensive line repeats the drill.

Sample Daily Practice Plan for Friday					
Meeting Time: 3:15–3:30 p.m.—Written test.			**Formation:** Right		
Specialists: 3:35–3:45 p.m.			**Dress:** Helmets and sweats		
Period	**2B and 3B**	**Quarterback**	**4B and X**	**Y**	**Offensive Line**
1	Pregame warm-up practice				
2					
3					
4	Extra points and field goals				
5	Punt and punt return	Hash mark drill	Punt and punt return		Review blocking assignments
6					
7	Kickoff and kickoff return	1. Ball security 2. Option pitch drill	Kickoff and kickoff return		Review blocking assignments
8					
9	Two-minute drill; tag off #1 offense vs. #1 defense #2 offense vs. #2 defense 5 minutes each group				
10					
11	Run script (first 15 plays) vs. scout team				
12					
13					
14	Run each running play and each pass protection scheme vs. tires aligned in opponent's defense. #1 offense runs a play, then #2 offense runs same play				
15					
16					
17					
18					
	5:15 Entire team meets on field for game day instruction				

Figure 14-22. Sample daily practice schedule for Friday

Two-minute offense is reviewed in periods 9 and 10. Offense #1 goes against defense #1 and offense #2 against defense #2. Defenders tag off on receivers, and linemen step to their assignments and stop so that no contact is made. The 800 formation is used for the two-minute attack. It provides four quick receivers, but retains the potential for the run game.

Periods 11 through 13 have the offense practice the first 15 scripted plays for the game. Tires or shields are laid on the ground aligned in the opponent's primary defensive look. The offense operates from right formation. Offense #1 runs all 15 plays in rapid sequence; after that, offense #2 repeats the plays.

Right formation is used for periods 14 through 18. All run plays and passes not included in the first 15 scripts are run against the tires. During this time, offense #1 runs a play. Then offense #2 steps up and runs the same play. The units continue to alternate until all plays are run. When additional players beyond the second unit are involved, they are alternated into the second offensive group.

Practice ends at 5:15 p.m. after 18 periods. The entire team gathers around the head coach for game day instructions and reminders before being dismissed.

On game day, a walk-through of running plays and pass protection assignments is held before the team goes to the field for warm-up. This step may be done in the gym or on the field. Players can be in street clothes. Scout teams are used for defense. This approach serves as a final review before the game.

The entire offense with the exception of weekly special plays should be installed in the pre-season. While not every play will be polished in pre-season, new plays will not have to be added once the regular season begins. Figure 14-23 is a timetable for installing the offense. This schedule is based on the availability of 12 pre-season practices. Implementation of the offense could change based on more or fewer preseason practice opportunities.

Schedule for Teaching the No-Huddle Multiple Offense				
Practice	**Formations Shifts/Motion**	**Run Plays**	**Pass Protection/Quarterback Actions**	**Patterns**
1	Right: 500, 600, 780, 800, 900 Shifts Cadence and snap	10 13 14	50 60	3 8
2	Left	11 38 39	80 (fake 14) 883, 783	2 4
3	Right zac motion	49 29 19	west 626	6 1
4	Left zin motion	28 30	east 727, 627, 827, 927	7 0
5	Right flip motion	35 15	90, 697, 797, 897, 997	7 Peoria
6	Left flop motion	22 31	70, 777, 677, 877	5
7	Right jet motion	18 36 30G	jet east 817 south 746	4 Utah Bubble screens 760 Frank 960 Fred
8	Left	33 25 30 base	western 526	9
9	Right	24 34 16	eastern 534 80 (fake 24) 688	9 Iowa WR screen 650 Frank 850 Frank
10	Left	47 46	685 Ohio north 725 825 flip 625	8 Texas Ohio
11	Right	26 27	80 Denver 780 Denver 680 Denver 880 Denver 980 Denver	3 two
12	Left	11G 17 09		6 whip

Figure 14-23. Timetable for offense installation

Practice one of the pre-season is covered in Figure 14-24. A 25-minute meeting prior to going on the field is used to cover right formations 500, 600, 700, 800, and 900. Cadence and shifts are discussed. Following the meeting, specialists go to the field for 10 minutes.

During period one, the team performs the agilities that will be covered in period one of a normal practice week. These exercises include high knees, lunges, shuffle, carioca, backward run, and strides.

<table>
<tr><th colspan="6">Sample Pre-Season Practice Plan Day 1</th></tr>
<tr><td colspan="3">Meeting Time: 25 minutes</td><td colspan="3">Formation: Right</td></tr>
<tr><td colspan="3">Specialists: 10 min.</td><td colspan="3">Dress: Helmets/shoulder pads</td></tr>
<tr><td colspan="3">Quarterbacks: Learn signals</td><td colspan="3">Plays Introduced: 13, 14, 10, 53, 68</td></tr>
<tr><th>Period</th><th>2B and 3B</th><th>Quarterback</th><th>4B and X</th><th>Y</th><th>Offensive Line</th></tr>
<tr><td>1</td><td colspan="5">Agility</td></tr>
<tr><td>2
3</td><td>1. Hitch
2. Seam</td><td>One-man routes</td><td>1. Hitch
2. Fade</td><td>1. Hitch
2. Seam</td><td>Blocking rules: 13, 14, 50, 60</td></tr>
<tr><td>4
5
6</td><td colspan="5">Extra points and field goals</td></tr>
<tr><td>7
8
9
10</td><td colspan="5">Team offense vs. air
1. Cadence
2. Formations: 500, 600, 700, 800, 900
3. Shifts
4. Run 10
5. Signals</td></tr>
<tr><td>11
12</td><td colspan="5">Introduce scout team alignments in a 43 defense vs. right formation</td></tr>
<tr><td>13
14</td><td colspan="2">Option reads: 13, 14</td><td>1. Stalk block
2. Ball security</td><td colspan="2">1. Five-man sled
2. Boards</td></tr>
<tr><td>15
16</td><td>1. Block two-man sled
2. Ball security</td><td colspan="3">Unit pass patterns vs. air
Right formation: 8, 3</td><td>1. Zone blocks
2. Sweep-and-down</td></tr>
<tr><td>17
18
19</td><td colspan="4">7-on-7 vs. defense
Defense plays cover 3
#1 offense (10 minutes)
#2 offense (5 minutes)</td><td>1. Set, punch, grab, pass block
2. Block twists</td></tr>
<tr><td>20
21
22</td><td colspan="5">Half-line option vs. scout team
613, 713, 813, 514, 614, 714</td></tr>
<tr><td>23
24
25
26</td><td colspan="5">Team offense vs. defense (thud tempo)</td></tr>
<tr><td>27</td><td colspan="5">Team conditioning: 40-yard sprints</td></tr>
</table>

Figure 14-24. Pre-season practice one

In periods two and three, the quarterbacks take snaps from the center and throw one-man routes. The 2-backs and 3-backs execute hitch and seam cuts. The 4-backs and X-receivers run hitch and fade routes, while Y-receivers practice hitch and seams. The offensive line receives instruction in blocking rules for 13 and 14, the inside veer plays, and cover 50 and 60 pass protection rules.

Extra points and defending extra points is covered in periods four through six. Two units are used on offense and defense.

The offense aligns in right formation 500, 600, 700, 800, and 900 in periods 7 through 10. The team shifts from 500 to the other formations. The quarterback sneak, 10, is then run from each formation. Cadence is taught. Formations and 10 are signaled to the quarterbacks. At least two offensive units alternate. If additional personnel are available, more offensive units may be used. This period is practiced on air with no defense.

Scout team alignments in a base 4-3 with a cover 4 secondary are introduced in periods 11 and 12. The first offensive unit lines up in right formation. The second offensive players are then aligned in a base 4-3 defense. The 4-back and X-receiver are corners. The quarterback and 2-back play safeties. Offensive tackles play defensive ends, and the offensive guards align as defensive tackles. The Y-receiver and 3-back are outside linebackers with the center playing middle linebacker. The first offensive unit then aligns as a scout defense with the second offensive unit in a right 600 set. It is important to emphasize the positive role that the scout team must play throughout the season.

The 2-backs, 3-backs, and quarterbacks run 13 and 14 as option reads from right formation in periods 13 and 14. The 4-backs and X-receivers practice stalk blocks and run ball security drills. Y-receivers and the offensive line practice takeoffs on the five-man sled and block on the boards.

During periods 15 and 16, 2-backs and 3-backs block the two-man sled and run the ball security drill. Quarterbacks, 4-backs, X-receivers, and Y-receivers run unit pass patterns versus air. Right formation is used, and the 8 and 3 patterns are practiced. Offensive linemen zone block and run the down-and-sweep drill.

The 7-on-7 drill against the defense is conducted in periods 17 through 19. Offense #1 goes against defense #1 and offense #2 works against defense #2. Right formation is used. The defense plays cover 3. Plays run are 868, 853, 658, 663, 768, 753, and 953. Offensive linemen pass block. They work a set, punch, and grab drill and block twists. Footwork for pass protection is also practiced.

Periods 20 through 22 are team periods. The half-line option drill is introduced versus a scout team. Right formation is used to run 613, 713, 813, 514, 614, and 714.

The offense and defense work against each other in periods 23 through 26. Right formation is used, and plays 510, 514, 613, 658, 614, 663, 714, 768, 713, 963, 753, 813, 858, and 868 are executed. Offense #1works against defense #1 and offense #2 practices against defense #2. A thud tempo is used.

During period 27, 40-yard sprints are run for conditioning. The entire team runs 10 40-yard sprints.

Practice number eight of the pre-season is shown in Figure 14-25. The pre-practice meeting of 20 minutes is used to introduce 533, 525, 530 base, western 526, and the nine pattern. Left formation is used for practice, and full pads are worn. Specialists and quarterbacks are on the field 10 minutes prior to start of the official practice.

Sample Preseason Practice Plan Day 8					
Meeting Time: 20 minutes			**Formation:** Left		
Specialists: 10 min.			**Dress:** Full pads		
Plays Introduced: 33, 25, 30 base, western 526, 9 pattern					
Period	**2B and 3B**	**Quarterback**	**4B and X**	**Y**	**Offensive Line**
1	Agility				
2	1. Mesh 0 2. 5-yard flat 3. Wheel	One-man routes	1. Hitch 2. 6-yard out 3. Post curl	1. Mesh 0 2. Slant 3. 8-yard hook	1. Five-man sled 2. Down-and-log 3. Down-and-fold
3					
4	Kickoff and kickoff return	Hash mark drill	Kickoff and kickoff return		Blocking rules: 33, 25, 30 base, western
5					
6					
7	Team offense: introduce new plays vs. scout team 33, 25, 30 base, western 526, 859 (wheel), 9 route				
8					
9					
10	Option reads: 13, 11, 39, 14, 38		1. Stalk block 2. Gauntlet 3. Cut block	1. Boards 2. Zone blocks	
11					
12	Pass block vs. linebackers	Unit pass vs. air Left formation: 9, 5, 4			1. Sweep-and-down 2. Trap, corner,shuffle
13					
14	Half-line option vs. scout team 13, 11, 39, 14, 38				
15	9-on-9 vs. defense 13, 11, 22, 39, 14, 38		One-man routes vs. corners 4, dig, post, post corner	9-on-9 vs. defense	
16					
17	7-on-7 vs. defense Defense cover 2				Pass block 1-on-1 vs. defensive line
18					
19					
20	Buck series and belly series vs. defense (thud tempo)				
21					
22	Power series and zone series vs. defense (thud tempo)				
23					
24	Quick series and dropback series vs. defense (thud tempo)				
25					
26	Goal line offense vs. defense (live) 533, 525, western 526, 519, 514, 539				
27					

Figure 14-25. Pre-season practice eight

Agility drills are performed in period one. For periods two and three, the 2-backs and 3-backs run five-yard flat cuts, wheel routes, zero mesh pattern. Y-receivers practice the 0 mesh with the backs, run slant cuts, and execute eight-yard hook routes over center. The 4-backs and X-receivers work on six-yard out cuts, hitches, and post curl routes. Quarterbacks throw to the receivers after taking snaps from the center. Offensive linemen block the five-man sled and practice the down-and-log and down-and-fold drills.

Periods four through six are used for kickoffs and kickoff returns. Quarterbacks run the hash mark drill. Offensive linemen work on blocking rules for 533, 525, 30 base, and western pass protection versus a scout team.

New plays 533, 525, 30 base, western 526, and 859 (wheel) are introduced and practiced against scout teams in periods seven through nine. Left formation is used, and scout teams hold shields.

Option reads are run from left formation in periods 10 and 11. Plays practiced are 13, 11, 39, 14, and 38. The 4-back and X-receiver stalk block, cut block, and run the gauntlet drill. Y-receivers and the offensive linemen block on the boards and work on zone blocks.

During periods 12 and 13, the 2-back and 3-back pass protect versus the linebackers. Quarterbacks, 4-backs, X-receivers, and Y-receivers run unit pass versus air from left formation. Patterns practiced are 9, 5, and 4 pass concepts. Offensive linemen run the sweep-and-down, trap, combo, and shuffle drills.

The half-line option is practiced against scout personnel in period 14. Left formation is used to run 13, 11, 39, 14, and 38. Thud tempo is used.

A 9-on-9 segment with the offense going against the defense is held in periods 15 and 16. Quarterbacks, 2-backs, 3-backs, Y-receivers, and offensive linemen run 13, 11, 22, 39, 14, and 38 from left formation. This contact period is live. The 4-backs, X-receivers, and one quarterback practice 1-on-1 pass routes against the cornerbacks. Receivers run the 4 route, post, dig, and post corner.

A 7-on-7 drill is run from left formation versus the defense playing cover 2 in periods 17 through 19. Passes run during 7-on-7 are 860, 783, west 626, east 727, 997, zac 797 Peoria, 877, jet east 817, zac south 746, western 529, 859, 864 Utah, 665, 658, 762, and 961. Offensive linemen practice 1-on-1 pass blocks versus the defensive line. Left formation is always used.

Buck series and belly series are emphasized during periods 20 and 21. Plays practiced are zac 749, zac 735, zac 815, zac 722, zac 777, zac south 846, zin 728, zin 730, zin east 827, 519, 830, 960 Fred.

Zone and power series are run in periods 22 and 23. Plays run are 629, flip west 626, jet 818, jet east 817, 929, 533, 525, western 526, 530 base, 759, 860, and zac 760 Frank.

Emphasis in periods 24 and 25 is on quick and dropback passes. The plays practiced include 859, 861, 863 Utah, 752, jet 883, 658, 765, zac 968, 853, 652, 864, and 669.

The final two periods, 26 and 27, are devoted to goal line offense versus the defense. These periods are live. The 500 series is used and plays practiced are 533, 525, western 526, 519, 514, and 539.

Pre-season practice plans should be completed prior to the start of pre-season practices. Doing so will help to ensure that all skills are covered thoroughly and that the offense is completely installed. All practice plans should be duplicated so that each coach has a written plan available for his use. It is good policy to post the day's practice plan in the locker room so that players can check it. The time frames need to be adhered to strictly. The head coach keeps practice plans in a permanent form, which allows him to look back year-to-year to see what worked well and what needs to be changed. Ideally, each coach has input into the daily practice plan. This approach may not be possible in situations where some coaches are not available for planning periods.

CHAPTER 15

Game Planning

Offensive football must be attacking and calculating. The risk/reward dynamic of offensive play should be in the forefront when making decisions about what play to run next. This process is proper game planning. Games are won or lost by paying attention to this most important detail; it should not be left to chance. Every well-run and organized football program must put in due diligence and have a plan for every facet of the program. This includes a well thought-out and thorough game plan.

This chapter will address the following questions. Why a game plan? How to game plan? What should be in a game plan? This attempt to help a coach determine his game plan is far from the ultimate; the suggestions are not etched in stone. The information is simply an attempt to get a coach to think about the task of calling plays in a more intelligent and efficient manner. The quest for a perfect game plan may never be attained, but the effort to get there is what should drive a coach in everything he does in pursuit of victory.

The thoughts presented in this chapter have been influenced by contacts with many great coaches. Coaches are often little more than beggars and thieves in what they do. Three coaches that deserve being researched on the subject of game planning are Bill Walsh, Brian Billick, and Homer Smith. Much of what is presented is from these three sources. Bill Walsh's book Finding the Winning Edge is a must-have for any coach's library. Brian Billick's book Developing an Offensive Game Plan is required reading for this subject, and any of the many thought-provoking writings of Homer Smith will improve a coach's skill as teacher and coach.

Why put the effort into setting a plan of attack for game day, versus the idea of calling plays based on gut feel or some other method of delivery? Some advantages that proper game planning affords a coach include the following:

- It allows a coach to make decisions away from the constant stress of the game.
- It reduces the amount of guesswork involved.
- It takes pressure off the signal caller.
- It allows a coach to set his formations, motions, and personnel groupings in a sequenced manner.
- It allows a coach to set the percentage of run/pass, inside/outside run, play-action pass, three-step, five-step, sprint pass for all situations.
- It gives confidence to all that the team is prepared.
- It provides an opportunity to break tendencies.
- It allows a coach to plan to create confusion.

No matter the situation, everyone knows what the team is going to do. The game plan becomes the blueprint for the daily practice plan. No coach can afford to waste practice time, so he must become efficient in his use of this limited resource. Proper allocation of time based on what will be done in the game is the best way to structure a practice plan. The job of the coach is to place his players in the best position he can to have a chance to be successful against all opponents. Without a proper game plan, the odds of achieving success become very limited.

Game planning does not begin the week of or two weeks before the game. If a coach waits until then, he has lost a great advantage. Proper game planning begins early in the off-season. It is then that a coach can decide the size and scope of his offense for the next season. Football is a game of situations pressured by the ever-shrinking game clock. Early in the season, a coach must study each situation and each one of his opponents, along with their philosophy in regard to those situations to identify offensive needs. The time a coach has to meet, teach, and practice will be the biggest factor in determining the size and scope of the offense. It is necessary to determine how much time is needed to practice each situation involved in a game, as well how much time is needed to effectively teach and master each of these situations. These factors will limit the size and scope of the offense. Early on, the capabilities of the team must be determined and decisions made about the best methods of teaching the offense to players. Homer Smith at UCLA was once asked, "How much offense should a team have, and how much offense should it carry each week?" His response was simple yet profound: "How much time does the team have to practice?"

Time can be very limited at the high school level. Often, players must play both sides of the ball. A coach cannot afford to waste time. He should determine what is best for him and his team by identifying individual situations and breaking down the game field into zones.

Individual down-and-distance situations include:

- First-and-10-plus
- First-and-10
- First-and-five or less
- Second-and-15-plus
- Second-and-long (8 to 14)
- Second-and-medium (three to seven)
- Second-and-short (one to two)
- Third-and-12-plus
- Third-and-long (5 to 11)
- Third-and-medium (two to four)
- Third-and-short (one or less)
- Fourth-and-eight-plus
- Fourth-and-long (four to seven)
- Fourth-and-medium (two to three)
- Fourth-and-one

The game field may be broken into the following zones:

- Backed up (–1 to –10)
- Coming out (–11 to –25)
- Open field (–26 to +35)

- Red zone (+34 to +11)
- Goal line (+10 in)

A coach should identify other situations and specific plays to be included in the game plan, such as the following:

- Two-point plays
- Two-minute offense plays
- Four-minute offense
- Overtime plays
- Special or trick plays and when to call them
- Blitz-beaters
- Last three plays of the game from the +50-yard line
- Last three plays from –50-yard line

A script of 10 to 15 opening plays should also be included in the plan.

In his book Developing an Offensive Game Plan, Coach Billick said, "You will be surprised when you go back and study yourself as to the actual number of plays you ran and needed in each of these situations." He guaranteed that if a coach went back and checked the numbers for each situation, they would be very similar to his numbers of actual plays run in each of the situations he mentioned. For example, he said, "You will only get on average one third-and-short play per game." A coach does not need 10 plays for that situation, nor for any of the other situations identified. A limited and definable number of plays is needed for each situation, and that is the key in setting a plan. The identified number of plays may get the necessary reps in practice for players to master them. Time is a scarce resource. It should not be wasted on plays not needed for what a team will do in a game. Only an offense large enough to cover the identified game situations is necessary.

Another off-season task is to check out how opponents handle each situation identified. A coach needs to know what systems opponents employ in each situation. What tendencies do they have in each situation? What special problems do they present that will need to be worked on? It is necessary to know how they line up on defense and what systems they employ. More importantly is how they play the defense, if they play it correctly, and if they can do what they say they are going to do. This information becomes most helpful in formulating ideas on how to attack these opponents in the fall. Homework in the off-season is important to set the size and scope of the offense and to have an idea of how to teach and practice it efficiently and effectively. It is not what coaches know or understand, but only what players can execute that counts.

In his book Developing an Offensive Game Plan, Coach Billick points out that in the NFL four statistics really determine the outcome of a game:

- Turnover margin: If a team was plus one in turnover margin, it won at a 75 to 85 percent clip. Plus two and higher percentages were even more in the team's favor up to the point where it becomes impossible to lose.

- Explosive plays (runs of 12-plus and passes of 16-plus yards): If a team was plus two in that category, it had an 80 to 85 percent chance of victory.
- First down efficiency: If a team ran for four or more yards on first down 45 percent of the time and if it completed passes at a 60 percent rate on first down, it was efficient. Better teams ran for four or more yards 50 percent of the time.
- An efficiency rate of 80 percent in the red zone: This rate means scores over possessions. Touchdowns are always the goal, but a coach should not give up an opportunity for three points.

These statistics are a huge factor in determining success at any level of ball. Everything possible should be done to prevent turnovers, create explosive plays, and be as efficient as possible on first down and in the scoring zone in order to win.

Coach Billick also states that a coach must be aware of the success ratios for third-and-long (20 to 25 percent), third-and-medium (45 to 50 percent), and third-and-short (75 to 85 percent). These percentages should shape what play to call in any given situation. A punt is a great offensive play. Coaches should not force actions that are not needed. Coach Billick also reveals that 65 to 75 percent of made first downs come from first and second downs. Only 25 to 35 percent of made first downs come from third-down situations. This is not to say that third down in not important, but to keep the chains moving, a team needs chunks of yards on first and second downs. No matter the level of ball being played, the longer the drive needs to be to score, the lower the chance that the team scores. These percentages factor into how to set a game plan. Homer Smith pointed out that offensive players and offensive football must be offensive. A coach must not lose that mindset. The amount of risk for each situation should always be evaluated, and that is nearly impossible to do effectively on the field with the pressure of the game clock. Making these decisions in the office with ample time to think is the better choice.

In his book, Coach Billick also lists the actual number of plays for each situation that may arise in a game. Coaches should read his book for those numbers. He states that the number of plays in the NFL and high school are closer than the NFL and college due to the length of the game and rule differences. The game of football continues to evolve with the advent of many up-tempo and no-huddle teams and greater reliance on the pass. A coach should study himself to find the exact numbers of plays he needs, as those presented by Coach Billick may not apply to his situation. A coach will find the appropriate numbers by studying past games over a number of years.

Homer Smith was asked when a coach knows to call a run or pass or just what kind of run or pass. He replied that the game of football is a math problem. He said, "What is the percentage chance of this play or another play getting the desired results against the anticipated defensive look in that situation?" Any risk taken must be an educated risk. A coach needs to play the odds. He needs to know when and why to take the risk. It is as if the coach were in Las Vegas, except he wants to be the house not the gambler because over time the house always wins and the sucker always ends up broke. Hotels are constantly being built in the desert for those who can never quite figure it out.

Setting a game plan each week requires a lot of study. A coach must watch hours of the opponent's game tape and hours of practice tape to see if the game plan is being executed. White boards and notepads will become filled with ideas on just how to get it done. The entire offensive staff must have a say and be part of the planning. This process can lead to passionate debate, but it is necessary to gain input from all involved. The staff needs to look at the opponent's structure, tendencies, and techniques, and evaluate match-ups. How do the opponent's players react? When do they employ certain looks and schemes? Are any tips available on what they may do? Are any defensive personnel present who may be attacked? By doing all this and more, the staff can gain as much knowledge as possible. This information becomes vital for putting the plan together.

So what does a game plan look like? The plan should prepare for situations that have been identified. The team will have x number of plays to run in the game. A decision must be made regarding the total number of plays to be run, and the run:pass ratio for the game should be determined. Is there a need for the team to be balanced? Does the team need to run more often or run a lot more often? Is there a need to pass more or pass a lot more? The coach should come up with a percentage overall for the game and work from there.

The game plan should address first down in each field zone. For example, the coach should consider first down in the open field. What should the run/pass percentage be for first down? What runs give the best chance at four-plus yards, and what formations or motions should be employed for the defense anticipated for in this given situation? Assuming that he has 10 open field first downs, the coach may want a run:pass ratio of 60 to 40. Six of the 10 plays would be runs he feels will be successful. They need not be six different plays. He may choose to run inside, off-tackle, and outside. A decision will be made as to how many runs will be weakside or strongside and how many will be left or right. The coach chooses formations that give the best chance for success. If plays are repeated, they can be dressed up with motion to give a different look. That leaves four plays that would be passes in this situation. The coach must decide what would be a high-percentage throw to use and what kind of explosive play could be created from a play-action pass. Two play passes from the same run formations and actions could be used to give a chance for big plays. A pass that looks like a run is the best counter available in football. The pass keeps the runs effective for the entire game. That leaves two additional passes, and one could be a three-step drop that has a high percentage of completion in this situation. Because first down is a balanced down for the defense, the coach may choose a formation that suggests run to the defense for the three-step pass. For the last play, he may choose a sprint pass that will give the defense something else to worry about and to change the launch point for the quarterback. This same procedure can be employed for all situations identified in every field zone for every down-and-distance.

Other considerations that factor in would be what defensive weakness does the offense wish to attack and how. What players are to be attacked or avoided in any given situation? Are playmakers getting the ball enough times in positions for them to make big plays? Does the coach plan to attack the wideside of the field or boundary, and with what plays? When does he run special plays, and where on the field are they to be run? What are the chances of these plays being successful? Backed up in third-and-long, the chances of getting a first down are slim, so it must be determined what the best chance is to get a first down with the least amount of risk involved. That may change if the team is behind with very little time to catch up. That scenario requires the coach to be more aggressive.

For openers (the first 10 to 15 plays of the game), the coach decides the run-pass percentage he wants to present to the defense. These plays are often those that present a high chance of being successful. Many times, an explosive type of play will be included and perhaps a trick play as well. A coach wants to script confidence into these openers through success on the team's behalf and defeat for the opponent's defense. Often, the offense may attempt to break tendencies from previous games. Plays are selected that will give the offense some rhythm. The coach selects formations and motions from which to run plays that will give a clue as to how the defense is going to play. The play caller stays with the script until he gets into a situation where the scripted play would have little chance of success. The coach then goes to the rest of the game plan to find the play he feels will be successful in that scenario and runs it instead. He then returns to the script for the next play. For example, if the coach finds the offense in a third-and-short situation and the script calls for a play with a low percentage chance of success, he will go to a third-and-short segment of the game plan and select from that. The offense will then return to the script. At times, a coach may see an opportunity with one of the plays down the list that he intended to run later. He decides to run it before the defense corrects the problem that the coach has identified. The play caller and staff need to be disciplined and stay on script. The offense can be flexible, but the coach must have a good reason to come off script, and he should return to the script if he has veered off.

The following are some thoughts on play calling in general:

- Get a first down. When Mark Richt was the offensive coordinator at Florida State University, he pointed out that it was their philosophy on second-and-short to get a first down and not use it as a waste down. He said that when a team is that close to a first down, it should not take the ball off the line of scrimmage. A shotgun no-huddle offense can go under center in that situation and run the quarterback sneak even if the offense does nothing else under the center.
- Third down is very important. The percentages on third down are not in the offense's favor until it arrives at third-and-short. This is not to say that the coach must be a conservative play caller. Far from it. He must be an aggressive play caller, but he must also weigh the options and decide when the risk is worth the reward. Not many coaches can make those decisions under the stress of the ever-shrinking clock time and be correct most of the time. These decisions require thought and planning and are nearly impossible to make with a high chance of success as the play clock winds down. The offense wants to create explosive plays, not just hope

to bust the trap. As stated earlier, if the team is plus two in the explosive category, it has an 80 to 85 percent chance to win. Only turnovers decide more games.

- Coach against turnovers. All players and coaches must know how they play a role in causing turnovers, such as missed assignments, bad decisions with the ball, not handling the ball properly, and in the case of coaching, putting the team under undue pressure. A coach must first teach a team how not to lose a game before he can teach them how to win one. Mistakes will happen. Teams cannot afford to make a mistake that could have been avoided with proper planning.

Goal line offense starts from the +10 because, under high school rules, overtime begins at the +10. In this way, a coach can cut down on the number of plays needed in these two situations by combining them.

Coming out from the goal line (–1 to –15), the thought process should be to get at least two first downs to give the offense a chance to punt. A coach could take a shot downfield as a change-up, but he would normally minimize the risk with short drops, quick screens, boots, sprints, or waggle types of plays to avoid having to hold protection for long periods of time. An offense would not want to take a sack or penalty that might result in a safety or worse, or put it deeper in the field position hole. Screens often are helpful if placed in a passing situation. Run choices often attempt to minimize the risk of fumbles by using few option plays and staying away from plays that require players to hold blocks for long periods to avoid holding penalties.

In the coming out zone (–11 to –25) a play caller would open it up a little more and try to get chunks of yards in the passing game. Play-action is very good in this case, and the coach could include more option plays in the run plan. The open field zone is a freewheeling zone (–26 to –35) for the team with everything in the offense at its disposal. In the red zone (+34 to +11), a coach should use plays that keep him from getting into long down-and-distance situations and from taking the team out of field goal or scoring range. For example, he can use more of the quick passing game to avoid sacks or holding penalties in this zone. The play caller may go with play-action passes that present a chance for a quick score but give protection for the longer routes being run. Sprint passes work well in this zone. Quick screens are a good choice in all zones for most situations. The play caller may reduce some option runs to keep possible fumbles to a minimum. Run plays that require players to hold blocks for extended periods of time may not be selected due to the possibility of a holding penalty taking the offense out of field goal range.

In third-and-long, an offense wants to throw the ball using routes that have the best shot of getting the needed yards for the first down. It is always better for the quarterback to take what the defense is giving. It is okay to punt. Either runs that give the best opportunity to get the needed yardage or runs that really add yardage to the punt should be selected. Situations dictate when it is time to force the issue and take more risk or time to become more conservative.

What does a game plan sheet look like? The coach may use a word processing program to enter everything on a computer, or he may choose to use a spread sheet format. He begins by typing in openers from the formations and motions intended to be used, as well as his choice of plays for the run:pass ratio desired. The opening script should test the defense's ability to adjust to varying formations, shifts, and motions.

Next, the open field calls for each down-and-distance situation should be entered. The plays are entered in two columns of run or pass and listed in the order that they are to be called. The run:pass ratio is set, and the types of run or pass plays for each situation are listed. This approach makes it easy to put the plan together with a limited number of plays needed for each situation. The coach repeats this process for each field zone and each down-and-distance situation. Two-point plays are listed under goal line plays. Two or three two-point plays should be sufficient for the season. These plays should be practiced on a daily basis. The offense should choose these plays in the off-season and dress them up with different motions and formations to keep them fresh. Although the numbers tell the coach he will have only one true second- or third-and-short situation per game, he should list a play-action pass for each.

Special plays intended to be run are listed, along with notes as to when they are called. A blitz-beater segment with ideas on how to combat anticipated blitzes is listed. The coach needs to ask himself the following questions. Is he giving his team the best percentage chance to accomplish his goal? Is the offense attacking the weakness of the defense or its weaker players? Is the offense getting the ball to its best players or running back behind its best blockers often enough to make the big plays? The risk/reward question must always be kept in mind when selecting just what to do next.

Two-minute calls to be used in the appropriate down-and-distance situations are listed. Two-minute offense may be the most difficult concept in coaching football. Books have been written on this subject, and yet every week at every level mistakes are made that could have been avoided. A coach would be wise to read Homer Smith's words on this subject. Smith describes two-minute offense as the Mount Everest of football. He is right. This is another strong reason for spelling out the offensive game on paper.

The last three plays of the game are listed for end-of-game situations. Four-minute offense is scripted with the best runs from the best formations and the passes that have a high percentage rate of completion to get the yards needed and to keep the clock moving. Every coach should decide what is best for him and his ball club in any given situation and what gives the team the best chance in each situation to attain victory.

Other considerations to include in the game plan are plays to begin drives. Does the offense have a play that the defense has not seen and wishes now to show? The play caller must decide when to unleash that attack. What should the offense do if it gets behind early in the game by more than two touchdowns or if it is ahead by more than two touchdowns? When should the team go to the four-minute or two-minute offense? What are the two-point plays? Do injuries to his team or to the opponents require a change in the offensive plan? The offense may need to adjust if weather conditions become bad.

Proper game planning requires a lot of work, and there is no guarantee that work will always produce victory. An offense must be disciplined to work and to stay with the plan. It is wise to remember the adage: If you fail to plan, then you are planning to fail. Homer Smith said, "To be a good coach, your job is to put your players in the best position you can to win." A coach is judged by how well he does. Victory depends on it.

APPENDIX

Principles of Coaching

Over 50 years of coaching, certain principles have stood the test of time. These principles relate to the X's and O's of the game, practice techniques, or relationships with players and coaches. They are presented in this chapter in no particular order.

- *Play performance, not potential.* It is easy to fall into a trap where a great-looking athlete who does not perform is played in place of a smaller or less-talented player who outperforms the potentially superior player. Performance should always be the basis for determining playing time.
- *Don't tell me what a player can't do; tell me what he can do!* A coach cannot worry about what a player is unable to do. He must find out what the player can do and utilize those attributes to contribute to the team's performance.
- *Discipline the stars first.* If the star player is required to follow a prescribed set of rules, those of lesser ability will generally fall into line. When exceptions to rules are made for the star, team discipline will quickly fall apart.
- *Treat the least talented player on the team with the same respect and care as the best player is treated.* The ability of the coach to treat all players equally builds strong team bonds.
- *Coach on every repetition during practice.*
- *Correct errors, but don't berate players.*
- *Encourage, praise, and reward effort.* Positive reinforcement always leads to the best results in performance.
- *Set a positive tone every day by being enthusiastic and excited.* Players may have days when they are down, but coaches can never be less than excited about every practice and game. This attitude is contagious, and players respond positively to it. Following losses, it becomes even more important for coaches to be enthusiastic and excited about practice.
- *On a platoon football team, the offense should get first choice of players for the quarterback and tailback positions.* The defense, however, should get the pick of the next 11 positions. This selection process allows for the use of the two best athletes on offense, while emphasizing the importance of defense.
- *Play your best athletes on special teams.* This principle is especially true for punt, punt return, and kickoff teams. Special team players create field position and create scoring opportunities.
- *The true test of effective coaching is seen by how much the team improves over the course of a season.* Some teams will possess more talent than others and thus have more potential. But whatever the starting point, the effectiveness of a coaching staff can be judged by the level of improvement by the team over the course of a season.
- *Use a whole-part teaching method.* Give the player an overall view of a play or skill, and then break it down to a step-by-step sequence. If a player has a big picture first, he will be more likely to understand the need for the step-by-step teaching sequence.

- *Have a limited number of rules, but be willing to enforce them for everyone.* A rule such as "Do the right thing" encompasses many situations and allows for flexibility in interpretation and enforcement. Team rules are probably most effective if players have a voice in setting those rules. A perception of fairness is the product of even-handed enforcement of team rules.
- *Never publicly argue with or berate an assistant coach or any support personnel. Issues between the head coach and members of his staff must be dealt with in private.* If players see the head coach criticize assistant coaches or support personnel, the players may lose respect for these individuals.
- *Be willing to talk to parents about their child, but hold fast to the rule: "Never discuss playing time."* A coach needs to be available to discuss issues about a player with parents. This approach fosters a better understanding of an individual player and some of the problems he may have. Playing time (or lack of playing time) is never open for discussion with parents. It may be a topic of conversation between the coach and a player.
- *Always give a player an out if he is disciplined or criticized in front of his peers.* Don't back a player into a corner from which the only face-saving way out is rebellion. When faced with a rebellious player, send him to the showers and have him meet with you after practice. This approach gives the player a chance to cool off and reflect on the situation. It also gives the coach a chance to consider and weigh his response.
- *Never criticize the quarterback in front of his teammates.* Criticism of the quarterback should be done in private. It is important for his teammates to have confidence in him. This confidence can be undermined by coaches offering negative criticism of the quarterback in front of the team. If this player is expected to lead, he must enjoy the confidence of the team.
- *A coach must care about his players as people.* Players don't care how much you know until they know how much you care. In many cases, the football coach may be the only positive male role model in a young man's life. The chance to be a positive influence is great for a football coach. The player's welfare should always be placed first.
- *The coach must be available to players away from practice.* An open-door policy is the best policy. This should apply not only during the season, but on a year-round basis.
- *Provide the very best player equipment that the budget will allow.* Helmets and shoulder pads particularly should be of the highest quality. A program should be established for replacing some of each equipment item yearly. A sound reconditioning program should be followed each year. Equipment safety must be the guiding principle in purchasing and reconditioning.
- *All coaches in the football program must set a good example for players.* This example includes dress, appearance, language, dedication, enthusiasm, and treatment of players, other coaches, and support personnel.

- *Make a special effort to treat all support personnel well.* This treatment of personnel includes trainers, equipment men, custodians, secretaries, and ground crews. These people are the individuals who can make the coach's job easier or harder, depending on how they feel about the coach and his program. Take every opportunity to thank them for their help. Be friendly and cooperative with them, and find ways to reward them for their assistance.
- *Respect your opponents, but don't fear them.* Fear inhibits athletic performance. A team must learn never to fear opponents, but to look forward to competing against them. Teach the team to respect any opponent that it faces and expect their best effort.
- *Demand that players respect each other and their coaches.* The golden rule for relationships between players and between players and coaches is for everyone to treat others in the way they would want to be treated.
- *Be honest with players, and give honest answers when asked questions.* Honesty is always the best policy. If players know a coach is not telling them the truth, the coach will lose their respect and trust.
- *Each player should be evaluated every day in practice, as well as in games.* The coach should use video and observation to make these evaluations. The evaluations should be made available to players.
- *A high school coach must continually recruit in his school and in the lower grades in his district.* Potential recruits may be found in physical education classes and intramurals. Other sports such as track, basketball, and baseball may yield potential football players.
- *The coach should understand the systems he uses well enough to be able to adjust them when things go wrong.* Game situations may dictate the need for adjustments. A coach must be able to make these adjustments in games. He also must understand his system well enough to adjust it to the talent he has available from year to year.
- *A coach's integrity and character can be judged by how he reacts following a loss, not when the team wins.* A coach needs to be gracious in defeat as well as in victory.
- *A head coach should prepare his assistant coaches to take his job.* Most young assistants hope to become head coaches. It is the responsibility of the head coach to prepare his assistants to achieve this goal. Most head coaches have had a mentor who taught them how to be head coaches.
- *Character is who you are when no one is watching you.* Coaches must be role models for their players, and a good role model needs to be a person of good character.
- *In crucial game situations, the coach should think of players, not plays.* When a game is on the line, the coach should get the ball into the hands of his best players. He should remember how he got to where he is.
- *A coach should always think of the worst thing that could happen and have a plan to approach that situation.* Over a lengthy career, a coach will face almost every tough situation he can imagine. He should accept this as inevitable and prepare ahead for the challenge.

- *Create a family atmosphere within your team.* Creation of a family atmosphere may be developed by having older players take younger players under their wing. Coaches can assign mentors or big brothers for young players. All individuals want to belong to a group in which they are liked and respected. This element is the chief appeal of the gang culture. The football team has to provide that family feeling for young men. Many youngsters today come from dysfunctional homes and hunger for the stability of a family unit.
- *Individual and group periods are for teaching.* Team periods are for performance. Coaches teach and correct in group or individual periods. If a player needs instruction, it is done at this time.
- *Get as many repetitions as possible in team periods.* The more plays that can be run in team periods, the better it is. Action should never be stopped to talk to players. If instruction is needed, the player should be replaced so that action can continue.
- *Play more than one player at a position in practice and in games to build depth and maintain interest.* The one exception to this principle is the quarterback position. A coach should play three guards, three tackles, two Y's, two tailbacks, two 3-backs, and three wide receivers. Thus, 17 offensive players are regularly employed. When injuries occur, backup players have already gained experience.
- *Devote at least 20 minutes every day to special teams.* On Mondays, Thursdays, and Fridays the coach should devote 25 minutes to special teams so that every possible situation is covered. Nothing should be left to chance. The most efficient way to practice special teams is to have different personnel on the punt and kickoff teams than are on the punt return and kickoff return teams. This idea allows the first punt return team to work against the first punt team, and is also true for the kickoff versus kickoff return teams and the field goal or extra point teams versus first defense. This procedure allows for more repetitions of each phase of the kicking game in less practice time.
- *Have a time schedule for practice, and stick to it.* Use five-minute periods as the basis for that schedule. Practice plans should be printed out so that each coach, manager, trainer, or equipment man has a copy. A copy of the practice schedule should be posted in the locker rooms for all players to see.
- *Repeating skills fewer times each day is more effective than practicing a skill extensively one day and ignoring it in the next practice.* Drills are based on a time limit, not repetitions.
- *Drills should teach skills that are used in game situations. Improvement in these skills should be apparent on game tape.* Break skills into step-by-step movements, and teach those movements sequentially.
- *Demand effort on every repetition in practice.* Effort does not take talent; it only takes desire.
- *Create competitive situations in practice as often as possible.* Competition in drills as well as in group and team situations keeps players' attention. Every opportunity to create competition helps develop the competitiveness of players that is essential for success.

- *Work the #1 offense against the #1 defense whenever possible.* Working against the best competition available allows players to develop their skill level versus good players.
- *Coach on the run. Don't hold up practice to talk.* This principle is especially true during team periods. Some instruction may be given during individual periods, but team periods should not be slowed to do this. If a coach must talk to an individual player, he should pull the player out of the group and replace him with another player while he has the conversation.
- *Try to make practice fun when possible.* Football is a tough, demanding game, but whenever possible practice should be fun. Creating competition in drills, group work, and team work can make practice more enjoyable. Making sure that practice keeps all players involved and on the move helps. The worst thing a coach can do is to let large numbers of players stand around doing nothing.
- *Skills common to all positions are best taught through a circuit skills program using sleds, dummies, and live bodies.* An example of such a circuit for a team that must play players both ways might include: tackle the two-man sled, shed on the five- or seven-man sled with a fumble recovery at the end, block on boards, and an agility station. Break the squad into four groups with one group starting at each station, and rotate them every four minutes. In 16 minutes, basic skills have been covered in a fast-paced environment.
- *It is not possible to have full contact in all practices and drills if a team is to remain healthy.* Dummies and hand shields may need to be used at times. Players must be taught what is meant by thud tempo, where ballcarriers are not taken to the ground, but blocking and shedding are done at full speed.
- *Football games are won by teams that pursue on defense, shed blockers, and tackle well.* Offensively teams who block, practice ball security, and feature a strong running game will succeed. Practice drills must emphasize these fundamental football techniques on a daily basis.
- *Team defense and offense should be practiced from the hash marks at least 80 percent of the time.* This principle is about the percentage of the time that the ball will be on a hash mark in any game. Too often, coaches practice from the middle of the field the majority of the time.
- *Every defensive drill should be started with ball movement and every offensive drill with cadence.* The defense must react to ball movement in game situations and the offense moves on cadence.
- *Group and team drills should always end with a whistle.* If a coach expects players to play until the whistle, he should use the whistle to end drills and team practice.
- *Physical toughness must be taught through individual, group, and team drills.* Physical toughness is not a natural attribute for most young men, but it can be taught and developed. It generally stems from a player developing confidence in his ability to hit.
- *Field position and turnovers are the two most important factors in winning football games.* Ball security is emphasized on offense and creating turnovers is emphasized defensively. Strong special teams lead to positive field position. Offensive drives

that start inside the offense's 10-yard line result in scoring by the offense about 3 percent of the time. If the drive starts inside the opponent's 10-yard line, a score results about 70 percent of the time. A drive that begins between the offense's 40- to 50-yard line results in a score about 20 percent of the time, while starting between the opponent's 50- to 40-yard line results in a score approximately 33 percent of the time. Offensive series starting inside an opponent's 35-yard line yield a score at about a 50 percent rate.

- *The punt is the most important single play in any football game.* More yardage is gained or lost from this play than any other. Blocked punts are especially devastating to the kicking team and present the return team with good field position at the least and possible scoring opportunities.
- *Every offense should include an option series.* The dive option is the best structure since it requires a defense to assign personnel to the dive, quarterback, and pitchman. The threat of the option forces defenses to devote practice time to defending it. It also tends to dictate fewer coverages, fronts, and stunts because of the need to be sound in defending all facets of the option. The option does not need to be the principal part of the offense in order to force the defense to cover it.
- *A team will either improve or get worse*. It never remains the same. Good coaching should find the team improving over the course of the season. If it does not improve, its performance will deteriorate.
- *Focus on the fact that the next play is the only play.* What happened in the past cannot change the need to have everyone focus on the next play. By the same token, it is not good to place focus on the future. Take care of the next play. This philosophy will lead to a team focus on each play as it occurs.
- *A team should be known for something on offense and defense.* Most offensive and defensive systems can be successful. A coach wants to be consistent with the systems he uses.
- *A leadership council elected by the players should meet regularly with the head coach to address player concerns.* This group should have representatives from each class, freshmen through seniors. It should also include players from the offense, defense, special teams, and scout teams.
- *Players should have input in the establishment of team rules.* If players help determine team rules, it is easier for the team as a group to buy into them.
- *Each player should know what his role is on the team.* Players want to know what their role on the team will be. Everyone has an important place and role on the team. When this role is communicated to the player, he will be more accepting of his place. It is important to emphasize that all players are important to the team.
- *Players should be required to memorize assignments, and that learning should be checked by weekly written tests.* It is particularly important that blocking rules be memorized and tested each week. Offensive players need to know blocking rules so well that they don't have to think about them. They should be able to apply the rules to any unusual defense they may confront.

- *Not all players develop physically at the same time.* Some players are physically developed at a young age, and others take longer. A coach should not give up on a young player's slow physical development.
- *Each player should be taught to be accountable for his actions.* Many young people want to make excuses when they make mistakes. They blame other factors for their failure. The coach needs to encourage players to be accountable for their failures as well as their successes. This accountability is one of the most valuable character traits that a coach can help players develop.
- *Most individuals learn best through performance of a skill.* Talking to players about how to do things has its place, but it is a relatively ineffective teaching method. Demonstration and film study also can be used, but having players actually perform the activity is the best teaching method.
- *Lack of self-confidence leads players to a lack of respect for themselves and others.* Players who are confident of themselves find it easier to respect others as well as themselves. The coach's role is to help build the confidence of all the young men who play for him.
- *Some players have a sense of entitlement.* These individuals struggle with responsibility. Adversity and conflict are not something to which they are accustomed. Football is a game that can teach responsibility.
- *Involve the team in at least three community projects each year.* The benefits of community participation are many. It helps players feel good about themselves as they are doing something worthwhile for others. It helps build team spirit through cooperation with others. The team will gain community support through such endeavors. Some possible projects include the following:
  - ✓ Help with Special Olympics.
  - ✓ Clean up a park or other public facility.
  - ✓ Volunteer to read at a preschool or elementary school.
  - ✓ Conduct a food drive for a food pantry.
  - ✓ Volunteer to work at a non-profit agency such as a food pantry, a homeless shelter, an animal shelter, or a nursing home.
  - ✓ Conduct a youth football camp.
- *Remember, you can never arrive.* There is always the next challenge. A team should always strive to improve. Remember this adage: "There is always someone better than you!" As a result, a team and/or player must continue to grow.

ABOUT THE AUTHORS

Born in Akron, Iowa in 1935, **Vince McMahon** attended school in Sioux City, Iowa. He graduated from Leeds High School in 1954, where he played on a football team that won 25 games in a row. He graduated from Morningside College in 1958 and earned a master's degree from the University of South Dakota in 1963.

In 1958, McMahon started a 50-year coaching career at Climbing Hill, Iowa. This was followed by positions as assistant football coach in Sioux City and Rochelle, Illinois. The Rochelle football team won 35 games in a row during his time there.

McMahon became head football coach and athletic director at Vermillion State Junior College (Ely, MN) in 1967. This was followed by a three-year period as head football coach and athletic director at St. Peter (MN) High School. For the next four and a half years, he served as an assistant football coach and head baseball coach at the University of Wisconsin–Superior. In 1975 he accepted the position of head football coach at Illinois Valley Community College in Oglesby, where he also served as athletic director. After 16 seasons, he moved to Joliet (IL) Junior College to become head football coach, athletic director, and assistant dean of students.

After retiring in 1994, Coach McMahon continued as an offensive assistant coach at Aurora University and Benedictine University in Illinois until 2008.

During 20 years as a head junior college coach, he compiled a record of 127 wins and 73 losses. His teams appeared in numerous bowl games and posted a 17-game winning streak. McMahon was named conference coach of the year for the North Central Community College Conference five times.

Upon his retirement, Coach McMahon was inducted into the National Junior College Athletic Association Football Hall of Fame. He was also elected to the NJCAA Region IV Hall of Fame and the Illinois Valley Community College Hall of Fame. Coach McMahon is the author of *Coaching the Option Wing Offense* published by Coaches Choice in 2003. He is a 35-year member of the American Football Coaches Association.

Vince McMahon and his wife Pat, a former high school English and French teacher, currently reside in DeKalb, Illinois. Their son Kurt lives in DeKalb and is a member of the computer science faculty at Northern Illinois University in DeKalb. Their daughter Kara, her husband Jim, and their son Ryan live in Elgin, Illinois. She is the chief academic officer for schools in District 300, Carpentersville, Illinois.

Kevin McMahon was born in Sioux City, Iowa, and graduated from East High School in Sioux City. He is a graduate of the University of Northern Iowa and has a master's degree in physical education from Nova University. Coach McMahon has spent his entire 35-year career coaching high school football in Florida. He served as an assistant coach at Boyd Anderson High School in Ft. Lauderdale, Centennial High School in St. Lucie West, and for 10 years at Vero Beach High School under legendary coach Billy Livings.

McMahon served as head football coach at George Jenkins High School in Lakeland for four years and at Westwood High School in Ft. Pierce for 11 years. McMahon is now retired.